Analytical Issues in Debt

Edited by
Jacob A. Frenkel, Michael P. Dooley, and Peter Wickham

International Monetary Fund

Library of Congress Cataloging-in-Publication Data

Analytical issues in debt / edited by Jacob A. Frenkel, Michael P.
Dooley, and Peter Wickham.
    p. cm.
    Includes bibliographical references.
    ISBN 1-55775-041-6
    1. Debts, External—Developing countries. 2. Debt relief—
Developing countries.   I. Frenkel, Jacob A.   II. Dooley, Michael
P. III Wickham, Peter.
HJ8899.A53 1989
336,3'435'091724—dc20   89-19749
                                                  CIP

Price: US$26.50

CONTENTS

iii

CONTENTS

An Introduction to Analytical Issues in Debt

JACOB A. FRENKEL, MICHAEL P. DOOLEY, and PETER WICKHAM*

IN THE AUTUMN OF 1982 Mexican banks in New York encountered increasing difficulties in meeting their obligations to repay maturing interbank loans. This announcement sent a strong pulse through the delicate web of international financial markets. A liquidity crisis for a debtor as important as Mexico placed the economic viability of other developing countries in doubt as well and threatened to disrupt the trust that a modern credit market operates on. While Federal Reserve officials took the threat very seriously, there were well-known and tested procedures to handle such contingencies. The Fed quickly stepped in to protect the system and provide time to find a more permanent solution.

After eight years, the international economic system is still in search of a lasting solution to the debt problem. The general outlines of the problem are by now familiar. Countries that the Fund classifies as having recent debt-servicing difficulties have seen their external debt grow from US$538 billion in 1982 to US$726 billion at the end of 1988. To get some feel for the size of this debt, the end-1988 debt total was equal to about 47 percent of GNP for these countries. Interest payments made equaled about 18 percent of exports. For a variety of reasons the economic performance of these countries has been far below their historical norms. Real GNP has grown at an average rate of only 2 percent since 1982, while per capita GNP has grown even more slowly. Inflation has in many cases soared as fiscal authorities have attempted to cope with internal demands and debt service payments.

* Mr. Frenkel is Director of the Research Department of the International Monetary Fund.

Mr. Dooley, Chief of the External Adjustment Division in the Research Department of the IMF, is a graduate of Duquesne University, the University of Delaware, and the Pennsylvania State University.

Mr. Wickham is Assistant to the Director of the Fund's Research Department. He did his undergraduate work at the University of Essex and pursued his graduate studies at the University of British Columbia and the Johns Hopkins University.

The management and staff of the Fund have focused much of their effort in recent years on coming to grips with these problems. Even a cursory investigation of the issues immediately points up the diversity of problems facing debtor countries. Low income countries in Africa, owing the bulk of their debt to official creditors, face problems fundamentally different from those of middle income countries in Latin America with heavy debt to commercial banks. The Fund's case-by-case approach in assisting member countries reflects the fact that no rigid and universal prescription will fit the needs of all member countries.

Nevertheless, research efforts in the Fund have also focused a great deal of attention on the common analytical elements that might be useful in clarifying thinking about the debt problem. A sample of this work, a sample that we hope will have lasting value, is reproduced in this volume. The last chapter is not a simple blueprint for a solution to the debt problem. We do not believe that a simple answer exists. But we do believe that, as we go to print in the summer of 1989, new initiatives involving debt and debt-service reduction techniques hold the best promise thus far in finding a lasting solution to the problems of debtor countries. We hope that the reader will be struck by the development of thinking on the problem and recognize that the end of the volume is not the end of the story. The support given to research at the Fund will continue to allow further development of these important analytical problems.

The selection of papers for this volume was difficult and involved a degree of arbitrariness. We have tended to favor papers dealing with the conceptual issues involved in analyzing debt problems, at a cost, however, of having to omit papers dealing more directly with operational issues and implications. We would like to acknowledge in particular the work undertaken in the latter area by colleagues in the Fund's Exchange and Trade Relations Department under the direction of Alan Whittome (Counsellor and Director) and Helen Junz (Deputy Director).

The following section of the introduction contains a guide to the book with a summary of each paper and an examination of the links to be found between them. A final few paragraphs bring matters up to date.

About two years had elapsed since U.S. Secretary of the Treasury Baker's speech at the 1985 IMF-World Bank Annual Meeting in Seoul when Max Corden and Michael Dooley wrote the first paper in this volume. The Baker Plan, as the proposals on the debt strategy made in the speech became known, was concerned with the disappointing growth performance in heavily indebted developing countries and argued for more comprehensive programs of reform by the debtors, which, together with substantial additional financial support from official and private creditors, would permit countries to grow out of their debt problems. Against this background the authors set out to review the options for dealing with developing countries' debt. The paper they prepared, a revised version of which appears here, served as a basis for a seminar of the Fund's Executive Board held in February 1988. Starting out with a review of the debt situation as they then saw it, the authors next examined how a country might grow out of debt and what effect concerted lending by commercial banks and "better" policies might have in heavily indebted countries. They followed this with an examination of market-based ways of transforming debt (e.g., debt buy-backs and debt-equity swaps), before turning to debt relief, and the possible establishment of an international debt facility. Many readers will find this nontechnical paper an excellent and evenhanded overview of the issues involved in the "debt crisis."

Joshua Greene reminds us in his paper that while much of the literature has concerned commercial debt and the debt problems of middle-income countries, mounting debt and debt-servicing difficulties in low income countries, where official debt predominates, have become worrying. His paper focuses particularly on the situation in sub-Saharan Africa, detailing both the origins of the problem, its size, and the initial response to it from countries in the region and the international community. He then looks at recent initiatives from the Fund and the World Bank to provide concessional finance for adjustment programs, as well as the June 1988 Group of Seven agreement in Toronto to reduce debt-service obligations. His paper concludes by analyzing further steps that might help countries in the sub-Saharan region.

Concern with the fall of investment in many of the heavily indebted middle-income developing countries after 1982 motivates the next paper in the volume. Michael Dooley argues that the markets' current valuation of existing debt may well have discouraged real investment in these countries. Potential investors must consider what will happen to their new financial claims if existing claims are trading at a discount in the market. The cost of investing in physical plants and equipment will not be affected by the discount, but since new financial claims will not be subordinated voluntarily to old financial claims, their prices will be equalized at near the market discount. Many domestic investment projects that would have been viable when claims were valued at par become unprofitable when there is a market discount; the result will be a fall in real gross investment.

There follow two theoretical papers that extend the literature on international lending and country risk. In the first of these, Joshua Aizenman starts from the premise that country risk associated with lending to sovereign states brings about an equilibrium in international credit markets in which flows are limited by the default or repudiation penalties. The best approach that a borrower can take to attracting funds appears to be a pre-commitment not to default on contracts, but the author considers that the commitment cannot be regarded as credible since a time-consistent policy would weigh the costs and benefits of default at each point in time. Default penalties take the form of restrictions on trade in goods, services, and financial assets, and can be expected to be higher the more open the economy is to such trade. Aizenman then argues that policy measures to increase the openness of the economy, can, by making potential default penalties higher, influence the calculus of creditors and lead to larger flows of foreign credit to the economy than would otherwise take place.

In the second of the two papers, Aizenman and Eduardo Borensztein start from the position in which country-risk considerations have already led to effective credit rationing and to low investment in developing countries. The authors seek to identify conditions under which renewed lending may benefit both developed and developing countries by taking advantage of the trade repercussions of financial flows. The latter stem from the fact that an increase in lending generates an increase in the debtor countries' demand for imported capital goods. Therefore, a basis exists for mutually beneficial loans, provided a substantial part of these resources is used for investment. To ensure this, it may be necessary to attach conditions to the new loans. Even then, a further obstacle must be overcome. The increase in export demand, or more generally a favorable shift in the terms of trade, made possible by the new loans, benefit the creditor countries overall but not the banks directly. Aizenman and Borensztein therefore conclude that there may be a policy role for creditor country governments to induce the private banks to be forthcoming with new loans.

A third paper by Michael Dooley provides a framework for analyzing market pricing of external debt, which can be used to evaluate proposals to execute buy-backs or similar debt operations. Central to the paper and to others that follow in this volume is the notion that the aggregate market value of claims on a debtor country reflect the expected present value of transfers that will be made available over time by the country to creditors. With buy-backs financed by third parties, additional resources are available to a debtor country. As a result, the buy-back operation will not only reduce the contractual value of debt but will reduce the market discount, leading to capital gains for creditors and a possible increase in domestic investment. Self-financed buy-backs, on the other hand, do not increase resources available to the debtor, so that such operations, while reducing the contractual value of debt, may not improve the investment climate and can increase the market discount.

Max Corden makes his second contribution to the volume with his "An International Debt Facility?" paper. He was intrigued by the various proposals to set up a facility or authority that would buy up debt at a discount and write down its contractual value. But, in typical fashion, he wondered whether the pros and cons had been fully thought through: note his insistence on a question mark in the title. The result of his musings is the present dispassionately argued paper, which analyzes how the debtor countries, the creditor banks, and the "owners" of the debt facility are each affected by the debt transactions undertaken. Particular attention is paid to the prices at which debt transactions may take place, whether remaining debt held by creditor banks is subordinated or not, whether debtor countries' access to the facility should have strings attached, and how the problem of moral hazard can be confronted. The reader will appreciate the importance of these issues in light of proposals to modify the debt strategy that attracted so much attention at the Spring 1989 Meetings of the Governors of the International Monetary Fund and the World Bank.

The next three papers examine the nature of debt contracts associated with loans to sovereign countries and the theoretical issues concerned with modifying or renegotiating the terms of the contracts. In the first of these, Guillermo Calvo shows that in drawing up debt contracts there may be incentives for lenders to settle on relatively low default penalties and thus for the borrowers to take on more debt than they otherwise would. But even if contracts are optimal in terms of interest rates and default penalties, it is argued that they are bound to be time inconsistent because it will always be in the interest of creditors to maximize the probability of repayment by raising the stakes after the contract is signed. There is strong reason, it is argued, for an arbitrator to exercise caution if called in by the contending parties in a contract dispute. The author then proceeds to argue that debt relief could very well be a characteristic of optimal debt contracts. First he considers that contracts are normally contingent on the likely "states of nature." If actual events are widely out of line with expectations held when the contracts were entered into, then there is a prima facie case for reexamining the contract's provisions. In the case of bad "states of nature" from the borrower's viewpoint, this reexamination means considering debt relief. The argument can be strengthened further if recognition is given to the notion of implicit contracts in international lending agreements.

Jeremy Bulow and Kenneth Rogoff extend their earlier work on debt recontracting to include multilateral bargaining among debtors, private lenders, and creditor-country governments. Each of the parties faces different benefits and costs in the event of debt repudiation. The repudiating debtor risks losing future access to international financial markets and being forced by sanctions to trade inefficiently. Apart from arguments based on the need for a response "pour encourager les autres" to keep paying, private creditors do not gain directly from cutting a country's access to the international financial markets. However, exporters and consumers in creditor countries may well suffer if trade sanctions are imposed, so that, in the interest of many of their constituents, creditor-country governments may regard debt rescheduling as desirable. Creditor-country governments may even be tempted into making sidepayments to encourage rescheduling, although to which of the other parties the benefits accrue depends critically on whether the sidepayments are anticipated or not.

In his paper on debt renegotiation, Kenneth Kletzer examines the issue of whether in the face of recalcitrant behavior by sovereign debtors the optimal response by creditors is to provide additional loans. He considers the argument that additional loans can reduce the probability of default on outstanding debt. With symmetric information, he finds in his model that renegotiating contracts will reduce current debt service but will never result in additional inflows. Under information asymmetries, an equilibrium may exist in which new inflows occur but this will depend on the occurrence or otherwise of good "states of nature" over time.

The next group of papers explores theoretical aspects of voluntary debt reduction and relief and centers on incentives facing creditors and debtors. These papers consider whether debt reduction or other forms of debt relief increase the incentives for a debtor country to "adjust" and invest (reform) to the benefit of debtors and creditors alike. Max Corden analyzes the concept of "capacity to pay," which he defines as the excess of income over some minimal consumption level with debt service and investment forming claims on the excess each period. Using simple graphical tools he shows that in certain circumstances it may indeed be advantageous for creditors to grant relief. However, he also shows that the conditions required will not necessarily be satisfied.

Paul Krugman organizes his thoughts about debt forgiveness around the idea of a "debt relief Laffer curve." Just as governments may sometimes actually increase revenues by reducing tax rates, creditors may sometimes increase expected payments by forgiving part of a country's debt. The argument that debt relief benefits all parties presumes that the debtor country is over the hump and on the wrong side of the "debt relief Laffer curve." Krugman then considers various market-based schemes for debt-reduction, which are often pictured as being able to harvest secondary-market discounts to the benefit of both creditors and debtors. He concludes that this will be the case only if the debtor country is again over the hump in the Laffer curve, the same circumstances under which unilateral debt forgiveness is in the interests of creditors.

Elhanan Helpman's paper provides a painstaking and systematic approach to the issues involved in voluntary debt reduction. His model shows that debt reduction may raise or lower investment, depending on the degree of international capital mobility and the degree of risk aversion. In addition, the possibility of multiple equilibria at different investment levels cannot be excluded. Understanding these interactions can help to identify circumstances in which voluntary debt reduction in the collective interest of creditors may take place. The author then considers if cooperation among creditors is necessary in order for creditors collectively to provide any debt reduction warranted. This will not be the case, he argues, if multiple equilibria are absent and the face value of debt is sufficiently high.

There follows in the volume a series of more narrowly focused papers dealing with the means and ways of transforming or reducing debt.

Michael Blackwell and Simon Nocera provide a concise appraisal of how debt-equity swaps operate, who benefits from them, and how they influence the country operating the program. While acknowledging the benefits that creditors and indebted countries can realize from debt-equity swaps, the authors point out that such conversions do not necessarily provide additional foreign funds and can, through the implications for monetary and fiscal policy in the debtor country, lead to inflation.

Debt buy-backs and exchanges are the focus of attention in the next two papers. Carlos Rodriguez considers the case in which a country runs a fixed trade surplus which it devotes to debt service, an amount that falls short of that required to fully service outstanding debt. There is thus excess debt which will grow over time through interest rollovers with consequent effects on the price at which debt can be traded. The country is assumed to have an additional amount of cash which it can use for buy-backs now and in the future. Competitive creditors are assumed to have full information on the excess debt buy-back strategy which brings with it the implication that the debt can be recovered not at a discount but only at par. Only if creditors are myopic or if they have less than full information about the debtor's buy-back plan can excess debt be repurchased at a discount.

The paper by David Folkerts-Landau and Carlos Rodriguez analyzes the Mexican debt exchange operation undertaken in 1987. It prices the new partly secured bond using the observed market price on restructured bank debt and derives the reduction in the existing stock of debt achievable through the exchange of secured for unsecured debt. The main lesson from the paper is that, in general, debt exchange operations are equivalent to cash buy-backs in terms of debt and interest rate reduction with a given amount of resources.

The penultimate paper in the volume considers the additional difficulties faced by countries with debt-servicing problems caused by the increased volatility of international interest rates during the 1980s. The interest cost of bank debt to these countries is largely tied to LIBOR, but considerations of creditworthiness and a lack of readily available international reserves have denied indebted countries the opportunity to hedge their exposure to the volatility in LIBOR. David Folkerts-Landau discusses this problem and suggests the use of modified interest rate swaps as a solution to interest risk management by indebted developing countries. He shows that credit risk can be virtually eliminated from the swap contract by marking the swap to market periodically. Unlike many other derivative markets, the swap market has enough depth, liquidity, and sufficiently lengthy maturities to accommodate large scale use by sovereign debtors. Hence, it may be the most promising avenue for risk management currently available.

The final paper in the volume by Michael Dooley and Steven Symansky is also a revised version of a paper prepared for a seminar of the Fund's Executive Board held in January 1989. The paper outlines a framework for evaluating debt reduction in cases where a debtor country is expected to continue to rely on creditors to finance some part of its debt service obligations. It argues that a partition of payments between interest payments on contractual terms and buy-backs of debt and market terms can be thought of as a basic renegotiation of existing contracts. Once this blend of debt reduction and contractual payment is established, market participants can, and presumably do, price alternative menu instruments by equating their expected market values. Thus, the exchange ratio between two financing instruments can be established by pricing their attributes relative to existing debt, for which there is an easily observed market price, and cash.

A renewed sense of urgency in dealing with the debt strategy and the debt situation was underlined by U.S. Secretary of the Treasury Nicholas F. Brady shortly before the April 1989 meeting of the Interim Committee of the International Monetary Fund. At that meeting, it was agreed that the Fund and the Bank should provide appropriate financing to help debt reduction operations in countries undertaking sound economic reforms. In May 1989 the Fund's Executive Board adopted broad guidelines for the provision of Fund support, and by late July 1989, Fund arrangements involving debt reduction operations had been approved for Mexico, Venezuela, Philippines, and Costa Rica. A general description of the Fund and Bank's approach to the challenges raised by this new initiative can be found in the August 1989 issue of *Finance and Development* (Washington: International Monetary Fund and World Bank).

Needless to say, many of the different analytical issues raised in this volume remain in the forefront. A few that seem particularly important include: the "free rider" problem that limits collective behavior by creditors; the negotiating structure and the role of third parties in shaping bargains; the relationship between the "domestic debt problem" and the "extended debt problem"; the relationship between debt reduction and access to new credit and that between debt-service reduction implied by a reduction in the stock of debt and similar relief brought about by a reduction in the rate of interest. Moreover, the linkages between internal and external credit markets and, more generally, the economic linkages among debt, external credit markets, and economic performance in debtor countries deserve further study.

Indeed, in such an important and rapidly growing subject, it is difficult to pause to take stock of existing knowledge. What we know, or think we know, is frequently overtaken by events. We hope this volume spurs others to join in the search for better understanding of these problems and ultimately to write a final chapter to the debt crisis.

Issues in Debt Strategy:
An Overview

W. MAX CORDEN and MICHAEL P. DOOLEY*

This paper touches on many topics relating to the debt strategy that are also discussed elsewhere in this book. Because of the market discount on debt, an inadequate share of world savings may be going to indebted countries. Various "growing out of debt" scenarios are expounded, and the roles of concerted lending and of the policies of debtor countries in affecting the availability of new funds are discussed. The paper outlines the essential features of buy-backs, of securitization, of debt-equity swaps and of the transformation of debt into contingent claims, and also the implications of debt relief for debtors and creditors and of an international debt facility.

THIS PAPER REVIEWS options for dealing with developing countries' debt problems. The paper does not attempt to make the case for or against any of the options reviewed but rather tries to clarify the issues.

The paper as a whole focuses on debtor countries' relationships with private credit markets. The first section provides an overview of four aspects of the current debt situation. The second section looks at the current strategy and qualifications to it. It outlines several "growing out of debt" scenarios. The role of policy improvements by problem debtor countries is stressed as is the need for the international system to accommodate export expansion by them. The third section reviews a number

*At the time he wrote this paper Mr. Corden was Senior Advisor in the Research Department of the IMF, on leave from the Australian National University. He taught at Oxford University from 1967 to 1976. From 1989 he will be Professor of International Economics at the School of Advanced International Studies of the Johns Hopkins University.

Mr. Dooley, Chief of the External Adjustment Division in the Research Department of the IMF, is a graduate of Duquesne University, the University of Delaware, and the Pennsylvania State University.

of supplementary approaches to the debt problem, beginning with various market-based approaches, notably buy-backs, debt-equity swaps, and securitization. It then deals with debt relief, emphasizing the long-term implications for creditors and debtors.

Most figures in this paper refer to a category of developing countries—now 65 in all—called here "problem debtors" or "problem debtor countries," these being the group described as "countries with recent debt service problems" in the IMF's *World Economic Outlook,* April 1988, p. 106. They are defined as " . . . those countries which incurred external payments arrears during 1985 or rescheduled their debt during the period from end-1983 to end-1986 as reported in the relevant issues of the Fund's *Annual Report on Exchange Arrangements and Exchange Restrictions.* "

I. Aspects of the Debt Situation

Disruption of Financial Markets Avoided

One initial problem associated with the inability of some countries to tap private credit markets in 1982 was the threat of instability and disruption of financial markets. Avoiding this threat, and the threat that the crisis might spread to a wider range of debtor countries, was one important priority in dealing with the debt crisis. Indeed, the term "crisis" seems appropriate to a situation in which the solvency of important financial institutions was called into question. Since it is clearly in the interests of both debtor and creditor countries to maintain an open and viable international payments system, any strategy to deal with debt issues must be evaluated with this in mind.

It is in these respects that the current strategy has probably best served the interests of both debtors and creditors. The potential costs of a breakdown in international financial markets have been avoided. Private lenders are in a much stronger position to absorb potential losses on their credits than was the case in 1982 when some debtors for the first time seemed unable to service their obligations. The capital-asset ratios for banks in nine industrial countries increased, on average, by about 16 percent from 1982 to 1986, namely from 4.4 to 5.1 percent. Moreover, as a result of a decline in U.S. banks' claims on developing countries, their ratio of capital to these claims had doubled since 1982 to about 95 percent in 1986. For banks outside the United States the depreciation of the U.S. dollar has probably also generated substantial improvements in this ratio.[1] Over the longer horizon the debt strategy seeks to restore economic growth in problem debtors and restore these countries' normal access to international credit markets.

Current and Future Consumption in Debtor Countries

The servicing of debt obligations built up over the years of high borrowing has reduced consumption levels in some problem debtor countries below where they might have been otherwise and has clearly reduced the level of investment, thus limiting future consumption. Gross capital formation as a percent of GDP averaged 25 percent during 1970–82 for this group and since 1983 has been only around 19 percent. Estimates reported in the April 1987 *World Economic Outlook* suggest that the steep decline in investment ratios for problem debtors has allowed per capita consumption expenditures to remain roughly unchanged since 1982. It is clear, however, that for a number of debtor countries consumption per head has declined over the period. By contrast, per capita consumption expenditures in developing countries without debt-servicing problems increased by about 15 percent over the 1982–86 period. The buildup of debt would not have had this effect if all the debt incurred had been utilized for investment that finally ended up yielding rates of return at least equal to the interest rates on the loans. But, in most cases output in debtor countries has not grown as rapidly as expected, the value of purchasing power over imports even less so, and interest rates have turned out much higher than expected.

Thus, borrowing was based on expectations of both debtors and private and official creditors about the terms of trade, world real interest rates, and the economic growth in developed countries that—with hindsight—were too optimistic, even though they may have appeared reasonable at the time. Furthermore, it must be remembered that during the period of high borrowing savings ratios in many of the problem debtor countries fell; in other words, borrowing allowed them to sustain or raise consumption levels so that the reduction in consumption that was compelled later by the debt crisis was to some extent a consequence of higher consumption levels earlier—levels that, at least in retrospect, were too high.

Even without increased debt service, the decline in the terms of trade would have called for reductions in present or future consumption. The debt service obligations have added to this. Clearly this situation has set up severe strains.

[1]Watson and others (1988), p. 39.

Distribution of Savings Internationally

Another important aspect of the current situation is the possibility that an inadequate share of world savings is going to developing countries.

First of all, one must distinguish the so-called resource transfer from the transfer of savings. The resource transfer *out* of a debtor country is usually defined as the current account surplus plus all interest payments to nonresidents. The transfer of savings from a debtor, however, is measured by the current account balance plus the inflation premium in interest payments. The inflation premium can be measured by considering the portion of interest payments required to keep the real value of debt unchanged. For problem debtors the transfer of real savings is estimated to have been about $4 billion in 1987, assuming the relevant inflation rate to be 3.3 percent a year.[2]

It is reasonable to expect that a country will make interest payments to nonresidents for a period when it has in a previous period been absorbing large capital inflows. If the funds have been efficiently utilized they would have raised the real value of the country's output by more than the subsequent payments needed to service interest on the debt. This is, after all, the logic behind placing interest payments to nonresidents among other service payments to nonresidents. Interest payments are payments for the use of nonresidents' savings. Thus, the resource transfer is simply the cost that goes with the benefit of higher output. The problem with funds that were borrowed in the 1970s and early 1980s is that they did not always lead to the necessary rise in output. They were used either to sustain consumption levels or invested on the basis of expectations about interest rates and terms of trade that were widely held but unfortunately turned out to be quite wrong.

Problem debtor countries had a cumulated current account deficit of $82 billion from 1983 to 1987, but this does not imply that they were net borrowers in real terms from the rest of the world. While their nominal debt did rise as a counterpart of the current account deficit, the real value of that debt was eroded by inflation. Thus, about $100 billion in the interest payments recorded over this period represented amortization of debt rather than service payments for the use of nonresident savings. In other words, if account is taken of the inflation premium implicit in interest payments, problem debtors transferred real savings to the rest of the world that cumulated to about $18 billion from 1983 to 1987.

In effect, there has therefore been some net repayment of borrowing

---

[2]The appropriate choice of a deflator will vary according to the question investigated. For expositional purposes, the U.S. GNP deflator is used here.

by the group as a whole. Over 1983–87 the decline in real debt came entirely from private sources as the real value of official credits to problem debtors rose while the real value of private credits fell by about 7 percent.[3]

From the point of view of world efficiency, funds should move internationally in response to prospective relative returns on investment opportunities whether in the public, the parastatal, or the private sector. Put very broadly, countries should be able to borrow if the expected risk-adjusted rate of return in terms of extra national output resulting from the new investment measured at expected and undistorted prices exceeds the world rate of interest. But the existence of market discounts suggests that the incentive structure discourages the flow of new funds to problem debtors.

The problem is that, in evaluating new investment opportunities in an indebted country, a resident or nonresident investor would consider his standing relative to existing creditors. When existing debt sells at a discount in secondary markets, potential investors might assume that new claims would also trade at a discount. This could be offset by relatively high expected earnings, but there are probably a limited number of investment opportunities that would be expected to yield this relatively high rate of return. In these circumstances, expectations that bring about the market discount will affect the distribution of new savings around the world, reducing the flow of new funds on a voluntary basis to problem debtor countries. This helps to explain the decline or even cessation of new lending.

Many developing countries have been able to maintain a normal relationship with their creditors, and it is not assumed here that it is beyond the grasp of those that have experienced difficulties to regain that status, as already shown by some countries. Moreover, it cannot be automatically assumed that the inflow of net new funds has been inadequate in all cases (i.e., that expected risk-adjusted rates of return at the margin generally exceed the world rate of interest). If countries have borrowed so much in the past that there has been an undue rise in their debt ratios, it may well be prudent to cease borrowing or even to reduce their indebtedness. Projects that yield the necessary rate of return may not exist. There is no presumption that all developing countries must be consistently net borrowers, and, for some, any addition to their indebt-

---

[3]In fact, nominal debt is estimated to have risen by more than the cumulated current account deficits for problem debtors over this period. This discrepancy may reflect valuation changes that do not appear in balance of payments data or errors in one or both sources of data. Both sources of data suggest that the real value of private claims on these countries declined over the period although debt statistics suggest that the real value of total debt rose somewhat.

edness at market interest rates may currently be quite unwise. This is not to say that they may not be in desperate need of extra current resources to maintain present levels of per capita consumption or even to prevent a decline. But this really represents a need for concessional finance, for a change in domestic policies, or for both. Thus the decline of new lending may have some justification, especially if new funds would be used for the maintenance of consumption or if domestic policies or economic prospects are poor.

When interpreting the causes and implications of market discounts, some attention needs to be given to the characteristics of the instruments being traded and the structure of the market. For example, observed discounts on existing syndicated credits might reflect not only the market valuation of alternative new claims on the debtor country but also the characteristics and status of these particular financial instruments. Existing syndicated credits are illiquid instruments and prices quoted in these markets are in some cases not transactions prices but only prices that the intermediaries believe are representative of market conditions. They are not structured as "trading" assets—indeed the legal structure may create impediments, thus raising the cost of trading and thus resulting in a higher discount than tradable securities. For these reasons the secondary market for existing commercial bank syndicated credits may understate the value of claims on debtor countries. But the secondary market is likely to provide at least an indication of how investors at the margin view the relative returns required for general balance of payments lending to different countries. They may not reflect, however, the return that investors require from other forms of lending to the debtor countries, such as negotiable securities. Indeed, an underlying premise of market-based approaches to the debt problem is that alternative methods of financing could be more attractive to creditors.

Finally, there is some evidence that the market values of commercial banks' stocks reflect the banks' exposures to those debtor countries whose debts are heavily discounted in secondary markets. Thus, the very well developed market for bank equity seems to reflect the same valuations of the external debt as observed in secondary markets for syndicated credits.

Fiscal Problems of Debtor Countries

Another feature of the current situation is that external debt obligations represent a present and future expected fiscal commitment in the debtor countries. Interest payments accounted for about 16½ percent of fiscal expenditures of problem debtors in 1987, and for several of these countries interest payments accounted for more than 40 percent of total expenditures. These ratios reflect the fact that in most cases the external debt of developing countries was originally—or subsequently became— an obligation of the government. This fiscal obligation is likely to reduce domestically financed investment both directly through restricting capital formation by the government, and indirectly, since private investment may be a relatively attractive tax base. Higher taxes may also distort resource allocation. There are a number of different effects here.

First, expenditures on public investment have declined and, indeed, with inadequate gross investment the public capital stock may well have depreciated in some countries. Against this, it has to be borne in mind that some public investment in the recent past has been highly uneconomic, and the reduction of such investment could even be a blessing.

Second, there is an internal transfer problem—that is, a need to raise taxes now and in the future to finance service on the public external debt. Raising taxes involves familiar collection costs and distortions in relative prices and incentives. Particularly important is the effect of future tax liabilities on the extent and form of domestic investment.

Productive investment in domestic real capital is a relatively visible activity and hence liable to be taxed heavily in direct and indirect ways, and this could lead to a sub-optimal share of domestic savings going into such investment. This prospect produces incentives both for capital flight—the investment of domestic savings abroad—and for excessive investment in nonproductive assets. Furthermore, savings may be discouraged. Prospects of high taxation also discourage the inflow of new foreign capital into the private sector. Finally, the fiscal problem generates uncertainty as to the extent to which the government will resort to inflation in order to generate internal transfers to the government.

A fiscal problem is nothing new for governments, whether developed or developing, and as the debt service obligation may be just one out of many causes of such a problem, one needs to put the role of debt service in perspective. But for many countries the increased debt service obligations have been combined with a severe deterioration in the terms of trade that has eroded the tax base. Tax liabilities are likely to reduce investment unless the burden of earlier mistakes or misfortunes is to be borne wholly by cuts in consumption. The burden must be borne somewhere, unless it is possible to increase output sufficiently by supply side measures.

II. Debt Strategy

The present strategy is that debtor countries should grow out of their debt situation with the help of (i) improved policies that are expected to raise their rates of growth, (ii) official support from governments and multilateral agencies, (iii) new money from private lenders, and (iv) growing and open markets in the industrial countries for debtor countries' exports. We discuss the role of domestic policy changes below. With regard to official funds, problem debtors have received about $124 billion in net new credits from 1982 to 1987. Increased efforts by official creditors (e.g., the Fund's enhanced structural adjustment facility) hold substantial promise for the low income countries whose debt is small in absolute terms though not relative to their capacity to pay, but official credits are not likely to provide a significant offset to the reduced availability of private credit to the middle income debtors.

Given the availability of official finance, the key issue is whether it is possible for debtor countries to meet their current debt service obligations and yet gradually grow out of debt.

Growing Out of Debt: Possibilities

To start with, one particular scenario might be considered. This is perhaps closest to the scenario implicit in the current strategy. Suppose that a debtor country gets sufficient net new funds annually so that its nominal external debt grows at the rate of inflation in the country in whose currency the debt is denominated (e.g., the United States) or—which is the same thing—its real external debt remains constant. If the country's debt/GDP ratio is 50 percent (roughly the average, net of official reserves, for the problem debtors) and if the real rate of interest on its debt is 4 percent, then the debtor country would have to make payments equal to 2 percent of its GDP annually to its foreign creditors. For the "average" problem debtor this would equal about 16 percent of exports.

One view is that this is not a great burden and is feasible. With real growth of, say, 3 percent a year, the debt/GDP ratio would steadily fall and after ten years it would be only about 37 percent. Given the same 4 percent real interest rate, only about 1½ percent of GDP would be paid to nonresident creditors. The country would be well on the way toward having grown out of debt. Both consumption and investment as a proportion of GDP could increase over time, and the rise in investment might further increase the growth rate.

Another view, however, is that this scenario would entail serious difficulties for many debtor countries. A payment of even 2 percent of GDP for an extended period would be quite large by historical standards. Moreover, these figures are based on averages for problem debtors. In fact about one quarter of all problem debtors have debt/GDP ratios that exceed 100 percent so that the ratios look twice as serious. Furthermore, it cannot be assumed that the real interest rate would stay at 4 percent or that problem debtors could borrow at market rates of interest. If, for example, the average problem debtor could attract private funds only by paying a 2 percent risk premium, then 3 percent of GDP and 24 percent of exports would have to be paid to nonresident creditors in order to keep real external debt constant. Finally, an important factor in recent years has been that declines in the debtor's terms of trade have reduced the foreign currency value of their GDPs. Thus, a given foreign currency payment to nonresidents represents a larger share of the debtor's output.

A crucial and essentially arbitrary assumption of this scenario is that real debt stays constant. One might consider some alternative scenarios.

One of these conceivable scenarios is that the nominal debt stays constant—that is, that the current account stays in balance, with no net new money being provided, some inflow from official sources being offset by net nominal amortization of commercial debt. The real debt will then decline in line with world inflation. If the nominal interest rate was 9 percent, then 4.5 percent of GDP and 36 percent of exports would initially be paid to nonresident creditors annually.

Compared with a constant real debt, this means greater payments to nonresidents now at the cost of reduced consumption or investment. If we suppose that the extra burden would be borne by consumption and not by investment we can assume the same growth rate as before, and the debt/GDP ratio will then fall more rapidly. The debt service burden will be heavier earlier but lighter later—a redistribution of the pattern of consumption over time. If some of the burden of the amortization of real debt is borne by reduced investment, the growth rate will decline and, to an extent, the burden will be borne by future rather than present consumption.

One might also consider the possibility that the country, even though already heavily in debt, increases its real debt further. Here the possibility can be considered that it borrows net in real terms to finance part of its debt service—that is, to avoid a decline in consumption that might otherwise be necessary.

If the rate of interest paid on external debt is equal to the rate of growth of nominal GDP and stays so indefinitely, the country could allow its debt to grow at the rate of interest (by borrowing all interest payments) while the debt/GDP ratio would remain at its initial level. The baseline scenario in the *World Economic Outlook,* April 1988, suggests that GDP growth in problem debtor countries might average 4.3 percent over the 1990–92 period. Real interest rates on dollar-denominated short-term debt might average about 4 percent. Thus, assuming moderate spreads over LIBOR and no changes in the terms of trade, the debt/GDP ratio would remain about unchanged if problem debtors as a whole reborrowed their interest payments.

The problem is that in the real world conditions change: one cannot rely on the interest rate payable by a debtor country staying indefinitely at or below the rate of growth, as the experience of the early 1980s has shown. The initial size of the debt is highly relevant. When the debt/GDP ratio is around 50 percent or more it may be desirable that it be reduced over time because of the possibility that the real interest rate might rise or the growth rate fall in the future, hence imposing a serious debt servicing burden.

Finally, there is the scenario where a country deliberately amortizes its debt not only in real but also in nominal terms. It may choose to do so not only when rescheduling cannot be negotiated and new funds are not available, but also when it takes a long view about its prospects and chooses for some time to reduce its indebtedness even though new funds would be available. The debt/GDP ratio may be too high and the aim may be to reduce it to a more reasonable level even at the cost of considerable sacrifice in the immediate future. It may be thought desirable to finance domestic investment wholly from domestic savings, and, in addition, to use some savings to reduce the debt. The aim would be to reduce the debt service burden in the future and to work rapidly toward the reestablishment of full creditworthiness.

Thus, many debt scenarios are possible and the one that is chosen will inevitably differ by country. The choices that authorities make will depend both on external circumstances—notably the availability of funds, the possibility of rescheduling, interest rates, and the terms of trade—and on domestic preferences—notably the weight given to future welfare relative to current welfare. The choices also have implications for policies, a matter to be discussed further below.

Availability of Funds from the Market: Role of Banks

The first growing out of debt scenario presented above assumes that some net new nominal money will be available, even though real debt stays unchanged. Over time, the debtor country would then grow out of debt and regain normal access to credit markets. But one could take a more pessimistic view and regard a scenario involving little or no net new money, and possibly even net outflows, as being more consistent with the current preferences of private external creditors.

One interpretation of the current situation is the following. The market discount and the buildup of substantial loan loss reserves indicate a lack of market confidence in the repayments prospects of problem debtor countries. When there is a discount it cannot be in the interests of any individual bank to provide new money—or indeed to reschedule—at interest rates that do not fully compensate for this discount. A reluctance to provide new money at reasonable interest rates, and attempts by individual banks to "get out" as quickly as possible, are then not at all surprising. Moreover resident investors in the debtor country might also prefer offshore investments. This interpretation is, of course, subject to doubts about the full significance of secondary market prices of commercial-bank syndicated claims given the characteristics of the claims and the structure of the market.

Here it has to be stressed that the market discount on debt and the expectations that cause it are not determined exogenously. As noted below, they are influenced by policies of the debtor countries themselves. Furthermore, even for given policies these are influenced by the atmosphere of confidence or lack of confidence created by policymakers and others in the debtor countries. With respect to the scenarios, there is perhaps an element of circularity. The theme of the first scenario presented earlier is that, provided sufficient new funds are available to keep the real debt approximately constant, it would be possible for countries to avoid undue sacrifices in consumption and investment in the near future and gradually to grow out of debt. If their authorities see this clearly they can plan rationally and with a long view, and with every intention of meeting their debt service obligations. This prospect should then inspire confidence in the minds of the creditors—hence reducing the discount and making available new money. Yet the promise of new money is needed in the first place if the scenario is to be realized.

Role of Concerted Lending

The logic of concerted lending is that the reluctance of individual private creditors can be overcome by coordination of lending. When any one bank provides extra funds, it generates favorable spillover effects for other banks. It provides funds for the debtor country to pay interest on the debts that the country owes others. (For the group of banks as a whole this is defensive lending.) In addition, it may finance new investment that raises future taxable capacity, hence raising the ability to repay all banks in the future. Given these favorable overspill effects that banks create for each other through new lending, there is a familiar argument for coordination of banks' lending. But, of course, the precondition for banks' willingness to participate is that they expect to gain as a group.

The question is whether concerted lending (or the availability of official funds) can reduce the market discount and so eventually make concerted lending itself unnecessary. One view is that the scope for further concerted lending has not been exhausted. The need is for continued initiatives designed to coordinate bank lending and "internalize" the overspill effects. In effect, a convincing pledge of private or public lending to a debtor country would convince creditors that the existing debt will eventually be serviced on a normal basis. An alternative view is that concerted private lending, at least in its current form, would not be sufficient to ensure an adequate growth path for some or even any of the problem debtors, so that alternative approaches need to be considered.

Policies of Debtor Countries

Each of the growing out of debt scenarios is based on the assumption that future growth in external debt will be quite limited as compared with its growth in the 1970s and early 1980s. The effect that this will have on domestic capital formation and economic performance in debtor countries depends on their economic policies. As discussed above, limiting the growth in debt would require significantly greater fiscal effort. If, for example, payments to nonresidents are to be financed by domestic borrowing, the government would capture a larger share of domestic savings. The resulting crowding out of private domestic investment might place the growth objective, the essence of the strategy, out of reach. Financing through monetary expansion would cause or increase inflation—as indeed it has in some of the largest problem debtors. Finally, reductions in government expenditures or measures that increase revenues should be designed to limit the detrimental effects on capital formation and growth.

In choosing a debt strategy for an individual country it is crucial, therefore, that the availability of external finance be consistent with a policy framework that can be credibly maintained by the debtor government. For example, if the amortization scenario is chosen, the typical problem debtor would have to make substantial adjustments in its fiscal stance in order to carry out its debt service commitments to nonresidents. At the same time, the real exchange rate would have to be sufficiently depreciated to ensure the appropriate relative price of tradables to nontradables needed for the payment. If the constant real debt scenario is chosen, smaller adjustments in the debtor's fiscal and exchange rate policies would be required in the near term, but a larger amount of external financing or better terms on existing debt would be necessary under this scenario.

A related part of the present strategy has been an emphasis on improved market-based policies in debtor countries. The aim has been to improve the efficiency of resource allocation, including the allocation of new investment, as well as the efficiency of state and parastatal enterprises, in some cases through their privatization. The objective is to raise the level of output and rate of growth even for given availability of foreign savings and a given domestic propensity to save.

In all countries, debtor or otherwise, industrial or developing, there is always scope for policy improvements, but what is possible and desirable clearly varies among countries as does the extent of actions that have been taken. In a number of the debtor countries there have been major changes, for example in trade policy, though no simple generalizations as to what has been achieved are possible. It can be argued that the productive potential of most of the problem debtor countries is sufficient to make possible full servicing of debts provided this potential is realized. Useful examples are set by some other indebted countries which, owing to sound policies, are not problem debtors.

If the real debt stays constant, the more policy changes are successful in raising domestic savings, investment, and efficiency—and hence the rate of growth—the quicker will be the decline in the debt/GDP ratio. Furthermore, the better the growth prospects on account of the implementation and success of these policies, the more justification there is for allowing the real debt to increase somewhat. Some new borrowing can then finance current debt service, hence possibly allowing a maintenance of or increase in per capita consumption that would not otherwise have taken place. In other words, some of the burden of the existing debt would be shifted forward in time. This is rational if the harvest of improved policies is expected to be reaped some years hence. Whether this is possible depends, of course, on there being willing lenders.

A crucial question concerns the effects of improved policies on the availability of new money. It is highly likely that signs of improved policies would in due course affect the market's perceptions favorably and so make funds more readily and cheaply available. This is at the heart of the first scenario sketched earlier and the view that the current strategy can be successful. But the policy improvements have to be credible, that is, it must be expected that they will be consistently applied and they must have sufficiently wide support in the debtor countries. The commitments by governments must be clear and sustained. There is thus a connection between two parts of the present strategy: the availability of new money from the private sector and improved policies.

The requirements that have been set out here are easier to state than for policymakers to bring about: it is not just a matter of the present implementation of new policies—itself not usually easy—but also the creation of the necessary credibility. In this respect, Fund conditionality can play an important role. In particular, if debtor countries commit themselves to sound policies, the terms on which they can borrow from private creditors are likely to be improved. As discussed above, these better terms would in themselves make it more likely that the debtor countries could eventually outgrow their problems.

Implications for World Trading Patterns

If indebted developing countries are to keep their real debt constant over a prolonged period, or if real debt is actually to fall, this would have to be accompanied by prolonged outward resource transfers by them, that is, by trade surpluses. (The term "trade surplus" is used here as shorthand for "non-interest current account surplus" since the surplus required to finance interest payments can be obtained not just from net trade flows but also from the net flow of services other than interest payments.) Other countries would have to be prepared to accept the implications; some countries must be content to run trade deficits. Such deficits will inevitably emerge, but the question is whether they will lead to tensions in the form of protectionist measures in industrial countries that would limit growth. In a world perspective the orders of magnitude are quite small. In 1987 exports of goods and services of the problem debtor countries were about 9 percent of world exports. One might envisage for some time a trade surplus of 2 percent of world exports. Even if the surplus were, say, doubled, the effect would not be large in world terms (though effects for particular product categories may be significant).

Increased trade surpluses by developing countries of these magnitudes need not create overall unemployment in industrial countries. In the short run a shift toward greater surpluses by debtor countries might increase unemployment in particular industries in industrial countries that compete in domestic or foreign markets with the products of the debtors. But that cannot be the whole story. Higher trade surpluses would be associated with increased real interest or debt repayments, which would increase spending power elsewhere, no doubt primarily in the industrial countries themselves. The marginal shift into trade deficit in the industrial countries as a whole that is required if developing countries (or some of them) are to shift into surplus would involve some contraction of tradables industries in the industrial countries, but also expansion of nontradables.

The argument applies in reverse if the indebted countries do obtain debt relief or more new funds so that they can allow themselves trade deficits. In an overall sense, reduced spending resulting from reduced interest payments received by banks and others in industrial countries would be compensated by higher spending by the developing countries themselves. The shift in the industrial countries would be marginally into tradables.

Industrial countries can make adjustment by debtor countries more difficult through protectionist measures designed to discourage the latters' export expansion, in effect worsening their terms of trade. A similarly adverse effect would result from slow economic growth in industrial countries even without an increase in protectionism. Whatever is the precise nature of the debt strategy, developing countries' exports will have to increase, and the less they get debt relief or new funds, the more this is necessary. Given official transfers and the availability of new funds from the private sector, the trade balance outcome will have to fit in with the requirements of debt service. If export expansion is made too difficult, either by protectionism or by slow growth in industrial countries, the debtor countries would have to concentrate their adjustment on reducing the growth of imports relative to GDP growth. This would be much more painful for them, especially when imports are crucial inputs into local production.

With regard to current account imbalances, in whatever direction they move as a result of developments in the debt situation, the relatively modest orders of magnitude involved from a global point of view should be noted. In 1987 the aggregate current account deficit of the problem debtors is estimated to be $19 billion, which can be compared with the U.S. deficit of $152 billion and the Japanese surplus of $85 billion.

Finally, one might consider the case of industrial countries that have trade surpluses. If they did not wish to see their tradable sectors decline or did not wish to reduce their national savings or increase domestic investment—that is, if they wished to stay in trade surplus—while other industrial countries were not willing to accept offsetting trade deficits then, one way or another, funds would have to be channeled to developing countries to allow them to run the deficits. The problem is that, given the market discount and the expectations that have given rise to it, such funds will not necessarily flow through the normal market processes. Overseas development assistance by the surplus countries, or government guarantees involving a potential commitment of government funds, would be needed. But this means that the governments would have to borrow some of the excess of domestic private savings over investment to finance the aid.

III. Supplementary Approaches

Various supplementary approaches to the current debt strategy will now be considered. It is not strictly accurate to call them new since some are already under way and might be regarded as part of the current strategy, or at least as being consistent with it.

First, there are versions of a market-based approach. These developments are, in fact, already under way to a small extent, and it is worth considering what the implications would be if this approach is pursued on a much larger scale than now.

Second, there is debt relief. This is also not new since rescheduling can be regarded as a form of partial relief, even without interest rates being reduced. The concessional nature of such agreements is even more apparent if the new terms are compared with market discounts on existing debt. Furthermore, there are well-known cases of *non*-negotiated, partial relief, that is, unilateral actions designed to lead to relief. A debt strategy proposal that would provide relief and which has been frequently suggested is the idea of an international debt facility. Often it is suggested that it should be run by, or associated with, the Fund or the World Bank, or both. Proponents imply that the debt situation might be resolved by methods that involve financial support or guarantees from the members of the Bank or the Fund as a whole or, possibly, industrial countries only.

Market-Based Approaches

The bulk of private lending to developing countries in recent years has been intermediated by commercial banks in the form of medium-term syndicated credits. One response to recent difficulties in expanding this type of lending has been a search for alternative forms of private lending. Such initiatives involve the exchange of syndicated credits for an alternative liability of the debtor country or, less frequently, for cash.

In cases in which existing syndicated credits sell at a discount in the secondary market, the yield to maturity to a buyer is higher than the contractual yield. In this section, a number of cases are examined in which the debtor itself is the buyer of existing debt. If the debtor is to finance a buy-back of syndicated credit with borrowed funds, the cost of which is less than the yield on repurchased debt, or with the sale of assets that yield less, the contractual value of the debtor country's outstanding debt and the interest payments on that debt would be reduced. The magnitude of the savings would depend on the discount at which the debt were purchased, the amounts that were purchased, and the cost of the borrowed funds.

Alternatively, the debtor country could use resources obtained through a current account surplus or a reduction in reserves, or from sales or conversions of alternative financial instruments, to buy existing debt at a discount. New financing could take the form of debt-equity swaps, proceeds from concerted lending packages, concessional assistance, sales of bonds, or any other transaction that places additional funds in the hands of the debtor country.

The cost of using reserves (or earnings from a current account surplus) to retire existing debt would depend on the best alternative use of funds. This might be measured by the return on foreign financial investments, by the potential cost of holding an inadequate level of reserves, or by the rate of return on domestic investment. To the extent that other instruments of external finance are used to finance the retirement of existing debt, the cost of such financing would tend to approach the effective cost of existing syndicated debt unless the country is able to differentiate the characteristics of the new external claims in a way that such claims would be seen as having less risk, higher seniority, or other advantages over existing debt. For example, a country might declare that the alternative financing instruments would receive priority when they pay interest (or dividends). Alternatively, the new instruments might not be subject to rescheduling and would not be included in the base for any future new money packages. On the other hand, if the country borrowed new funds at the same effective interest rate as prevailed in the secondary market for syndicated credits (i.e., taking into account the market discount), it would simply exchange instruments with the same contractual value.

The credibility of declarations designed to differentiate new debt, and thus the potential relative financing cost advantages of the alternative financing instruments, will depend on a number of factors. The smaller the amount outstanding of such instruments relative to the amount outstanding of syndicated credits, the greater the credibility that the debtor can maintain preferred treatment of such claims. Of course, the larger the debt servicing problem facing the country, the lower would be the credibility of such declarations.

Although a country may be able to reduce total interest payments and the total book value of external claims using other lower-cost financing instruments, other considerations should be taken into account. If additional external resources should be required in the future to service external claims, and if some form of concerted lending is needed, it may be more difficult to obtain sufficient resources because of a smaller concerted lending base. In particular, if the money center banks become net sellers of debt, they will have less to gain from defensive lending since the favorable overspill effects will go to many other holders of the debt as well as to themselves. Moreover, since the holders of the debt become more dispersed, they will find it more difficult to organize themselves, and thus they lose some of the bargaining power in relation to the debtors. These problems would be reduced if the new securities were bought by fringe creditors rather than the major lenders. In this case, the narrowing of ownership of a country's debt could facilitate concerted lending.

Buy-Backs Financed by Current Account Surpluses or Sales of Reserve Assets

A relatively straightforward transaction would be for the debtor government to repurchase its own debt for cash acquired through a current account surplus or sales of reserve assets. From the debtor country's point of view amortization at a discount is certainly preferable to amortization of debt at its contractual value. But there remains the basic question as to whether amortization, even at a discount, is desirable. It would be desirable if the savings on interest and principal on retired debt exceeded the benefits that could be derived from alternative uses of the funds that financed the buy-back. Since the buy-backs are voluntary transactions between debtors and creditors, they could be important vehicles for avoiding conflict. But the scope for such transactions is limited by provisions in syndicated credits that specify that all participants in the credit share in such a buy-back.

Buy-backs would allow the banks to dispose of some of their debt in the market and is a natural response to a changing perception of the value of the debt held in banks' portfolios. Loan loss provisioning has made it possible for commercial banks to realize the losses that accompany sales of developing country debt. While the size of bank reserves currently varies across creditor countries, there has been a widespread increase in reserves in 1987.

Alternatively, a cash buy-back might be financed by foreign donors. When there are several donors and they act through a multilateral agency and the buy-back takes this last form , this is, in fact, the proposal for an international debt facility, which will be discussed below.

Securitization

In its purest form, securitization consists essentially of a process that increases the tradability of existing claims. But as argued above, it could also involve larger changes that would make the new claims more desirable than existing claims for other reasons. An example would be the assignment of collateral to new securities. As with buy-backs for cash, exchanges of new securities for existing debt would benefit debtors as long as the cost of the new security is less than the implicit yield on existing debt.

Securitization could reduce the cost of debt because it would increase its marketability and would make developing countries' debt available to investors who might value it more highly than do current holders. Insurance companies, mutual funds, pension funds, and so on, as well as individual investors, might bid for new instruments and thus increase their market value. It is sometimes argued that commercial banks are not the best vehicles for the flow of private funds to sovereign borrowers, other than for short-term trade credit. In particular, in the 1970s the banks played an unusually prominent role in the light of historical experience. Thus, a return to bond-financing, as well as an increase in direct investment, would be a movement back toward a historical norm.

Debt-Equity Swaps

A typical debt-equity swap involves a straightforward set of transactions. In most cases the debtor government offers to swap its debt for domestic currency on the condition that the currency be used to purchase local equity. First, the investing company acquires existing debt in the secondary market or, in the case of commercial banks, utilizes its own holdings. Then it exchanges this debt with the debtor government for local currency so that the debt is retired. Finally, it uses the domestic currency to purchase local equity or finance approved domestic projects. As far as the debtor country is concerned, some of its foreign-currency-denominated debt has been retired early. This expenditure can be financed in a number of ways, and this is explained further below. From the point of view of the debtor country's balance of payments, a prospective flow of public sector interest payments is replaced by a flow of private sector dividend payments. This has a number of implications both for the time-profile of payments and for the degree of risk-spreading involved. When there are dividend rather than interest flows, more of the risks of terms of trade changes, for example, are likely to be shared by the creditors.

The incentives that lead investors to participate in swaps vary from case to case. In some instances, investors have been able to purchase existing debt in the secondary market at a lower price than the price at which the government is willing to redeem it. If an investor purchases a foreign-currency-denominated debt instrument at a 50 percent discount and sells it to the debtor country authorities for 100 percent of the equivalent domestic currency price, the government can be thought of as offering a favorable exchange rate for this transaction. Thus, as compared to a cash purchase of equity, the debtor government has provided more domestic currency to the investor than he could have obtained at prevailing market prices. It is not necessarily the case, however, that such an incentive is required since, in most debtor countries, a simple removal of controls on foreign investment could also provide an incentive for the purchase of equities or direct investment.

An important issue is whether the net result of a debt-equity swap is that the country obtains more or less funds in total. On the one hand it is retiring debt, and to that extent there are less funds; on the other hand the attractiveness of direct private investment has been improved and this—on its own—is likely to increase the net inflow of such investment. Thus, if one thinks only of direct investment, "additionality" can be expected. But if one takes into account the retirement of debt, there is no general presumption that a net increase or decrease of inflow of funds would result.

Residents of the debtor country might also be encouraged to exchange their assets held offshore for their government's debt in order to swap for domestic equities if the government agreed to waive any penalties or tax liability that might be associated with repatriation. Changes in regulatory constraints or policy changes that encouraged residents to repatriate so-called flight capital could play an important role in solving the foreign exchange problems of some debtor countries. Because debtor governments are often unable to tax earnings on such assets, official interest payments to nonresidents cannot be financed by private interest receipts on foreign assets that have resulted from capital flight. Again, it is clear that the fiscal problem faced by debtor country governments is an important aspect of the debt problem.

Opening domestic equity markets to foreign direct investment could bring benefits in terms of technology transfers and related benefits that exceed the "additional" capital inflow that might accompany such measures. Moreover, the capital stocks of most debtor countries are large relative to their external debts so that the potential for equity sales in exchange for debt is considerable. For these reasons some observers consider debt-equity swaps a potentially important part of the solution to the debt problem, even though swaps have totaled only about $4.5 billion through June 1987, or about 2 percent of the outstanding bank debt of countries with active conversion schemes.

An important constraint on debt-equity swaps is the fact that in most instances the equity attractive to private investors is owned by the private sector of the debtor country while the debt is owed by the government. It follows that the debtor government must finance the swap as it would any other expenditure. It must increase taxes or reduce expenditures, borrow on domestic credit markets or print money. The internal fiscal problem discussed earlier, which is at the heart of the debt problem, remains and is brought forward in time. It is a frequent concern that the method of financing would be through monetary expansion and hence would be inflationary. An alternative means of financing is for the debtor government to sell domestic-currency-denominated securities to domestic residents. But the ability of the domestic credit market to absorb such sales may limit the scope for debt-equity swaps. Indeed, it can be argued that if a country has a fiscal problem in paying interest on its debt, it must have an even greater immediate problem in trying to finance what is, in effect, a buy-back of its debt.

The fiscal problem could be avoided if publicly owned enterprises were privatized and the equity of the privatized enterprises were then swapped for debt. If privatization of public enterprises led to increases in efficiency, the debtor government would gain from a reduction both in its external debt and in the need to subsidize the public enterprise. However, if the government swapped debt for equity in currently profitable public enterprises, the reduction in the government's future tax receipts would have to be set against the reduction in payments on external debt.

Proponents of debt-equity swaps usually have more in mind than a simple exchange of financial claims. In most cases some additional incentives, or the removal of existing disincentives, for the private investor are an integral part of such proposals. In some cases this might involve a direct subsidy by the debtor government or perhaps more frequently the relaxation of administrative controls over nonresident investment in the debtor country or repatriation of capital by residents of the debtor country. The debtor country might gain substantially from relaxing barriers to equity investments by nonresidents or by privatization. It is important to stress that such policy improvements (generally supported by the Fund) and the resultant benefits need not be linked to swaps of debt for equity.

In order to understand more precisely what is involved in a debt-equity swap, it is useful to think of it as being equivalent to a debt-for-cash swap, or buy-back, coupled with policy reforms that induce nonresidents to purchase equity in the debtor country. Provided the equity purchases are not actually subsidized—or that the firms or industries concerned are not excessively protected relative to other industries—there are likely to be clear benefits to the debtor country from such policy reforms quite independent from their association with a buy-back scheme, which in itself may or may not be beneficial.

Contingent Claims

The transformation of existing debt into equities or tradable securities would provide an opportunity to make future payments by debtors contingent on developments that will affect their ability to service debt. Since problem debtors would share in improvements in their economic performance, this could provide better incentives for economic adjustment. For example, a contingent contract might link interest payments to growth in exports. Moreover, since existing floating rate contracts are contingent on market interest rates, it might be beneficial to insulate interest payments from this source of uncertainty.

While existing contracts may be poorly suited to the needs of developing countries, contingent claims are better suited to allocate the risk of changes in the economic environment in advance than to allocate a loss after conditions have changed. Thus, an important lesson from the difficulties that have confronted many developing countries is that their contractual obligations should henceforth better reflect the uncertainties surrounding their ability to service debt. Nevertheless, an exchange of debt for contingent claims would not necessarily help to resolve the existing debt problem: the addition of a contingency clause to an existing claim would not necessarily change its market value.

Debt Relief

Debt relief can be defined as any change in the contractual arrangements that is favorable to the debtor. While market-based solutions transform the debt, debt relief is defined as reducing the contractual value of the debt in terms of present value.

Relief can be brought about as a purely voluntary act of the creditor, or it can result from a bargaining process in which the threat of delay or default—possibly partial default—plays a role. An extreme threat would involve debt repudiation.

Relief can take the form of the contractual value of the principal being written down, or it can take the form of rescheduling at reduced spreads over market interest rates. It can also involve a shifting forward of the payments stream. For example, for a limited period, part or all of interest payments might be capitalized at rates that do not reflect market conditions, so that the debt increases, the implication being that it will be easier to pay later than now, but that eventually—possibly a long time ahead—all interest and principal will be paid.

At least two questions arise here. First, is it to the advantage of creditors to grant relief and, in particular, to grant it voluntarily rather than under threat? Second, is it in the interest of debtor countries to obtain relief, especially when it can only be obtained with threat of default or with actual, possibly temporary, default? It is unlikely that there is a general answer applying to all cases. Following are some relevant considerations.

Point of View of Creditors

For the creditors as a group there is always a strong argument against reducing the contractual value of the debt—that is, providing voluntary debt relief—even when the chances of ever getting full debt service payments over the lifetime of the loan are considered quite slim. The reason is simply that the contractual value sets the "ceiling" to what might be paid back, and since there is always at least a slight chance that capacity or willingness to pay will turn out to be favorable, there would be a potential loss in reducing the ceiling. Even when banks write down the value of a loan in their books on the basis of their expectations of a possible loss, it is not necessarily in their interests to give up the possibility of full repayment. For an individual bank the argument against writing down the contractual debt is even stronger. If it does so while others do not, its share of eventual repayments will be reduced.

In general, "voluntary" relief will have to be tied to some other change in the outlook. The situation would be transformed from the creditors' point of view if the reduction of the contractual value is associated with an increased probability of full or substantial repayments of the debt that remains. The problem is to provide the credible assurance. Proposals for the provision of debt relief as part of an agreement with debtor governments backed by Fund surveillance or conditionality really involve this kind of bargain. The key issue is whether any arrangements can be made that would yield assurances backed with sufficient credibility. It should be noted here that the more commercial debt becomes dispersed in the market the more difficult it becomes to strike bargains of this kind. These bargains clearly hinge on creditors acting as a group.

With the prospects of better policies, debt relief that effectively reduces actual debt service payments in the near future is likely to increase investment in the debtor country. This has already been discussed. It may do so through reducing the market discount on debt, through increasing the resources available to the debtor government for public investment and for support of private investment, and through reducing the prospective tax rates (including inflation tax) and so raising the expected profitability of private investment. Increased investment and hence growth in the debtor countries would increase the repayment prospects and hence, in this respect, benefit creditors. Of course, the possibility cannot be ruled out that the gains to debtors from debt relief would simply be used to increase consumption rather than improving repayment prospects of the remaining debt or increasing investment.

Another motive for relief from the point of view of the creditors could be the threat of some degree of default or subordination of existing credits. If it is clearly seen that there is a good chance that a country will not be able or willing to meet its full contractual payments, is there any argument from the point of view of the creditors for reducing the contractual value (apart from the consideration just discussed)? One argument is that it avoids the unpleasantness of default and so gives the creditors some goodwill that may stand them in good stead in later years when economic conditions in the debtor country have changed; giving something up that is likely to be lost anyway also reduces the costs of bargaining. Furthermore, it is at least possible that once serious default is contemplated it may not be partial, so that creditors may be better off by offering partial relief. In addition, default may involve penalties (e.g., deprivation of trade credits) that also impose some costs on creditors or others in creditor countries. Here again, the more commercial debt becomes dispersed, the less likely is it that creditors will be able to take all these considerations into account.

The willingness of commercial banks to grant debt relief will also be affected by the regulatory environment, by tax arrangements, and possibly by accounting conventions. This is a complex subject, which can only be touched upon here.

The accounting issue is straightforward. Market perceptions of a bank's solvency may be influenced by accounting conventions—for example, whether debt on the books has to be written down when some similar debt has been sold at a discount or when relief in some form has been given, and whether it can be written down gradually or must be written down immediately. But such conventions do not affect the realities of the worth of the assets a bank holds. Presumably, it is always desirable that the accounts give a true picture.

The more important issue is the extent to which the cost of debt relief (given that there is a cost to the creditors) is shared by governments of the creditor countries. It may be shared in three ways. First, there may be direct or indirect subsidization of buy-backs, conceivably through the intermediation of an international debt facility. This will be discussed further below. Second, if debt relief is so great as to "use up" the whole of a bank's capital (which appears highly unlikely for most banks in present circumstances), the security of deposits would be threatened, and governments would come to the rescue through deposit insurance and possibly lender-of-last resort action.

Third, and most important, are the tax implications. In most countries, credit losses, whether on domestic or foreign loans, involve tax relief, the details varying. This means that the government shares the losses. In this regard it may be particularly important if governments allow provisions against possible or expected losses to be set against current earnings when calculating taxable income. Such allowances can create incentives for provisioning since the bank would gain tax relief before losses are actually realized. It would, of course, also reduce the incentive for declaring a loss. But, by strengthening banks' after-tax earnings, this could strengthen their bargaining power in their dealings with debtor countries.

Point of View of Debtors

For a debtor country, the benefits of debt relief voluntarily granted may seem obvious. After all, investment is likely to increase, and in addition more resources for current consumption will become available. But the long view must also take into account the effect on future creditworthiness. If circumstances induced creditors to grant relief this time, it could happen again, and the expectation of a repetition is likely to affect the availability of funds and their spreads in the future. Thus it may not be in a debtor country's interests to obtain relief, or to apply pressure for relief.

The debtor country needs to assess both the likelihood that it will be in the market again within a reasonable time and how exceptional the circumstances of the last years that have given rise to the need for or offer of relief have been. If the circumstances are recognized in later years as having been exceptional, future potential creditors will attach only a low probability to a repetition of debt relief having to be provided. It can, of course, be argued that the combination of recession in 1981–82, high real interest rates, and then severe declines in the non-oil primary product terms of trade, combined with the severe and widely unexpected decline in the oil price recently, has been exceptional.

It is possible that some countries face interest payments that are so high relative to their ability to pay that there seems little likelihood that the country will regain access to additional credit in the foreseeable future. In such cases unilateral actions by the debtor country, such as interest moratoria or more extreme actions, may be considered. However, unilateral actions by debtors—as distinct from relief voluntarily granted—run the risk of substantial additional costs. The most important of these would be loss of access to trade credits and the international payments mechanism. This would result from the possibility that any payment made through the payments mechanism would be subject to the legal claims of creditors. In this event, the debtor would be unable to finance its trade or to make payments through normal channels. In the extreme the debtor country would be forced to barter its goods internationally.

The associated loss of world trade and efficiency would reduce the welfare of debtors, of their trading partners, and of creditors. For this reason, all parties have strong incentives to avoid this mutually costly outcome. Thus, it is desirable that creditors cooperate in setting conditions that will induce debtors to participate in strategies that minimize confrontation. For their part, debtors, in their own interest, should avoid actions that will ultimately result in their exclusion not only from private credit markets but also the international payments system. The international community has an important stake in ensuring that this option is not exercised since it is clearly not in the interest of either party or their neighbors.

International Debt Facility

A common proposal designed to deal with the developing countries' debt problem is to set up an international debt facility that would buy debt at a discount and then write down its contractual value, hence providing debt relief. Similar proposals would have the facility guarantee repayment of credits that remain in private hands. The facility could be envisaged on a large or a small scale, possibly applying to only a few countries. Many of the general considerations associated with voluntary debt relief apply here as well. A difference, however, is that an officially supported facility is likely to involve some contribution or some guarantees from its owners. There are three main parties involved in a typical proposal, namely the debtor governments, private creditors, and the owners of the facility. It is then necessary to analyze how the costs and benefits of a typical proposal might accrue to the various parties.

The groundwork for the discussion can be established by considering a very simple case in which the expected capacity to pay off the debtor and the probability distribution around its capacity to pay remain unchanged and in which debt that is not sold to the facility is not subordinated to debt that is sold to the facility. The facility would offer to buy the debt of a developing country and would announce in advance that some part of the purchased debt would be forgiven.[4] In this case private

---

[4]If, alternatively, a part of the debt were not actually bought by the facility, but were only guaranteed by it—so that the private holder would have the right to sell the debt to the facility at contractual value or some discount—the effects would be roughly the same. The market value of debt that is not guaranteed would rise while the facility would have incurred an expected cost.

creditors will gain at the expense of the facility because the market price of debt will rise as the result of the forgiveness. This happens because, following the forgiveness by the facility, there will be a smaller stock of contractual claims on an unchanged expected capacity to pay. This is an example of the general proposition that it is generally inappropriate to assume that market prices would remain unchanged given any important change in the economic environment. In addition, the debtor country will gain because of the "ceiling effect" mentioned earlier. That is, the contractual value of the debt sets a ceiling on what the debtor country would pay and this will be reduced by debt relief.

Thus the various proposals for an international debt facility really have two aspects. First, there is a gain to the banks reflected in the higher market price, and resulting essentially from a transfer of risks from the private creditors to the facility. Second, there is a gain to the debtors owing to the reduction in the contractual value of the debt. Both these gains are obtained at the expense of the owners of the facility who acquire the new reduced debts with the inevitable risks they involve.

The likely gain to private creditors at the expense of the facility could be avoided if debt retained by private creditors is subordinated to debt purchased by the facility. There may be legal obstacles to this, but if it is brought about, the market price of debt remaining in the hands of private creditors might not rise following forgiveness of the part of the debt bought by the facility. In effect the potential increase in the value of the remaining debt owing to forgiveness could be offset to some extent by a fall in price owing to subordination of this debt relative to that held by the facility.

A full analysis of the potential costs and benefits of a facility is considerably complicated if likely total repayments (interest and amortization) are altered by the existence of the facility. For example, the operation of a facility could be combined with conditionality or other arrangements which reduced the risk of low payouts. In this case all creditors, including the facility, and perhaps even the debtor country itself, could be made better off. Creditors might be made better off since the likely payoffs on remaining debt would in the aggregate be higher than they were initially. The debtor country may also be made better off if conditionality allows it to commit itself convincingly to policies that it plans to undertake in any case. To the extent that such commitments are more credible this would allow the country to face a market discount which was more appropriate or which better reflected the country's likely policy choices.

On the other side of the coin, it could be pointed out that debt facility proposals present a moral hazard problem. Debtors have an interest in the facility's purchase price being reduced as much as possible. Thus the valuation of debt prior to the facility's purchase may be manipulated by the debtor government. A constraint on such behavior is that it could involve a loss of credibility and perhaps a long-run cost to the debtor governments involved. It may be possible to overcome the moral hazard problem by establishing a purchase price above the market price or perhaps using the market price that prevailed at a specified day before the possibility of the facility was considered.

If a facility was to purchase a significant part of the commercial debt of the developing countries that currently have problems (as is sometimes proposed), this would involve a very large transfer of risk internationally from private creditors to governments or multilateral institutions. The governments that underwrite the facility directly or that underwrite the multilateral institution that operates the facility have to be prepared for their taxpayers to assume the risk. There would also be the problem of deciding which countries would be provided with the option of making use of the facility. In particular, such proposals can be viewed as benefiting countries that have not made adjustment efforts relative to countries that have made such efforts.

REFERENCES

International Monetary Fund, *World Economic Outlook: A Survey by the Staff of the International Monetary Fund,* World Economic and Financial Surveys (Washington, April 1987).

———, *World Economic Outlook: A Survey by the Staff of the International Monetary Fund,* World Economic and Financial Surveys (Washington, April 1988).

Watson, Maxwell, and others, *International Capital Markets, Developments and Prospects,* World Economic and Financial Surveys (Washington: International Monetary Fund, January 1988).

External Debt Problem of
Sub-Saharan Africa

JOSHUA GREENE*

The massive external debt burden of sub-Saharan Africa has gained wide-spread attention as a serious policy issue during the past few years. This paper reviews recent trends in the debt levels and economic performance of sub-Saharan countries and assesses a number of proposals for reducing their external debt service obligations. There is also a discussion of the modalities of various debt relief proposals that have been advanced.

M OST OF THE RECENT discussion of external debt problems of developing countries has centered on middle-income countries, particularly those in Latin America. Apart from the studies by Krumm (1985), Lancaster and Williamson (1986), and Feldstein and others (1987), relatively little attention has been paid to the external debt of African countries, in particular that of sub-Saharan nations. During the past year, however, a number of papers have appeared on this subject, including studies by Helleiner (1989), Humphreys and Underwood (1988), Lancaster (1989), Mistry (1988), Stymne (1988), the United Nations (1988), and Weerasinghe (1988). Perhaps more significantly, the Group of Seven countries have acknowledged the seriousness of the problem through their decision at the June 1988 Toronto summit and at the annual meetings of the Fund and the World Bank in September 1988 to provide more extensive debt relief for very low-income countries. Under this initiative, low-income countries will be able to reschedule their debt over longer periods, enjoy lower interest rates on rescheduled debt, or receive partial debt forgiveness as ways of reducing their increasingly severe debt burdens.

* Mr. Greene, an Economist in the Developing Country Studies Division of the Research Department, completed undergraduate studies at Princeton University and holds both a law degree and a doctorate in economics from the University of Michigan.

The external debt of sub-Saharan countries has received less attention than that of middle-income countries in part because it poses less of a threat to the international banking system. In recent years, upwards of 75 percent of the publicly guaranteed external debt of sub-Saharan countries has been owed to bilateral or multilateral institutions, compared with well under half the debt of most Latin American countries. At the end of 1987 only about 21 percent of total external debt for sub-Saharan countries was owed to financial institutions, and the bulk of that represented loans to a few countries, such as Côte d'Ivoire and Nigeria that have had significant access to international financial markets.[1] Consequently, the debt service problems of sub-Saharan countries are more a concern of donor governments and international institutions than of commercial banks.

The mounting debt levels of sub-Saharan countries are nevertheless serious. Rising debt service levels severely limit the ability of these countries to finance critical imports and new development projects. In addition, the increasing difficulty of these countries in meeting debt service obligations poses a particular problem for multilateral agencies, such as the Fund, which had SDR 4.9 billion in credit (excluding Trust Fund loans of SDR 0.3 billion) outstanding to sub-Saharan countries as of the end of 1988.[2] The same is true for the World Bank, whose outstanding IBRD loans and IDA credits to sub-Saharan countries approached US$18 billion at the end of 1988, and for the African Development Bank, among other multilateral creditors. These agencies depend heavily on recycling their assets for financial operations and may not be able to obtain additional funds readily in the event of loan or operations losses.[3] The primary exception is the World Bank's IDA facility, which requires periodic replenishment of its resources because of the very long maturities (50 years' repayment, with 10 years' grace) of its credits.

This paper assesses the debt problems of sub-Saharan African countries and examines various proposals for reform. Data for this analysis are based on the 44 Fund member countries in sub-Saharan Africa,

---

[1] Other major market borrowers include the Republic of the Congo and Gabon. In past years, however, a number of other sub-Saharan countries including Kenya, Liberia, Malawi, Senegal, Zaïre, Zambia, and Zimbabwe made significant use of commercial borrowing.

[2] Data obtained from International Monetary Fund (1989), p. 36.

[3] The World Bank does borrow on the international capital market, but mostly to supplement funds for its IBRD facility, which is used for middle- and higher-income countries and thus is not available to most sub-Saharan countries.

excluding South Africa.[4] These countries are of special interest because of their very low per capita incomes and their general dependence on only a few primary commodities for export earnings. Most of these countries have experienced severe economic setbacks during the last decade as a result of the weakness in primary commodity markets. In addition, more than half have required debt rescheduling or incurred arrears on debt service obligations since 1980.

The plan of the paper is as follows. Section I describes the dimensions of the debt problem facing sub-Saharan Africa, reviewing recent developments in debt and debt-service levels, and comparing them with other countries identified for their debt-service difficulties. Recent trends in economic indicators are also presented. Section II examines the origins of the sub-Saharan Africa debt problem, while Section III reviews the initial donor responses, focusing on Fund and Bank assistance and debt rescheduling from bilateral and commercial bank creditors. Section IV discusses more recent debt initiatives, including the formation of the Fund's Enhanced Structural Adjustment Facility (ESAF), and the Group of Seven proposal to reduce debt service burdens for low-income countries. Section V then analyzes a number of alternative proposals for lessening the debt burdens of sub-Saharan African countries. Measures that sub-Saharan African countries could take on their own are also considered. Conclusions are presented in Section VI.

I. Dimensions of the Sub-Saharan African Debt Problem

How severe is the sub-Saharan debt problem? Tables 1 and 2, which draw on the Fund's World Economic Outlook (WEO) data base, provide some indication. These figures abstract from the significant differences among individual country debt positions. Thus, they obscure the relative success of a few countries, such as Botswana, Lesotho, Swaziland, and Zimbabwe, in limiting their debt buildup and in remaining current on their debt-service obligations. Nevertheless, the aggregate information reported here indicates a substantial increase both in the stock of sub-Saharan debt and in debt-service levels since the early 1970s, although the data for years before 1980 must be treated with caution. The aggre-

---

[4] The countries are Benin, Botswana, Burkina Faso, Burundi, Cameroon, Cape Verde, Central African Republic, Chad, Comoros, Congo, Côte d'Ivoire, Djibouti, Equatorial Guinea, Ethiopia, Gabon, the Gambia, Ghana, Guinea, Guinea-Bissau, Kenya, Lesotho, Liberia, Madagascar, Malawi, Mali, Mauritania, Mauritius, Mozambique, Niger, Nigeria, Rwanda, São Tomé and Príncipe, Senegal, Seychelles, Sierra Leone, Somalia, Sudan, Swaziland, Tanzania, Togo, Uganda, Zaïre, Zambia, and Zimbabwe.

Table 1. External Debt and Debt Service of Sub-Saharan Africa, 1970-87[1]

(In billions of U.S. dollars; at end of period)

	1970 Est.	1975 Est.	1980	1981	1982	1983	1984	1985	1986	1987
Aggregate external debt	6.0	15.8	54.0	64.1	73.1	82.0	85.5	97.2	112.7	126.5
Medium and long-term debt										
Including Fund	5.8	15.2	47.9	57.2	63.6	71.4	76.2	87.6	105.3	119.2
Excluding Fund	5.8	14.7	45.1	52.8	58.5	65.0	69.3	80.8	98.9	113.3
Publicly guaranteed	5.4	13.8	41.8	48.2	53.6	60.1	63.9	74.7	92.3	106.4
Not publicly guaranteed	0.4	0.8	3.2	4.5	5.0	4.9	5.4	6.1	6.6	6.9
Fund	—	0.5	2.8	4.4	5.1	6.4	6.9	6.9	6.4	5.9
Short-term debt	0.2	0.6	6.1	6.9	9.5	10.6	9.3	9.6	7.4	7.3
Debt-service payments	0.7	2.1	6.4	7.3	8.1	8.3	10.7	12.2	9.9	9.2
To non-Fund agencies	0.7	2.0	6.0	6.8	7.5	7.6	9.8	11.2	8.5	7.9
To the Fund[2]	—	0.1	0.5	0.5	0.6	0.7	0.9	1.0	1.4	1.3
Memorandum items:										
Estimated impact of rescheduling	—	—	0.8	1.4	0.5	3.5	2.8	3.1	11.1	11.1
Estimated stock of arrears	—	0.5	0.6	1.3	5.6	10.6	11.7	14.3	16.6	18.0
Publicly guaranteed debt owed to (In percent)										
Governments	53.7	46.9	40.4	40.0	41.9	41.6	42.6	44.9	48.8	49.2
Multilateral institutions	16.7	22.4	26.2	28.0	29.0	29.7	30.8	29.5	27.7	28.4
Financial institutions	5.6	17.5	26.2	26.2	23.0	21.7	19.0	17.4	16.7	15.3
Other creditors	22.2	14.0	7.4	8.6	6.0	7.4	7.6	8.2	6.8	7.0

Sources: International Monetary Fund, International Financial Statistics (1988); and Fund staff estimates.
[1] Defined as Africa excluding Algeria, Angola, Morocco, Namibia, South Africa, and Tunisia.
[2] Repurchases and charges; excludes payments on Trust Fund and SAF loans.

Table 2.   *Debt Burden Indicators for Sub-Saharan Africa and Debt-Distressed Countries, 1970–87*[1]

(In percent)

	1970 Est.	1975 Est.	1980	1982	1985	1986	1987
Ratio of external debt to exports of goods and services							
Sub-Saharan Africa	65.4	65.2	94.1	190.9	253.6	335.5	352.4
Countries with recent debt-servicing problems[2]	131.7	111.0	155.6	247.0	282.3	322.6	317.0
Fifteen heavily indebted countries[3]	162.5	133.9	169.5	271.9	301.2	361.0	347.6
Ratio of external debt to GDP							
Sub-Saharan Africa	14.1	17.1	27.2	38.7	51.2	62.8	81.6
Countries with recent debt-servicing problems[2]	18.7	18.8	34.2	44.6	51.1	51.7	54.2
Fifteen heavily indebted countries[3]	19.6	18.5	33.1	43.0	47.8	49.2	51.3
Ratio of debt-service payments to exports of goods and services[4]							
Sub-Saharan Africa	7.7	8.2	11.1	21.1	31.8	29.5	25.6
Countries with recent debt-servicing problems[2]	19.4	20.8	27.8	40.2	35.8	39.1	32.6
Fifteen heavily indebted countries[3]	24.8	27.7	30.0	40.3	40.3	46.4	38.3

Source: International Monetary Fund, *International Financial Statistics* (1988); and Fund staff estimates.
[1] Ratios for debt are based on aggregate debt excluding arrears.
[2] Average for capital-importing countries that experienced external arrears in 1985 or that rescheduled debt during 1984–86.
[3] Average for Argentina, Bolivia, Brazil, Chile, Colombia, Côte d'Ivoire, Ecuador, Mexico, Morocco, Nigeria, Peru, Philippines, Uruguay, Venezuela, and Yugoslavia.
[4] Data for 1970 and 1975 exclude payments to the Fund.

gate external debt of sub-Saharan countries, excluding arrears, has grown from an estimated US$6 billion in 1970 to more than US$126 billion at the end of 1987, more than a 650 percent increase in constant (1980) U.S. dollar terms. Over the same period their real GDP per capita has fallen by about 11 percent[5] (Table 3 and Figures 1 and 2). Total debt-service payments on medium- and long-term external debt for these countries are estimated to have grown from less than US$1 billion in 1970 to more than US$12 billion in 1985 before falling to US$9 billion in 1987. This includes more than US$1 billion a year in payments to the Fund during 1985–87.

As shown in Table 2, this rise in total payments represents an increase in the ratio of debt-service payments to exports of goods and services from an estimated 8 percent in 1970 to 26 percent in 1987, after declining from a peak of 32 percent in 1985. These debt-service ratios understate the true debt-service burden facing sub-Saharan countries, however, because they reflect only payments and not scheduled obligations. Once debt relief (estimated at US$11 billion in 1987, for example) and arrears (estimated at US$1–2 billion in 1986 and 1987) are taken into account, scheduled debt-service obligations probably exceeded 50 percent of exports of goods and services during 1986 and 1987. Moreover, some preliminary estimates suggest that with the region's current ratio of total debt to exports exceeding 350 percent, even full rescheduling of forthcoming principal payments over the next five years would allow no growth in nominal imports if export earnings grow at a plausibly conservative rate of 3 percent a year.[6] Given the need for real import growth to allow a recovery in real output per capita, these figures suggest that the region as a whole is far from being able to meet forthcoming debt-service obligations without continuing debt relief on a scale more massive even than that granted in recent years.[7]

Table 2 and Figures 3–5 also compare the debt burdens of sub-Saharan Africa and of two groups of countries distinguished by their debt problems—countries with recent debt-servicing problems[8] and a group

[5] The decline is 6 percent if Nigeria is excluded.
[6] Stymne (1988).
[7] Stymne (1988), referring to the composition and terms of sub-Saharan external debt, suggests that a ratio of debt to exports of goods and service higher than 150 to 180 percent is excessive for African countries, because this figure corresponds to a debt-service ratio of about 25 to 30 percent. This is the debt-service ratio for those sub-Saharan countries now barely meeting their scheduled debt-service obligations.
[8] These are defined in the October 1988 *World Economic Outlook* report as capital-importing developing countries that incurred external payments arrears in 1985 or that rescheduled their debt at any time during 1984–86. See International Monetary Fund (1988), p. 54.

Table 3.   Selected Economic Indicators for Sub-Saharan Africa, 1970–87[1]

(Index: 1980 = 100)

	1970 Est.	1975 Est.	1980	1982	1985	1986	1987
Sub-Saharan Africa							
Real GDP	72.4	90.7	100.0	101.5	101.7	104.6	107.1
Real GDP per capita	97.0	105.8	100.0	96.1	89.1	89.2	88.8
Consumer prices	21.5	38.1	100.0	144.1	266.8	308.8	369.4
Export value	15.2	41.1	100.0	64.6	66.6	55.6	58.4
Export volume	94.9	97.6	100.0	70.4	81.4	85.8	82.9
Import volume	55.5	75.8	100.0	101.0	80.1	71.3	66.6
Export unit value	16.1	42.1	100.0	91.6	81.9	64.8	70.4
Import unit value	28.3	59.7	100.0	91.3	83.4	94.7	104.0
Terms of trade	56.8	70.6	100.0	100.3	98.2	68.4	67.7
Non-oil commodity prices	37.2	54.7	100.0	75.1	77.9	80.5	78.7
Gross capital formation[2]	19.2	23.8	20.0	17.2	11.6	13.5	13.0
Sub-Saharan Africa, excluding Nigeria							
Real GDP	75.4	88.9	100.0	104.7	108.4	112.2	114.8
Real GDP per capita	100.0	103.0	100.0	98.9	94.2	94.8	94.3
Consumer prices	19.7	33.6	100.0	154.8	291.0	359.7	452.3
Export value	26.6	50.9	100.0	83.9	86.4	87.7	90.1
Export volume	91.2	97.0	100.0	100.6	107.6	115.7	115.8
Import volume	76.8	85.0	100.0	95.8	87.2	84.4	83.4
Export unit value	29.2	52.5	100.0	83.4	80.3	75.8	77.8
Import unit value	27.0	58.3	100.0	91.4	83.2	93.8	102.4
Terms of trade	108.2	90.0	100.0	91.2	96.6	80.8	76.0
Non-oil commodity prices	37.7	55.0	100.0	75.4	77.6	80.8	78.9
Gross capital formation[2]	21.7	22.9	19.8	19.0	17.0	17.7	17.6

Source: International Monetary Fund, *International Financial Statistics* (1988); and Fund staff estimates.
[1] Defined as Africa excluding Algeria, Angola, Morocco, Namibia, South Africa, and Tunisia.
[2] As a percent of GDP.

Figure 1. *Sub-Saharan Africa: Per Capita Real GDP and Debt-Service Ratio, 1978–87*

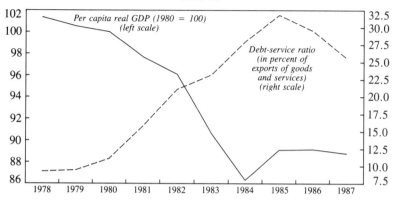

Source: International Monetary Fund, staff estimates.

Figure 2. *Sub-Saharan Africa, Excluding Nigeria: Per Capita Real GDP and Debt-Service Ratio, 1978–87*

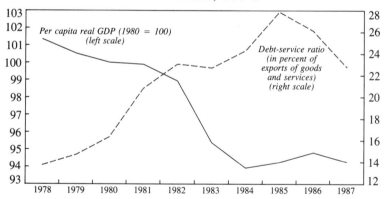

Source: International Monetary Fund, staff estimates.

of 15 heavily indebted countries.[9] As indicated, in recent years the ratio of aggregate external debt to exports of goods and services for sub-

[9] As defined in the October 1988 *World Economic Outlook* report, the countries are Argentina, Bolivia, Brazil, Chile, Colombia, Côte d'Ivoire, Ecuador, Mexico, Morocco, Nigeria, Peru, Philippines, Uruguay, Venezuela, and Yugoslavia.

Figure 3. *Total Debt to Exports Ratio for Sub-Saharan Africa,*
Fifteen Heavily Indebted Countries, and Countries with Recent Debt-Servicing
Problems, 1978–87

(In percent of exports of goods and services)

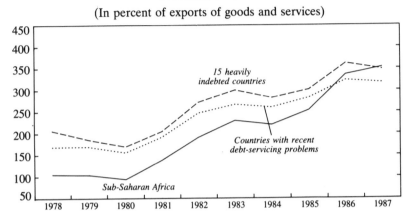

Source: International Monetary Fund, staff estimates.

Figure 4. *Total Debt to GDP Ratio for Sub-Saharan Africa,*
Fifteen Heavily Indebted Countries, and Countries with Recent Debt-Servicing
Problems, 1978–87

(In percent of gross domestic product)

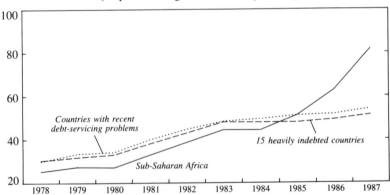

Source: International Monetary Fund, staff estimates.

Saharan countries has risen dramatically, reaching 335 percent in 1986
and exceeding 350 percent in 1987. This last figure is higher than the
comparable ratios for countries with recent debt-servicing problems and
for the group of 15 heavily indebted countries. The ratio of external debt
to GDP for sub-Saharan countries has also risen steadily, from 27 per-

Figure 5. *Debt-Service Ratio for Sub-Saharan Africa, Fifteen Heavily Indebted Countries, and Countries with Recent Debt-Servicing Problems, 1978–87*
(In percent of exports of goods and services)

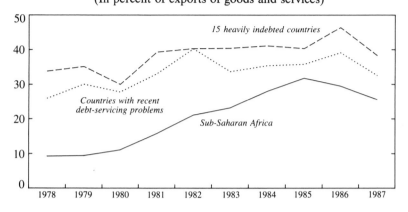

Source: International Monetary Fund, staff estimates.

cent in 1980 to 82 percent in 1987, a level more than one and one half times that for the other two groups of debt distressed countries. The ratio of actual debt service payments to exports of goods and services for sub-Saharan countries, which has exceeded 20 percent since 1983, has remained less than that for the two groups of debt distressed countries. As mentioned earlier, however, the ratio of scheduled debt-service obligations for sub-Saharan countries is significantly higher, given the extent of debt relief and arrears among these countries. In view of these observations and the estimates pointing to the region's inability to maintain even its current, compressed level of real imports without continuing and massive debt relief, it seems fair to call the entire sub-Saharan region debt distressed.

II. Origins of the Sub-Saharan Debt Problem

The sub-Saharan debt problem can be traced largely to government actions, in particular, the accumulation of external debt for development projects. Since independence, sub-Saharan countries have undertaken public projects in attempting to strengthen their economies, frequently with donor support and generally with heavy use of foreign financing in the form of loans. Many of these development projects have been designed to improve domestic industry and infrastructure rather than to boost export production directly. The assumption was that national economies would grow over time, and that commensurate increases in

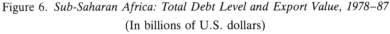

Figure 6. *Sub-Saharan Africa: Total Debt Level and Export Value, 1978–87*
(In billions of U.S. dollars)

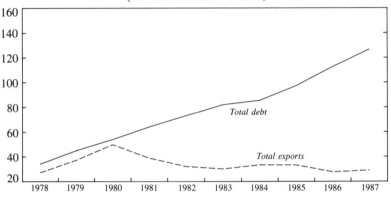

Source: International Monetary Fund, staff estimates.

export production and reasonable trends in export prices would allow the debt-service obligations arising from these projects to be met. This assumption is consistent with the results from standard growth models that incorporate external debt (see, for example, the survey article by McDonald (1982) and papers by Bardhan (1967), Hamada (1969), and Blanchard (1983)). These assumptions became increasingly unrealistic in the light of the two oil price shocks during 1973–74 and 1979–80 and the subsequent depression in non-oil commodities markets during the 1980s. Indeed, as shown in Figures 6 and 7, total debt levels have risen steadily since 1978, while export earnings in 1987 were barely above their dollar level nine years earlier.

Following the first round of oil price increases in 1973, prices for a number of other primary commodities, in particular cocoa, coffee, tea, sugar, groundnuts, sisal, phosphate, and uranium, experienced sharp increases followed by steep declines.[10] These price developments affected a number of sub-Saharan African countries, including Burundi, the Central African Republic, Ethiopia, Kenya, Madagascar, Sierra Leone, and Tanzania (all coffee growers); Ghana (cocoa producer); Côte d'Ivoire (cocoa and coffee exporter); the Gambia (groundnut exporter); Senegal (producer of groundnuts and phosphate); Malawi (sugar and tobacco producer); Niger (uranium producer); and Togo (phosphate producer).

[10] See Krumm (1985), p. 7.

Figure 7. *Sub-Saharan Africa, Excluding Nigeria: Total Debt Level and Export Value, 1978–87*

(In billions of U.S. dollars)

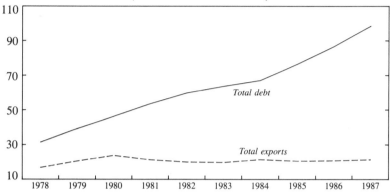

Source: International Monetary Fund, staff estimates.

Many of the affected countries responded to the initial commodity price increases by sharply expanding public expenditure.[11] Revenues from commodity taxation, though higher, did not rise as fast, and governments used foreign borrowing to meet the remaining costs of particular spending projects. When commodity prices subsequently fell, expenditures were not reduced commensurately, and previous borrowing was often supplemented with new loans to maintain expenditure levels. At the same time, several countries dependent on minerals, such as copper (Zaïre and Zambia) and iron ore (Liberia and Mauritania), whose prices declined during the 1970s, were able to borrow externally on the assumption that prices would subsequently recover. External debt also accumulated in several oil-producing countries during the mid-1970s as a result of declining real prices (Gabon) and production difficulties (Republic of the Congo).[12] Moreover, after 1977, the leading sub-Saharan African oil producer, Nigeria, began to borrow heavily in commercial markets, with its total Eurocurrency commitments approaching US\$3 billion during 1978 and 1979.[13]

The trend toward rising sub-Saharan debt burdens accelerated during the 1980s in the wake of the second oil price shock of 1979–80. Reflecting a concerted effort by industrial countries to contain the resulting

[11] See Larrecq (1980).
[12] Krumm (1985), p. 8.
[13] Krumm (1985), p. 48.

Figure 8. *Sub-Saharan Africa: Import Volume and Debt-Service Ratio,*
1978–87

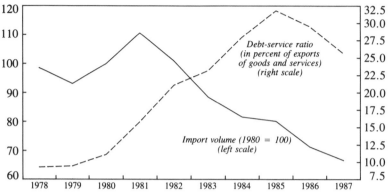

Source: International Monetary Fund, staff estimates.

inflationary repercussions, industrial country growth since then has been
considerably more sluggish than during the 1970s. As a result, prices of
non-oil primary commodities have not risen, and in many cases have
fallen precipitously since 1980. By 1987 the terms of trade for sub-
Saharan countries excluding Nigeria were 24 percent below the level of
1980 (Table 3).[14] In 1987, aggregate export earnings for the sub-Saharan
nations excluding Nigeria were 10 percent below their nominal levels in
1980, despite a 16 percent rise in export volume.[15] At the same time,
debt-service obligations more than doubled between 1980 and 1987,
reflecting both the overhang of debt incurred during the 1970s and
continued borrowing since then. With diminished export earnings, and
with import prices by 1987 significantly above their 1980 levels, sub-
Saharan countries found it increasingly difficult to meet their debt-
service burdens while maintaining an acceptable volume of imports
(Figures 8 and 9). This was particularly true for countries, such as
Zambia, that had expanded import-intensive manufacturing industries
during the 1970s and thus had become even more dependent on imports
of raw materials and intermediate goods in later years.

  Another factor that contributed to sub-Saharan debt burdens during
the 1980s was the rise in interest rates. Although less important than for
market borrowers, because of the predominantly official character of

---

[14] With Nigeria included, the decline in the terms of trade was 32 percent.
[15] Including Nigeria, the decline in export earnings was 42 percent, reflecting
an 18 percent drop in export volume.

Figure 9. *Sub-Saharan Africa, Excluding Nigeria: Import Volume and Debt-Service Ratio, 1978–87*

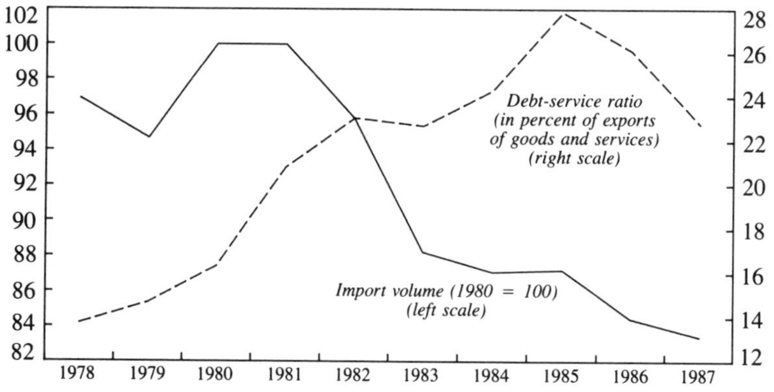

Source: International Monetary Fund, staff estimates.

sub-Saharan debt, rising interest rates nonetheless affected a number of countries that had made significant use of commercial borrowing, in particular Botswana, Côte d'Ivoire, Kenya, Liberia, Malawi, Mauritius, Niger, Nigeria, Senegal, Zaïre, Zambia, and Zimbabwe.[16] Although some of these loans carried fixed rates, an increasing proportion was either denominated in floating rates or renegotiated at the new and higher fixed rates, which averaged 13 percent in nominal terms (and 4 percent in real terms) during 1979–82, compared to 9 percent (and −2 percent in real terms) during 1973–78.[17] According to Krumm (1985), higher real interest rates may have increased debt levels for the Côte d'Ivoire, Malawi, and Zambia by more than 10 percent during 1979–83.[18]

Still another factor affecting the ability of sub-Saharan countries to meet debt service obligations was the decline in real net capital inflows, including external assistance, during the 1980s. As shown in Table 4, combined net external borrowing and non-debt-creating flows, including estimated debt relief and arrears, rose from US$6 billion in 1975 to US$13 billion in 1980 and US$17 billion in 1982, before falling sharply

[16] Krumm (1985), p. 14.

[17] Krumm (1985). These real interest rates were calculated using the wholesale price index for the United States as the price deflator. Stymne (1988), using export unit values for sub-Saharan Africa as the price index for calculating real interest rates, estimates far higher real interest rates for these countries during the post-1979 period, because of the decline in export prices of most primary commodities.

[18] Krumm (1985), p. 15.

Table 4. *External Financing Flows for Sub-Saharan Africa, 1970–87*

(In billions of U.S. dollars)

	1970 Est.	1975 Est.	1980	1982	1985	1986	1987
Sub-Saharan Africa[1]	1.9	6.1	12.9	16.8	8.2	14.2	13.2
Net non-debt-creating flows	1.0	2.4	3.6	4.1	4.5	5.2	5.5
Net external borrowing[2]	0.9	3.7	9.3	12.7	3.7	9.0	7.7
Long-term borrowing from official creditors	(0.6)	(1.8)	(4.5)	(6.0)	(5.7)	(12.4)	(7.5)
Reserve-related liabilities[3]	(—)	(0.5)	(0.4)	(5.2)	(2.1)	(2.1)	(0.8)
Other borrowing	(0.3)	(1.4)	(4.4)	(1.6)	(−4.1)	(−5.5)	(−0.6)
Memorandum item:							
Total flows, excluding estimated impact of rescheduling and arrears	1.9	5.9	13.0	12.0	2.9	0.7	0.8

Source: International Monetary Fund, *International Financial Statistics* (1988); and Fund staff estimates.
[1] Defined as Africa excluding Algeria, Angola, Morocco, Namibia, South Africa, and Tunisia.
[2] Includes estimated impact of debt rescheduling and arrears.
[3] Includes use of Fund credit and arrears.

to US$8 billion in 1985. Total inflows recovered to US$13–14 billion in 1986 and 1987, largely because of debt relief, estimated at US$11 billion during each of these years. Absent debt relief and arrears, the figures suggest a decrease in net capital flows from US$11–13 billion a year during 1980–82 to less than US$1 billion a year during 1986–87. Within these totals was a sharp redistribution of funds toward official sources, as other borrowing (mostly from private creditors) fell from US$4.4 billion in 1980 to minus US$5.5 billion in 1986 and minus US$0.6 billion in 1987. Official grants and borrowing from official sources increased during the period, but by less than the decline in net borrowing from private sources.

Domestic policies have also been a major cause of debt accumulation in sub-Saharan countries. As noted earlier, many countries opted for major development programs and highly expansionary fiscal policies during the commodity boom years of the late 1970s, acquiring external debt as spending increases outpaced the rise in tax receipts. These spending policies continued for some time after the post-1980 collapse in commodity prices. A few countries, such as Zambia, also used external commercial borrowing to maintain consumption in the face of deteriorating export earnings. In addition, several oil producing countries, such as Gabon, Nigeria, and the Republic of the Congo, used their access to foreign capital markets to support major public investment schemes during the 1980s. When oil prices plummeted early in 1986, many of these countries found themselves hard pressed to meet their debt-service obligations.

Besides expansionary fiscal policy and outright borrowing for consumption, many sub-Saharan countries pursued policies that weakened their external positions. Growing fiscal deficits and surging private credit demand led to rapid monetary expansion in many countries. This, in turn, contributed to higher inflation, with consumer prices rising on average by more than 20 percent a year during the 1980s. Because most of these countries did not depreciate their currencies to offset this inflationary impact, many currencies became overvalued. This inhibited exports and encouraged the formation of parallel exchange markets. Also limiting exports was the common practice of marketing crops through monopolistic public sector agencies that offered low producer prices as a way of meeting costs and raising government revenue. In many countries, producer prices lagged far behind inflation, discouraging production and promoting smuggling.

Domestic economic policies also promoted imports, through overvalued currencies and other measures. Many countries subsidized imported food, fertilizer, and petroleum products as a matter of policy. In addition, tariff legislation encouraged the growth of inefficient, import-intensive manufacturing establishments by imposing high tariff rates or quantitative restrictions on imports of finished goods, while tariffs on imported raw materials and intermediate goods were low or nonexistent.

Negative real interest rates in many countries discouraged domestic savings, encouraged capital outflows, and contributed to debt accumulation by requiring substantial borrowing to finance investment projects. In addition, high inflation rates, capital controls, and extensive restrictions on investment discouraged direct investment and the growth it might have generated. Altogether, these policies increased borrowing needs and lowered export earnings, thus reducing the ability of sub-Saharan countries to meet rising debt-service obligations. These efforts were then compounded during 1986–87, when the failure of commodity prices to match the increase in dollar-denominated import costs led to a 20 percent deterioration on the terms of trade for sub-Saharan countries excluding Nigeria.[19]

III. Initial Responses to the Problem: Economic Adjustment and Debt Relief

With the temporary booms in non-oil commodity prices largely over by 1980, a significant number of sub-Saharan countries found themselves unable to meet debt-service obligations while maintaining existing trends in payments for imported goods and services. Many of these countries responded to this situation by adopting adjustment programs aimed at bolstering export earnings, curbing domestic absorption, and reducing inflation. In a number of cases, the Fund supported these programs through stand-by and extended arrangements. As summarized in Zulu and Nsouli (1985), the adjustment programs receiving Fund support frequently included measures to improve competitiveness through exchange rate adjustments. Also included were measures to reduce fiscal deficits through expenditure cuts and higher revenues, and policies to curb monetary expansion while directing a larger share of new credit to the private sector. In many cases structural problems were also addressed, including large and often unprofitable public enterprises that had expanded rapidly during the 1970s.

The initial response of the donor community to the growth of debt-servicing problems of sub-Saharan countries focused on financial assistance from the Fund and accompanying debt relief from bilateral

---

[19] With Nigeria included, the decrease was 32 percent.

creditors. The World Bank, however, through its structural adjustment lending, initiated in 1980–81, also provided significant assistance to many sub-Saharan countries. This type of lending was frequently designed to supplement the Bank's project lending, by helping establish the economic conditions needed for project success. In some cases it also served to supplement the resources of the Fund, by supporting adjustment programs developed in conjunction with the Fund.[20]

The Fund, as the major international institution for balance of payments support, stood ready to assist sub-Saharan countries in adjusting to adverse external developments. Moreover, with the exception of Zaïre in 1976, sub-Saharan countries did not make significant use of Fund resources in the stand-by, extended, and compensatory financing facilities during the 1960s and 1970s. In 1980, the Fund had substantial resources available to assist member countries, as quotas had more than doubled to SDR 59.6 billion in 1977. SDR 12.3 billion in additional funds were available from the General Arrangements to Borrow and the supplementary financing facility, and outstanding use of Fund credit was less than SDR 8.0 billion at the end of 1979.

Early in 1977 the Fund had authorized members to make cumulative purchases outside the special facilities exceeding 200 percent of their quotas, using the combined resources of a member's credit tranches and entitlement to supplementary financing facility.[21] The cumulative ceiling was raised to a maximum of 500 percent of quota following the introduction of the policy on enlarged access in 1981. Consequently, when significant numbers of sub-Saharan Africa countries began to request Fund arrangements in 1980 and 1981, the Fund could offer relatively large amounts of financial assistance. Outstanding use of Fund credit, excluding Trust Fund loans, to sub-Saharan Africa countries increased from SDR 1.3 billion at the end of 1979 to SDR 5.4 billion at the end of 1984 (Table 5). Fund arrangements also served as a catalyst for obtaining debt relief from bilateral creditors and commercial banks, in particular from Paris Club countries that generally made a Fund arrangement in the upper credit tranches a condition for the approval of debt rescheduling. A detailed list of sub-Saharan Africa countries receiving debt relief from the Paris and London Clubs appears in Table 6. Over the five years 1980–84 the impact of debt relief for sub-Saharan countries is estimated to have totaled US$9 billion.

---

[20] See Thomas and Chhibber (1989).

[21] The total, set at 247 percent of quota prior to the implementation of the 1977 quota increase, was reduced to 202.5 percent of quota after that increase became effective.

Table 5. *Fund Purchases, Repurchases, Charges, and Net Use of Fund Credit in Sub-Saharan Africa, 1970–87*

(In billions of SDRs)

	1970	1975	1980	1981	1982	1983	1984	1985	1986	1987
Sub-Saharan Africa										
Net use of Fund credit[1,2]	—	0.4	0.4	1.4	1.0	1.4	0.5	0.1	-0.3	-0.5
Purchases	—	(0.5)	(0.7)	(1.7)	(1.3)	(1.8)	(1.0)	(0.7)	(0.6)	(0.3)
Repurchases	(-0.1)	(-0.1)	(-0.3)	(-0.3)	(-0.2)	(-0.4)	(-0.5)	(-0.6)	(-0.9)	(-0.8)
Fund charges	—	—	0.1	0.1	0.3	0.3	0.4	0.3	0.3	0.2
Memorandum item:										
Outstanding use of Fund credit[2,3] in the General Department	0.1	0.6	1.5	2.9	3.6	4.9	5.4	5.5	5.2	5.0

Source: International Monetary Fund, *International Financial Statistics* (1988); and Fund staff estimates.
[1] Totals may not add because of rounding.
[2] Excludes Trust Fund loans and SAF loans.
[3] At end of period.

Table 6. *Sub-Saharan Africa: Amounts Restructured in Paris Club and Commercial Bank Debt Restructurings, 1976–87[1]*

(In millions of U.S. dollars)

	1976	1977	1978	1979	1980	1981	1982	1983	1984	1985	1986	1987
Central African Republic												
Paris Club	—	—	—	—	—	72	—	13	—	14[2]	—	—
Commercial banks	—	—	—	—	—	—	—	—	—	—	—	—
Congo												
Paris Club	—	—	—	—	—	—	—	—	—	—	756	—
Commercial banks	—	—	—	—	—	—	—	—	—	—	217	—
Côte d'Ivoire												
Paris Club	—	—	—	—	—	—	—	—	230	213	370	567[2]
Commercial banks	—	—	—	—	—	—	—	—	501	—	691	—
Equatorial Guinea												
Paris Club	—	—	—	—	—	—	—	—	—	38	—	—
Commercial banks	—	—	—	—	—	—	—	—	—	—	—	—
Gabon												
Paris Club	—	—	—	—	—	—	—	—	—	—	—	387
Commercial banks	—	—	—	—	—	—	—	—	—	—	—	39
Gambia, The												
Paris Club	—	—	—	—	—	—	—	—	—	—	17	—
Commercial banks	—	—	—	—	—	—	—	—	—	—	—	—
Guinea												
Paris Club	—	—	—	—	—	—	—	—	—	—	196	—
Commercial banks	—	—	—	—	—	—	—	—	—	—	—	25
Guinea-Bissau												
Paris Club	—	—	—	—	—	—	—	—	—	—	—	25
Commercial banks	—	—	—	—	—	—	—	—	—	—	—	—
Liberia												
Paris Club	—	—	—	—	35	25	—	17	17	—	—	—
Commercial banks	—	—	—	—	—	—	30	—	—	—	—	—

Table 6 (concluded). *Sub-Saharan Africa: Amounts Restructured in Paris Club and Commercial Bank Debt Restructurings, 1976–87*[1]

(In millions of U.S. dollars)

	1976	1977	1978	1979	1980	1981	1982	1983	1984	1985	1986	1987
Madagascar												
Paris Club	—	—	—	—	—	140	107	—	89[2]	128[2]	212[2]	—
Commercial banks	—	—	—	—	—	147	—	—	195	—	—	—
Malawi												
Paris Club	—	—	—	—	—	—	25	26	—	—	—	—
Commercial banks	—	—	—	—	—	—	—	57	—	—	—	—
Mauritania												
Paris Club	—	—	—	—	—	—	—	—	—	74	27	90
Commercial banks	—	—	—	—	—	—	—	—	—	—	—	—
Mozambique												
Paris Club	—	—	—	—	—	—	—	—	283	—	—	361[2]
Commercial banks	—	—	—	—	—	—	—	—	—	—	—	140
Niger												
Paris Club	—	—	—	—	—	—	—	36	26	38	34	—
Commercial banks	—	—	—	—	—	—	—	—	27	—	52	—
Nigeria												
Paris Club	—	—	—	—	—	—	—	—	—	—	6,251	—
Commercial banks	—	—	—	—	—	—	—	1,935	—	—	4,250	—
Senegal												
Paris Club	—	—	—	—	—	75	74	72	—	122	65	79
Commercial banks	—	—	—	—	—	—	—	—	78	20	—	—
Sierra Leone												
Paris Club	—	—	39	—	37	—	—	—	25[2]	—	86[2]	—
Commercial banks	—	—	—	—	—	—	—	—	25	—	—	—

Somalia											
Paris Club	—	—	—	—	—	—	—	—	—	127	153[2]
Commercial banks	—	—	—	—	—	—	—	—	—	—	—
Sudan											
Paris Club	—	—	487	—	—	203	518[2]	249[2]	—	—	—
Commercial banks	—	—	—	498	55[3]	—	790[3]	838[3]	—	920[3]	—
Tanzania											
Paris Club	—	—	—	—	—	—	—	—	—	—	—
Commercial banks	—	—	—	—	—	—	—	—	1,046	—	—
Togo											
Paris Club	—	—	260	—	232	—	300[2]	75[2]	—	27	—
Commercial banks	—	—	—	69	—	—	84	—	—	—	—
Uganda											
Paris Club	—	—	—	—	30	19	—	—	—	—	170[2]
Commercial banks	—	—	—	—	—	—	—	—	—	—	—
Zaïre											
Paris Club	270	210	1,040	—	500	—	1,497[2]	—	408[2]	429[2]	671[2]
Commercial banks	—	—	—	402	—	—	58[4]	64[4]	61[4]	65[4]	61[4]
Zambia											
Paris Club	—	—	—	—	—	—	375	253[2]	—	371[2]	—
Commercial banks	—	—	—	—	—	—	—	74	—	—	—

Source: Fund staff estimates.

[1] Debt restructuring with commercial banks is recorded in the year of agreement in principle; debt restructuring with Paris Club official creditors is recorded in the year in which the Agreed Minute is signed.

[2] Includes the restructuring of previously rescheduled debts.

[3] Modification of 1981 agreement.

[4] Deferment agreement.

Net Fund credit to sub-Saharan Africa began to slow in 1984 and turned negative in 1986 and 1987, with net outflows from sub-Saharan countries to the Fund approaching SDR 1 billion a year during this period after the inclusion of Fund charges. The Fund continued to serve, however, as a catalyst for debt rescheduling and for new commitments of donor assistance. As noted in Table 1, during 1986 and 1987 alone, sub-Saharan countries were estimated to receive more than US$20 billion in debt relief. Thus, the Fund continued to have a net positive impact on external capital flows to Africa, even if its own exposure to sub-Saharan Africa was decreasing during this period.

While the Fund's direct financial assistance to sub-Saharan Africa diminished after 1983, the Bank's adjustment lending increased substantially. Disbursements from the Bank's adjustment loans and credits to sub-Saharan countries totaled US$0.4 billion in 1985 and increased to an average of more than US$1 billion a year during 1986 and 1987. Much of this increase can be traced to the establishment of the Bank's US$1 billion sub-Saharan Africa facility in 1985. Disbursements from this facility totaled US$0.3 billion in 1986 and US$0.4 billion in 1987. Net transfers (disbursements less principal and interest payments) from the Bank to sub-Saharan countries also increased over the period, from US$0.5 billion in 1980 to US$1.4 billion in 1987.[22] Net transfers from other multilateral institutions fell, however, from US$1.0 billion in 1980 to US$0.7 billion in 1987.

Despite the availability of debt relief and the continuing attention of donor countries and international organizations, economic conditions in sub-Saharan Africa continued to deteriorate during the mid-1980s, and by 1987 the position of most sub-Saharan countries had become precarious. Average export earnings stood at barely 64 percent of their 1980 levels, and real per capita GDP was estimated to have fallen below the 1970–71 level. Real aid flows (in constant 1980 U.S. dollars) had also fallen considerably from the start of the decade, and net capital flows were positive only because of the effect of debt relief. Moreover, even debt rescheduling was of little use to an important subset of sub-Saharan countries such as Uganda and Zambia, most of whose debt was owed to international organizations, and by convention nonreschedulable.

Partly in response to these developments the Fund in 1986 established its structural adjustment facility (SAF), to provide assistance on very concessional terms (interest rates of ½ of 1 percent, with repayment over a ten-year period including a grace period of four and a half years) to very low-income (basically, IDA-eligible) countries undertaking pro-

[22] See World Bank (1989), pp. 6–9.

grams of comprehensive macroeconomic and structural adjustment. Through the end of 1987, however, the amounts available under this facility were relatively low, totaling only 63.5 percent of members' quotas over a three-year period. In addition, Paris Club donor countries agreed to consider more generous terms for debt rescheduling and to approve debt reschedulings for countries having only a SAF arrangement with the Fund, rather than the traditional stand-by or extended Fund arrangement. Neither of these initiatives did much to reduce the debt burdens of countries with substantial obligations owing to international organizations. Moreover, the combined funds available for external assistance left many sub-Saharan Africa countries in unmanageable balance of payments positions.

IV. Recent Debt Initiatives

During the last half of 1987, the Fund and the World Bank undertook further measures to address the debt problems of very low income countries. The Fund obtained resources from a number of member countries to allow a substantial expansion of its structural adjustment facility. The expanded SAF, termed the enhanced structural adjustment facility (ESAF), stands to provide much larger amounts of financial assistance to qualifying countries, in the order of 150 percent of members' quotas over a three-year period, and in some cases up to 350 percent of quota where the need arises. This facility became effective in January 1988; as of the end of May 1989, ESAF arrangements had been approved for ten sub-Saharan African countries—the Gambia, Ghana, Kenya, Madagascar, Malawi, Mauritania, Niger, Senegal, Togo, and Uganda. The World Bank has also secured commitments from major donors to provide substantial co-financing for its Special Program for Africa, aimed at debt-distressed countries. As of the end of 1988, more than US$2 billion of the US$5.2 billion in funds committed had been allocated, and about US$1 billion had been disbursed.

In addition to the Fund and World Bank initiatives, in 1988 the Group of Seven countries agreed on measures to reduce the bilateral debt-service obligations of very low-income countries. Under the terms of the agreement reached at the June 1988 Toronto economic summit and detailed at the September 1988 annual meetings of the Fund and the World Bank, Group of Seven creditors have agreed to provide countries eligible for World Bank IDA credits one of three types of more extensive debt relief: (a) forgiveness of one third of the debt service due on obligations rescheduled through the Paris Club, with the remainder rescheduled over a 14-year period, including 8 years of grace; (b) rescheduling of all eligible obligations over a 14-year period, including 8 years of grace, at interest rates 3.5 percentage points below market rates, or at one half of market rates if these rates are less than 7 percent; and (c) a rescheduling of all obligations at market interest rates, but over 25 years, including a 14-year grace period.

At present, it is uncertain whether existing aid sources can provide sufficient relief for the debt problem of sub-Saharan Africa. The new Fund facility and World Bank program for Africa remain to be used by most sub-Saharan countries. Moreover, the magnitude of resources available from these two sources and the Fund's SAF facility is small compared with the total debt-service obligations of these countries. Total SAF and ESAF resources, for which sub-Saharan countries represent only some of the potential claimants, are SDR 8.7 billion (equivalent to about US$11.3 billion as of early 1989). Co-financing for the World Bank's Special Program for Africa totals another US$6.4 billion, of which only about half is estimated to represent new projects. Moreover, the ultimate benefit from the recent Group of Seven initiative remains to be determined, although for the five low-income countries granted exceptional debt relief during 1988, it is estimated that the Group of Seven initiative will reduce interest payments by a total of only US$15 million a year.

In 1987 alone debt-service payments of sub-Saharan countries exceeded US$9 billion, and scheduled obligations exceeded US$20 billion. Unless these programs are supplemented by additional resources in future years, the available funds may only provide significant debt relief to sub-Saharan countries for a few years. If their terms of trade improve and they achieve major structural adjustments in their economies, sub-Saharan countries may find these funds sufficient to cover their external financing gaps until their overall external positions strengthen considerably. It may take many years, however, for sub-Saharan countries to diversify their export bases, phase out import-intensive manufacturing concerns, and establish new and efficient import-substitution industries, if the experience of past adjustment programs supported by the Fund and the World Bank is any guide. Moreover, primary commodity prices seem unlikely to rise significantly during the next few years, based on recent trends in commodity prices and the likelihood of moderate economic growth and continued implementation of anti-inflation policies among the industrial countries. Thus, the current resources for debt relief may well run out before sub-Saharan countries can begin to handle their debt-service obligations.

V. Alternative Debt Proposals

What more could be done to help debt-distressed sub-Saharan African countries? Many ways of reducing their debt-service obligations can be considered, ranging from debt relief for obligations to international organizations to various forms of outright debt forgiveness. A broad range of such proposals can be found in Helleiner (1989). This paper focuses on a few specific proposals for alleviating the debt-service burdens of sub-Saharan countries to official creditors. Some of these measures would represent major departures from current practice. They would also require substantially more foreign assistance from bilateral donors, which might be difficult to obtain given the climate of budget stringency facing most industrial countries.

Besides the proposals for official debt considered here, proposals for reducing debt to commercial banks and private lenders could also be considered. Among these are debt buy-backs, which are now under consideration for a few sub-Saharan countries, such as Mozambique and the Republic of the Congo.[23] These proposals are of particular importance for the few African countries with substantial amounts of debt to private sector creditors. For most sub-Saharan countries, schemes to reduce commercial debt would provide relatively limited assistance. Accordingly, these proposals are not discussed further in this paper.

Assisting Low-Income Countries in Meeting Debt Service Due to International Organizations

One idea that has been suggested is to provide assistance to low-income countries in meeting debt-service obligations to international organizations. This proposal would be of particular use to sub-Saharan countries, for whom debt to international organizations represents a large proportion of their total external debt. As noted earlier, international organizations do not, as a rule, reschedule outstanding debt-service obligations, in large part because they rely to a significant degree on the recycling of existing resources to fund new programs. Moreover, few donors or agencies are willing to provide cash assistance or aid that can be used to meet these obligations. Countries with large obligations to international organizations therefore have no choice but to meet these

---

[23]For theoretical discussions of debt buy-backs, see, for example, Dooley (1988) and Corden, "An International Debt Facility?" below.

obligations or to fall into arrears. Falling into arrears is not an attractive alternative, however, since it typically leads to a cut-off in funds from the organization involved and may cause other donors to reconsider their own aid programs with the country.

A number of mechanisms could be envisaged for providing debt relief for obligations due to international organizations. One possibility would be for donors to raise additional funds to allow international organizations to replace existing loans with loans offering more concessional terms.[24] As with more formal debt rescheduling, the replacement of outstanding loans would give borrowers more time to meet their debt-service obligations. This could make it easier to fulfill debt-service obligations. To increase the chance of loan repayment, access to softer loans could be conditioned on the implementation of a satisfactory economic adjustment program, as is now true for the use of Fund resources.

To be of greatest use in relieving debt burdens, assistance in meeting debt-service obligations to international organizations should be commensurate with the magnitude of these obligations. The most direct way to achieve this would be through formal rescheduling of these obligations. However, most international organizations lack the capital to provide substantial debt relief without in some way curtailing their primary objective of offering new loans and programs. Obtaining new capital from major donors would seem essential for these organizations to consider formal rescheduling. Whether such funding can be secured under the current economic environment facing most donor countries is highly uncertain.

Another option would be to create a new international facility charged with buying the outstanding debt owed to international organizations, and then replacing existing debt-service obligations with new loans on more concessional terms. This would be similar to proposals made earlier regarding a facility for buying commercial bank debt.[25] A debt-buyout facility of this sort would have the advantage of providing debt relief to low-income countries without requiring international organizations to provide new loans themselves. This would enable these institutions to concentrate on their existing functions. To avoid reducing the

---

[24] The recent study by the United Nations (1988), for example, recommends for low-income countries refinancing outstanding IBRD obligations at highly concessional terms and refinancing Fund purchases through the ESAF facility. The Fund, however, has indicated that ESAF resources are intended to increase the amount of external financing available to low-income countries in pursuing growth-oriented adjustment programs, rather than to replace outstanding debt obligations.

[25] See, for example, Corden, "An International Debt Facility?" below.

funds available to these organizations for new lending, however, an international facility would have to purchase existing loan obligations at par. At a minimum, this would require a large initial capitalization from donor countries to cover the difference between obligations due to international organizations and payments received from outstanding borrowers. A new international organization would also face considerable start-up costs, including the need to screen and supervise new loans to debt-distressed countries. For these reasons, it seems unlikely that this approach to meeting debt-service obligations due to international organizations would be followed.

A third option for relieving the debt service obligations of low-income countries to international organizations would be for bilateral lenders to relax their normal rules regarding aid and provide funds themselves that are targeted for this purpose. This could involve either a direct payment to the country or a payment made on that country's behalf to an international organization. To ensure that the resources were properly used, donor countries might require that the recipients be implementing a satisfactory economic adjustment program, as is now the case for countries seeking bilateral debt relief.

Having donors assist debt-distressed countries in meeting external debt-service obligations would have an advantage in allowing donors to oversee the selection of countries and tailor the degree of assistance to each country's apparent needs. One disadvantage would be the need for donor countries to decide, in each case, how much financial support each donor should provide to qualifying debtors in meeting their obligations to international agencies. This could prove far harder than the alternative of giving multilateral agencies the funds and authority to arrange rescheduling themselves. Another disadvantage would be in requiring donors to supervise a number of countries in this position, particularly if payments to international organizations were released in tranches, following evidence of "good" country performance.

The major drawback to any proposal for debt relief on obligations to international organizations is that bilateral donors would inevitably be required to provide the necessary funding. In recent years debt-service payments to these organizations from sub-Saharan countries have exceeded US$3 billion, or about one and one-half times the yearly total of bilateral loan disbursements since 1984 (Table 7). Covering any substantial part of this amount would thus require either a significant increase in bilateral aid or some cutback in other aid activities. The likelihood of a major increase in donor aid to support this type of activity seems uncertain, given the present budgetary positions of the leading donors. Consequently, the idea of increasing the resources of existing interna-

Table 7. Sub-Saharan Africa: Estimated Debt Service Payments to International Organizations, 1975–87[1]

(In billions of U.S. dollars)

	1975	1980	1981	1982	1983	1984	1985	1986	1987
International organizations	0.3	0.9	1.0	1.2	1.4	1.8	2.1	3.0	3.1
Multilateral agencies, excluding the Fund	0.2	0.5	0.5	0.6	0.7	0.9	1.1	1.6	1.8
Principal	(0.1)	(0.2)	(0.2)	(0.3)	(0.3)	(0.5)	(0.6)	(0.8)	(0.9)
Interest	(0.1)	(0.3)	(0.3)	(0.3)	(0.4)	(0.5)	(0.5)	(0.8)	(0.9)
Fund	0.1	0.4	0.5	0.6	0.7	0.9	1.0	1.4	1.3
Repurchases	(0.1)	(0.3)	(0.3)	(0.3)	(0.4)	(0.5)	(0.6)	(0.9)	(1.0)
Charges	(—)	(0.1)	(0.2)	(0.3)	(0.3)	(0.4)	(0.4)	(0.5)	(0.3)
Memorandum items:									
Loan disbursements from bilateral donors	1.4	2.5	3.4	2.7	3.1	2.1	1.9	2.0	2.0

Sources: World Bank, *World Debt Tables*; staff estimates; International Monetary Fund, *International Financial Statistics*; and Fund staff estimates.

[1] Totals may not add because of rounding.

tional organizations to cover outstanding debt-service obligations or, alternatively, to fund a new institution to "buy out" existing loans, seems quite doubtful. Any such program would probably thus displace at least some of the funding available for new aid programs to low-income countries. This would mean a reallocation of existing aid resources, not only among functions but also across countries in favor of those with large debt-service problems. As a large number of sub-Saharan countries fall into this category,[26] however, the change might be advantageous for the region as a whole.

Bilateral Debt Forgiveness

A more radical approach to assisting debt-distressed sub-Saharan African countries would be to establish large-scale debt forgiveness programs among bilateral donors. This could be considered an extension of UNCTAD Resolution 165 (S-IX) of March 1978 calling for retroactive conversion into grants (or equivalent action) of past official development assistance lending to the least developed countries and for future bilateral aid to these countries to be in the form of grants. Several African donors have already forgiven certain debts owed by sub-Saharan Africa countries. Moreover, at the September 1988 annual meetings of the Fund and the World Bank, the Group of Seven countries agreed to a more wide-ranging proposal for debt relief, including the option of forgiving as much as a third of the debt service on outstanding bilateral debt owed by low-income countries to these nations. Some research also suggests that some degree of debt forgiveness may be necessary to enable sub-Saharan countries simply to maintain existing nominal import levels, in view of current debt levels and the likelihood of continued sluggish growth in export earnings.[27]

Debt forgiveness of strictly government obligations might not provide large savings to some countries already receiving debt rescheduling, because many of these countries have already been granted full or nearly total debt relief on their current external obligations and arrears to national governments and export guarantee agencies. Significant savings could nevertheless arise from eliminating the moratorium interest obligations on rescheduled debt, however. This is particularly true for countries that have repeatedly undergone debt rescheduling, and thus

[26] Of the 44 sub-Saharan countries, only 11 (Botswana, Burundi, Djibouti, Ethiopia, Kenya, Lesotho, Mauritius, Rwanda, Seychelles, Swaziland, and Zimbabwe) did not incur arrears or resort to debt rescheduling during 1984–86.

[27] See Stymne (1988).

accumulated a much larger stock of debt on which these interest payments are calculated.

Debt forgiveness would also eliminate the sizable administrative burdens associated with periodic debt reschedulings. In addition, it would stop the steady accumulation of debt to bilateral governments that results from repeated debt reschedulings and the resulting capitalization of interest and arrears. What effect debt forgiveness would have on the ability of donor countries to provide new assistance is unclear, however. On the one hand, few major donors rely on the recycling of earlier aid to fund new programs, with the exception of export credit guarantee agencies like the U.S. Export-Import Bank, which are self-financing and would need budgetary transfers to restore capital lost through debt forgiveness. On the other hand, some governments might view debt forgiveness as tantamount to foreign aid and reduce new aid allocations by a comparable amount. For these donors, a decision to waive interest payments and postpone principal repayments might provide equivalent relief without raising the more difficult issues posed by outright debt forgiveness.

To succeed, debt forgiveness would have to be limited to very low-income countries and be conditioned on the pursuit of appropriate economic adjustment programs, perhaps with a certain amount of forgiveness occurring each year after the successful completion, say, of a Fund-supported economic adjustment program. Neither requirement seems particularly difficult, since both are already accepted as conditions for receiving debt relief on exceptional terms from Paris Club donor countries. To guard against future debt problems, new bilateral aid would also have to come in the form of grants, rather than loans. Donor countries might be less willing to accept this proposal, although in the last year many donors have been willing to increase the percentage of aid given as grants to low-income countries, such as Uganda, that are undertaking major economic adjustment programs.

Eliminating Sub-Saharan African Debt and Providing Only Grants

Perhaps the most extreme debt relief proposal for sub-Saharan African countries would be to forgive all external debts, including those to international organizations, and (as in the aforementioned UNCTAD resolution) to restrict all future assistance to outright grants. Such a strategy would, of course, eliminate the sub-Saharan debt problem. However, the resources required to forgive all outstanding sub-Saharan external debt far exceed the present or foreseeable aid budgets of industrial countries. In addition, channeling all future aid as grants would require a major change in policy for international organizations, virtually all of which restrict their financial assistance activities to loans or their equivalents.

Simply to repay the estimated end-1987 debt to international organizations of sub-Saharan countries would require more than US$29 billion. This is more than twice the sum of official grants and net official loan disbursements to these countries during 1987, and it is hard to imagine the creditor countries committing such a sum just to eliminate nonreschedulable debt. Thus, from an aid flow perspective sub-Saharan countries might do better receiving the much smaller sum of money (perhaps US$1–3 billion annually, based on the most recently published World Bank debt tables and current projections of net Fund repurchases and charges) needed to cover that part of the nonreschedulable debt service due to international organizations each year that is deemed "excessive" or to fund a comparable debt rescheduling program. This approach would leave bilateral donors with significantly more resources to finance new aid projects. Sub-Saharan countries, in turn, would receive more funding for imports, development, and structural reform. As mentioned earlier, however, it might be difficult for donors to raise even this smaller amount of money, given the present budgetary constraints facing most industrial nations.

As regards international agencies, any attempt to shift operations to providing grants would require periodic replenishments of these agencies' capital to ensure sufficient funds for new operations. Given the fiscal pressures facing many donor countries, this may be hard to achieve. The most that seems possible is for these agencies to review the terms of their lending activities, restrict new loans to the most concessional of terms, and make a more careful analysis of the ability of countries to service additional debt. Even this change would probably mean fewer new lending programs for sub-Saharan countries, a serious drawback from the standpoint of maintaining capital inflows to these countries. This approach could, however, reduce the risk of future sub-Saharan debt crises.

Actions for Sub-Saharan African Countries to Take

In addition to policies for creditor nations, sub-Saharan countries must themselves take steps to lessen their debt burdens. As noted earlier, much of the problem resulted from the accumulation of external debt for development projects that were not, in retrospect, self-financing. During their first years of independence many sub-Saharan countries lacked the means to generate significant domestic savings for development projects. These projects thus required large amounts of external financing. Two decades later, however, most of these countries still rely primarily on external finance for capital projects. A significant number have also come to require external finance for current expenditure and an important share of critical imports.

One way for sub-Saharan countries to reduce their external debt burden is to increase domestic savings for capital projects. This can be achieved in two ways: by encouraging private savings and by increasing public savings through fiscal retrenchment. Encouraging private savings would require measures to make saving an attractive alternative to consumption. Since many sub-Saharan countries have high inflation rates and very low nominal interest rates, this may require substantial increases in these interest rates, so that real rates become positive. This step may prove difficult in many African countries, where efforts to raise interest rates often encounter strong opposition. It will also require serious measures to reduce inflation itself, through strong policies of fiscal and monetary adjustment. As for boosting public savings, this will require measures to decrease the government's budget deficit, through revenue increases and appropriate cuts in current expenditure. Achieving higher revenues may require significant reforms both in tax laws and in revenue administration and enforcement, while expenditure cuts in many countries will require more stringent monitoring systems. Appropriate spending cuts will also require a willingness to contain certain politically attractive types of spending, such as subsidy payments and military outlays, to preserve funds for payment of essential staff and for maintenance of existing facilities.

Besides measures to increase domestic savings, sub-Saharan countries may also have to reconsider certain well-entrenched views about the desirability of undertaking new concessional borrowing. Current thinking in the world financial community is that low-income countries should avoid new nonconcessional debt, but that additional debt on concessional terms is acceptable for financing worthwhile projects. However, many debt-distressed sub-Saharan countries might ask whether *any* increase in their current debt burdens is appropriate, given the difficulty they have experienced in meeting existing concessional and nonconcessional debt-service obligations. Just as donor countries might be encouraged to provide new external assistance in the form of grants, debtor countries might consider refusing even new loans on concessional terms, or at least applying a careful cost-benefit analysis to concessional loan proposals aimed at restricting new loans to those for projects likely to generate enough foreign exchange to meet the related debt-service obligations. "Taking a pledge" to restrict even new concessional borrowing could encourage bilateral donors to be more willing to provide new assistance in the form of grants. Refusing all loans, however, would preclude low-income countries from receiving additional support from multilateral agencies such as the World Bank and the African Development Bank, whose charters preclude them from providing grants rather than loans. Thus, it may not be realistic for low-income countries to rule out any new borrowing, as opposed to avoiding all but the most concessional of new loans and credits for projects likely to generate future foreign exchange.

VI. Summary and Conclusions

The evidence on African debt and debt burdens clearly indicates that sub-Saharan African countries face a serious and growing external debt problem. External debt as a ratio to GDP or to exports of goods and services for sub-Saharan countries has risen more than threefold since 1980 and now exceeds the comparable ratios for countries with recent debt-servicing problems and for the 15 heavily indebted countries identified in the Baker initiative. During the past five years more than half the sub-Saharan countries have incurred arrears on debt-service obligations or sought debt rescheduling. In 1987, without debt relief, scheduled debt-service obligations would probably have exceeded 50 percent of exports of goods and services.

Several initiatives have been developed during the last two years in an attempt to address the growing debt burden of sub-Saharan Africa. These include the Fund's SAF and ESAF facilities, the World Bank's Special Africa Program, and the Group of Seven initiative providing greater debt relief to very low-income countries. In addition, in July 1989 the United States announced its intention to forgive its overseas development assistance (ODA) debt from low-income African countries that were implementing adjustment programs, following a similar announcement by France. Together, these facilities have expanded the resources available for relieving African debt burdens. However, the total resources available to these facilities (US$12 billion for the SAF-ESAF fund and US$6.4 billion for the Special Africa Program) and the estimated additional relief arising from the Group of Seven proposal (possibly less than US$0.1 billion a year) are small compared to the estimated yearly debt-service obligations sub-Saharan countries (US$21 billion a year),[28] of which these countries are now paying less than 50

---

[28] Weerasinghe (1988), p. 180.

percent. Moreover, with the exception of the recent U.S. and French announcements, none of these proposals would reduce the outstanding stock of debt of sub-Saharan countries, although the Group of Seven initiative would enable some countries to forego debt service obligations on a portion of their bilateral debt.

To supplement these recent donor initiatives, a number of other debt relief proposals for sub-Saharan Africa have been suggested, of which this paper has considered three types of measures. These are proposals to assist countries in meeting debt-service obligations to multilateral organizations, measures for bilateral debt forgiveness, and more general debt forgiveness measures aimed at eliminating both bilateral and multilateral debt and providing all future assistance in the form of grants.

The first group of proposals, aimed at alleviating debt service due to nonrescheduling creditors, could provide significant debt relief to an important subset of sub-Saharan countries for which these obligations represent a large percentage of total debt-service obligations. A variety of mechanisms could be envisaged for providing this assistance, ranging from the replacement of existing loans with credits from new facilities to payments from bilateral donors on behalf of debt-distressed, low-income countries. Any such scheme is likely to require additional financing on the order of US$1–3 billion a year from donor countries, however, because most international organizations do not have the resources to undertake a large-scale refinancing of existing obligations without curtailing ongoing activities. Given the fiscal pressures facing many donor countries, such financing appears unlikely in the immediate future.

The second set of debt-relief proposals, which involves a broadening of debt forgiveness by bilateral donors, would assist debt-distressed countries by eliminating the moratorium interest obligations and administrative burdens now arising from repeated debt reschedulings. Except perhaps for loans to export credit guarantee agencies, some of which operate as self-funding enterprises, the budgetary cost of bilateral loan forgiveness sub-Saharan countries would probably be small. Accordingly, some increase in bilateral debt relief beyond that envisioned by the Group of Seven countries seems conceivable, although the extent may depend on the percentage of central government obligations in the stock of bilateral debt. This option has some risk, however, to the extent that creditor governments viewed debt forgiveness as tantamount to foreign assistance and reduced new aid commitments accordingly.

The final class of debt relief proposals, involving the forgiveness of debt to multilateral organizations as well as bilateral donors, seems highly unlikely under current circumstances. The sheer cost of forgiving sub-Saharan debt to multilateral organizations would be more than twice the annual sum of total grants and loan disbursements received by these countries in recent years. Thus, even apart from the broader questions raised by this proposal, it appears financially infeasible. In sum, therefore, some broadening of bilateral debt forgiveness seems the most likely new initiative to be forthcoming to assist debt-distressed sub-Saharan countries. This might be accompanied by a small program of bilateral aid toward meeting a portion of their debt-service obligations to multilateral agencies.

Beyond greater debt relief, a fundamental rethinking of the adjustment strategy for sub-Saharan Africa may be needed, to help these countries escape the poverty now associated with being exporters of primary commodities. It is beyond the scope of this paper to suggest strategies for diversifying the exports of sub-Saharan countries, promoting efficient industrialization schemes, or encouraging trade liberalization among the industrial countries. Nevertheless, the success of many Asian countries in industrializing their economies during the last two decades may provide some lessons for sub-Saharan countries. In addition, international organizations and the countries financing them may wish to follow the lead of the Fund in reconsidering the terms of their current lending facilities, so that assistance can be provided for longer time periods, as is now done by the Fund's SAF and ESAF facilities. Donors should also acknowledge that sub-Saharan Africa is likely to require far longer to achieve external viability than was previously anticipated. Thus, substantial new commitments of foreign assistance will be needed. Without these changes it is difficult to foresee an end to the sub-Saharan African debt problem, much less the underlying problems of poverty and stagnation that still cripple many, if not most, sub-Saharan countries more than two decades after their independence.

References

Bardhan, Pranab K., "Optimum Foreign Borrowing," in *Essays on the Theory of Optimal Economic Growth*, ed. by Karl Shell (Cambridge, Massachusetts: MIT Press, 1967), pp. 117–28.

Blanchard, Olivier, "Debt and the Current Account of Brazil," in *Financial Policies and the World Capital Market: The Problem of Latin American Countries*, ed. by Pedro Aspe Armella, Rudiger Dornbusch, and Maurice Obstfeld (Chicago: University of Chicago Press, 1983), pp. 187–98.

Dooley, Michael P., "Self-Financed Buy-Backs and Asset Exchanges," International Monetary Fund, *Staff Papers* (Washington), Vol. 35 (December 1988), pp. 714–23.

Feldstein, Martin, and others, *Restoring Growth in the Debt-Laden Third World* (New York: Trilateral Commission, 1987).

Hamada, Koichi, "Optimal Capital Accumulation by an Economy Facing an International Capital Market," *Journal of Political Economy* (Chicago), Vol. 77 (July–August 1969), pp. 684–97.

Helleiner, G.K., "The Sub-Saharan African Debt Problem: Issues for International Policy," (unpublished; Toronto: University of Toronto, April 1989).

Humphreys, Charles, and John Underwood, "The External Debt Difficulties of Low Income Africa," (unpublished; Washington: World Bank Working Paper, September 1988).

International Monetary Fund, *World Economic Outlook* (Washington: IMF, October 1988).

――――, *International Financial Statistics,* Vol. 42 (Washington: IMF, February 1989).

Krumm, Kathie L., "The External Debt of Sub-Saharan Africa," (unpublished; Washington: World Bank Staff Working Paper No. 741, 1985).

Lancaster, Carol, "Debt and Development in Low-Income Africa: Issues and Options for the United States," (unpublished; Washington: Institute for International Economics, May 1989).

――――, and John Williamson, eds., *African Debt and Financing* (Washington: Institute for International Economics, May 1986).

Larrecq, Kathryn, "The Commodity Boom and the Response of Governments," (unpublished; Washington: World Bank Report No. 3088-WA, June 1980).

McDonald, Donogh C., "Debt Capacity and Developing Country Borrowing: A Survey of the Literature," International Monetary Fund, *Staff Papers* (Washington), Vol. 29 (December 1982), pp. 603–46.

Mistry, Percy S., "Sub-Saharan Africa's External Debt: The Case for Relief," unpublished paper presented at the Symposium on Swedish Development Cooperation with sub-Saharan Africa in the 1990s (Saltsjobaden, Sweden, September 1988).

Stymne, Joakim, "The Accelerating Growth of the African Debt Burden," (unpublished; Washington: International Monetary Fund, October 1988).

Thomas, Vinod and Ajay Chhibber, "Experience with Policy Reforms Under Adjustment," International Monetary Fund and The World Bank, *Finance and Development* (Washington), Vol. 26, No. 1 (March 1989), pp. 28–31.

United Nations, *Financing Africa's Recovery*: Report and Recommendations of the Advisory Group on Financial Flows for Africa (New York, May 1988).

Weerasinghe, Nissanke E., "External Debt of Sub-Saharan Africa," *IMF Survey* (Washington), Vol. 17, Supplement (June 1988), pp. 177–91.

World Bank, *World Debt Tables, 1988/89* (Washington: World Bank, 1989).

Zulu, Justin B. and Saleh M. Nsouli, *Adjustment Programs in Africa: The Recent Experience,* Occasional Paper No. 34 (Washington: International Monetary Fund, 1985).

Market Valuation of External Debt

MICHAEL P. DOOLEY*

Investment in debtor countries depends upon residents' and nonresidents' expectations about the future. The market discount on existing debt also reflects the expectation that existing creditors may share a loss. Because it is difficult in international credit arrangements to differentiate between new and old debt, it may not be possible to insulate returns on new investment from an expected loss on existing debt. This inability to "let bygones be bygones" is a potentially important market failure that may lead to misallocation of domestic savings and constrain growth in debtor countries.

FOR 15 HEAVILY INDEBTED COUNTRIES, real gross investment relative to GNP has fallen by about one third in recent years compared with its level in the three-year period before 1982. While many factors have contributed to this decline, the markets' valuation of the existing debt of these countries may have been an important independent factor in discouraging investment. This argument is based on the proposition that, in evaluating new physical investment opportunities in an indebted country, a resident or nonresident investor must consider his standing relative to existing creditors. When the "property rights" of existing creditors are poorly defined, it is impossible to spell out clearly the rights of new creditors. Since a new credit cannot be convincingly differentiated from existing credits, potential investors must assume that the market value of their new claims will immediately become identical to the value of existing claims. This value is summarized by the market discount on existing debt. The cost of new capital goods does not depend upon the price at which financial claims on existing capital are currently traded. Thus, the fact that claims on new capital will trade at roughly the same discount as existing claims has the result of restraining real investment.

*Mr. Dooley, Chief of the External Adjustment Division in the Research Department of the IMF, is a graduate of Duquesne University, the University of Delaware, and the Pennsylvania State University.

The relevance of market valuation of existing debt to new real investment decisions is a fundamental issue in analyses of the debt crisis. Much of the analytical work on the debt issue has focused on the determinants of countries' ability and willingness to service their external debts. While such analysis may be useful in choosing among policy options that would alter the debtor's ability or willingness to service its debt, it tends to distract attention from the fact that the market's current evaluation of the debtor's situation is summarized in the price of existing debt. More important, it is this market valuation of existing debt that determines economic behavior.

I. Valuation of Debt

The contractual value of a debt can be defined as the present value of the stream of payments set out in the initial contract between the debtor and creditor on the assumption that such payments will be made with certainty. The market valuation of that contract is the present value of the market's expectation of the stream of payments that will actually be made under the contract. In most cases the contractual value will be somewhat above the market valuation to cover the possibility that, at some future date, the debtor may be unwilling or unable to carry out his obligations as set out in the contract. For example, if a country pays a 2 percent premium over LIBOR (London Interbank Offer Rate) on a floating rate credit, the contractual value of its debt instruments is above the market's valuation even at the inception of the contract.

The fact that a country's debt "sells" at a discount relative to its contractual value is always a problem in the sense that the country would have a larger stock of investment projects that are profitable if there were a smaller discount. This condition, which holds to some extent for most countries, can become a crisis in circumstances where most new domestic investment projects are unprofitable when "penalized" by factors equal to the market discount on existing debt.

Although it seems natural to focus on external debt, it is argued here that all existing debt of residents (private and official) of the debtor country represents a claim on the future output of that country. For this reason substantial market discounts on external debts can be associated with high real interest rates in the debtor country's domestic credit markets. If external credits are traded at a discount that reflects the expectation that contractual obligations will not be completely satisfied, it is very likely that *all* existing credits to residents of the debtor countries, including those held by other residents, are also subject to some doubt. In fact, all activities and forms of wealth that are potentially taxable by the debtor country should earn a rate of return that reflects the expected effects of those future taxes. If external debt carries a higher market yield (larger discount) than internal debt, residents should attempt to sell internal debt and purchase external debt (thereby making it internal) until their yields (discounts) are equalized. This arbitrage would be unprofitable only if resident and nonresident investors expected equivalent penalties on similar credits.

II. Existing and New Credits

The importance of the market valuation of existing debt derives from the earlier stated proposition that claims on new physical capital will immediately fall to the same discount as the existing claims. In fact, the problem is even more serious if potentially successful investments are likely to be more heavily taxed in order to satisfy "old" creditors.

The institutional framework that allows such a situation to persist is seriously deficient. In circumstances in which contractual obligations are not expected to be honored, property rights among creditors and debtors are poorly defined. In normal circumstances the hierarchy of claims is established by contract. But if it is expected that all such obligations cannot or will not be discharged, there is no way to tell who will suffer the expected loss. This situation creates uncertainty among new investors as to whether they will be forced to share an expected loss, and is therefore disadvantageous for the borrowing country.

The inability to subordinate existing credits to new credits is the factor that distinguishes the current international debt crisis from the more familiar problems presented in domestic financial arrangements. It is quite common for debtors and creditors to enter into agreements that, in some future circumstance, will be impossible to carry out. The value of such agreements is that they are simple and not dependent, or "contingent," upon the large number of factors that might affect the debtor's willingness or ability to carry out the terms of the agreement. The development of contracts that do not depend upon a large number of future conditions facilitates secondary trading of the obligation, thus making such contracts more attractive to creditors. Should the debtor be unable to satisfy the terms of the contract, however, both parties would be uncertain as to how the situation would be resolved.

In the case in which both debtor and creditor share a national legal residence, the conflict is resolved by the courts in a bankruptcy proceeding. Since the general outlines of this solution are known to both parties at the outset, it is reasonable to include this mechanism as an implicit element of the original agreement. Moreover, in the event that some contracts are subordinate to others, it is known how the courts will enforce the property rights of various creditors. The procedure by which a debtor asks the courts to "protect him from his creditors" serves to free the debtor (at perhaps considerable cost) from his obligations.

The view that this procedure "benefits" the domestic debtor derives from the fundamental problem faced by such a debtor in obtaining new credits. In the absence of a bankruptcy proceeding, the debtor's problem in obtaining new finance is that all potential new creditors will be subject to sharing in the existing "expected" loss, the difference between the market's valuation of the debtor's obligations and their contractual value. Regardless of the debtor's willingness or ability to fulfill his obligations, the behavior of creditors is shaped by the market valuation of the debt. It may be possible to assure some new creditors that their investments will be protected from the legal claims of existing creditors, but it seems unlikely that such assurances would be completely or widely credible as long as substantial discounts on existing credits remain.

The above argument suggests that a key ingredient in the current international debt crisis is the lack of a legal structure that comes into play in cases in which the market valuation falls to a point at which the debtor country is unable to attract new investments in productive capital. In fact, it is not clear which of several national legal systems would decide the property rights of various creditors. In this environment it is impossible convincingly to subordinate existing claims to new claims regardless of what forms these new credits might take.

III. An Investment Problem

The inability to shield the returns on new investments from being tainted by the expected loss on existing credits may result in a slowdown of new investment. Because the debt crisis occurred at a well-defined point in time it seems natural to assume that once some threshold of creditworthiness is reestablished, the situation will return to normal. The "best" solution to the investment problem would be to alter the market valuation of existing credits by improving the outlook for the debtor country. In particular, in cases in which changes in economic policies or structures can contribute to such a revaluation, the implementation of a sound adjustment program is the first priority.

Nevertheless, while some changes in the economic environment could lead to an immediate return to a normal investment climate, not all eventual cures for the debt problem will have this property. In particular, solutions characterized by gradual amortization of debt and a slowly rising market value for remaining debt may not change for a long time the depressed state of domestic investment in debtor countries.

IV. Four Approaches

The distinction between the "investment problem" and the "debt problem" can be illustrated by considering four strategies that could be undertaken by debtors or creditors. Each strategy might eventually eliminate or allocate the expected loss on existing debt, and in that sense resolve the "debt problem," but these strategies will have different effects on the climate for future real investment in debtor countries. One way to calculate the success of a given strategy in dealing with the "investment problem" would be to consider whether the strategy would alter the market discount on existing debt in order to encourage rates of capital accumulation consistent with acceptable targets for economic growth.

Wait and see. The commercial banks that hold the debt may have strong incentives to carry the existing debt at book value and limit new lending to a portion of accrued interest payments. A popular explanation for this stategy is that, given time, the banks and debtor countries will eventually grow out of the debt problem. Here a distinction must be made between real interest payments and payments that, although classified as interest, in reality reflect accelerated amortization owing to inflation. In an inflationary environment, commercial banks could shrink their exposure by diverting amortization payments implicit in the inflation premium to the purchase of alternative investments, even though the nominal value of the banks' claims continue to grow at a rate less than the rate of inflation.

For banks whose capital might be exhausted by realizing (writing off) the losses on existing credits, there is no doubt that the strategy of waiting to see whether a good outcome for the country could save the bank from liquidation is preferred to a solution that would involve realizing expected losses immediately. In the interim, as long as governments implicitly or explicitly insure the value of bank liabilities, the banks can continue to attract deposits and carry on normal business. Moreover, by postponing action the nonbank public also avoids the disruption to the payments mechanism that might accompany the failure, or expected failure, of one or several money center banks.

The "wait and see" strategy has an important negative impact on the debtor country. As argued above, the expected but "unallocated" loss on existing external credits will affect current investment decisions. Nonresident investors will assume that their claims will be merged with existing credits. Perhaps more disturbing are the implications for the decisions of residents in allocating their savings. If the government is not expected to be able to service its internal and external debt, a successful domestic investment project would provide an attractive tax base for a hard-pressed fiscal authority. To avoid this potential tax liability residents might choose to send their savings overseas or to direct them to unproductive domestic investments that are difficult for the debtor country's fiscal authority to tax.

Thus, even as this strategy is successful in "wearing down" the debt, it involves a smaller capital stock for the debtor country for an extended period in cases in which the gap between the market value of existing debt and its contractual value narrows slowly as the existing debt is amortized. The consequences for the capital stock can be quantitatively important because debtor countries stand to lose not only new foreign savings but also some part of the productive domestic investment made possible by domestic savings.

Creditors share expected losses. If creditors were to write off the expected loss without altering the debtor country's legal obligations, their capital would be partially or completely lost. This strategy is generally not in the interest of the creditor banks. Moreover, the debtor country is no better or worse off as compared to the "wait and see" option discussed above since both the market and contractual values of existing debts are unchanged.

The nonbank private residents of creditor countries may be better off since the uncertainty as to how losses will affect various institutions is removed. Nevertheless, they would also suffer whatever ill effects are associated with the impact of the losses realized by commercial banks on the payments mechanism. This solution does not seem to be clearly in anyone's interest.

Loss-sharing and debt relief. A third strategy would be for the creditors to write off the expected loss *and* to relieve or forgive debtor countries' legal obligations to pay. As argued above, some level of forgiveness would in most cases create conditions under which physical investments profitable in their own right would be undertaken. It seems unlikely that existing creditors will see it in their interest to undertake such an action voluntarily, either as individuals or as a group. It follows that some third party would have to force creditors to take the loss and renegotiate the credits, or what seems more promising, purchase the existing credits and then forgive some part of the debt.

One plan would be to offer to purchase a certain type and amount of debt at an auction where sellers submit offers to sell various amounts at different prices. The purchaser of the debt could also announce that it would replace the existing debt with obligations that had a present value somewhat below the current contractual value, perhaps equal to the auction price. Market participants would anticipate the need to revalue debt not sold and this would of course affect their offers. By manipulating the size of the offer to buy at the auction, the discount on existing debt could be reduced to a level consistent with real investment objectives. The cost of this operation would be the difference between the buying and selling prices obtained by the purchaser.

As part of this strategy, new credits could be better designed to reflect the risks inherent in the debtor's ability to pay. The value of such credits, however, would probably not be much higher than the expected value of existing credits. Thus, a restructuring of the debt toward equity-type instruments might serve to avoid future problems, but would not in itself significantly reduce the loss that must be realized in order to restore the desired climate for real investment.

This strategy is clearly attractive to the debtor country. Moreover, if we consider banks and nonbanks of creditor countries together, they may, as a group, be better off. A difficult question is whether such a write-off would damage existing debtors' reputation regarding their willingness to pay or lead other debtors to demand similar treatment. Such considerations may be sufficient to make this an unattractive alternative.

Unilateral partial default. A debtor country could partially default on its obligations in that some payments would be made but the existing legal contracts would not be fully honored. The creditor banks would retain a legal claim on the country, and although this claim would probably be judged "nonperforming" by the regulatory authorities, it is unlikely that the debt would be formally forgiven by creditors. The debtor country would suffer a reduction in its reputation as a potential borrower. Thus, although a partial default might make the country a good risk in terms of ability to pay, creditors (old and new) might doubt the country's willingness to pay. Moreover, the legal claims on the debtor country would remain and continue to threaten new creditors. The greatest problem with a repudiation strategy is that the long-term reputation of the debtor is damaged.

V. Overview

The market value of existing debt plays a central role in the analysis presented above. This value is important because it summarizes the forecasts of many actual and potential owners of claims on a debtor country. Thus, it provides a ready guide and frees creditors from the need to calculate the true value of external debt. It is useful to provide a model of the factors that might lie behind the market valuation of debt since this allows analysis of the factors that might alter that valuation. But ultimately market valuation depends on the collective wisdom (or ignorance) of those who are willing to risk their wealth in acquiring claims on debtor countries. This is the forecast that will determine the economic behavior of debtors and creditors.

It is sometimes argued that the market value of the external debt of developing countries is depressed by the behavior of existing creditors. For example, commercial banks may face regulatory constraints over the amount of loans to individual countries, creating uncertainty about future lending to a country. If all banks reach this position, or if their desired position is for some reason reduced, the country might be said to have experienced a liquidity crisis. If no new creditors enter the market at this point, the market value of the country's debt will fall and voluntary new credits will stop. It has been argued that new creditors will not enter the market because, while the new credits will increase the value of the existing credits, most of the benefit will go to the existing creditors who are sometimes called free riders.

This idea is intuitively appealing but ignores straight-forward arbitrage opportunities. Suppose that the market value of claims on a country has fallen to 50 percent of its contractual value, not because the outlook for the country has changed, but because existing creditors are unwilling or unable to provide new credits. A potential new creditor knows that new credits would increase the present value of the existing debt. His strategy should be to agree to buy some of the existing debt at the market discount and then advertise and grant additional new credits. This would cause the market value of existing debts to rise. The new creditor would realize capital gains until the market value of debt again reflected the unchanged outlook for the debtor country. It follows that if an arbitrage opportunity exists, that is, if the expected value of existing debt is above the market valuation, it will be exploited by new creditors. Free riders would be bought out.

Finally, the market value of existing debt is not a good indicator of the extent to which the contractual value of debt would have to fall in order to restore the debtor to normal status in credit markets. At a minimum, as the discussion above suggests, the market's valuation of debt remaining after a default or some forgiveness of existing debt would depend on a whole set of new expectations about the future behavior of the debtor country and its creditors.

Investment, Openness, and Country Risk

JOSHUA AIZENMAN*

This study draws attention to the linkages between country risk and the openness of an economy and demonstrates that in the long run the openness of an economy is endogenously determined by the interaction between endowments and policies. The presence of country risk poses a problem for the smooth operation of international credit markets: the ex-ante first best policy is for countries to pre-commit themselves to no-default policies. Such a commitment, however, may not be credible because it may not be the optimal ex-post policy. This suggests, as a way to increase the credibility of a no-default commitment, a special role for policies leading toward investment in openness. The paper studies the optimal implementation of these policies.

THE EVOLUTION of external debt during the 1970s and 1980s demonstrates the unique dimension of international banking in the presence of country risk. The lack of simple enforcement mechanisms for debt repayment tends to reduce the international credit market to an equilibrium in which the volume of international credit is limited by the effective penalties associated with defaults. These penalties are the results of potential embargoes and are associated with restrictions on the flow of both temporal (goods) and intertemporal (financial assets) trade.

To pre-commit itself to no-default is the borrower's "first best" policy (i.e., the policy that will maximize the expected welfare of the borrowing nation) because a default is associated with a net waste of resources

* Joshua Aizenman, a consultant at the Research Department of the IMF, is Associate Professor of Economics at the Hebrew University and was formerly Associate Professor of Business Economics at the University of Chicago. He is a graduate of the Hebrew University and received his doctorate from the University of Chicago.

(resulting from the embargo) that is not captured by any party and thus results in welfare losses. The problem with a no-default commitment is that it is not credible, because it is time inconsistent. The time-consistent policy regarding the default decision is based on a periodic cost-benefit assessment. The literature has in fact focused on analyzing the properties of the time-consistent equilibrium. Typically, the default decision is arrived by comparing the saving resulting from the default to the default penalty, taken as exogenously given.[1]

This paper focuses on the role of investment policies in the presence of country risk. This issue is important because a trade embargo can eliminate the gains from trade. Thus, a default penalty is tied directly to the openness of the economy. In the long run the openness of an economy is endogenously determined by the interaction between endowment and investment policies. These policies, in turn, may affect the supply of credit facing the economy. Our analysis examines the linkages between investment policies and country risk.

As is commonly mentioned in the time-consistency literature, welfare benefits associated with a credible commitment will allow the attainment of the first best equilibrium.[2] We can move toward such an equilibrium by designing investment policies that will increase the openness of the economy, thereby raising the cost of deviations from a no-default commitment.[3] To examine these policies we construct a simple two-period analysis of country risk. Borrowing in the first period finances consumption and investment in various activities that differ in their exposure to international trade, owing to varying degrees of reliance on imported inputs or on external markets for sales of output. The country will default in the second period if the default penalty falls short of the debt. The international credit market is dominated by risk-neutral lenders who will supply sufficient credit to equate the expected yield on their international lendings to the exogenously given risk-free interest rate. Since domestic agents are small enough to be price takers in the domestic credit market, they treat the interest rate facing them as exogenously given. The default decision against external creditors is made by a centralized decisionmaker, such as the central bank, whose policy is guided by an attempt to maximize the expected welfare of a representative consumer. The source of country risk is thus transfer risk. Agents are

[1] For an analysis of country risk, see the list of further readings at the end of this volume.

[2] For an analysis of time consistency see Calvo (1978) and Kydland and Prescott (1977).

[3] Investment in openness may serve as a credible commitment as long as installed capital is sector specific.

assumed to be rational and fully informed about the default decision rule guiding the central bank. We study the factors determining the supply of credit facing the economy, the private sector consumption and investment, and the policies needed to attain the optimal allocation.

Our analysis demonstrates that the supply of credit is determined by aggregate borrowing and by its decomposition among consumption and various investment activities. The supply curve slopes upward and may include a backward bending portion. The investment in a given sector is determined by the expected incidence of country default and by the relative exposure of the sector to international trade. A rise in country risk is associated with more frequent defaults and consequently with a lower level of investment. The resultant drop in investment is larger in activities with greater reliance on international trade.

Financial policies in the presence of country risk are important because competitive equilibrium is inefficient in the presence of international debt. The presence of country risk is shown to introduce a distortion arising individual borrowers' treating the rate of interest as given even though, from the perspective of the country as a whole, the rate of interest varies with the volume of borrowing and investment because of the change in the probability of default. Each small consumer overlooks the change in the probability of default induced by his marginal borrowing and marginal investment. The change in the probability of default creates an externality because of the consequent change in the expected default penalty inflicted on all domestic consumers.

The presence of country risk calls for financial policies. These policies take the form of a tax on borrowing for consumption and a tax on borrowing for investment. The tax internalizes the effect of the activity financed by the borrowing on the probability of default. The optimal tax should be higher in proportion to the increase in the probability of default resulting from that activity. For example, the optimal borrowing tax on investment in intermediate goods that must be exported for final assembly should be lower than that on investment in the production of final goods. Similarly, investment in export substitutes or nontraded goods should be taxed more than investment in exportable goods. This outcome is consistent with the notion that, in the presence of country risk, a country can more easily finance export-led growth biased toward the production of intermediate goods rather than toward final goods, or inward growth biased toward import substitution.

Unlike the case of borrowing for consumption, borrowing for investment has two opposite externality effects. First, marginal borrowing raises total indebtedness, thus increasing the probability of default. Second, investment in the traded sector also opens the economy and raises its productive capacity, thereby changing the default penalty and the probability of default. The optimal tax on investment borrowing balances these two effects. The stronger the openness effect, the lower the optimal tax on investment borrowing; and if this effect dominates, the optimal policy takes the form of an investment subsidy. Consequently, in the presence of country risk the marginal use of funds plays a key role in determining appropriate policies.

A final topic of our analysis is a study of the nature of country risk in the presence of equity finance. We demonstrate that swapping nominal debt for equities may have useful consequences for reducing country risk, but it cannot eliminate the fundamental problems associated with international credit. If the random shocks affect output and the default penalty in the same way, we obtain the strong result, by correlating the repayments with the default penalty, that equity finance will eliminate defaults up to the credit ceiling. The debt-equity swap, however, cannot eliminate the resulting need to impose a ceiling on the available credit, but may allow an increase in the credit ceiling. These results should be viewed as a special case of a more general economic environment: in the presence of several shocks that affect output and the default penalty in different ways, the move to equity finance may be beneficial, but it will not eliminate defaults.

I. Credit Market Equilibrium

Let us construct a simple framework for the analysis of country risk and investment policy in the presence of default risk. This can be done in a two-period, multi-sectorial economy. Suppose that the value added in sector i depends on the realization of a productivity shock, on the decision regarding default (if default raises the costs of imported inputs, it will tend to depress output), and on the capital stock, which in turn is determined by past investment. We can summarize the value added in sector i at time t by:

$$Y_{i;t} = \begin{array}{l} Y_{i;t}(\Psi; n, K_{i;t}), \text{ if no default occurs,} \\ Y_{i;t}(\Psi; d, K_{i;t}), \text{ if default occurs,} \end{array} \tag{1}$$

where Ψ is the state of nature, reflecting a productivity shock $(\partial Y_i / \partial \Psi > 0)$. The second term stands for the default position of the economy. It can have values of n and d, for the default and no-default position, and $K_{i;t}$ is the stock of capital in sector i at time t. For expositional simplicity we assume that the economy is a price taker in the international market, and we normalize all prices of final goods to unity.

We also assume a common productivity shock for all sectors, and we assume that the density function of the productivity shock (denoted by $f(\Psi)$) is common knowledge. The GNP in our economy is the sum of the value added in all activities, being given by $Y_t(\Psi; s) = \sum_{i=1}^{q} Y_{i,t}(\Psi; s, K_{i,t})$; where $s = n$ or d (no default or default, respectively) and there are q sectors.[4]

We define the default penalty (denoted by Δ) as the drop in the GNP resultant from the default: $\Delta = Y_t(\Psi; n) - Y_t(\Psi; d)$. Let us assume that the default penalty is larger in goods states of nature (i.e., $\partial\Delta/\partial\Psi > 0$).[5]

Aggregate indebtedness in the second period ($t = 2$) is denoted by B, and the interest rate on that indebtedness is r^*. Aggregate borrowing is the result of consumption borrowing (denoted by B_c) and investment borrowing in sector i (denoted by I_i, where $1 \leq i \leq q$). For simplicity of exposition we assume that all the investment in period one is financed via external borrowing. In such a case $B = B_c + \sum_{i=1}^{q} I_i$, and, assuming no depreciation, we obtain that $K_{i;2} = K_{i;1} + I_i$.[6]

The default decision in period two can be summarized by the following simple rule: default if the penalty falls short of the payment due:

no default if $\quad B(1 + r^*) < \Delta$,

default if $\quad B(1 + r^*) > \Delta$.

Let us denote by Ψ_0 the marginal value of the productivity shock being associated with default (i.e., Ψ_0 is defined by the requirement that $B(1 + r^*) = \Delta$). Consequently, the probability of no default is the probability that the productivity shock exceeds Ψ_0. Let us denote this probability by Π.[7] Assuming that the international banking sector is dominated by risk neutral agents we can characterize the supply of credit by the combination of B and r^* that solves:

$$1 + r_f = (1 + r^*)\Pi, \tag{2}$$

where r_f is the exogenously given risk free interest rate.[8] We can sum-

---

[4] Note that the GNP Y_t is a function also of the vector of capital ($K_{1,t}, \ldots K_{2,t}, \ldots, K_{q,t}$). For notational simplicity this vector is suppressed.

[5] This assumption reflects the presumption that in goods states of nature we expect greater volume of international trade, thereby raising the default penalty.

[6] To simplify we neglect the potential role of initial indebtedness by assuming it to be zero. For an analysis regarding a partial default decision in period zero owing to initial indebtedness see Krugman (1985).

[7] Formally, $\Pi = \int_{\Psi_0}^{\infty} f(\Psi) \, d\Psi$.

[8] The probability of no default is a function of the following variables $\Pi = \Pi(\vec{B}, r^*; \vec{K}_2)$; where the signs above the variables stand for the sign of the partial derivatives, and $\vec{K}_2$ stands for the vector of the capital stock in the various activities (in the second period).

Figure 1. *Supply of Credit to an Economy*

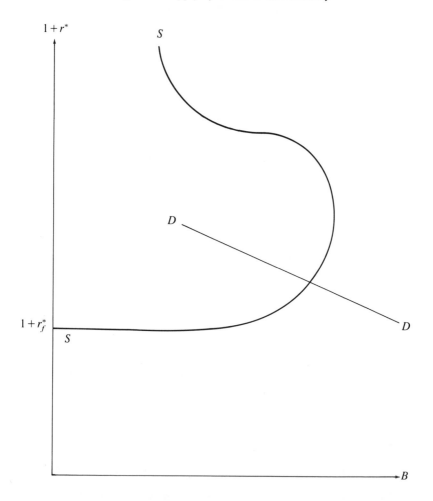

marize the supply of credit facing the economy by curve SS in Figure 1.
The supply schedule is upward sloping for intermediate levels of credit.
It may include also a backward bending portion, reflecting the fact that
a rise in the interest rate has two opposing effects on expected returns—
for a given probability of no default it increases the expected yield, but
at the same time it reduces the probability of payment, depressing the
expected yield. If the second effect dominates, we will operate on the
backward bending portion of the supply schedule. Direct application of
(2) reveals that the elasticity of the supply of credit ($d \log (1 + r^*)/d \log$

B) is determined by the elasticity of the probability of no default with respect to the interest rate, denoted by $-\varepsilon$ (i.e., $\varepsilon = -d \log \Pi / d \log (1 + r^*)$). It can be shown that $d \log (1 + r^*)/d \log B = \varepsilon/(1 - \varepsilon)$.[9] The term ε is a measure of the segmentation of the domestic credit market from the international market, being determined by the nature of the distribution of the default penalty. A lower ε is associated with greater capital market integration, and $\varepsilon = 0$ corresponds to the case in which country risk is absent. We restrict the economy to operate along the upward sloping portion of the supply of credit schedule (where a rise in indebtedness is associated with a rise in the interest rate).[10]

We would like to use our framework to evaluate optimal policies in the presence of country risk. We can do this by comparing the optimality conditions determining the consumption and investment from the point of view of the consumer and of the centralized planner. A comparison between the planner's and the consumer's solutions reveals that the planner applies the social interest rate, whereas the consumer applies the private one (see the Appendix for the derivations of these results). The social interest rate is defined as the total marginal interest cost associated with borrowing for consumption and for investment in activity i, given by

$$(1 + r^*)\left[1 + \frac{B}{B_c} \frac{d \log (1 + r^*)}{d \log B_c}\right]; \ (1 + r^*)\left[1 + \frac{B}{I_i} \frac{d \log (1 + r^*)}{d \log I_i}\right];$$

$i = 1, \ldots, q$, respectively. Note that the social planner may face different social interest rates for the various activities. The key difference between the individual agent and the social planner is that the latter is internalizing the marginal changes in the interest rate facing the economy resulting from marginal borrowing. These changes in turn are determined by the use of these funds and are reflected in the second term in the social interest rates. The percentage difference between the private and the social interest rate equals the elasticity of the interest rate $(1 + r^*)$ with the respect to the borrowing. Logarithmic derivation of (2) gives us that the elasticity with respect to consumption borrowing is

$$\frac{d \log (1 + r^*)}{d \log B_c} = \frac{\varepsilon}{1 - \varepsilon} \frac{B_c}{B} > 0.$$

[9] Thus, we operate on the upwards sloping portion of the supply of credit as long as $\varepsilon < 1$, and we reach the credit ceiling where $\varepsilon = 1$. For further details on the factors determining the supply of credit in the presence of country risk, see Aizenman (1986).

[10] This assumption is consistent with welfare maximization: it can be shown that an equilibrium on the backward bending portion of the supply of credit schedule is inefficient. Ruling out such an equilibrium may require policies in the form of optimal borrowing taxes (Aizenman (1986)).

This elasticity equals the elasticity of the supply of credit ($\varepsilon/1 - \varepsilon$) weighted by the relative importance of the consumption borrowing to the entire volume of borrowing. Applying a similar derivation we can infer that the elasticity with respect to investment borrowing is:

$$\frac{d \log (1 + r^*)}{d \log I_i} = \frac{\varepsilon}{1 - \varepsilon} \left(\frac{I_i}{B} - \frac{I_i}{K_i} \frac{\lambda_i}{\varepsilon} \right),$$

where λ_i is the elasticity of the probability of no default with respect to the stock of capital in sector i (i.e., $\lambda_i = \partial \log \Pi / \partial \log K_i$). We can view λ_i as a measure of the openness associated with the investment in sector i. An investment project raising the openness will have the consequence of increasing the probability of no default, thereby raising λ_i. Consequently, the magnitude of λ_i is a measure of the importance of this effect. We will further investigate this interpretation in the next section.

The difference between the interest rate of the private consumer and the social planner suggests that in the absence of policies the presence of country risk implies a distortion. From the social point of view, the equilibrium is associated with "excessive" borrowing for consumption because the private interest rate falls short of the social one. This situation provides the rationale for policies. The distortion arises from individual borrowers treating the rate of interest as given, even though from the perspective of the country as a whole the rate of interest rises with the volume of consumption borrowing owing to the rise in the probability of default. Each small consumer overlooks the marginal rise in the probability of default induced by his marginal borrowing. The rise in the probability of default entails a negative externality because of the consequent rise in the expected default penalty inflicted on all domestic consumers. Therefore, the role of policies is to internalize this externality. An optimal tax on borrowing for consumption (denoted by ρ_c) is needed to yield equality between the social and private interest rates. This tax is defined by the condition that

$$1 + r_c = (1 + r^*) \left[1 + \frac{B}{B_c} \frac{d \log (1 + r^*)}{d \log B_c} \right],$$

where r_c is the domestic interest rate defined by the borrowing tax (i.e., $1 + r_c = 1 + r^*(1 + \rho_c)$). Applying our previous results yields the optimal tax to be[11]

---

[11] Note that as ε approaches 1, the optimal tax approaches infinity, corresponding to an effective quota on external borrowing implemented by the central bank. This quota has the consequence of ruling out inefficient equilibrium on the backward bending portion of the supply of credit. For more details see Aizenman (1986).

$$\rho_c = \frac{\varepsilon}{1-\varepsilon} \frac{1+r^*}{r^*} > 0. \tag{3}$$

By following a similar approach we can determine that the optimal borrowing tax for investment in sector i (denoted by ρ_i) is

$$\rho_i = \frac{\varepsilon}{1-\varepsilon} \frac{1+r^*}{r^*} - \frac{\lambda_i}{1-\varepsilon} \frac{B}{K_i} \frac{1+r^*}{r^*}. \tag{4}$$

Notice that unlike consumption borrowing, marginal investment borrowing affects the borrowing externality in two opposing directions. First, marginal borrowing for investment raises the total debt, thus increasing the probability of default. This effect is captured by the first term in (4) and is similar to the one reported in (3) for consumption borrowing. Second, the investment in the traded sector also opens the economy and raises its productive capacity, thereby increasing the default penalty and reducing the probability of default. This effect is captured in the second term, and is proportional to the measure of the investment in openness, λ_i. The optimal borrowing tax balances these two effects. The stronger the investment effect, the lower the optimal tax on investment borrowing.

The optimal taxes have a simple diagrammatic interpretation in Figure 2. Let MC stand for the social marginal costs of consumption borrowing. The consumption borrowing tax is defined by the vertical distance between the supply SS and the marginal cost. Note that the location of the supply schedule is determined by the vector of the capital stock in the economy (denoted by $\vec{K}$). Borrowing for investment purposes has the consequence of raising $\vec{K}$ to $\vec{K}'$, thereby shifting the supply and the corresponding marginal cost schedules to SS' and MC', respectively. The optimal investment borrowing tax is defined by the vertical distance between SS' and the new marginal cost schedule.[12]

A relevant implication of country risk is that the marginal use of funds plays a key role in determining the appropriate policies because the role of policies is to internalize the marginal contribution of the activity to the probability of default. If one activity raises this probability by more than another, borrowing for that activity should be taxed at a higher rate. This is the rationale for the differential taxation of borrowing for consumption versus various investment projects. A possible consequence of our

---

[12] If the investment financed by the borrowing is highly effective in raising the default penalty, the shift to the right of the relevant schedule may result in a policy of subsidizing that investment relative to the initial no policy equilibrium. This will correspond to the case in which the MC' schedule is to the right of the original SS.

Figure 2. *Marginal Cost of Credit*

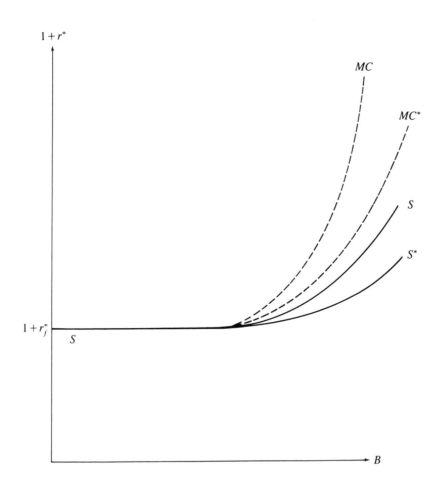

analysis is that investment in openness should be treated favorably relative to investment that does not affect openness or borrowing for consumption. For example, investment in intermediate goods that must be exported for final assembly may be associated with a different contribution toward country risk than investment in the production of a final good. Consequently, the social interest rate and the corresponding tax on borrowing or subsidy rates will differ across these activities. To derive this result more formally we should impose further structure on our model. This is done in the next section by specializing the model to deal with an economy in which a default results in a rise in the price of imported inputs and in which the various sectors differ in their dependency on importable goods.[13]

II. Investment and Imported Inputs

The simplest example to deal with country risk with endogenous choice of openness can be constructed in a two-sectorial economy. The two sectors differ in terms of their reliance on international trade. For example, consider an economy in which output in sector i (denoted by X_i) is produced by the following process:

$$X_i = \Psi\, C_i\, (K_i)^\alpha\, (M_i)^{\beta_i}; \qquad \alpha + \beta_i < 1, \tag{5}$$

where K_i and M_i are the capital and the imported inputs used in sector i, and C_i is a constant. The only difference between the two sectors is that they differ in their dependence on international trade. One of them, suppose sector 1, is more dependent on international trade (i.e., $\beta_2 < \beta_1$). Thus, we can refer to β_i as a measure of the "openness," or the reliance on international trade of activity i. In the short run the stock of capital is exogenously given. We denote the price of the imported input by P_m, and we assume that P_m is determined by the policies of the country. In the absence of default, the country faces the international price of P_m, assumed to be unity. A default will have the consequence of triggering a penalty owing to a trade embargo. A simple way to capture the penalty is to assume that it will raise the price of imported inputs by a factor of $p_m > 0$, such that in states of default the effective costs of importables for the country is $exp\,(p_m)$.

Producers in each sector maximize profits in two ways. In the first period producers will choose the optimal investment that will determine the capital stock in the second period. Within each period the stock of capital is given, and producers will choose the imported input M in order to maximize profits. As is shown in the appendix, the default penalty can be approximated by the sum of output in the various sectors in states of no default weighted by a measure of the reliance on trade (β_i) times the

---

[13] An example of such an economic environment may be the case of Turkey in the 1970s, when, as a consequence of credit difficulties, imports of energy were reduced. Our discussion should be viewed as only one example for modeling external dependency. While the focus of the analysis here is on the inputs linkages, similar analysis can apply for output linkages, where various sectors differ in the share of exports.

increase in imported inputs prices, p_m. Formally, the default penalty can be approximated for small values of p_m by:

$$\Delta \approx (\beta_1 X_{n;1} + \beta_2 X_{n;2}) p_m, \tag{6}$$

where $X_{n;i} = c_i (\Psi)^{1/(1-\beta_i)}(K_i)^{\alpha/(1-\beta_i)}$ for $i = 1,2$ (c_i are constants).

Reliance on international trade (as measured by the importance of the imported input, β_i) determines in large measure the relative importance of sector i in the aggregate default penalty. A sector that is shielded from international trade has little to do with the determination of the aggregate default penalty. These factors help determine the optimal tax on borrowing for investment in sector i. Investment in an activity with a larger openness index β_i will increase the default penalty, raising the probability of no default. Thus, we expect sectors with larger exposure to trade to be associated with a larger elasticity of the probability of no default with respect to capital (denoted by λ_i). Let us recall that this λ_i was referred to as a measure of the openness associated with investment in sector i. A larger λ_i was shown to be associated with a lower tax on investment borrowing (see (4)). Applying (6) we show in the appendix that the value of λ_i equals $s_i \varepsilon \alpha/(1 - \beta_i)$, where s_i is a measure of sector i's share in the aggregate penalty. This measure is proportional to the reliance on imports, β_i. Consequently, we can derive the reduced form of the optimal tax on investment borrowing for activity i:

$$\rho_i = \frac{\varepsilon}{1 - \varepsilon} \left[1 - \frac{s_i \alpha B}{(1 - \beta_i) K_i} \right] (1 + r^*)/r^*. \tag{4'}$$

The optimal tax depends negatively on the openness of activity i to international trade. A smaller openness is associated with smaller values of s_i and β_i, implying a higher investment borrowing tax. An activity with no contribution to the default penalty ($\beta_i = s_i = 0$) should be treated similarly to a borrowing for consumption.[14]

A default is associated with a penalty that results in a lower productivity of capital. To gain further insight regarding the adverse consequences of country risk on investment it is useful to consider a special case. Suppose that investment is conducted by risk neutral agents who equate the expected cost of capital to the expected marginal product, and let us assume that the logarithm of the productivity shock is normally distributed ($\log (\Psi) \sim N (O,V)$) with mean zero and a small variance V.

---

[14] Note that (4') also implies that the condition for subsidizing investment in sector i is that $K_i/B < s_i \alpha/(1 - \beta_i)$. Thus, a higher aggregate indebtedness as well as a higher reliance of activity i on international trade will increase the likelihood of subsidizing investment in sector i.

In the appendix we demonstrate that in a competitive equilibrium the stock of capital can be approximated by

$$K_i \approx d_i \left[\frac{1 - \beta_i p_m (1 - \Pi)/(1 - \beta_i)}{1 + r_f} \right] \frac{1 - \beta_i}{1 - \beta_i - \alpha}, \tag{7}$$

where d_i is a constant. Equation (7) has a simple interpretation: the stock of capital depends positively on the term in the bracket, which is the ratio of expected net productivity (net of the default penalty) over the expected cost of capital.[15] The expected cost of credit is the risk-free interest rate, and this is the cost element in that equation. Thus, as long as we operate below the credit ceiling, country risk does not change the expected cost of borrowing (being equal to the risk-free rate). Instead, country risk operates by reducing the expected marginal product of capital, thereby reducing investment.

The adverse consequences of country risk affect the various sectors differentially. Investment drops more in the sectors more heavily dependent on international trade. Formally, one can show that a marginal increase in the probability of default will reduce investment in sector i by a factor of $\beta_i/1 - \alpha - \beta_i$, in proportion to the relative openness of sector i.[16]

III. Debt Versus Equity Finance

Recently we have observed the emergence of schemes intended to swap existing debt for equities. A typical loan in the 1970s and 1980s was in the form of a nominal interest rate contract, not allowing for contingencies. It is hard to believe that such a contract is optimal, and a purpose of the debt-equity swap is to overcome some of the difficulties associated with loans with limited price contingencies by replacing a noncontingent with a contingent contract.[17] Indeed, it is somewhat of a puzzle as to why the growing awareness of the welfare benefits of contingencies has oc-

---

[15] Note that $1 - \Pi$ is the probability of default, and $\beta_i p_m/(1 - \beta_i)$ is the percentage drop in output and in the productivity of capital attributed to default. Consequently, $\beta_i p_m (1 - \Pi)/(1 - \beta_i)$ has the interpretation of the expected drop in output and in the productivity of capital owing to default (see (6)).

[16] Formally, $d \log K_i/d (1 - \Pi) \approx - \beta_i p_m/(1 - \alpha - \beta_i)$.

[17] One standard argument for debt contracts is the costs of monitoring the behavior of the borrower and other informational costs. This argument cannot, however, explain the lack of contingencies that use public information that is exogenous to the borrowers (such as the price of oil and other commodities, the real interest rate in the United States, and the growth rate of industrialized nations).

curred only recently.[18] We turn now to an application of our model, in which we analyze the nature of country risk in the presence of equity finance. The present analysis will demonstrate that swapping nominal debt for equities may have useful consequences in reducing country risk, but it cannot eliminate the fundamental problems associated with international credit.

It is useful to start with the case of a one-sector economy ($q = 1$), where for notational simplicity we suppress the sectorial index. Consider an initial equilibrium in our economy with an initial level of indebtedness of B. A debt-equity swap will replace the debt B with claims on an equivalent fraction of the value added. We denote that fraction by τ. A default in the equity scheme will occur if its benefits (in the form of no payments to foreign investors) exceed the default penalty. Thus, a default will occur if, and only if, $\tau(1 - \beta) X_n > \beta X_n p_m$, where the left-hand side stands for the foreign equity income paid in case of no default, and the right-hand side stands for the default penalty. Consequently, the condition assuring no default is that the foreign ownership share τ does not exceed $\beta p_m/(1 - \beta)$. This condition is useful in yielding the maximum equity investment in period one, which is determined by the expected net present value of the foreign equity income extracted for $\bar{\tau} = \beta p_m/(1 - \beta)$ which can be approximated by $\beta p_m c(K)^{\alpha/(1-\beta)}/(1 + r_f)$. This defines the equivalent of a credit ceiling for the case of equity investment. It is given by a portion $\beta p_m/(1 + r_f)$ of the expected output. It can be shown that a useful property of the equity scheme is that it increases the correlation between the income of foreign investors and the default penalty, thereby reducing the incidence of default. In our example, for equity investment below the ceiling defined above we obtain no default because the equity scheme leads to a unitary correlation between the default penalty and the income to foreign owners. It can be also shown that the switch from debt-to-equity finance has the consequence of increasing the credit ceiling available to the economy. Furthermore, as long as the foreign investment is below the ceiling, an equity scheme will increase the optimal investment.[19]

Our discussion should be viewed only as an example for the benefits of the debt-equity swap. Because we allow the random shock to affect output and the default penalty in the same way we obtain the strong

---

[18] One of the first attempts to use such contingencies was the rescheduling plan between the International Monetary Fund and Mexico in the summer of 1986, in which the future supply of credit was made conditional on the price of oil.

[19] Formally, the optimal capital stock with equity investment is given by equation (7), for the case where we replace p_m with 0 (assuming that we operate below the credit ceiling).

result that equity finance will eliminate defaults up to the credit ceiling. This is done by correlating the repayments with the default penalty. The debt-equity swap, however, cannot eliminate the impact of country risk and the resulting need to impose a ceiling on the available credit. Instead, it allows us to increase the credit ceiling. In the presence of several shocks which affect output and the default penalty in different ways, the move to equity finance will not eliminate the incidence of default but may be beneficial to the degree that it increases the correlation between the default penalty and the repayment. It can be shown that the general optimal contract in the presence of country risk is not an equity finance but rather a loan contract that optimally indexes the repayment to the default penalty, and the credit ceiling subject to such a contract is the expected net present value of the penalty (discounted at the risk-free interest rate).[20]

IV. Concluding Remarks

This study has drawn attention to the linkages between country risk and the openness of an economy and demonstrated that in the long run the openness of an economy is endogenously determined by the interaction between endowments and policies. The presence of country risk poses a problem for the smooth operation of international credit markets: the ex-ante first best policy is for countries to pre-commit themselves to no-default policies. Such a commitment, however, may not be credible because it may not be the optimal ex-post policy. This suggests a special role for policies leading toward investment in openness as a way to increase the credibility of a no-default commitment.

APPENDIX

This appendix summarizes the derivation of the results reported in the paper. We start by formulating the problem as a welfare maximization of the representative agent and the central bank. We then derive the optimal credit market and investment policies.

Suppose that the utility of the representative agent is given by (to simplify notation we suppress the consumer index):

$$U = u(C_1) + \delta u(C_2), \tag{8}$$

---

[20] For further discussion of the optimal contract in the presence of country risk and equity finance see Aizenman (1987).

where δ stands for the subjective rate of time preference and C_t is the consumption of traded goods at time t ($t = 1, 2$). We allow for domestic policies in the form of a borrowing tax and lump-sum transfers. The domestic interest rates are defined by

$$r_c = r^*(1 + \rho_c), \qquad (9)$$

$$r_i = r^*(1 + \rho_i), \qquad (10)$$

where r^* is the interest rate facing the country and ρ_c is the domestic tax on consumption borrowing. Similarly, r_i is the interest rate for investment borrowing in sector i, defined by ρ_i. The budget constraints facing the representative agent are

$$C_1 = Y_1 + B_c, \qquad (11)$$

$$C_{2,n} = Y_{2,n} + R - B_c (1 + r_c) - \sum_{i=1}^{q} I_i (1 + r_i), \qquad (12)$$

$$C_{2,d} = Y_{2,d}, \qquad (13)$$

where subscripts n and d correspond to the cases of no default and default, respectively, and R is a lump-sum transfer (to be specified later). The aggregate investment borrowing and consumption borrowing (B) is obtained as the sum of B_c and I across all the individual borrowers. Equations (12) and (13) are the budget constraints for period two for the cases of no default and default, respectively. Domestic agents are assumed to be small enough to be pricetakers in the domestic credit market. Each faces a given interest rate.

The agent's problem is to allocate consumption and investment so as to maximize his expected utility subject to the budget constraint. Let V denote the value of the expected utility of a representative consumer. It follows that

$$V = u(C_1) + \delta \int_0^{\Psi_0} u(C_{2,d}) f^d \Psi + \delta \int_{\Psi_0}^{\infty} u(C_{2,n}) f^d \Psi. \qquad (14)$$

The agent chooses investment I and indebtedness B_c so as to maximize his expected utility (14). Because each agent is a pricetaker in the credit market, Ψ_0 is viewed by the consumer as given. Solving the optimal consumption and investment plan for a representative agent yields the following first-order conditions:

a. $MU(C_1) = \delta E[MU(C_2)|N.D.](1 + r_c)$,

b. $E[MU(C_2)|N.D.](1 + r_i) = E[MU(C_2) MPK_{2,i}]$, $\qquad$ (15)

for $i = 1, \dots, q$,

where $MU(C_t)$ stands for the marginal utility of consumption in period t ($t = 1,2$), $MPK_{2,i}$ stands for the marginal product of capital in period two in activity i, and $E[Y|N.D.]$ stands for the expected value of a variable Y conditional on no default (i.e., conditional on $\Psi > \Psi_0$).[21] Equation (15) represents two types of intertemporal arbitrage conditions. The first concerns the equality of the marginal utility of consumption at period one to the discounted expected marginal utility of future consumption (conditional on no default) times the interest

[21] Formally, $E[MU(C_2)|N.D.] = \delta \int_{\Psi_0}^{\infty} u'(C_{2,n}) f^d \Psi$ and $E[MU(C_2) MPK_{2,i}]$ $= \delta \int_0^{\Psi_0} u'(C_{2,d})(\partial Y_2/\partial K_{2,i}) f^d \Psi + \delta \int_{\Psi_0}^{\infty} u'(C_{2,n})(\partial Y_2/\partial K_{2,i}) f^d \Psi$.

rate. This is the condition under which the benefit of increasing first period consumption by borrowing equals the future costs associated with repayment.[22] The second arbitrage condition concerns optimal investment borrowing: the expected cost of borrowing (in terms of expected marginal utility in the second period) should be equated with the expected marginal utility of investment. This is the condition under which the benefit of increasing the investment by borrowing equals the cost associated with repayment.

To gain insight into the potential role of optimal policies let us evaluate the solution of the optimal consumption path by a centralized decision maker. Potential deviations between the planner's and the consumer's solutions will justify policies to support optimality. These policies will be shown to be in the form of optimal borrowing taxes. We assume that the lump-sum transfer R is used to rebate to consumers the proceeds generated by the borrowing taxes.[23] The planner's problem is to choose consumption borrowing (B_c) and investment borrowing (I_i) that will maximize the welfare of the representative consumer. A key difference between the consumer's and the planner's problems is that the centralized planner is not a pricetaker in the credit market, and he is aware that the choice of borrowing will have an impact on the interest rate via the supply of credit. Consequently, (14) implies that the condition for optimal borrowing and investment from the planner's perspective is

a. $MU\,(C_1) = \delta\,E[MU(C_2)|N.D.\,](1+r^*)\left[1+\dfrac{B}{B_c}\dfrac{d\,\log\,(1+r^*)}{d\,\log\,B_c}\right],$

b. $E[MU(C_2)|N.D.\,](1+r^*)\left[1+\dfrac{B}{I_i}\dfrac{d\,\log\,(1+r^*)}{d\,\log\,I_i}\right]$

$$= E[MU(C_2)\,MPK_{2,i}], \tag{15'}$$

for $i = 1,\ldots,q$.

A comparison between the planner's and the consumer's solutions reveals that the two differ in that the planner applies the social interest rate, whereas the consumer applies the private one. The social interest rate is defined as the total marginal interest cost associated with the borrowing for consumption and for investment activities, given by:

$$(1+r^*)\left[1+\frac{B}{B_c}\frac{d\,\log\,(1+r^*)}{d\,\log\,B_c}\right]\text{ and }(1+r^*)\left[1+\frac{B}{I_i}\frac{d\,\log\,(1+r^*)}{d\,\log\,I_i}\right], \tag{16}$$

respectively. Note that the social planner faces different social interest rates for the various activities. The key difference between the individual agent and the social planner is that the latter is internalizing the marginal changes in the interest rate facing the economy owing to marginal borrowing. These changes in turn are determined by the use of these funds and are reflected in the second

---

[22] Note that since repayment occurs only in states of no default, the expectation operator in (15') is conditional on no default.

[23] Note that this implies that the lump-sum transfer to the consumer is $r^*\,(\rho_c\,B_c + \sum_{i=1}^{q}\rho_i I_i)$. Consequently, the budget constraint that is relevant for the policymaker in the absence of default is $C_{2,n} = Y_{2,n} - (B_c + I)(1 + r^*)$. $\tag{12'}$

term in the social interest rates. The percentage difference between the private and the social interest rates equals the elasticity of the interest rate $(1 + r^*)$ with respect to the borrowing, which in turn define the optimal taxes, as reported in (3) and (4).

We turn now to an overview of the derivation of the equations reported in the section on investment and imported inputs. Short-run profit maximization with respect to the use of importable M yields the following value for output

$$X_i = c_i \left[\frac{\Psi}{(P_m)^{\beta_i}} \right]^{1/(1-\beta_i)} (K_i)^{\alpha/(1-\beta_i)}, \tag{17}$$

where $c_i = [C_i(\beta_i)^{\beta_i/(1-\beta_i)}]$. Thus, a raise of P_m from 1 to $exp\,(p_m)$ is associated with a change of output at a rate of:

$$exp\,\{ - [\beta_i/(1 - \beta_i)]p_m \} - 1 \approx - [\beta_i/(1 - \beta_i)]p_m. \tag{18}$$

Note that a portion β_i of output is spent on the imported input. Thus, the value added is $Y_i = (1 - \beta_i) X_i$, and (18) implies that the drop in value added in sector i resulting from the default is $(1 - \beta_i) X_{n,i} [\beta_i/(1 - \beta_i)]p_m = \beta_i X_{n,i} p_m$. Aggregating the drop in the value added across sectors gives us equation (6) in the text.

We turn now to the derivation of the value of λ_i that is applied in (4). Applying (6) and the definition of the marginal value of the productivity shock that is associated with default (Ψ_0) we get that Ψ_0 is the solution to

$$(1 + r^*) B = p_m \sum_{i=1}^{2} \beta_i c_i \left[\frac{\Psi_0}{(P_m)^{\beta_i}} \right]^{1/(1-\beta_i)} (K_i)^{\alpha/(1-\beta_i)}. \tag{19}$$

Note that $\lambda_i = \partial \log \Pi / \partial \log K_i$. Recalling that $\Pi = \int_{\Psi_0}^{\infty} f(\Psi)\, d\Psi$ we obtain by logarithmic derivation that

$$\lambda_i = -f \frac{\Psi_0}{\Pi} \frac{\partial \log \Psi_0}{\partial \log K_i}. \tag{20}$$

Logarithmic derivation of (19) yields that:

$$\frac{\partial \log \Psi_0}{\partial \log K_i} = - \frac{\alpha s_i/(1 - \beta_i)}{s_1/(1 - \beta_1) + s_2/(1 - \beta_2)}, \tag{21}$$

where s_i is the i's sector share in the aggregate penalty at the marginal default (i.e., $\Psi = \Psi_0$): $s_i = \beta_i X_{n;i}/[\beta_1 X_{n;1} + \beta_2 X_{n;2}]$, where the X's are obtained by (17) evaluated at $\Psi = \Psi_0$ and $P_m = 1$. Applying similar derivation we get also that

$$\varepsilon = - \frac{\partial \log \Pi}{\partial \log B} = -f \frac{\Psi_0}{\Pi} \frac{\partial \log \Psi_0}{\partial \log B} = f \frac{\Psi_0}{\Pi} \frac{1}{s_1/(1 - \beta_1) + s_2/(1 - \beta_2)}. \tag{22}$$

Applying (22) and (21) to (20) yields that $\lambda_i = s_i \varepsilon \alpha/(1 - \beta_i)$, which the result applied in the text to derive (4').

We turn now to the derivation of (7). Equation (17) implies that the marginal product of capital is given by:

$$MPK_i = c_i' \left[\frac{\Psi}{(P_m)^{\beta_i}} \right]^{1/(1-\beta_i)} (K_i)^{\alpha/(1-\beta_i)-1}, \tag{23}$$

where $c_i' = [\alpha/(1 - \beta_i)]c_i$. Denoting by ψ the value of log (Ψ) we obtain that

$$MPK_i = \begin{array}{ll} c_i \ exp \ [\psi/(1 - \beta_i)] \, (K_i)^{\alpha/(1-\beta_i)-1}, & \text{no default} \\ c_i \ exp \ [(\psi - p_m\beta_i)/(1 - \beta_i)] \, (K_i)^{\alpha/(1-\beta_i)-1}. & \text{default.} \end{array} \qquad (24)$$

Optimal investment is made so as to yield equality between the expected cost $(1 + r_f)$ and the expected marginal product of capital. Note that for small shocks we can approximate $exp \ [(\psi - p_m\beta_i)/(1 - \beta_i)]$ by $1 + (\psi - p_m\beta_i)/(1 - \beta_i)$. Applying this approximation we obtain that the expected marginal product of capital is

$$E \ (MPK_{i;2}) \approx c_i' \left[1 - \frac{E \ (p_m\beta_i | \Psi < \Psi_0)}{1 - \beta_i} \right] (K_i)^{\alpha/(1-\beta_i)-1},$$

$$= c_i' \left[1 - (1 - \Pi) \, \frac{p_m\beta_i}{1 - \beta_i} \right] (K_i)^{\alpha/(1-\beta_i)-1}. \qquad (25)$$

The optimal stock of capital is obtained by solving the K that equates (25) to $1 + r_f$, yielding (7) in the text.

REFERENCES

Aizenman, Joshua, "Country Risk, Incomplete Information, and Taxes on International Borrowing," *Economic Journal* (London), 1989 forthcoming.

———, "Country Risk and Contingencies," *Journal of International Economics* (Amsterdam), 1989 forthcoming.

Calvo, Guillermo A., "On the Time Consistency of Optimal Policy in a Monetary Economy," *Econometrica* (Chicago), Vol. 46 (1978), pp. 1411–28.

Krugman, Paul, "International Strategies in an Uncertain World," in *International Debt and the Developing Countries,* ed. by Gordon W. Smith and John T. Cuddington (Washington: World Bank, 1985), pp. 79–100.

Kydland, E. Finn, and Edward C. Prescott, "The Inconsistency of Optimal Plans," *Journal of Political Economy* (Chicago), Vol. 85 (1977), pp. 473–93.

Debt and Conditionality Under Endogenous Terms of Trade Adjustment

JOSHUA AIZENMAN and EDUARDO R. BORENSZTEIN*

Conditions under which renewed international lending will benefit both the developed and the developing countries are identified. We evaluate how the presence of terms of trade adjustment and distorted credit markets affect the conditions for the existence of beneficial lending. We demonstrate that in the presence of endogenous terms of trade adjustment, there are cases in which a competitive international banking system may not revitalize lending for investment purposes, even if such renewed lending is socially desirable. Renewed lending may require the appropriate conditionality, and the presence of endogenous terms of trade adjustment puts greater weight on investment conditionality.

THE INTERNATIONAL capital market is presently characterized by effective credit rationing to developing countries. Most developing countries cannot obtain new credits from the international banking sys-

* Mr. Aizenman, a consultant in the Research Department of the Fund, is Associate Professor of Economics at the Hebrew University and was formerly Associate Professor of Business Economics at the University of Chicago. He is a graduate of the Hebrew University and received his doctorate from the University of Chicago.

Mr. Borensztein, an economist in the Research Department of the Fund, is a graduate of the University of Buenos Aires and received his doctorate from the Massachusetts Institute of Technology.

The authors thank Sebastian Edwards, Elhanan Helpman, Assaf Razin, Sweder van Wijnbergen, participants in the NBER conference on "International Trade and Finance with Limited Global Integration" and in a Research Department seminar, and colleagues in the Fund for helpful comments.

102

tem. This situation contrasts sharply with that in the 1970s, when the international banking system engaged willingly in substantial resource transfer to the developing countries. This remarkable switch from a functioning international credit market to a market characterized by credit rationing reflects the growing awareness of the country risk involved in further lending to developing countries. Most developing countries have reached a point where their willingness or ability to service their debt is questionable, thereby increasing the reluctance of the international banking system to extend new credits. This situation is further complicated by the drop in export prices experienced by the developing nations in recent years, a process that has further reduced their ability and willingness to service their debt.

A significant literature has evolved in recent years that attempts to study the unique characteristics of international country risk. The lack of simple enforcement mechanisms for international debt repayment tends to reduce the international credit market to an equilibrium in which the volume of international credit is limited by the effective penalties associated with defaults. These penalties are potential embargoes that restrict the flow of both temporal and intertemporal trade (that is, trade in goods and financial assets, respectively).[1]

While the above literature has provided clues regarding the problems of country risk, it has raised important policy questions of what can be (or should be) done in the present situation characterized by "overborrowing" and debt overhang.[2] An open question is the degree to which the international system is capable of revitalizing the resource transfer for investment purposes from the developed to the developing nations.

This paper identifies conditions under which renewed lending may benefit both the developed and the developing countries. We evaluate how endogenous terms of trade, that is, terms of trade between debtor and creditor nations that are significantly affected by the financial flows between them, affect the conditions for the existence of beneficial lending. This analysis has special relevance because a competitive international banking system does not internalize terms of trade effects and may not revitalize lending for investment purposes, even in cases in which renewed lending is socially desirable. This may suggest an important role for policymakers in imposing appropriate conditionality (that is, in im-

---

[1] The list of further readings at the end of this volume contains a number of works analyzing country risk.

[2] The literature on solutions to the debt situation is also quite impressive. Important studies that summarize advantages and disadvantages of existing proposals include Krugman (1985), Dornbusch (1987), Fischer (1987), Feldstein and others (1987), and Bergsten and others (1985).

posing guidelines for domestic policies that should follow renewed lending). We will attempt to evaluate conditions under which such a role is desirable.

The relevance of terms of trade effects for the debt situation depends on the answer to the following question: Do debtor countries face a downward-sloping demand curve for their export products? There are two reasons to believe that they do. The first is that although perhaps all debtor countries can be considered small economies, often they are all simultaneously affected by the same shocks, and their joint response is of a large magnitude. For example, the increasing unavailability of foreign borrowing since 1982 affected most debtor countries; their response included a general increase in exports, and a terms of trade deterioration followed.[3] This means that even if the actions of each individual debtor country cannot affect its terms of trade, on occasions the debtor country may find falling prices every time it tries to increase the volume of its exports because other debtor countries are doing the same.

The second reason is that an increasing portion of debtor countries' exports are manufactured products, the markets for which are, in many cases, well described by a differentiated-products structure. In a differentiated-products framework (such as Spence (1976)),[4] there is a whole continuum of goods that can be produced by a given industry, each of them differing only slightly from the point of view of consumer preference. With increasing returns, each firm will specialize in a different product on the continuum, and it will command a certain degree of market power.[5] If this is the case, the manufactured exports from debtor countries will face a downward-sloping demand curve, irrespective of size considerations.

Econometric studies of the elasticity of demand for developing country exports by industrial economies have usually taken developing countries as a group. Estimates of this import demand elasticity range from somewhat less than 1 to over 4.[6] The studies use, however, different aggregations for the definition of the import commodity and different aggregations for the importer economy, apart from different sample periods. Despite that fact, it appears that a number slightly above 1 is a

---

[3] The link between real commodity prices and debt service is suggested in Feldstein and others (1987).

[4] An extensive analysis of this market structure in the context of international trade can be found in Helpman and Krugman (1985).

[5] Alternatively, the differentiation could arise from reputational or learning problems.

[6] This range is taken from the survey included in Marquez and McNeilly (1988).

reasonable synthesis of econometric estimates of import demand elasticity. It is remarkable that the median (across products) elasticity estimated by Grossman (1982) is equal to 1.2, the median (across countries) elasticity estimated by Marquez and McNeilly (1988) is also equal to 1.2, and the elasticity estimated by Dornbusch (1985) for the aggregate of non-oil developing countries is also equal to 1.2.[7] Such a figure is also in line with estimates of import price elasticities for industrial goods irrespective of the country of origin of exports (see Goldstein and Khan (1985)). This elasticity applies, however, to the aggregate of developing country exports, although for some particular goods a few exporters account for most of the supply.

We start our analysis by describing a model of the international credit market characterized by insolvency on the part of debtor countries. This means that repayments do not suffice to cover all obligations and therefore become more closely related to available resources in the debtor economy than to existing debt. As a consequence, the debtor countries cannot borrow as much as they would like to[8] and find themselves credit rationed. In these circumstances, we assume that debtors and creditors negotiate agreements, which we will call contracts, by means of which creditors offer increased lending and debtors pledge to undertake certain actions concerning productive investment and debt repayment. This simple framework is intended to capture some of the main features of the current rescheduling negotiations.

The debt negotiations are assumed to take place in the context of a two-period, two-good world economy composed of two blocks of nations: creditors and debtors. Each block produces one good and consumes both. In the first period, debtors and creditors try to reach a deal, or contract, to increase lending. The contracts are defined as a resource transfer to the developing nations in the first period that specifies a marginal propensity to invest out of the transfer and a marginal propensity to repay out of the proceeds of the new investment in the second period. A contract is a Pareto-improving contract if both blocks of nations benefit from the marginal resource transfers. We obtain the conditions for the existence of Pareto contracts and describe them.

In the absence of terms of trade effects (perfect substitutability between the two goods) the key results can be summarized in the following way. The condition guaranteeing the existence of Pareto contracts is that the marginal productivity of capital in the developing countries should

---

[7] The estimates reported by Khan and Knight (1988) also lie between 1 and 2.

[8] That is, as much as necessary to equate the domestic interest rate to the international rate.

exceed that in the developed countries. In the absence of distortions (other than the situation of international insolvency) this condition is identical to the requirement that the interest rate be higher in the developing than in the developed nations. The larger the excess of the marginal productivity of capital in the developed countries, the larger the range of Pareto contracts. The presumption is that this condition is indeed satisfied because the interest rate in the heavily indebted countries tends to be higher than in the industrial countries. Nevertheless, in a real world situation, the marginal resource transfer will not occur in the absence of either appropriate incentives or conditionality on the debtor country.

We turn then to the analysis of the consequences of endogenous terms of trade adjustment owing to limited goods substitutability on the region of Pareto contracts. We show that the Pareto region is enlarged for strict conditionality contracts (contracts that require high marginal propensity to invest in the debtor country) and is reduced for contracts requiring low marginal propensity to invest on the part of the debtor country. We also analyze an alternative type of contract between debtors and creditors. In this case the amount of the repayment is the only variable to be agreed upon, and investment is assumed to be undertaken in an optimal manner by the developing country. We show how, in this framework, the existence of endogenous terms of trade modifies the region of Pareto-improving contracts.

The terms of trade effect is not internalized by the international banking system, with the result that in the negotiation process the interests of the banking system may diverge from those of a representative consumer in the creditor country. This possibility may suggest an important role in the debt renegotiation process for governmental institutions that may provide the international banking system with the proper incentives needed to implement the desirable contracts.

I. Framework of Analysis

Our analysis identifies conditions under which an increase in the resource transfer from developed to developing countries would be beneficial and studies the consequences of endogenous terms of trade adjustment. The simplest framework to deal with these issues is, as mentioned in the introduction, a two-period, two-good world economy composed of two blocks of nations: developed and developing nations. Each block produces one good, and consumes both. For simplicity of exposition it is convenient to assume that in the long run the relative price of the two goods is exogenously fixed by the technology of production. In the short run the supply is given, and the relative price of the two goods is determined by the prevailing demand conditions. We will identify the short run with the first period and the long run with the second.

On the supply side, let X and Y denote the good produced by the developed and the developing nations, respectively. Let $\overline{X}_i$ and $\overline{Y}_i$ denote the output level of the two goods in period i, $i = 1,2$. The output level is exogenously given in the first period. In the second period, the output level is determined by investment carried out in the first period, which is denoted by I. We assume an asymmetric environment: good X can be either consumed or invested to increase the future output of both good X and Y, while good Y can only be used for consumption purposes. The investment technologies also differ. In the developed economy, second-period output is linked to investment according to:

$$dX_2 = (1 + r)\ dI,$$

where I refers to investment in the production of good X by the developed economy, and r is the interest rate in the developed country. Thus, optimality conditions ensure that the marginal product of capital is always equal to the interest rate in the developed economy. The supply level of a good is indicated by a bar over its name. In the debtor economy, investment translates into output according to:

$$d\overline{Y}_2 = m\ (I^*)\ dI^*,$$

where I^* refers to the use of good X for investment purposes in the developing country, and m is a function of the volume of investment, displaying decreasing returns. We do not make the assumption that the marginal product of capital equals the interest rate in the developing economy. Instead, the volume of investment is determined by an economic authority, and it is the subject of bargaining between debtor and creditor. Specifically, we assume that a fraction β is invested out of every extra dollar of net borrowing:

$$\frac{dI^*}{dB} = \beta, \tag{1}$$

and that the value of β is subject to debt negotiations. In fact, the actual subject of the debt negotiations could be an economic policy package for the debtor economy, which contains a set of measures (say taxes and subsidies) that ensure that the level of investment in the economy is consistent with the given value of β.

Note that the domestic interest rate in the debtor country (which we will denote by r^*) will not be equal to the interest rate in the creditor country, r. This is a consequence of the situation of insolvency in which we assume the debtor country to be. This situation implies that, in the first period, the debtor country can obtain net foreign resources only up to a certain limit B, which it cannot control. Thus, if this is a binding constraint, the debtor country is credit rationed, and r^* will exceed r.

The situation of insolvency also implies that repayments by the debtor country will fall short of its obligations and will thus be linked to the debtor's capacity to pay. Specifically, we assume that, in the second period, the debtor country repays an amount R, which is linked to its available resources by

$$\frac{dR}{d\overline{Y}_2} = \chi. \tag{2}$$

The value of χ is determined by negotiations between the debtor country and its creditors. We assume that there exists previous indebtedness, contracted before the first period, of a level larger than any value that R can attain. Note that this also implies that R can be larger or smaller than $(1 + r)B$. In the absence of credit rationing and insolvency, interest rates would be equalized, and repayment would equal total existing debt (plus the corresponding interest).

Let $P_{z,i}$ denote the price of good z in period i, where $z = X, Y$, and $i = 1,2$; and by Q_i ($= P_{Y,i}/P_{X,i}$) the relative price in period i. It is convenient to use good X as the numeraire, normalizing $P_{X,1}$ to 1. We will assume that the future relative price of the two goods is constant, say $Q_2 = 1$. The basic motivation is to concentrate on the terms of trade effects in the first period, when international resources flow from the developed country to the developing country. The constancy of terms of trade in the second period would be consistent with an environment in which there exists a technology in the second period that costlessly transforms good Y into good X at a fixed rate (say, 1).[9] The assumption is also consistent with the idea that the second period represents a long-run position and that the long-run supply elasticities are larger than the short-run ones. In the Appendix, we relax the assumption of constancy of terms of trade in the second period, however, and show that allowing for endogeneity of terms of trade in the second period enlarges (and shifts) the area of feasible Pareto-improving contracts described in the main body of the paper.

---

[9] Credit rationing would prevent the exploitation of arbitrage oportunities that would emerge from different rates of return to capital and a fixed relative price for the two goods.

The budget constraints faced by the developing country are

$$X_1^* + QY_1^* + \frac{X_2^* + Y_2^*}{1 + r^*} = Q\overline{Y}_1 + B - I^* + \frac{\overline{Y}_2 - R}{1 + r^*} \tag{3}$$

$$X_1^* + QY_1^* = Q\overline{Y}_1 + B - I^*, \tag{4}$$

where all variables are defined in terms of good X, B stands for net borrowing by the developing nations from the developed nations in the first period, R stands for the flows of payments in the second period from the developing to the developed nation, and r^* is the domestic interest rate in the debtor economy. Stars identify a variable as corresponding to the debtor country. Q is used as shorthand for Q_1. Equation (3) is the standard lifetime budget constraint faced by the representative agent in the debtor country. In addition, the credit constraint puts a separate restriction on the debtor country in the first period, namely that the debtor country cannot borrow beyond the exogenous limit B. This restriction is represented by equation (4).

Similarly, the budget constraints faced by the developed economy are

$$X_1 + QY_1 + \frac{X_2 + Y_2}{1 + r} = \overline{X}_1 - B - I + \frac{\overline{X}_2 + R}{1 + r} \tag{5}$$

$$X_1 + QY_1 = \overline{X}_1 - B - I. \tag{6}$$

Debt Negotiations

We assume that negotiations may take place over the value of two parameters: β and χ, that is, over the proportion of new lending that is devoted to investment and over the proportion of the increase in debtor country's GDP that will be paid back to creditors. We will identify values of β and χ for which both the debtor and the creditor countries will find it worthwhile to engage in increased lending. In the presence of risk of debt repudiation, there are reasons to believe that the optimal contract may not be implemented by a competitive banking system. Consequently, it may be useful to identify conditions under which policy actions can lead to such contracts.

Let us assume that utility functions of the representative consumer in the developing and the developed countries are given by

$$U^*(X_1^*, Y_1^*, X_2^*, Y_2^*) = u^*(X_1^*, Y_1^*) + \rho u^*(X_2^*, Y_2^*) \tag{7}$$

$$U(X_1, Y_1, X_2, Y_2) = u(X_1, Y_1) + \rho u(X_2, Y_2). \tag{8}$$

We can obtain the welfare effects on the creditor and debtor economies derived from increased lending by differentiating (7) and (8) and making use of the standard optimality conditions on the marginal rates of substitution and of the budget constraints (the detailed derivation is presented in the Appendix):

$$\frac{dU^*}{dB}\frac{1}{u_{1,x}^*} = Y_1\frac{dQ}{dB} + 1 - \beta + \frac{\beta(1-\chi)m}{1+r^*}. \tag{9}$$

The first term in equation (9) measures the welfare consequences of the change in the terms of trade, given by the volume of exports $(Y_I = \overline{Y}_1 - Y_1^*)$ times the improvement in the terms of trade. The other terms reflect the increase in consumption. Consumption goes up in the first period by $1 - \beta$, and in the second period by $m\beta(1-\chi)$. The second-period increase in consumption stems from an increase in output equal to βm, with a fraction χ of that increase being paid back to the developed countries.

The same procedure applied to the developed economy leads to

$$\frac{dU}{dB}\frac{1}{u_{1,x}} = -Y_1\frac{dQ}{dB} - 1 + \frac{\beta\chi m}{1+r}. \tag{10}$$

Equation (10) shows that welfare in the developed countries changes in proportion to the amount of imports owing to the terms of trade effect, decreases owing to the direct drop in wealth resultant from the transfer, and increases owing to the increase in repayment from the developing nation in the second period.

Pareto-Improving Contracts

Are there conditions under which an increase in lending would be attractive to both debtors and creditors? The international capital market setup is one in which the debtor country cannot service its obligations in full (or cannot be forced to do so). Its creditors may nevertheless be willing to provide additional resources, perhaps as a defensive strategy for previously contracted loans (Krugman (1987)). In this context, we assume that debtors and creditors bargain over the conditionality attached to any additional lending. This conditionality is summarized by the two parameters (β and χ) that determine investment and repayment.[10]

---

[10] We abstract from monitoring problems, assuming that contract conditions are perfectly enforceable.

We will now try to identify the range of values of the parameters χ and β for which both blocks of nations could benefit from increased resource transfers to the developing nations. We will call this region the region of Pareto-improving contracts. A region of Pareto-improving contracts will exist if additional lending increases the world's total welfare. We can compute the global change in world welfare generated by an increase in international lending by adding up the welfare changes in each block, equations (17) and (18):

$$\frac{r^* - r}{(1 + r)(1 + r^*)} \beta \chi m + \beta \left(\frac{m}{1 + r^*} - 1 \right). \tag{11}$$

The first term measures the consequences of shifting resources from developed to developing nations. It is proportional to the interest rate differential and to the marginal investment rate in the developing countries (β). This corresponds to the fact that resources are being transferred from a low to a high interest rate country, where more productive investment projects exist. The second term measures the potential distortion in the capital markets of the developing countries. In the absence of distortions—other than the international credit market situation—this term is zero, because investors will equate the marginal product of capital (m) to the interest rate $(1 + r^*)$. In the presence of distortions, the term in parentheses is a measure of the distortion wedge, and the change in welfare is proportional to the distortion times the change in the distorted activity (β).[11] Note that the overall change in world welfare is proportional to the marginal investment rate in the developing country. If no new investment is triggered by the transfer, there are no aggregate wealth changes.

We start our analysis considering the limiting case in which the two goods are perfect substitutes ($dQ/dB = 0$), and we will later evaluate the consequences of imperfect substitutability on the region of Pareto contracts.

Pareto-Improving Contracts with Perfect Substitutability

To obtain the region of Pareto-improving contracts we start by tracing an indifference curve on the (β, χ) plane. This curve is the locus of the pairs of values of β and χ for which the country is indifferent with respect

---

[11] Note that the consequence of credit rationing is under-investment in the developing nations relative to the first best. The distortion wedge is measured by the interest rate differential. The change in welfare is the result of multiplying the distortion by the change in the distorted activity.

to (marginal) additional lending. The curve forms the boundary of the region where the country benefits from a marginal increase in the resource transfer. Applying the same procedure to the two countries allows us to identify the conditions under which the region of (β, χ) where both countries will benefit from resource transfer is not empty.

The configurations of χ and β for which the developing nations are indifferent with respect to increasing credit in the margin are obtained from equation (9):

$$\beta = \frac{1}{1 - \dfrac{m(1-x)}{1+r^*}}. \tag{12}$$

Equation (12) defines the curve DD in Figure 1. In Figure 1, a point like H corresponds to a contract that increases the credit available to the developing countries under the conditions that a fraction β_H of the marginal credit is devoted to investment and that a fraction χ_H of the increase in future output is paid to the developed countries. All points to the southwest of DD form the region for which the developing countries benefit from an increase in the resource transfer. Therefore, as long as $0 < \chi, \beta \leq 1$, the developing countries benefit for all possible contracts.[12]

In fact, the above configuration requires that $(1 - \chi)m/(1 + r^*) < 1$. It is natural to assume that this condition holds locally around the equilibrium position.[13]

The indifference curve for the developed countries is given by

$$\chi\beta = \frac{1+r}{m}. \tag{13}$$

This condition defines curve CC (Figure 1), drawn for the case in which the marginal productivity of investment in the developing nations exceeds the interest rate in the developed nations. All points to the northeast of CC form the region for which the developed countries will benefit from an increase in resource transfer. The interpretation of equa-

---

[12] But contracts with (β, χ) outside the unit square are also possible, and some of them benefit the debtor country.

[13] Otherwise, the implication is that the debtor country could increase its utility by borrowing and investing 100 percent of the loan. For such value of χ, there would hardly be any reason for credit rationing of the debtor country. Furthermore, one could support the above condition on an empirical basis. The sudden tightening of international borrowing conditions at the beginning of the debt crisis raised r^* without much short-run effect on m, which depends on the existent capital stock. (Notice that the above condition will hold if $1 + r^* \geq m$.) Also, if domestic capital markets are not very distorted, one could imagine m moving back to a value close to that of $1 + r^*$.

Figure 1

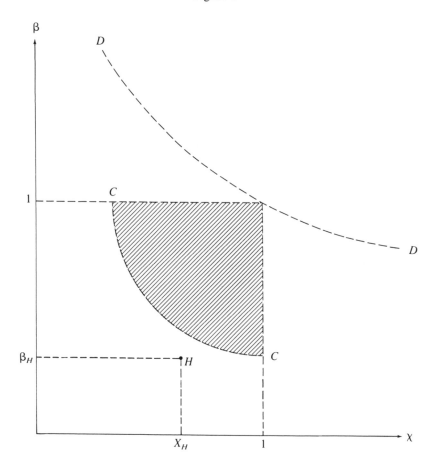

tion (13) is straightforward. An increase in lending in the first period of 1 dollar generates an increase in payoff in the second period of $\beta m \chi$. That implicit rate of return is compared with the domestic rate r to determine the convenience of increasing lending.

The area between the two curves in Figure 1 defines the Pareto contracts. The condition that guarantees the existence of Pareto-improving contracts is that the marginal productivity of capital in the developing countries exceeds that in the developed countries. The greater the excess of the marginal productivity of capital, the greater the area of Pareto contracts.

There is a strong presumption that this condition for the existence of

Pareto-improving contracts is indeed satisfied in the real world, because interest rates in heavily indebted countries tend to be much higher than in creditor countries, and presumably the divergence of the marginal product of capital with respect to the interest rate is not so large. In a real world situation, however, the marginal resource transfer will not occur in the absence of proper incentives or of conditionality on the debtor country to satisfy the terms (β,χ) of the contract.

Pareto-Improving Contracts with Imperfect Substitutability

Under limited goods substitutability, an increase in the resource transfer will have some impact on terms of trade. In the next section, we develop a model that determines the terms of trade effect explicitly. In the meantime, an approximate analysis can be made using only information on the sign of dQ/dB.[14]

From equations (9) and (10) we obtain the new boundaries of the sets of contracts that are advantageous to the debtor and the creditor country, respectively:

$$\beta = \frac{1 + Y_1 \dfrac{dQ}{dB}}{1 - \dfrac{m(1-\chi)}{1+r^*}} \tag{14}$$

$$\beta = \frac{1 + Y_1 \dfrac{dQ}{dB}}{\dfrac{\chi m}{1+r}}. \tag{15}$$

Consider first the case in which $-1 < Y_1\, dQ/dB < 0$. Both the CC and DD curves shift towards the origin. The set of contracts for which developing countries are willing to receive additional resources is in fact smaller. Some contracts in the upper left part of the unit square are no longer beneficial because the welfare effect of the terms of trade deterioration offsets the additional consumption possibilities generated by the increased lending. In contrast, the set of contracts for which developed nations are willing to increase lending is now larger, because the existence of a relative price effect is favorable to the developed countries.

We conclude that a deterioration in the terms of trade of developing countries has the consequence of shifting the location of the Pareto

---

[14] This analysis is not fully correct because dQ/dB will itself depend on the parameters β and χ.

region leftwards and downwards. This means that the developed countries may obtain "softer" conditionality terms, because part of the economic repayment is implemented via terms of trade adjustment. This effect would be larger the lower the substitutability between the two goods. From the point of view of the banking system, however, the curve CC continues to be the relevant contract indifference curve. This has the potential consequence that at the negotiation process the interests of the banking system may diverge from those of the other parties. Some Pareto-improving contracts exist, but they are associated with losses to the banking system. This possibility suggests an important role for policy actions that provide international banks with the proper incentives needed to implement such contracts.

Consider now the case in which dQ/dB is positive. Both the CC and DD curves will shift outwards. The developing countries will now be willing to accept some contracts that produce a negative payoff when evaluated at the domestic interest rate, because the terms of trade improvement more than compensate for that. From the point of view of creditor countries, however, the set of beneficial contracts is now smaller. This would be a situation in which the creditor country would attempt to regulate banks in order to restrain them from increasing lending under some contracts that generate profits for the banks but that make the creditor country worse off.

Consequently, the impact of endogenous terms of trade is determined by the direction of the terms of trade adjustment to the marginal increase in credit. We now turn to study the factors determining the sign of dQ/dB.

Model Linking Terms of Trade to International Lending

The framework of lending and investment is as described above, and the budget constraints (3) to (6) apply. We assume that the demand structure in the developed nation can be summarized by[15]

$$X_1 = E_1 g(Q), \qquad QY_1 = E_1[1 - g(Q)] \tag{16}$$

$$X_2 = E_2 g(1), \qquad Y_2 = E_2[1 - g(1)] \tag{17}$$

$$E_2 = \rho(1 + r)E_1, \tag{18}$$

---

[15] An example of a utility function that generates this type of demand function is

$$U(X_1, Y_1, X_2, Y_2) = \ln\left(\frac{X_1^{1-\gamma}}{1-\gamma} + \frac{Y_1^{1-\gamma}}{1-\gamma}\right) + \rho \ln\left(\frac{X_2^{1-\gamma}}{1-\gamma} + \frac{Y_2^{1-\gamma}}{1-\gamma}\right).$$

where E_i is total consumption expenditure in period i $(E_i = X_i + Q_i Y_i)$. The function $g(Q)$ determines the distribution of expenditure between the two goods as a function of the relative price.

The demand functions for the developing world are entirely symmetrical. However, we assume that each country may consume a larger proportion of the domestically produced good. This can be represented by

$$X_1^* = E_1^* ag(Q), \qquad QY_1^* = E_1^*[1 - ag(Q)] \tag{19}$$

$$X_2^* = E_2^* ag(1), \qquad Y_2^* = E_2^*[1 - ag(1)] \tag{20}$$

$$E_2^* = \rho(1 + r^*)E_1^*, \tag{21}$$

where $a \leq 1$. The parameter a measures the domestic bias in consumption.[16] To simplify further, it is useful to consider the special case in which the g functions are given by[17]

$$g(Q) = hQ^\alpha, \qquad h < 1. \tag{22}$$

Therefore, α is equal to the elasticity of demand with respect to the relative price of the two goods.

Regarding investment demand, we assume an asymmetric structure. In the creditor country, a linear technology transforms investment into output $d\overline{X}/dI = 1 + r$, r being a technological constant.[18] Therefore, in the creditor country, investment is the variable that adjusts to support the savings/investment/current account balance. By contrast, in the debtor country, investment is determined by the economic authority, as explained above.

Adjustment to an Increase in Net Borrowing

Given the demand and supply structure detailed above, the equilibrium of the system can be represented in the following way. In the first period, with the credit constraint binding, consumption in the debtor

---

[16] The case of $a = 1$ corresponds to the case in which there is no local habitat and the demand functions are the same in both countries. The case of $a < 1$ corresponds to the case in which each country prefers its own good.

[17] We assume that the range of values of Q is such that $hg(Q) < 1$ always.

[18] This linear technology serves the purpose of isolating intertemporal marginal rates of substitution in the developed economy from feedback from international lending to the developing world, which reflects our feeling about the magnitude of any such linkage. Our analysis can be generalized to the case where r is endogenously determined, without affecting the logic of our discussion.

country cannot exceed the exogenous limit $Q\overline{Y}_1 + B - I^*$. The domestic interest rate adjusts to obtain that level of consumption. The distribution of consumption across goods is given by equations (19) and (20). In the developed economy, consumption is set according to the level of wealth, but given the exogeneity of B, the investment level I has to adjust to satisfy the first-period budget constraint. This is of no consequence, because of the linear technology. Market-clearing in the first period implies

$$X_1 = (Q\overline{Y}_1 + B - I_Y)\,ag(Q) + (\overline{X}_1 - B - I_X)\,g(Q) + I + I^* \qquad (23)$$

$$Q\overline{Y}_1 = (Q\overline{Y}_1 + B - I^*)[1 - ag(Q)]$$
$$+ (\overline{X}_1 - B - I)[1 - g(Q)]. \qquad (24)$$

In the second period, there is effectively only one good, since supply can costlessly accommodate any combination of X and Y. Then, there is only an income/expenditure equilibrium condition in each country. Given the credit constraints, second period consumption, which is determined according to the intertemporal conditions (18) and (21) equals

$$Y_2^* + X_2^* = \rho(1 + r^*)[Q\overline{Y}_1 + B - I_Y(r^*)], \qquad (25)$$

$$X_2 + Y_2 = \rho(1 + r)(\overline{X}_1 - B - I_X). \qquad (26)$$

And consumption must equal income in each country, which is given by production and repayment:

$$\overline{Y}_2(I^*) - R(\overline{Y}_2) = \rho(1 + r^*)(Q\overline{Y}_1 + B - I^*) \qquad (27)$$

$$\overline{X}_2(I) + R(\overline{Y}_2) = \rho(1 + r)(\overline{X}_1 - B - I). \qquad (28)$$

Equilibrium can then be represented by equations (23) (or (24)), (27), and (28). These equilibrium conditions determine the value of the following endogenous variables: the first-period terms of trade, the interest rate in the developing countries, and investment in the developed countries (Q, r^*, and I). The levels of net borrowing B, and of investment by the debtor country I^* are exogenously determined in the debt negotiation process.

Suppose now that the developed nations initiate a marginal increase in the available credit ($dB > 0$), and let us evaluate the normative and positive aspects of the adjustment to such an increase in lending. The response of the terms of trade to the increase in lending, evaluated at $Q = 1$, is equal to[19]

---

[19] The derivation is contained in the Appendix.

$$\frac{dQ}{dB} = \frac{1}{\Omega}\left[-(1-h)\frac{dI + dI^*}{dB} + (1-a)h(1-\beta)\right], \qquad (29)$$

with $\Omega = ah\overline{Y}_1 + \alpha h(aE_1^* + E_1)$. This expression is positive for values of β that are in the Pareto region defined above curve CC (that is, for $\beta\chi m/(1+r) > 1$). The change in investment is given by

$$\frac{dI^* + dI}{dB} = \beta - 1 - \frac{1}{1+\rho}\left(-1 + \frac{\chi m\beta}{1+r}\right). \qquad (30)$$

Consider the case of $a = 1$.[20] The homotheticity of utilities and the absence of a local habitat effect imply that wealth increases or wealth redistributions will not affect the relative price Q. Therefore, the change in investment in the two countries will determine the change in terms of trade. From equation (30) it can be seen that the change in I^* is given by β, while the change in I is a one-for-one fall with the increases in lending and in consumption, where the latter is proportional to the change in wealth in the creditor country: $-1 + \chi m\beta/(1+r)$.

Note that equation (30) implies that, when $\chi m\beta/(1+r) = 1$ (which defines curve CC; that is, the lower bound of contracts acceptable to the creditor when terms of trade do not change), for $\beta = 1$ there is no change in aggregate investment and thus in Q, for $\beta < 1$ aggregate investment and Q fall, and for $\beta > 1$ aggregate investment and Q increase. This means that only when investment in the debtor country increases more than one for one with increases in borrowing will terms of trade turn in favor of the creditor country.

We can now use equations (14), (15), and (29) to determine the region of Pareto-improving contracts. The new boundary for the creditor country is defined by

$$\beta = \frac{1 + \dfrac{Y_1}{\Omega}\left[\dfrac{(1-h)\rho}{1+\rho} + (1-a)h\right]}{\dfrac{\chi m}{1+r}\left[1 - \dfrac{Y_1(1-h)}{\Omega(1+\rho)}\right] + \dfrac{Y_1}{\Omega}[(1-h) + (1-a)h]}. \qquad (31)$$

This means that with imperfect substitutability ($\Omega < \infty$), the curve CC rotates to a position like $C'C'$(see Figure 2). For values of $\beta < 1$, the terms of trade move in favor of the debtor economy, and this fact

---

[20] Note that, for $a < 1$, in the absence of new investment we get an improvement in the terms of trade of developing countries owing to the local habitat effect. This is in line with the classical transfer criterion (for analyses using transfer considerations, see Frenkel and Razin (1987) and van Wijnbergen (1988)). Note also that, with a unitary marginal investment ($\beta = 1$), the terms of trade adjustment is independent of any local habitat effect.

Figure 2

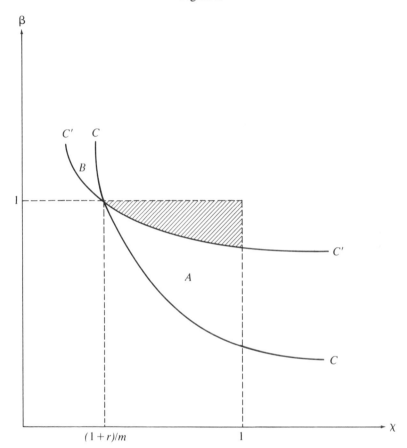

excludes some contracts that would be beneficial without the relative price change. Note that, for $\beta < 1$, there is now a region (labeled region A) of contracts that are profitable for banks (whose relevant cut-off continues to be CC), but not for the representative consumer in the creditor country. At $\beta = 1$ the two curves overlap because, as can be seen from equation (29), there would be no change in terms of trade. For values of $\beta > 1$, the terms of trade change in favor of the developed economy, and a typical consumer in the developed economy would benefit from contracts that are not acceptable to banks, such as those in region B.[21]

---

[21] The closer substitutes goods X and Y are, the smaller the terms of trade change that would occur, and the smaller the shift in the CC curve. This can be

Therefore, accounting for imperfect substitutability between goods produced by different countries changes the conditions under which a beneficial increase in lending may exist and creates a divergence of opinion between international banks and a representative consumer in the creditor country. In the context of the present model, this divergence of opinion can be summarized in the following way: for contracts with "softer" investment conditionality ($\beta < 1$), banks are more likely to find opportunities for increased lending, but the creditor country will find convenient contracts with "harder" investment conditionality ($\beta > 1$) and smaller repayment (χ) that actually produce losses to creditor banks.

An Alternative Framework

The model above assumed that debtors and creditors negotiate over the addition to investment (β) and to repayment (χ) that should be attached to an increase in lending.[22] Such framework appears to be in line with observed behavior in the recent rescheduling negotiations. Often in those negotiations, some conditionality on the debtor country's policies—usually within the framework of a Fund-supported program—is part of the agreement. In the model this policy conditionality is represented as a given value for the composition of spending; that is, the value of the parameter β. In addition, negotiations determine how much is paid and how much is rescheduled, a decision that is highly dependent on the economic performance of the debtor. In the model, this is represented by the parameter χ.

It can be argued, however, that negotiating over (β,χ) is not the best policy for the creditor. The creditor could leave the investment decision entirely up to the debtor, which (in the absence of distortions in the debtor economy) would maximize second-period output if the proper incentives are in place. In order to provide such proper incentives, repayment should be agreed as a fixed amount, because then the debtor can keep the return to any increase in investment that it achieves.[23]

---

seen from equation (32), where the elasticity of substitution is positively associated with Ω. Also, the larger the local habitat effect (represented by a smaller value of the parameter a), the larger the impact of the terms of trade change on the location of the Pareto region (that is, the larger the shift in curve CC).

[22] We thank Elhanan Helpman and Assaf Razin for comments that led to this section.

[23] In fact, the optimal policy for the creditor is dependent on the nature of uncertainty in the model, and on the possible existence of asymmetric information, as the results in Krugman (1987) and Froot, Sharfstein, and Stein (1988) show.

The alternative framework for negotiations would therefore not attach policy conditionality to the increased lending. In the absence of domestic distortions, investment in the debtor economy would therefore be determined by equating the marginal product of capital to the domestic interest rate r^*. The new contract being negotiated would simply determine the marginal repayment that will follow the increase in lending, which we will denominate Z. That is, Z is defined by

$$Z = \frac{dR}{dB}. \tag{32}$$

The equilibrium of this system is essentially the same as the one above. It is still represented by equations (23), (27), and (28), but now the effect of an increase in lending has to consider (32) and that investment in the debtor economy will be given by

$$\frac{d\overline{Y}_2}{dI^*} = m = 1 + r^* \tag{33}$$

$$\frac{dI^*}{dr^*} = \frac{1}{m'} < 0, \tag{34}$$

where $m = m(I^*)$. The effect on terms of trade of an increase in lending can now be computed:

$$\frac{dQ}{dB} = \frac{1}{\Delta}\left\{\Gamma\left[(1-h)\frac{\rho(1+r)+Z}{(1+\rho)(1+r)} + h(1-a)\right] \right.$$
$$\left. - \frac{1-ah}{m'}[\rho(1+r^*)+Z]\right\}, \tag{36}$$

where

$$\Delta = \Omega\Gamma + \frac{1-ah}{m'}\rho(1+r^*)\overline{Y}_1 > 0$$

$$\Gamma = \frac{(1+r^*)(1+\rho)}{m'} - \rho E_1^* < 0,$$

and Ω is as defined under equation (29). It can be shown that dQ/dB is positive for all relevant values of a.

The region of Pareto-improving contracts can now be determined. This region only refers to values of Z. If there are no changes in terms of trade, it is clear that the creditors would not accept any contract unless it sets $Z > 1 + r$, and debtors would not accept any contract unless it sets $Z < 1 + r^*$. As before, $r^* > r$ is the necessary condition for the existence of a non-empty Pareto-improving region. In Figure 3 we plot the region

Figure 3

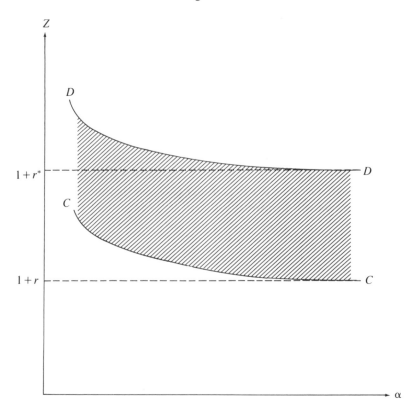

of Pareto-improving contracts as a function of α, which represents the degree of substitutability between the two goods. In the limit, as α goes to infinity and the two goods are perfect substitutes, there is no terms of trade effect, and the Pareto region is as described above. In contrast, for finite values of α, creditor countries require a value of Z exceeding $1 + r$ to engage in further lending, and debtor countries accept a value of Z higher than $1 + r^*$ because the terms of trade effect benefits the debtor country.

These results qualify the conclusions from the previous framework, in the sense that if investment is done in an optimal manner in the debtor country and debt negotiations provide the correct incentives to achieve such investment, there are no contracts that the creditor country would be willing to engage in that would not be achieved by a decentralized banking system. But, in addition, there is a set of contracts under which the decentralized banking system would engage in further borrowing that are not optimal from the point of view of the representative consumer in the creditor economy. Ultimately, the relevance of this and the previous framework depends on an explicit account of the reasons for credit rationing and under-investment. We suspect that the existence of defensive lending, different time horizons between governments and the private sector, distorted capital markets, and asymmetric information make the conclusions of the former framework the more relevant ones.

II. Concluding Remarks

This paper studied the conditions under which renewed lending to heavily indebted countries could be advantageous for both creditor and debtor countries. In dealing with the debt overhang issue it is useful to distinguish between the redistributive versus the efficiency issues. The purpose of our analysis was to highlight the potential efficiency losses emerging from the drop in investment in the developing countries owing to the presence of credit rationing, and to investigate mechanisms to revitalize the investment process. The analysis focused on the case where there are two dimensions for the conditionality: the determination of the marginal propensity to invest out of the new funds and of the marginal propensity to repay out of future output. We demonstrated the potential trade-off between these two dimensions and pointed out that endogenous terms of trade adjustment gives greater weight to investment conditionality. We now close the paper with some interpretive comments regarding qualifications and extensions.

Our discussion demonstrated that (in the absence of strict investment conditionality) renewed lending to developing countries tends to be associated with an improvement in the terms of trade of the developing countries and vice versa. This is consistent with the terms of trade deterioration observed in recent years. In the 1980s, there was a switch from a regime that transferred resources to the developing countries to a regime that transfers resources from the developing countries. The importance of the terms of trade adjustment stems from the observation that it has first-order welfare effects on the consumers in the creditor and debtor nations, despite a lack of internalization by the private banking system.

There are some qualifications to our results in this paper. The framework developed in the paper considers debt and credit rationing at the global level. Even if each indebted country has limited market power in its products, the group of indebted countries as a whole has significant market power. Because most indebted countries are presently facing similar constraints, we have used an aggregate version of a two-block world—creditors and debtors. If only the collective response of debtor countries is large enough to produce terms of trade changes, however, individual debtor countries would not be willing to accept a less favorable contract in consideration of the terms of trade effect. If this is the case, the set of contracts acceptable to debtors is not changed by the existence of a terms of trade effect of increased lending. Another qualification is that it is not entirely clear that the decisions of economic authorities are consistent with the representative consumer's interest when it comes to issues such as terms of trade changes. It appears that the protection of import-competing industries in industrial countries may be, in fact, more important for the authorities.

This last point suggests an interesting extension to the present framework. Some consistency is required between the conditionality attached to renewed credit and commercial policies adopted in the two blocks of countries, particularly in the creditor countries. Even in the absence of renewed lending, repayment of past loans will require consistent commercial policy (that is, intensive application of quotas may defeat any sincere attempt for debt repayment). This suggests that the incorporation of commercial policy actions to the policies considered in the debt negotiation process could have important implications for the design of mutually advantageous debt contracts.

APPENDIX

Some Derivations and Extensions

This Appendix provides the details of the derivation of two expressions used in the text of the paper and extends the application of the model to the case in which terms of trade are not fixed in the second period.

Derivations

The first expression concerns the effects of increased lending on utility. Differentiating the utility functions (7) and (8) we obtain

$$\frac{dU^*}{u_{1,x}^*} = dX_1^* + dY_1^* \frac{u_{1,Y}^*}{u_{1,x}^*} + dX_2^* \rho \frac{u_{2,X}^*}{u_{1,x}^*} + dY_2^* \rho \frac{u_{2,Y}^*}{u_{1,x}^*} \tag{37}$$

$$\frac{dU}{u_{1,x}} = dX_1 + dY_1 \frac{u_{1,Y}}{u_{1,x}} + dX_2 \rho \frac{u_{2,X}}{u_{1,x}} + dY_2 \rho \frac{u_{2,Y}}{u_{1,x}}. \tag{38}$$

We assume that marginal rates of substitution are given by the standard optimality conditions:

$$\frac{u_{1,Y}^*}{u_{1,x}^*} = \frac{u_{1,Y}}{u_{1,x}} = Q \tag{39}$$

$$\rho\frac{u_{2,X}^*}{u_{1,x}^*} = \rho\frac{u_{2,Y}^*}{u_{1,x}^*} = \frac{1}{1+r^*} \tag{40}$$

$$\rho\frac{u_{2,X}}{u_{1,x}} = \rho\frac{u_{2,Y}}{u_{1,x}} = \frac{1}{1+r}. \tag{41}$$

Making use of these marginal rates of substitution, we obtain

$$\frac{dU^*}{u_{1,x}^*} = dX_1^* + QdY_1^* + \frac{1}{1+r^*}(dX_2^* + dY_2^*) \tag{42}$$

$$\frac{dU}{u_{1,x}} = dX_1 + QdY_1 + \frac{1}{1+r}(dX_2 + dY_2). \tag{43}$$

Differentiating the budget constraint (3), we obtain

$$dX_1^* + QdY_1^* + Y_1^*dQ + \frac{1}{1+r^*}(dX_2^* + dY_2^*) - \frac{Y_2^* + X_2^* - (\overline{Y}_2 - R)}{(1+r^*)^2}dr^*$$

$$= \overline{Y}_1 dQ + dB - dI^* + \frac{1}{1+r^*}(d\overline{Y}_2 - dR). \tag{44}$$

Note that $Y_2^* + X_2^* = \overline{Y}_2 - R$ because of the credit constraint, which means that the change in the interest rate in the developing countries (r^*) does not generate a direct wealth effect. In fact, neither the domestic nor the foreign interest rate affect wealth of the debtor country. This is a consequence of the credit rationing/insolvency situation. Because of credit rationing, the country as a whole does not have a net position on assets carrying the domestic interest rate r^*, and because of insolvency, repayments R are not linked to interest rates. With "normal," fully integrated capital markets, an increase in the *world* interest rate reduces the borrower's wealth by the change in the interest rate times the external indebtedness position. The credit rationing and insolvency situation truncates this channel, because it de-links debt service from the world interest rate.

Finally, from equations (42) and (44), and making use of our assumptions regarding marginal investment and repayment rates in the debtor country, we obtain expression (9) in the main paper, and an entirely parallel procedure applied to the developed economy leads to equation (10) of the text:

$$\frac{dU^*}{dB}\frac{1}{u_{1,x}^*} = Y_1\frac{dQ}{dB} + 1 - \beta + \frac{\beta(1-\chi)m}{1+r^*} \tag{9}$$

$$\frac{dU}{dB}\frac{1}{u_{1,x}} = -Y_1\frac{dQ}{dB} - 1 + \frac{\beta\chi m}{1+r}. \tag{10}$$

The second expression this Appendix is concerned with is the change in the terms of trade generated by an increase in lending, dQ/dB. Recall that the system can be represented in the following way (the equation numbers are the same as in the text):

$$Q\overline{Y}_1 = (Q\overline{Y}_1 + B - I^*)[1 - ag(Q)] + (\overline{X}_1 - B - I)[1 - g(Q)] \tag{24}$$

$$\overline{Y}_2(I^*) - R(\overline{Y}_2) = \rho(1+r^*)(Q\overline{Y}_1 + B - I^*) \tag{27}$$

$$\overline{X}_2(I) + R(\overline{Y}_2) = \rho(1+r)(\overline{X}_1 - B - I). \tag{28}$$

These equilibrium conditions determine the value of the following endogenous variables: the first-period terms of trade, the interest rate in the developing nations, and investment in the developed countries (Q, r^*, and I). The levels of net borrowing B and of investment by the debtor country I^* are exogenously determined in the debt negotiation process. Differentiating the system, at $Q = 1$, we obtain

$$\frac{dQ}{dB}\,\overline{Y}_1 = (1 - \alpha h)\left(\frac{dQ}{dB}\,\overline{Y}_1 + 1 - \beta\right) + E_1^*\left(-a\,\alpha h\,\frac{dQ}{dB}\right)$$

$$+ (1 - h)\left(-1 - \frac{dI}{dB}\right) + E_1\left(-\alpha h\,\frac{dQ}{dB}\right) \tag{45}$$

$$m\beta - \chi m\beta = \rho(1 + r^*)\left(\frac{dQ}{dB}\,\overline{Y}_1 + 1 - \beta\right) + \rho E_1^*\,\frac{dr^*}{dB} \tag{46}$$

$$(1 + r)\frac{dI}{dB} + \chi m\beta = \rho(1 + r)\left(-1 - \frac{dI}{dB}\right). \tag{47}$$

It can be seen that there is some recursivity in the system, in that the variable r^* can be determined after the rest of the system is solved. The role of r^* is only to ensure that spending in the debtor economy, E_1^* is equal to the resources available in the first period, and only the level of E_1^* matters for the rest of the equilibrium. Collecting terms in (47), we obtain

$$\frac{dI}{dB} = \frac{-\chi m\beta - \rho(1 + r)}{(1 + r)(1 + \rho)}. \tag{48}$$

Using equations (48) in (45), we obtain

$$\frac{dQ}{dB}[\overline{Y}_1 ah + \alpha h\,(E_1^* + E_1)] = (1 - ah)\,(1 - \beta) - (1 - h)$$

$$+ (1 - h)\frac{\chi m\beta + \rho^* 1 + r)}{(1 + r)\,(1 + \rho)}. \tag{49}$$

And some further transformations produce equation (29) in the paper:

$$\frac{dQ}{dB} = \frac{1}{\Omega}\left\{-(1 - h)\left[\beta - 1 - \frac{1}{1 + \rho}\left(-1 + \frac{\chi m\beta}{1 + r}\right)\right] + (1 - a)\,h\,(1 - \beta)\right\}, \tag{29}$$

with $\Omega = ah\,\overline{Y}_1 + \alpha h\,(aE_1^* + E_1)$.

Extension: Endogeneity of Terms of Trade in the Second Period

We consider now the case in which there are terms of trade movements in both the first and the second period. We will show that terms of trade are likely to deteriorate for the debtor country in the second period, which enlarges the area of Pareto contracts relative to the case of no terms of trade effects.

We start by re-examining the effect of extra lending on world welfare, and the potential for Pareto-improving new loans. Equations (9) and (10) now become

$$\frac{dU^*}{dB}\,\frac{1}{u_{1,x}^*} = Y_1\frac{dQ_1}{dB} + \frac{Y_2}{1 + r^*}\frac{dQ_2}{dB} + 1 - \beta + \frac{\beta(1 - \chi)m}{1 + r^*} \tag{9'}$$

$$\frac{dU}{dB}\,\frac{1}{u_{1,x}} = -Y_1\frac{dQ_1}{dB} - \frac{Y_2}{1 + r}\frac{dQ_2}{dB} - 1 + \frac{\beta\chi m}{1 + r}. \tag{10'}$$

Adding up equations (9') and (10'), we get

$$\frac{r^* - r}{(1 + r)(1 + r^*)}\left(\beta\chi m - Y_2\frac{dQ_2}{dB}\right) + \beta\left(\frac{m}{1 + r^*} - 1\right). \tag{11'}$$

From equation (11') it is apparent that, if terms of trade deteriorate for the debtor country in the second period ($dQ_2/dB < 0$), the potential for Pareto-improving lending contracts increases. This is because second-period consumption is less valuable (more heavily discounted) in the credit-constrained debtor country.

In order to obtain the sign of dQ_2/dB, we need to solve the general equilibrium system, which now includes an additional second-period market clearing condition because of the differentiation of goods Y_2 and X_2. The system can now be represented by

$$Q_1\overline{Y}_1 = (Q_1\overline{Y}_1 + B - I^*)[1 - g(Q_1)] + (\overline{X}_1 - B - I)(1 - g(Q_1)) \tag{24'}$$

$$Q_2[\overline{Y}_2(I^*) - R(\overline{Y}_2)] = \rho(1 + r^*)(Q\overline{Y}_1 + B - I^*) \tag{27'}$$

$$\overline{X}_2(I) + Q_2R(\overline{Y}_2) = \rho(1 + r)(\overline{X}_1 - B - I) \tag{28'}$$

$$\overline{X}_2(I) = Q_2[\overline{Y}_2(I^*) - R(\overline{Y}_2)]g(Q_2) + [\overline{X}_2(I) + Q_2R(\overline{Y}_2)]g(Q_2), \tag{50}$$

where we make the assumption that $a = 1$, and we maintain the assumption that $g(Q) = hQ^\alpha$. Differentiating equations (24'), (27'), (28') and (50), at the point $Q_1 = Q_2 = 1$, we obtain

$$\frac{dQ_1}{dB}\overline{Y}_1 = -\alpha h\frac{dQ_1}{dB}(E_1^* + E_1) + (1 - h)\left(\frac{dQ_1}{dB}\overline{Y}_1 - \beta - \frac{dI}{dB}\right), \tag{51}$$

$$E_2^*\frac{dQ_2}{dB} + m\beta(1 - \chi) = \rho(1 + r^*)\left(\frac{dQ_1}{dB}\overline{Y}_1 + 1 - \beta\right) + \rho E_1^*\frac{dr^*}{dB}, \tag{52}$$

$$(1 + r)\frac{dI}{dB} + R\frac{dQ_2}{dB} + \chi m\beta = \rho(1 + r)\left(-1 - \frac{dI}{dB}\right), \tag{53}$$

$$\frac{dQ_2}{dB} = -\frac{1}{\Omega_2}\left[hm\beta - (1 - h)(1 + r)\frac{dI}{dB}\right], \tag{54}$$

with $\Omega = \alpha h(E_2^* + E_2) + h\overline{Y}_2 > 0$. We solve first for the change in investment in the industrial country:

$$\frac{dI}{dB} = \frac{-\chi m\beta - \rho(1 + r) - R\,dQ_2/dB}{(1 + r)(1 + \rho)}. \tag{55}$$

We can now obtain:

$$\frac{dQ_2}{dB} = -\frac{1}{\Omega_3}\left\{hm\beta + \frac{1 - h}{1 + \rho}[\chi m\beta + \rho(1 + r)]\right\}, \tag{56}$$

with $\Omega_3 = \Omega_2 + (1 - h)R/(1 + f) > 0$. It is apparent that $dQ_2/dB < 0$ always. This is because the additional lending increases investment and the supply of second-period debtor country good. Since there is no investment in the second final period and we are assuming no differences in preferences, the sign of dQ_2/dB is well determined.

This implies that allowing for endogenous terms of trade in the second period will expand the region of Pareto-improving contracts. In terms of our diagrams, the terms of trade changes in the second period shift both curves toward the origin, but the shift in DD (the debtors indifference curve) is of smaller magnitude, which enlarges the Pareto region. This can be seen from expressions analogous to (14) and (15) in the text of the paper:

$$\beta = \frac{1 + Y_1 \dfrac{dQ_1}{dB} + \dfrac{Y_2}{1+r^*} \dfrac{dQ_2}{dB}}{1 - \dfrac{m(1-\chi)}{1+r^*}} \tag{14'}$$

$$\beta = \frac{1 + Y_1 \dfrac{dQ_1}{dB} + \dfrac{Y_2}{1+r} \dfrac{dQ_2}{dB}}{\dfrac{\chi m}{1+r}}. \tag{15'}$$

Note that, since $r^* > r$ (that is, since the debtor country is credit constrained), the shift generated by dQ_2/dB is of larger magnitude in equation (15'); that is, for the creditor country.

As for the change in terms of trade in the first period, it will be the same as in the case of constant terms of trade in the second period if $R = 0$ or, alternatively, when the terms of trade change does not affect the value of repayments previously agreed to.[24] Therefore, the total effect of terms of trade endogeneity is an increase in the region of Pareto-improving contracts relative to the case of fixed terms of trade.

REFERENCES

Bergsten, C. Fred, William R. Cline, and John Williamson, *Bank Lending to Developing Countries* (Washington: Institute for International Economics, 1985).

Dornbusch, Rudiger, "Policy and Performance Links Between LDC Debtors and Industrial Nations," *Brookings Papers on Economic Activity: 2* (1985), The Brookings Institution (Washington), pp. 303–68.

————, "The World Debt Problem: Anatomy and Solutions" (unpublished; Washington, 1987).

Feldstein, Martin S., and others, "Restoring Growth in the Debt-Laden Third World: A Task Force Report to the Trilateral Commission," Triangle Papers, Report 33 (New York: The Triangle Commission, April 1987).

Fischer, Stanley, "Resolving the International Debt Crisis," NBER Working Paper 2373 (Cambridge, Massachusetts: National Bureau of Economic Research, September 1987).

---

[24] That is, prior to the new loan contract (β, χ) other payments from debtor to creditor might have been scheduled for the second period. We require that the value of those payments not be affected by the change in terms of trade. Such would be the case, for example, if those repayments were denominated in the currency of the creditor countries and the terms of trade change did not affect inflation in the creditor countries. If this is not the case, the sign of dQ_2/dB will still be indefinite and it will be more likely to be positive the larger the value of pre-scheduled repayment R.

Frenkel, Jacob A., and Assaf Razin, *Fiscal Policies and the World Economy: An Intertemporal Approach* (Cambridge, Massachusetts: MIT Press, 1985).

Froot, Kenneth, David Sharfstein, and Jeremy Stein, "LDC Debt: Forgiveness, Indexation, and Investment Incentives," NBER Working Paper 2541 (Cambridge, Massachusetts: National Bureau of Economic Research, March 1988).

Goldstein, Morris, and Mohsin S. Khan, "Income and Price Effects in Foreign Trade," Chapter 20 in *Handbook of International Economics*, Vol. 2, ed. by Ronald W. Jones and Peter B. Kenen (Amsterdam: North-Holland; New York: Elsevier, 1985).

Grossman, Gene, "Import Competition from Developed and Developing Countries," *Review of Economics and Statistics* (Amsterdam), Vol. 64 (May 1982), pp. 271–81.

Helpman, Elhanan, and Paul R. Krugman, *Market Structure and Foreign Trade* (Cambridge, Massachusetts: MIT Press, 1985).

Khan, Mohsin S., and Malcolm D. Knight, "Import Compression and Export Performance in Developing Countries," *Review of Economics and Statistics* (Amsterdam), forthcoming 1988.

Krugman, Paul R., "International Strategies in an Uncertain World," in *International Debt and the Developing Countries*, ed. by Gordon W. Smith and John T. Cuddington (Washington: World Bank, 1985), pp. 79–100.

———, "Private Capital Flows to Problem Debtors," paper presented at the NBER Conference on Developing Country Debt, (unpublished; Washington, 1987).

Marquez, Jaime, and Caryl McNeilly, "Income and Price Elasticities for Exports of Developing Countries," *Review of Economics and Statistics* (Amsterdam), forthcoming 1988.

Spence, Michael E., "Product Selection, Fixed Costs, and Monopolistic Competition," *Review of Economic Studies* (Edinburgh), Vol. 43 (1976), pp. 217–36.

Van Wijnbergen, Sweder, "Fiscal Policy, Trade Intervention, and World Interest Rates: An Empirical Analysis," in *International Aspects of Fiscal Policies*, ed. by Jacob A. Frenkel (Chicago: University of Chicago Press, 1988).

Buy-Backs, Debt-Equity Swaps, Asset Exchanges, and Market Prices of External Debt

MICHAEL P. DOOLEY*

*Buy-backs and asset exchanges that alter the amount and characteristics of
sovereign debt are evaluated in a simple framework. It is argued that the
terms on which existing debt can be purchased or exchanged depend upon
market prices for alternative instruments expected to prevail following the
transaction. These expected prices depend upon the the amount of debt,
the seniority of different classes of debt, and changes in the debtors' ability
to pay that are expected to prevail following a buy-back or exchange. The
costs and benefits of buy-backs and assets exchanges to debtors, creditors,
and third party benefactors are also identified.*

THIS PAPER develops a framework for evaluating a range of proposals
to "buy back" the external debt of developing countries. Sections I
through III focus on buy-backs and debt-equity swaps financed by third
parties. It is argued that the potential benefits of such proposals include
a reduction in the contractual value of the country's debt, capital gains
for creditors, and a possible increase in domestic investment in the
debtor country associated with reductions in market discounts on remaining debt. These benefits are compared with the cost of a buy-back
to the third party, measured by the expenditure necessary to induce
holders of a country's debt voluntarily to sell or exchange the existing
debt in circumstances in which they are fully informed about the new
amount and form of debt that will exist following the buy-back.

Two important insights emerge from the analysis of buy-backs fi-

---

*Mr. Dooley, Chief of the External Adjustment Division in the Research
Department of the IMF, is a graduate of Duquesne University, the University
of Delaware, and the Pennsylvania State University.

nanced by third parties. First, proposals that are successful in increasing the market price of debt, and therefore improve the climate for investment, also generate roughly equal increases in prices at which private investors will voluntarily sell or exchange these debts as the proposal is implemented. If, for example, a third party offers to buy a part of existing debt and forgives some or all of this debt, the price paid to purchase the debt will be the price expected to prevail following the forgiveness. Thus, market prices prevailing before the announcement of such a program will understate the expenditure necessary in order to purchase a given contractual value of debt.

This may be a particularly important consideration when initial market prices are low. Although it seems plausible that low-priced debt can be purchased and forgiven at a low "cost," it is clear that, if successful, such a proposition implies a large capital gain to any individual creditor holding his initially low-valued investment until after the forgiveness. It is illustrated below that in such cases the initial creditors stand to gain a large part of the benefits of such a program. In these cases it may be useful to consider conditional buy-back proposals for which claims that remain outstanding following forgiveness are in some way subordinated to new claims.

The second insight is that voluntary exchanges of existing contracts for new contracts with different attributes, such as "equity" content, will reflect the expected post-exchange values of alternative contracts. For example, if a third party offers to exchange equity for existing debt, a voluntary exchange will reflect the expected relative rights of debt and equity holders that will prevail following the exchange. An important determinant of this relative price would be the implicit or explicit subordination of the relative rights of holders of different types of financial contracts. It will generally be the case that increased value that might accrue to one type of contract will be matched by decreases in the value of other contracts. The effects of this change in relative values of existing credits to a given country may have little effect on the climate for investment in the debtor country.

An important assumption behind these results is that buy-backs financed by third parties do not reduce the capacity of the debtor country to make payments to nonresidents. In contrast, self-financed buy-backs analyzed in Section III usually reduce the debtors' ability to service remaining debt.[1] As a consequence, such buy-backs generally do not

---

[1] An exception would be the case where an unprofitable enterprise owned by the debtor government could be sold to a creditor. This would be possible if the change in ownership was expected to increase the profitability of the enterprise.

reduce the discount on remaining debt, nor do they reduce the expected value of debt service payments net of expected earnings on the asset sold. A self-financed buy-back does, however, reduce the contractual value of debt by some multiple of the value of the buy-back.

The intuition behind the different results is straightforward. If a country sells a real or financial asset to finance a buy-back, the earnings from that asset are no longer available to make payments on the remaining debt.[2] It follows that the reduction in the contractual value of its external debt is, to some extent, offset by a reduction in its capacity to make payments on that debt. It is shown below that, under fairly general conditions, the reduction in the expected value of the country's debt service payments dominates the reduction in contractual value of remaining debt so that the market discount *increases* slightly following a self-financed buy-back. The contractual value of debt and debt service payments are, in general, reduced by self-financed buy-backs.

If a country or third party dedicates a real or financial asset as collateral for a new class of external debt and then offers to exchange the collateralized new debt for old debt, the impact on net debt service payments and the market discount for old debt and the net contractual value of debt will be exactly equivalent to the effects of a buy-back using the same financial or real assets. This result is derived below for the self-financed case and is consistent with simple arbitrage conditions.

I. Aggregate Value of External Debt

The aggregate market value of claims on a debtor country depends upon the expected present value of resource transfers from the country that will be available to creditors. The expected resource transfer is determined by many factors, some of which are controlled by the debtor government and some of which are not. For buy-backs financed by third parties, it is assumed that these factors are not affected by the proposals discussed in the following pages. This assumption is to some extent unrealistic. For example, a buy-back that succeeds in increasing the market value of existing debt should improve the growth prospects for the debtor and, in turn, the payments to nonresident creditors the country could be expected to make. A more complete investigation of such linkages is left to future research.

[2] If a country sells its own liability (i.e., borrows), its ability to make future payments is reduced by the additional debt service on these new liabilities. If the market discount on new debt is equal to that on old debt, the exchange of identical liabilities clearly has no net effect and debt is not reduced.

In the analysis that follows, expected future payment streams are translated into expected present values. For the usual reasons, payoffs that are expected to occur far in the future are worth less today than are equal payoffs that will be received sooner. Nevertheless, investors are assumed to arbitrage claims on payment streams with the same present value so that their expected yields are equalized. This requires that some market participants can borrow and lend at any maturity at market interest rates. It is not necessary that the debtor be able to borrow and lend at market interest rates.

Suppose we observe that a country's debt is selling at 50 percent of its contractual value and that its total debt is $100 billion.[3] What value would the remaining debt carry if some part of the existing debt were forgiven? For example, if investors now value $100 billion of bonds at $50 billion, what value would they place on $75 billion worth of bonds remaining if $25 billion of the country's debt is forgiven? If we assume that the behavior of the debtor is unaffected by a partial forgiveness of its legal obligations, the answer to this question depends entirely on why investors valued the original $100 billion face value bonds at $50 billion.[4]

A simple way to characterize investors' expectations is to envision a probability distribution for the present value of various possible payoffs by a country to all its creditors. In the first example developed below, it is assumed that all creditors hold identical bond contracts and that each creditor expects to receive the average payment on the country's aggregate contractual obligation.[5] For example, if a uniform distribution for outcomes is assumed over aggregate payoffs with present values that range from zero to the entire contractual liability of $100 billion, each investor assumes that he will receive the same share of his contractual rights. Thus, the expected probability of receiving a payoff of $0.50 per dollar is equal to the expected probability of the country generating a payment stream to all creditors with a present value of $50 billion. The "payment stream" in the case of external debt can be thought of as net exports of goods and services.

---

[3] As argued in an earlier paper, there is probably little useful distinction between so-called internal and external debt at least in the context of this exercise. Thus the relevant stock of debt, $100 billion, in the above exercise should be thought of as the total government debt of the country concerned.

[4] For convenience it is assumed that the contractual value and the "face value" of the debt were identical when the debt was issued. This will not, in general, hold but does not affect the analysis as long as we interpret changes in the market discount as relative to the "at issue" discount.

[5] For convenience it is assumed that all the bonds have the same infinite maturity and are indexed to market interest rates.

II. Reductions in the Contractual Value of Debt

To explore the question of how a change in the contractual rights of creditors will alter the market value of credits, an auction can be imagined in which a benefactor would buy and forgive a portion of the existing debt. It is assumed that the funds made available by the benefactor would not otherwise be made available to the debtor country. The benefactor would then reissue a reduced stock of claims on the debtor country that would carry a lower contractual value. This procedure would, in most cases, generate conditions subsequent to the auction consistent with a reduced gap between the market value of the debt and its contractual value. The private sector's behavior with regard to an auction would depend upon expectations concerning the present value of the country's aggregate payments to creditors. For simplicity it is assumed in this analysis that these expectations are not changed by the auction. Thus, predicted changes in market prices reflect the fact that following the auction there will be a smaller value of contractual claims on expected payments.

Pricing for a Uniform Probability Distribution

In order to focus on the implications of debt forgiveness, a very simple probability distribution for aggregate payments is assumed. In particular, it is assumed that the present values of all payoffs, between zero and $100 billion inclusive, are believed to be uniformly likely to occur. Thus, the mean expected payoff is $50 billion and each dollar's worth of contractual value sells for $0.50.[6]

The benefactor offers to buy existing debt in a single auction and promises to forgive the difference between the auction price, PA, at which the benefactor purchases bonds and the contractual value of the bonds purchased.[7] The effects of such an auction can be illustrated for the uniform distribution ranging from 0 to 1 shown in Figure 1.

If the authorities purchase all the outstanding debt, the amount forgiven per dollar would be $(1-PA)$, the shaded area in Figure 1. The

[6] The assumption that market prices reflect the mean of the probability distribution of the present value of expected payment streams is maintained throughout the analysis.

[7] The benefactor can either hold the new bonds or sell them in the market. As long as the rights of the benefactor and other investors are identical, this would not affect market prices. In practice, the rights of the benefactor or his preferences for enforcing those rights may be different. Thus, the "cleanest" assumption would be that the benefactor sells the new bonds back to private investors.

Figure 1. *Uniform Probability Distribution*

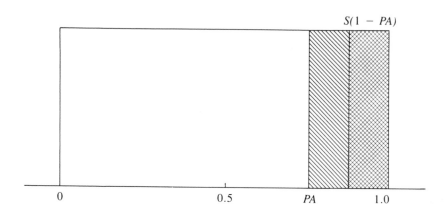

probability that new contracts would be paid off at contractual value (that is where PA equals one on the new contracts) is assumed to be the probability of all outcomes equal to or greater than PA for the old contracts. Since the auction price PA will be equal to one for the new contracts, the value of the new contracts is in part due to the probability of complete payoff which must be $(1-PA)$ *1 or simply $(1-PA)$.[8]

There will remain, however, some chance that the new contracts will not be completely paid off. This is assumed to be the probability of events to the left of PA for the original contracts. The mean of this probability density, the unshaded area in Figure 1, is $\frac{1}{2}PA$. The market price of the new contracts must therefore be:

$$PM = \frac{1}{2}PA + 1 - PA,$$

$$PM = 1 - \frac{1}{2}PA.$$

Competitive bids at the auction will ensure that the auction price is equal to the expected market price *following* the auction. If, for example, the auction price was higher than the market price subsequent to the auction, successful sellers at the auction would realize an immediate capital gain. Conversely, if the auction price were lower than the subsequent market price, successful sellers at the auction would experience

---

[8] Note that the value of this part of the new contract as a percentage of the auction price would be $(1 - PA)/PA$. This, however, is not of interest because the objective is to calculate the market discount on the new contractual value of debt.

an immediate capital loss. Assuming no collusion among bidders,[9] any expected gain would be eliminated as bidders competed against one another. It follows that the equilibrium auction price, PA, is that which sets the auction price equal to the subsequent market price, PM. For a uniform distribution where the benefactor buys and resells all the outstanding debt this would simply be:

$$PM = PA = \$0.66.$$

Although more realistic examples of auctions and probability distributions are considered below, all the important aspects of a forgiveness proposal financed by a benefactor are captured in this simple example. Any auction rule that generates the same amount of forgiveness would generate the same auction and post-auction price. The convention assumed here is therefore not crucial to the results. The benefactor incurs a cost of about \$22.2 billion in lowering the market discount on existing debt from 50 percent to $33\frac{1}{3}$ percent. The "investment" benefit of this reduction in market discounts would be the present value of future investment that would be undertaken at this discount but would not be undertaken at the initial 50 percent discount. This calculation would, of course, require an empirical estimate of the investment schedule in the debtor country.

The initial creditors enjoy a rise in the market value of their debt of \$16.6 billion since the market value of their bonds rose from \$50 billion to \$66.6 billion when the auction was announced.[10]

The debtor country gains the rights to payoffs above \$66.6 billion that would have gone without forgiveness to external creditors. In this example, the expected present value of these outcomes would be about \$5.6 billion.

Thus, the \$22.6 billion expenditure by the benefactor has three effects. First, the market discount is reduced from 50 percent to $33\frac{1}{3}$ percent. Second, the creditors realize an economic gain of \$16.6 billion. Third, the debtor realizes an expected gain with a present value of about \$5.6 billion. It should be noted that the initial creditors gain even though their *collective* rights to some relatively good outcomes have been trans-

---

[9] This is an important assumption. In practice, creditors may try to enforce noncompetitive bids by insisting that sales be allocated according to ownership shares rather than according to amounts offered for sale. Under these conditions the auction becomes a bilateral monopoly problem. In general, the sale price will be higher in this case and need not be equal to the expected post-forgiveness price.

[10] In selling their holdings the initial creditors would realize an accounting loss of \$33.4 billion assuming that the initial accounting loss of \$50 billion had not been realized.

ferred to the debtor country. This negative "income effect," from the point of view of creditors, is more than offset in this example by a "substitution effect" that results from the lower value of contractual debt following forgiveness. That is, the lower expected present value of payments by the debtor country will satisfy a larger share of credits following forgiveness.

This simple example of a buy-back proposal serves to highlight several important results that might be expected from such proposals. The relative strength (and for debt-equity swaps discussed in the next section even the signs) of these effects, however, are not invariant to assumptions about the probability distribution for payoffs. In the following discussion, these difficulties are explored further. In particular, it is argued that the income effect that was positive for the debtor in this example and negative for creditors as a group may not play an important role in some cases.

Partial Buy-Backs

It may not be realistic for the benefactor to offer to purchase all outstanding debt since this implies that all bids will be accepted regardless of cost. If the benefactor offers to buy less than the total outstanding debt, the reasoning is slightly more complicated, but the basic results hold. In this case, the securities not purchased at the auction will also increase in value following the auction, although their contractual value will remain unchanged. In this case, the benefactor would buy some share, S, of the existing debt, forgive $S(1 - PA)$ per dollar purchased, and sell the new securities to the market. Returning again to Figure 1, the contractual value per dollar of outstanding debt forgiven by the benefactor would be $S(1 - PA)$. Thus, by analogous reasoning the market value of *all* debt following the auction would be:

$$PM = \frac{1}{2}[1 - S(1 - PA)] + S(1 - PA).$$

And the equilibrium auction price is found by setting $PA = PM$ so that

$$PM = PA = \frac{1 + S}{2 + S}.$$

If, for example, the benefactor agreed to buy one half of the $100 billion described in Figure 1 the equilibrium auction price would be:

$$PM = PA = \$0.60.$$

The cost to the benefactor of "improving" the discount on debt outstanding following the auction from 50 percent to 40 percent is $12.0 billion. Corresponding to this, the creditors realize a capital gain of $10 billion while the debtor realizes an expected gain of $2 billion. It should be noted that the capital gain to creditors accrues both to those who participate in the auction and to those who choose not to participate.

An accounting loss may be realized by the initial creditors that participate in the auction although the rise in the post-auction market price would provide an economic benefit to initial creditors regardless of their participation in the auction. If the initial creditors have to be paid to realize the accounting loss, then we should expect an auction price above the expected subsequent market price in order to compensate for this. This might be important in cases where initial investors' relationships with regulators or their own creditors depend upon accounting as well as market prices.

Pricing for a Normal Probability Distribution

If the appropriate probability distribution over payoffs on existing debt was normal rather than uniform, there would be less value associated with payoffs near the extremes of 0 and 1. To illustrate this, consider a normal distribution, $F(x)$, of expected present values of resource transfers, x, that has a mean of 0.5 and 98 percent of the probability density between 0 and 1.0. As described above, the benefactor might purchase all the outstanding debt at PA and forgive $(1 - PA)$ of the debt. In this case the probability that repayment will exceed the reduced face value of debt is not $(1 - PA)$ as in the uniform distribution but $1 - F(PA)$, the shaded area in Figure 2. Moreover, the mean of the probability density of the remaining contractual value is not $\frac{1}{2} PA$ but the price corresponding to the mean of the truncated probability density from 0 to PA. If y is defined as the payoff per dollar of the new contractual value following the auction, then:

$$y = 1.0 \quad \text{if} \quad x \geq PA,$$

$$y = x/PA \quad \text{if} \quad x < PA.$$

The probability that $x < PA$ is $F(PA)$. The probability that $x \geq PA$ is $1 - F(PA)$. Thus the expected value of y will be the post-auction market price.[1]

$$E(y) = PM = 1 - F(PA) + \frac{1}{PA} \int_0^{PA} xf(x)dx,$$

where $f(x)$ is the probability density function of a truncated normal and, as before, since in equilibrium $PA = PM$ the solution can be solved numerically.

Figure 2. *Normal Probability Distribution*

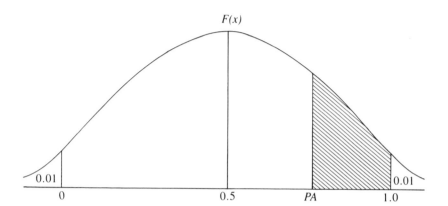

Suppose the auction price was $0.66 as was the equilibrium value for the uniform distribution. In this case, the market price following the auction would be slightly higher than $0.66, giving the sellers an expected loss in participating in the auction. Expected losses would induce sellers to drive the auction price up to about $0.69 per dollar bid. At this auction price the post-auction market price would also be about $0.69 per dollar of contractual value.

The cost to the benefactor of raising the market price of remaining debt from $0.50 and $0.69 would be about $21.4 billion.[11] Creditors receive a capital gain of $19 billion while the debtor regains control over expected payments with a present value of about $2.4 billion. It is interesting to note that the results are comparable to the uniform distribution discussed above. In fact, if we allow the variance of the normal distribution to become very large, the results converge to the uniform distribution. As the variance of a normal distribution becomes very small, it approaches the case in which there is a certain return of some present value on existing debt. We turn to this extreme in the next section.

---

[11] If the benefactor offered to purchase a share, S, of the outstanding debt the equilibrium auction price would be:

$$PA = PM = 1 - F[1 - S(1 - PA)] + \frac{1}{PA} \int_0^{[1-S(1-PA)]} xf(x)dx,$$

And if $S = \frac{1}{2}$,

$$PA = PM = 0.64.$$

Pricing for Single Value and Nonsymmetric Distribution

For simplicity it is assumed that all of the probability mass is concentrated on one payoff corresponding to \$.50 per dollar of contractual value. An auction along the lines discussed above would result in a post-auction market price which is simply \$.50 times the ratio of the initial and post-auction contractual values

$$PM = .50 * \frac{100}{100 - (1 - PA)100} = .50 * \frac{1}{PA}.$$

In equilibrium therefore

$$PM = PA = \$0.706.$$

Thus, the benefactor would incur a cost of \$20.6 billion in raising the market price by 20.6 percentage points. Moreover, creditors would realize a capital gain that is exactly equal to the expenditure of the benefactor, because there is no "income" effect in this example. The assumption that there is no probability that payments will exceed the new contractual value of debt of \$70.6 billion means that creditors, as a group, "lose" payoffs that have a zero chance of occurring. By the same logic, the debtor does not regain the rights to payoffs. Thus, in any circumstance in which the post-forgiveness contractual value of debt exceeds all probable payoffs, the creditors gain because of the "substitution" effect while the debtor gains only to the extent that investment is higher owing to the fall in market discounts.

A purchase with forgiveness seems particularly attractive when initial market prices are relatively low. In such cases, however, a large share of the benefits of forgiveness might accrue to the creditors. If, for example, the initial probability over outcomes was massed at \$0.10, the equilibrium auction price would be about \$0.316. In this case, the benefactor would incur a cost of \$22 billion in raising the market price by 22 percentage points. Nevertheless, there may be little or no increase in investment at a discount of 68 percent.

In this limiting case in which the variance of expected returns is zero, the benefactor can obtain a percentage increase in the market price of existing debt only by incurring a cost equal to the equivalent share of the contractual value of outstanding debt. This simply reflects the fact that creditors remaining after the auction and forgiveness expect to share the same distribution of payments. It follows that when the initial price is very low, an auction scheme reducing the market discount to a level that might be expected to encourage new investment would require the purchase of a sizable part of existing debt at a high cost.

Pricing for Bimodal Distributions

Another interesting distribution is an "all or nothing" possibility represented by a 0.5 probability that all creditors receive full payment and a 0.5 probability that creditors receive nothing. Such a distribution might be relevant when a single important change in the economic environment would either render the country unable to make any payments or make the existing debt small relative to the country's capacity to pay. The equilibrium condition for this auction would be:

$$PA = PM = 0.5 * 0 + 0.5 * 1.0,$$

$$= 0.5.$$

In this case, the market value debt will always remain at $0.50 regardless of the amount purchased by the benefactor. The benefactor would incur a cost of $25 billion, but would not succeed in narrowing the market discount. Therefore, the investment effect would be zero. The creditors in this case receive no capital gain while the debtor receives a capital gain of $25 billion.

The all or nothing probability distribution is often implicit in models that consider the effects of default on external debt. The framework developed here is not designed to address issues related to debtor countries' willingness to pay, only their ability, but the results for the bimodal distribution developed here suggest that the assumption of a bimodal probability distribution over outcomes has very special properties as compared with more general cases. It is likely, therefore, that the implications of default drawn from models that predict an all or nothing outcome would not apply if partial default is an option for debtors.

Comparison of Results

The results of this section are summarized in Table 1. It is clear that the distribution of benefits of a buy-back scheme financed by a third party depends upon the nature of the probability distribution over outcomes. In any case, however, the debtor stands to gain either from an improvement in the climate for investment or from an expected capital gain through debt reduction. Creditors gain to the extent that market prices rise as a result of the buy-back.

One way to alter the distribution of benefits for any of these distributions is to break the equality between the auction price and the expected post-auction market price. For example, the debtor country might specify that debt not purchased at the auction would not be fully honored.

Table 1. *Benefits and Costs of Buy-Backs*

(In billions of dollars)

Distribution	Probability Distribution			
	Uniform	Normal	Single value	Bimodal
Cost to benefactor	22.2	21.4	20.6	25.0
Investment effect (In percent rise in market prices)	+16.6	+19.0	+20.6	—
Expected gain for debtor	5.6	2.4	—	25.0
Realized gain for creditors	16.6	19.0	20.6	—

While this might be considered a partial default on the part of the debtor country, donor countries might reduce the expected cost of such an action to the debtor by refusing to assist creditors in enforcing payments for debt not purchased at the auction.

The difficulty in analyzing such schemes is that the probability distribution over payoffs is obviously changed by default or subordination of debt not bought at the auction. Default or subordination might succeed in reducing the market discounts with or without a buy-back. An extreme example of this would be the case in which the debtor defaults completely on all debt not purchased in the buy-back. If credible, this would allow all initial debt to be purchased at any positive price the debtor offers since the expected post-auction price of existing debt would be zero. It seems to follow that a buy-back under these conditions is analytically equivalent to a unilateral default on the part of the debtor combined with some compensation as provided by the buy-back.

III. Pricing for Different Types of Financial Contracts

In this section the assumption that all creditors receive the average payment is relaxed. As before, it is assumed that the aggregate value of financial claims on a country's resource transfers will reflect the present value of a range of possibilities for expected payment streams. Given this aggregate value, however, the value of each different type of claim on the expected resource transfers will depend on the "place in line" for payment granted to different types of creditors. For this reason individual creditors will be very interested in their rights relative to other creditors. It follows that creditors would welcome proposals that might move them up in line a place or two. However, such proposals may not affect the market valuation of a debtor's aggregate obligations.

Figure 3. *Normal Probability Distribution: Payoffs for Debt and Equity*

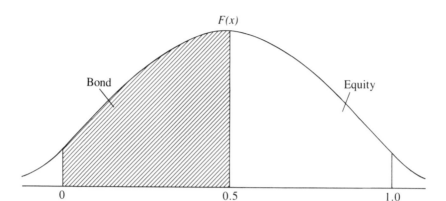

It has been suggested, for example, that equity could be substituted for debt in order to improve a country's financial position. One way to analyze such an idea is to imagine that a benefactor offered to purchase debt at the market discount and then reissue equity claims on the debtor country. The cost of such an auction would be the difference between the auction price of the bonds and the post-auction market price of the equities sold.

The introduction of two types of financial claims on the debtor country requires an assumption concerning the relative rights of the holders of these instruments. If it is assumed that bondholders will always be first in line for payment, then, from the bondholders' point of view, the substitution of equity for debt would be equivalent to a forgiveness of the outstanding debt purchased by the benefactor. For the normal distribution discussed above, this would mean that the post-auction value of the bonds would correspond to the mean of the shaded area of Figure 3, plus the probability of a payoff of 1.0 for all outcomes to the right of 0.5.[12]

$$P_B = 1 - F(S) + \frac{1}{s} \int_0^s x\, f(x) dx.$$

If one half of the initial debt is purchased, the equilibrium price would be $0.84. Thus, the benefactor would purchase $50 billion in bonds at a 16 percent discount, a total expenditure of $42 billion. The benefactor would then sell equities to the market. The value of the equities would

---

[12] Note that the integral's value is indexed by *s*, rather than *PA* in the earlier examples, since it is assumed that in valuing remaining bonds $(1 - s)$ of the contractual value of the initial debt is forgiven.

reflect the value of all outcomes that yield a payment after all bond-holders are satisfied. Note that in this case the value of outcomes above one would also go to equity holders.

If one half of the outstanding bond debt is purchased by a benefactor and reissued as equity, the value of the newly issued equity would be[13]

$$P_E = \int_S^\infty (x - s)\, \tilde{f}(x) dx,$$

$$= \$8.7 \text{ billion.}$$

Note that the price function differs from the bond pricing function because outcomes from 0 to S imply a zero price for the equity since for all outcomes when $x \leq S$ the payoff to equity holders would be zero. It should also be noted that, by assumption, there is very little probability weight above 1.0. For this reason, the value of the equity, $8.7 billion plus the value of the bonds, $42 billion, exceeds only slightly the market value of the original bond contracts. The benefactor would realize a total cost of $33 billion in narrowing the discount on debt from 50 percent to 16 percent. The lesson from this auction is that a conversion of debt into equity could lead to a substantial increase in the market value of remaining bonds but would do so at a considerable cost to the benefactor. Moreover, in this example the debtor has absorbed an expected income effect loss of $0.7 billion.

IV. Self-Financed Buy-Backs

In order to highlight the differences between self-financed buy-backs and those financed by a third party, the effects of an unanticipated and transitory increase in the debtor country's net worth are first analyzed.

Suppose, initially, an external debt of $100 billion and that expected payments on each dollar of a country's external debt are described by the unshaded uniform probability shown in Figure 4. If the debtor received an unexpected and transitory $10 increase in its current account balance, and if the debtor invested these funds in a financial instrument that yielded the same rate as the rate at which future payments were discounted, the uniform distribution would shift to the right by $0.10 as shown in Figure 4.[14]

---

[13] $\tilde{f}$ is the f density defined above, not truncated at 0 and 1 but defined from $-\infty$ to $+\infty$.

[14] If the country could obtain a rate of return higher than the rate at which foreign investors discount expected payments, then the initial surplus of $10 billion would have a present value of more than $10 billion. This, however, seems unlikely.

Figure 4. *Unexpected Current Account Surplus*

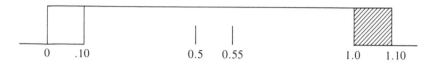

The initial price of debt was $0.50, the mean of the unshaded uniform distribution above. The shift of the distribution implies that the new market price, *PM*, would be:

$$PM = 0.9 * (0.55) + 0.1 * 1.0, \tag{1}$$

$$= \$0.595.$$

The increase in the market price of debt would occur as soon as creditors learn of the unexpected current account surplus.

If the debtor then finances a buy-back by selling the financial assets bought with the unexpected current account surplus, there are two changes in the situation. First, the probability distribution for the present value of expected payments shifts back to the zero to one interval as shown in Figure 5. Second, the contractual value of the remaining debt will be reduced by the $10 billion buy-back, *BB*, divided by the auction price, *PA*, at which debt is purchased by the debtor country. The equilibrium auction price is found by setting it equal to the expected post-auction market price.

$$PM = \tfrac{1}{2}(1 - BB/PA) + BB/PA, \tag{2}$$

setting $PM = PA$

$$PA^2 - \tfrac{1}{2}PA = BB/2,$$

$$PA \approx 0.585.$$

Figure 5. *Sale of Assets*

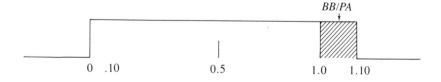

Thus, the $10 billion buy-back will result in about $17.1 billion in debt being repurchased and a fall in the market price of remaining debt from $0.595 to 0.585. The slight fall in the market price is the opposite of what would be expected if the buy-back had been financed by a third party. The market price falls slightly in this example because in some very good states of nature (the shaded area of Figure 1) the debtor would have been able to keep the present value of the returns on reserves. Following the buy-back, the earnings on reserves will always belong to former creditors. The gross *market* value of the debt is reduced by about $11 billion, $59.5 billion ($100 at 0.595) to $48.5 ($82.9 at 0.585). The market value of the assets sold is only $10 billion. The "extra" billion dollar reduction in market value of debt is matched by the decrease in the *expected* value to the debtor of the assets sold.

The *contractual* value of the country's debt is reduced by $17.1 billion. If the debtor had expected to fully service this debt, that is, if it did not believe that the probability distribution shown in Figure 5 was an accurate expectation, it follows that the debtor has managed to improve its position by utilizing $10 billion of reserves to retire $17.1 billion of debt. In general, a debtor country should not hold assets which earn a risk-free rate of return when it can retire liabilities on which it is paying a risk premium that it believes inappropriate.

Collateralization

There have been a variety of proposals that would dedicate some part of a debtor country's wealth to a specific type of new debt instrument. The asset pledged could be a financial asset or the proceeds from a given tax, or profits of a public enterprise. In each case, it is reasonable to assume that such assets had been expected to generate a part of the payments to the initial stock of old debt. It follows that, as with the buy-back, two factors will act on the post-auction price of old debt. The stock of old debt will be reduced and the expected payments to old debt will also be reduced. Such a scheme might be appealing because it appears to increase the amount of old debt that can be retired as compared with a cash buy-back financed by a sale of assets. It is shown below, however, that the amount of old debt retired is the same for both types of buy-backs.

In order to collateralize new debt, the debtor dedicates some asset exclusively to its service. To keep the analysis simple, it is assumed that the $10 billion financial asset discussed above is pledged as security for $20 billion contractual value of new bonds. It is further assumed that in

Figure 6. *Sale of Collateralized Assets*

all other respects, new and old bonds are identical.[15] In this case the auction would not involve an exchange of debt for cash but an exchange of old debt for new debt. Nevertheless, the equilibrium condition is determined by the *expected* cash prices of old and new debt following the auction. If the ratio of cash prices expected to prevail after the auction is not equal to the ratio at which contractual values of old and new debt are exchanged at the auction, there would be expected capital gains from holding one instrument or the other.

The post-auction price of old debt will again be based on the present values of expected payments over the interval zero to one (Figure 6), since the additional $10 billion earned through an unexpected current account surplus will not be available to make payments to holders of old debt. The contractual value of old debt remaining after the auction will depend on the exchange ratio between old and new debt that prevails at the auction. We prefer to refer to the ratio between old and new debt as an "exchange ratio" rather than a "price" because this ratio does not reflect the market cash price of either type of debt before or after the auction. There is no reason, for example, to compare the exchange ratio with the market price of debt before the auction is announced. The former reflects, in part, the arbitrary relationship between the value of collateral and the face value of new debt while the latter presumably reflects market expectations about the debtors' ability to pay.

The amount of old debt retired would be equal to the contractual value of new debt, *BB*, offered at the auction divided by the auction exchange ratio, *AR*, that is *BB/AR*. The market price of old debt following the auction will also reflect the share of new debt, which is also a claim on expected payments. Since it is assumed here that new and old debt are

---

[15] If the new securities are superior to old debt in other respects, their exchange value would be higher as compared to the example developed here. Subordination of old debt would, in general, increase the amount that can be retired relative to a direct buy-back. However, subordination as discussed above is equivalent to a partial default on the part of the debtor.

identical in all respects other than the collateral behind new debt, the contractual value of new debt not covered by collateral is equivalent to old debt. Thus, the total contractual value of claims following the auction (per dollar of the original contractual value) would be:

$$PACVN + PACVO = 1 - (BB/AR - BB + S) \qquad (3)$$

where $PACVN$ = post-auction contractual value of unsecured share of new debt,
   $PACVO$ = post-auction contractual value of old debt,
     BB = contractual value of new debt,
     AR = auction exchange ratio between contractual values of old and new debt,
      S = market value of collateral discounted at the same rate as expected payments.

The post-auction market price of old debt would thus be

$$PO = \tfrac{1}{2}(1 - BB/AR + BB - S) + BB/AR - B + S. \qquad (4)$$

The post-auction price of new debt would be

$$PN = S/BB + [(1 - S)/BB] \cdot PO. \qquad (5)$$

The equilibrium condition for the auction exchange ratio is that it be equal to the expected post-auction ratio of cash prices so that in equilibrium

$$AR = \frac{PO}{PN}. \qquad (6)$$

By substitution

$$AR^2(\tfrac{1}{2} + \tfrac{1}{2}S/BB + S - \tfrac{1}{2}S^2/B - \tfrac{1}{2}B) + AR(B - S - \tfrac{1}{2}) = \tfrac{1}{2}BB. \qquad (7)$$

In the example set out above, $BB = 0.2$ and $S = 0.1$ so that:

   $AR \approx 0.739.$

At the auction, investors will be willing to exchange $1.00 contractual value of new debt for $0.739 contractual value of old debt. It should be noted that the discount derived here of 0.261 is not a cash market discount on either type of debt.

To find the cash price of old and new debt, the equilibrium auction exchange rate, 0.739, must be substituted into (4) and (5), respectively. This yields:

   $PO = 0.585,$

   $PN = 0.7925.$

The price of old debt is identical to that which prevailed after the straight buy-back of $10 billion discussed above. This is not surprising since the new bond is simply a composite of two securities available to any investor.

The amount of old debt retired is about $27.1 billion, an amount $10 billion greater compared with the cash buy-back financed by the same $10 billion of assets. Since exactly $10 billion of the new securities issued are identical to old debt, however, there is no net gain in this respect. In general, increasing the size of BB relative to the collateral S has no effect on the equilibrium following the auction. The auction exchange rate would depend on the contractual value of new debt issued. For example, (7) implies that if $50 billion of new debt (backed by the same $10 billion collateral) was offered against old debt, the equilibrium exchange ratio would be about $0.876, somewhat higher as compared with the $20 billion buy-back. But the market price of old debt remaining would again be $0.585, and although $57.1 billion of debt is retired, the additional $30 billion retired is exactly matched by the $30 billion additional unsecured new debt issued. Thus, the auction exchange ratio is not a useful indicator of the value of debt or the effect of collateralization of a share of a country's external debt.

V. Limitations and Extensions

Several issues remain in an attempt to fully evaluate the proposals outlined in this paper. It has been shown that there is no typical distribution of benefits associated with buy-back proposals. Under plausible circumstances, both debtors and creditors could benefit substantially from buy-backs financed by a third party. It is possible, however, that almost all the benefits of such initiatives could go to the creditors in the form of a substitution effect, with little or no benefit to the debtor country in the form of investment or income effects. Buy-backs financed by the debtor itself are less likely to generate capital gains for either party and under plausible assumptions can lead to an increase in market discounts or remaining debt.

The distribution of benefits of buy-backs can be changed fundamentally by subordinating debt not purchased or transformed since this would break the link between auction prices and expected market prices. While it may be possible to tilt benefits toward the debtor country through conditional buy-backs, this could result in sanctions against the debtor and prejudice future access to private credit markets.

A more comprehensive evaluation of buy-backs would require the identification of the relevant alternative uses of funds. Suppose, for example, that the debtor used funds for imports and real investment. Alternatively, the funds could be used to service the existing debt in the usual way or to accumulate reserve assets. These alternatives or combinations of alternatives might be preferable in individual circumstances. At this point, it seems reasonable to conclude that there is no general rule as to whether buy-backs are an optimal strategy for individual countries. Each case would have to be judged against alternative uses of available funds.

Finally, the effects of any scheme on market discounts will reflect not only the initial offer, but also any information that might be inferred concerning future schemes. If, for example, investors believe that a benefactor will do what is necessary to maintain a given discount on a country's debt, the market discount will move to this level and the benefactor's actions then become endogenous to the system.

An International Debt Facility?

W. MAX CORDEN*

The proposal to set up an international debt facility to buy the debt of developing countries at a discount and then mark down its contractual value is analyzed. The paper considers the central question of how the debtor countries, creditor banks, and owners of the facility would be affected; in particular, what redistribution of gains and losses there would be among them. The "market price effect" and the "ceiling effect" are distinguished. A crucial consideration is whether debt retained by banks is subordinated to debt bought by the facility.

A COMMON PROPOSAL designed to deal with the developing countries' debt problem is that there be set up an "international debt facility" that would buy debt at a discount and then mark down its contractual value, hence providing debt relief. This facility could be envisaged either as a major scheme that would, over a period, deal with most or all outstanding commercial debt owed or guaranteed by governments, or as a more modest arrangement dealing with only small portions of debt, possibly only that which is owed by the governments of particular countries.

Many such proposals have been advanced. They vary in their details,[1]

*At the time he wrote this paper Mr. Corden was Senior Advisor in the Research Department, on leave from the Australian National University, where he is Professor of Economics. He is a graduate of the University of Melbourne and the London School of Economics and Political Science. He has taught at Oxford University and at various Australian and U.S. universities. He thanks Ken Rogoff and colleagues in the Fund for helpful comments.

[1] As far as I am aware, the first proposals of this general kind were advanced by Felix Rohatyn in *Business Week* (February 28, 1983) and by Peter Kenen in *The New York Times* (March 6, 1983). The proposal has been made by Sachs and Huizinga (1987) and by Percy Mistry, formerly of the World Bank (in *The Banker,* September 1987). In 1988, proposals of this general nature have been made by Dr. Sengupta, an Executive Director of the Fund, and by James Robinson, Chairman of American Express. There is an analysis of this kind of proposal in Feldstein and others (1987). The Omnibus Trade and Competitive-

and there are many difficulties, some major. Nevertheless, the frequency with which such proposals are made makes it worth examining them carefully in their many permutations.

I. Main Issues

There are three principal parties to the proposed transaction—the debtor governments, the creditor banks, and the "owners" of the facility. The central question is how the costs and benefits would accrue to various parties. Is there an element of "foreign aid" or of a "bank bail-out"? Alternatively, would the banks give up something? Could all three parties gain or, at least, could some gain without the others losing significantly, if at all? In other words, is there some systemic benefit?

The proximate redistributive effects—and possibly also the systemic effects—will depend crucially on three prices: the price at which the debt is bought, the price or value to which it is marked down, and the price or perceived value to which remaining debt that is retained in the private sector moves as a result of the whole operation. The full economic effects will depend, of course, on how the various parties react to or deal with the proximate gains or losses.

In considering the details of such a scheme there are many choices to be made.

• The debt might be bought by the facility at the minimum price required for the banks to part with it voluntarily; it might be bought at current market prices; it might be bought at the market prices that existed at some earlier "cut-off" date; or it might be bought at some other set of prices representing discounts on the contractual value. Conceivably it might even be bought at its contractual value.

• Purchased debt might be marked down to the cost at which the facility bought it, or to a higher or lower value than cost.

• The debt that is not sold by banks might maintain its present contractual status; it might be subordinated to the debt that the debtor countries will now incur to the facility; or it might be marked down by the debtors to an extent that would force the banks to sell all their debt to the facility.

A crucial question is how the facility would be financed. Here, also, there are differences among the various proposals, and the possibilities will be discussed shortly.

---

ness Act of 1988, passed by both houses of the U.S. Congress, included a provision for the Secretary of the Treasury to "study the feasibility and advisability" of establishing an "International Debt Management Authority."

II. A Simple Scheme

Let us suppose that the scheme applies to any one debtor country. The facility goes into the market and offers to buy given amounts of debt. In the detailed example spelled out below, it will be assumed that the facility offers to buy half the stock of debt. Of course debt is not homogeneous, so that various decisions would have to be made on which debt to buy. It is quite likely that the facility would have to pay more than the initial market price, but one can assume that the facility would buy debt at a discount from the contractual value. The important question of what would determine the price, and in which direction it would move, will be taken up later.

The facility pays for the purchased debt with new bonds guaranteed by its owners. The banks are thus able to dispose of debt with the original contractual value that is subject to default risk in exchange for debt of a lower contractual value that is subject to much lower, possibly zero, default risk. One's first thought is that those that sell could not be worse off as a result. After all, selling is voluntary; there is no compulsion in this scheme. This conclusion is not necessarily true, and will have to be looked at again in Section IV.

The facility would then mark down the contractual value of the debtor country's debt that it has acquired. It marks the debt down to the cost price to it—that is, the contractual value of the new bonds it has issued to the banks. No funds are thus required from the owners of the facility—that is, the governments that have underwritten the facility. But, of course, the facility's new assets are somewhat risky and, because of the guarantees on the bonds it has issued, this risk has been taken over by the facility's owners. Given this risk, there will be a potential need for funds from the owners, who may actually wish to finance contingency reserves specifically to allow for the risk. A major, and possibly overwhelming, obstacle to the establishment of a facility is the reluctance of governments to assume such risks. A question to be discussed below is whether this risk can be reduced or eliminated.

The debtor country apparently benefits because the contractual value of its debt has been reduced. But the gain to it will not necessarily be as great as it might seem at first. One possible view is that the market's perception of default risk, which led to the initial discount, was justified in the sense that this represented the true probability of default. In other words, there was a good chance in any case that the country would not repay the full contractual value of its debt. Reducing the contractual value as a result of the operation of the facility would not necessarily reduce actual payments (or the probability of actual payments expected to be made) to the same extent. Indeed, one might ask whether there is likely to be any gain to the debtor country at all.

III. How Debtor and Banks May Gain

This matter of the possible gain to the debtor, and also to the banks, can be analyzed more precisely if the concept of the debtor's "capacity to pay" is introduced. This is defined as the ability to make resource transfers abroad to cover interest payments and repayment of principal. It depends on the country's output over a period of time, on its minimum consumption level, and on its ability to transform output into tradables (exports and import-competing products) required to generate the transfer. It also depends on the terms of trade.

It will be supposed at this stage that capacity to pay can vary as the result of various exogenous, uncertain events—such as terms of trade developments—but does not vary because of changes in the policies of the debtor country itself, which are simply taken as given. This is the assumption of "exogeneity." It will also be assumed for the moment that expectations about capacity to pay are the same among market participants, debtor countries, and the decision makers of the facility. This is the assumption of "uniformity of expectations." These two simplifying assumptions are important for the analysis of gains and losses from the establishment of a facility and therefore will be reconsidered in Section VII.

There are two steps in the analysis. First I show why the banks might gain at the expense of the facility, and then I show why the debtor might gain. The second effect depends crucially on uncertainty.

Gain to the Banks

To begin with, there is the "market price effect."[2] It can be shown that the banks will gain at the expense of the facility, provided that the debt that they retain is not subordinated to the marked-down debt the facility now holds. The reason is that the market price of the debt will rise (the discount will fall). The argument is quite simple when there is complete certainty about the capacity to pay (or repay).

Let us suppose that the contractual debt is US$1,000 and the capacity

---

[2] This discussion builds on Michael Dooley's paper "Buy-Backs and Market Valuation of External Debt" in this volume.

to pay is $600. Assume at this stage that the latter is fixed. Hence the debtor country will neither gain nor lose; whatever happens, it pays $600. This is thought of as a single sum paid in a single future period, the sum consisting of principal and interest combined. Given the initial contractual debt, default or debt relief is then inevitable. The "default ratio" would be 40 percent.

The facility then offers to buy a proportion of the $1,000 in contractual debt from the banks at a discounted price. Here it will be assumed that it buys half the debt ($500) and that the price it pays is 80 cents to the dollar. Hence the facility pays $400 and marks the debt it has acquired down to its cost price. The contractual value of the total debt owed by the debtor country is thus reduced to $900. With the same capacity to pay as before, the default ratio becomes 33.3 percent. The facility will finally get 66.7 percent repayment of the debt it holds, thus making a loss of $133. The banks will get $333 for the debt they have retained (with a contractual value of $500), and when this is combined with the $400 they received from the facility they end up with $733, which is an improvement of $133 on what they would have received if the facility had not bought and marked down some of the debt. The discount on debt held by the banks has fallen from 40 percent to 33.3 percent.

In this example the facility's purchase price is 80 cents but the market price has risen only from 60 cents to 67 cents. The purchase price could therefore be reduced, leading to a bigger decline in the contractual value and, hence, to a further rise in the market price. The equilibrium price (where purchase and market prices are equal) would actually be 70½ cents when the facility buys half the debt. If it bought a greater proportion, the price would be higher. These results can be derived as follows:

$$C_2 = C_1(1 - q) + C_1 qp \tag{1}$$

$$p = R/C_2, \tag{2}$$

where
    C_1 = initial contractual value
    C_2 = contractual value after debt relief
    q = proportion of debt bought by facility
    R = capacity to pay
    p = purchase price (equal to market price after purchase) as proportion of initial contractual price.

From equations (1) and (2),

$$R/C_1 = (1-q)p + qp^2. \tag{3}$$

From equation (3),

$$p = \frac{-(1-q) + \sqrt{(1-q)^2 + 4qR/C_1}}{2q} .$$

There has been a pure transfer from the facility to the banks. All this will be reflected in the market price rising (discount falling) when the facility enters the market. It has to pay a higher price than the initial price to induce the banks to sell any debt to it. The banks will foresee that debt not sold would rise in value when some marking down takes place, and hence they will only sell at a sufficiently higher price. The price would not necessarily rise to its equilibrium value immediately, and could also overshoot, since banks and others in the market would not be able to predict this equilibrium in advance. The account given here, with its impression of precision, merely indicates likely tendencies.

The essential point can be restated as follows. When the contractual value of the total debt is reduced while total capacity to pay stays constant, each dollar's worth of contractual debt must be worth more in the market than before, provided that all dollars of contractual debt would be treated equally if there were some default.

Gain to the Debtor

Uncertainty about capacity to pay and the "ceiling effect" can now be introduced.[3] The mean expected repayment might be $600, but it could also be greater, up to a ceiling of complete repayment of $1,000, and it could be less, with a floor of zero. There is thus both upside and downside risk, and this will be taken into account in the market price. If the contractual value of the debt is reduced, say, to $900, the ceiling will be lowered to $900. If the terms of trade, for example, turn out to be quite favorable, so that capacity to pay is actually $950, the actual payment will be $50 less than if the contractual value had stayed at its initial level. Thus the debtor gains at the expense of creditors from a markdown of the contractual value because the downside risk remains as before, whereas the offsetting upside risk (or gain) becomes less.[4]

[3] In several papers Paul Krugman has discussed the uncertainty aspects; see especially Krugman (1985).
[4] The example that has been used is quite simplified, although sufficient to make the main points. As noted earlier, repayment is thought of as a single sum ($600, when there is certainty) paid in a single future period, the sum consisting of principal and interest combined. The analysis could be elaborated to allow for a stream of interest and amortization payments over time, in which case the sum should be thought of as the present value. There is then scope for changes in the time profile of payments. In that case a distinction between interest and principal

IV. Subordination: Can a Gain to the Banks Be Avoided?

An interesting question is whether a gain to the banks at the expense of the facility—that is, a "bank bail-out"—can be avoided. The key here is subordination of the debt retained by the banks relative to the debt now owned by the facility.

When one talks about a gain to the banks, one means a gain relative to the initial situation when there was already a discount in the market. Earlier, of course, the banks incurred a loss once the probability of some default or forced debt relief was perceived by them or the market. Presumably, as long as the banks get less than $1,000 they will have incurred some loss as normally defined, even though the margin above the London interbank offered rate (LIBOR) they charged originally must have taken into account the possibility of some default or of heavy pressure to provide some relief.

Suppose that, again, the facility buys half the debt and marks it down to cost. It buys it at 80 cents per dollar and so pays $400, total contractual debt being thus marked down to $900 as before. One now proceeds in two stages. First, let us assume that there is no doubt at all that the capacity to pay will be at least $400.

If it could be firmly established that, whatever is the capacity-to-pay outcome above $400, the debt held by the facility would always be paid first—that is, would be "senior" debt—then the facility would not make a loss, and its owners would run no risk. But the banks would lose potentially, and the debtors gain, because the "ceiling payment" has been reduced. Previously the maximum payment the banks could have received was $1,000, whereas now it is $500 for the debt they have retained plus the $400 they have already received from the facility. If capacity to pay turned out to be $950, previously the banks would have received $950, but now they can only receive $900. In contrast, the minimum they can receive remains $400.

Subordinating debt retained by the banks to facility-held debt thus ensures that the facility neither loses nor gains, taking on no risk, while the debtor countries gain potentially at the expense of the banks because

---

would have to be made. Debt relief may have an immediate effect in reducing interest payments, even though, if capacity to pay in total is really fixed, interest or amortization payments will increase later. Changes in the time profile of either interest or amortization payments that do not alter the present value leave the analysis presented above unchanged. The market discount is caused not only by the probability of default or forced debt relief as usually understood but also by the probability of forced rescheduling, pressures to participate in new money packages, and so on. These are all ways of changing the time profile and reducing the present value of repayments.

of the ceiling effect. The expected loss to the banks would be reflected in a decline in the market price.[5]

If it were desired for some of the loss to the banks to be shared with the facility, the latter could mark down the debt by more than the discounted purchase price, hence making a clear loss now. Alternatively, only part of its debt might be given seniority. Here there is scope for many variations in the details of such a scheme, and these may have significant effects on the gains or losses for the banks and the facility. The key point is that the banks and the facility combined must make a potential loss—that is, forgoing the benefits of a very favorable capacity-to-pay outcome. The risk of an unfavorable outcome has not been eliminated, but the possibility of a very favorable return (above $900) has.

The second stage of the analysis is to assume that capacity to pay could be less than $400. In that case there would be some possibility that even debt given senior status would not be fully repaid. Hence risk for the facility would not be completely eliminated. The conclusion that subordination of debt retained by the banks to the debt owned by the facility would eliminate all risk for the facility hinges completely on the assumption that some minimum total payment—equal to the value of the debt that the facility has bought ($400 in the example)—is utterly assured. But the larger the proportion of the initial total debt that the facility takes over and marks down, the less likely it is that all risk for the facility would be eliminated by giving the debt it holds senior status. If the facility had bought up all the debt, no one but the facility could assume the risk.

There can never be utter certainty about prospective capacity to pay, so that some risk for the facility is inherent in the scheme. This implicit risk is particularly relevant for proposals that would have the facility take over a large part of the foreign debt of a country. The inevitable risk helps to explain the reluctance of governments of creditor countries to support proposals for such a facility.

V. Reduction of Uncertainty

Another possibility, worth exploring carefully because it is implicit in some proposals, can now be considered. The suggestion is that the Fund or World Bank may be able to increase or ensure certainty of payment

---

[5] An issue that is clearly important for the various proposals is whether it would be legally possible for existing debt that is retained by the banks to be subordinated to that acquired by the facility. Of course there would be no difficulty in such subordination if it were done with the agreement of the banks.

at the new, marked-down value of the debt. The assumption maintained so far—that the actual repayment outcome depends only on exogenously determined capacity to pay, subject to the "ceiling" imposed by the contractual value—is relaxed. Repayment can also depend on policies.

Suppose that initially the mean expected capacity to pay was $600, with a probability of creditors getting more or less. If the total debt were marked down to $600, there would then be a $600 ceiling to the repayment. In addition, suppose that the Fund or World Bank were able to ensure that $600 also became the minimum repayment. This assurance might have been obtained with the aid of conditionality. Given this arrangement, there is no longer a necessary loss to the banks and the facility combined from the imposition of a reduced ceiling because that ceiling is associated with the imposition of a raised floor. Upside and downside risk have both been eliminated. Certainty has been obtained—or at least uncertainty has been reduced.

Certainty represents a net gain for the banks and the facility combined, given that they are risk averse. With subordination, the whole of this gain from certainty would go to the banks in the first case just discussed, in which a minimum repayment sufficient to cover the debt held by the facility was in any case ensured. But in the more general case, in which the facility has carried some of the risk previously (whether because no minimum was ensured or because there was no subordination), the gain would go partially to the facility.

It is often implied in debt relief proposals that the marked-down value of debt would have no more risk attached to it (or very little risk) because it would be close to the expected capacity to pay. It is doubtful whether this assumption is realistic. The implication is that willingness to repay—and the resolve to make the necessary adjustments—is not exogenous but rather can be made more "certain" in return for debt relief. Perhaps a commitment that would successfully reduce perceived default risk could be obtained from the debtor country in some way or other. Debtor governments could make certain policy commitments. No doubt the Fund's conditionality procedures can play a role here. Conditionality can conceivably reduce uncertainty and default risk, although it can surely not eliminate them.

A reduction in uncertainty of repayment without necessarily any net change in the mean expected repayment is clearly a gain to the banks and the facility. But it is not necessarily a gain for the system as a whole. If uncertainty in the capacity to pay—for example, uncertainty in terms of trade movements—could be reduced, that would be a net gain. But if uncertainty in capacity to pay continues while repayment becomes more certain owing to conditionality, there has simply been a transfer in the burden of uncertainty toward the debtor country. For example, if the terms of trade turned out to be particularly adverse, the country would have to bear the whole burden instead of sharing it with the banks or the facility through some degree of default or debt relief.

This approach assumes that the mean expected capacity or willingness to pay stays unchanged but that the floor is raised and the ceiling lowered. There are also two other possibilities.

The first is rather similar to the one just discussed. Conditionality may raise the mean without raising the floor: it may raise expected capacity to pay through bringing about an improvement in policies. Although the banks lose through the ceiling effect, they may then nevertheless gain.

The other, quite contrary possibility is that the probability of repayment is actually reduced when the facility takes over debt. As just noted, it is usually argued that, through associating conditionality with the establishment of a facility, the certainty of repayment can be improved. But a contrary view is that a facility that is subject to political pressure and that has no strong penalties available to it may be a less effective debt collector than private banks, which can threaten the withdrawal of trade credit as a potential penalty.

VI. Interests of the Debtor Countries and Moral Hazard

There are several ways in which the debtor country might gain from the arrangement. Some have already been referred to, but they will now be brought together.

Reducing the Default Ratio

A gain that seems obvious at first sight but turns out to be primarily cosmetic is the reduction in the default ratio. The default ratio, D, equals $1 - R/C$, where R is the actual debt repayment made—that is, the resource transfer—and C is the contractual value of the debt. D is reduced when the contractual value is marked down, even though the actual payment (which has been assumed to be exogenous so far) does not change.

Does it really matter if this default ratio falls, possibly to zero, when the resource transfer remains unchanged? One might say that the effect is purely cosmetic. If an emperor has few clothes, is it really necessary to proclaim the fact? Against this it can be argued convincingly that debt relief voluntarily provided by the creditors is always better than default.

There would clearly be a preference on the part of the debtor country for debt relief over default if penalties were associated with default.

Even in the absence of current penalties, reputation—and hence future creditworthiness—may be influenced by whether there has been formal default rather than debt relief. Note that it has been assumed here that default depends purely on exogenous capacity to pay; hence penalties related to the default ratio would seem less likely or reasonable. Because capacity to pay completely determines actual repayments, there would be no point in the creditors imposing penalties.

Lowering the Ceiling

The debtor country gains owing to the "ceiling effect." As has been pointed out, if capacity to pay turns out to be particularly favorable— above the new contractual value—the gain would go to the debtor rather than to the creditors because the ceiling for potential repayments has been lowered. This benefit to the debtor might disappear (and could even turn into a loss) if conditionality manages also to raise the floor for the repayment, shifting more of the risk toward the debtor country.[6]

Marking Debt Down Below Cost

The facility might mark the debt down by more than the cost price to it—possibly by much more—and the contractual value might then fall below the capacity to pay, even when the capacity to pay turns out to be quite low. At the limit, the debt might be marked down to zero. This would represent a straightforward transfer from the owners of the facility to the debtor countries—a case of foreign assistance. It is equivalent to the owner countries donating funds to the debtor country to buy back its debt.

Asymmetric Expectations

A fourth kind of gain has not been referred to so far but is implicit in much advocacy of debt relief and could be important. The markets, specifically the banks, may be pessimistic and believe that there is some

[6] There may be a touch of perversity in the ceiling effect brought about by debt relief. Whenever capacity to pay improves exogenously—owing, for example, to a terms of trade improvement—some of the gains inevitably go to the debtor even before debt relief (that is, when the ceiling is high). Similarly, some of the losses from a deterioration would be borne by the debtor, and not wholly by the creditors. In that case, lowering the ceiling as a result of debt relief increases the gains for the debtor when events, such as the terms of trade, turn out well but does not help when events turn out badly.

probability of default. Hence there is a market discount on the debt. But
the government of the debtor country may have no intention of defaulting. There are "asymmetric expectations." Capacity to pay, after all, is
not something clear-cut. The government foresees difficulties and adjustment problems and seeks debt relief but—possibly for fear of penalties—does not intend ever to default, even though it has not succeeded
in convincing the market of this. The issue of asymmetric expectations
will be discussed further below. Here it can be noted that, if the government of the debtor country has no intention at all of defaulting, the
whole of the fall in the contractual value of the debt brought about by
debt relief through the operation of the facility or in some other way
would represent a clear-cut gain to the debtor country in reduced prospective resource transfers.[7]

The creditors, however, having different expectations, do not perceive
this reduction in the contractual value—or all of it—as a loss to them.
They may expect to lose through the ceiling effect but also see some
virtue in an explicit recognition of what they believe to be realities—that
the country has limited capacity or willingness to pay, that the emperor
has fewer clothes than the initial contract specified.

Moral Hazard

For three of the four reasons given here (other than the third, marking
debt down below cost), the debtor country would want the price at which
the facility buys debt from the banks to be as low as possible. The lower
the price, the greater is the decline in the contractual value; hence, the
lower the default ratio, the lower is the ceiling applying when events turn
out favorably, and the lower are actual repayments if default is never
intended.

If this purchase price is equal to or closely related to the market price,
the debtor country therefore has an incentive to get the market price
down. This can be done by making "default noises"—just a hint here,
a threat there—and the banks will be glad to sell at a low price, in the

---

[7] There is an important qualification to this argument. If the debtor country's
government takes the long view, it will realize that debt relief through the facility
or otherwise—even though entirely voluntary on the part of the creditors and in
no way associated with actual default—could still have an adverse effect on its
country's future creditworthiness. After all, when investors look back they will
see that a $1,000 loan finally turned out to be worth less, for whatever reason.
The government will never have the opportunity to show that it would have paid
the full initial contractual value.

extreme case at any price above zero. This is the familiar "moral hazard" problem.

A possible solution from the point of view of creditors seems to be for the facility's purchase price not to be determined by the market price, or at least by the market price ruling once the likelihood of such a facility being established has become serious. Market prices at some earlier "cut-off" date might be taken. If the banks are to sell voluntarily, the purchase price will have to be no lower than the current market price. But it could be higher.

The problem is to fix a price that does not give a gain, or an undue gain, to the banks; otherwise there would be a bail-out. But what is a gain? Given the expectations created by their anticipation of the debtor country's capacity to pay, combined with the default noises made by the debtor government or others in that country, a sale of the debt to the facility at a very low price may still seem to be a gain to the banks. This is true even though the price is likely to represent a loss relative to the expectations at the time the loans were originally made. Presumably the facility should aim to avoid either gain or loss to the banks relative to the situation at some "pre-discussion-of-facility" date—that is, an appropriately early cut-off date.

Most proposals for a facility do not pursue in detail the critical question of how the price at which debt is to be purchased is to be determined, given that there is a moral hazard problem and that there must presumably be a separate price (discount) for each country. It is at this point that the greatest practical problems arise. Sometimes elaborate calculations, which are essentially estimates of capacity to pay, are proposed, but the political difficulties such estimates would involve cannot be ignored. Given the thinness of existing markets, actual market prices, whether current or at some earlier cut-off date, may not be adequate guides.

VII. Two Assumptions Reconsidered

At the beginning of this paper two crucial assumptions were made: that the debtor's capacity to pay was exogenously determined—for example, by the terms of trade—and that expectations about the capacity to pay were the same among all the relevant parties. Given these assumptions, a fairly straightforward analysis followed that showed that a facility would yield a gain to the banks because of the market price effect and a gain to the debtor because of the ceiling effect. These gains would be at the expense of the facility, which would be taking over a risk. It was further assumed that debt owed to the facility would not be given seniority over debt retained by the banks. If the latter were subordinated, a gain to the banks and loss to the facility might be avoided.

Subsequently, the two initial assumptions have been removed in particular ways. In Section V, the possibility was explored that the facility (or the World Bank or Fund acting on its behalf) could actually affect the debtor's policies so that capacity to pay would be improved to ensure certainty of repayment of the marked-down value of the debt. In other words, capacity to pay might no longer be exogenous. In Section VI, one case of asymmetric expectations was noted. The debtor government may have no intention of defaulting, but the market may not be convinced of this. In addition, moral hazard was introduced. Prospective repayment may depend not only on *capacity* to pay but also on *willingness* to pay (for given capacity), and threats of reduced willingness would affect the market price.

These complications to the initial approach are really special cases, but there are further cases that analysts of these issues sometimes have in mind. A more systematic approach is therefore needed.

First of all, the concept of expected capacity to pay determined by exogenous factors could be redefined as "expected total repayment" determined both by expected capacity to pay and by expected willingness to pay.[8] Both would be influenced, or even determined, by policies. When the original concept of capacity to pay is broadened in this way, it becomes more plausible. If the redefined concept is to apply to the initial analysis in this paper, it has to be assumed that expected policies are exogenous in the sense of not being expected to change as a result of the establishment of the facility or its activities.

The next step is to allow for endogenous policies affecting capacity and willingness to pay. The endogeneity of policies is central to many debt-strategy proposals. As noted in Section V, the basic idea is that the benefit to the debtor from debt relief provided through the intermediation of the facility would be reciprocated by improvements in the debtor's policies, and that some kind of assurance about these policies can be obtained, perhaps with the help of conditionality. In this way more certainty of repayment can be ensured.

With regard to endogenous willingness to pay, two points are usually made. The first, as noted above, is the moral hazard problem: threats of reduced willingness to pay can get the market price down. A second idea not mentioned so far is that, when the contractual value of the debt is partially forgiven so that it is brought down to a more realistic level, the

---

[8] All this should be thought of in present-value terms. See footnote 4 in Section III.

debtor government may have a greater willingness to repay the remainder. If the contractual debt was $1,000 and capacity to pay was $600, some default would be inevitable. It has then been argued that a large default is as bad—and incurs similar penalties—as a more modest default, so that willingness to pay in that case might fall to zero. But if the contractual debt were marked down to $600, there would be a good chance that default could be avoided, and willingness to pay might become 100 percent.

As regards asymmetric expectations about the capacity and willingness to pay, there are several possibilities worth noting. First, as already mentioned, the debtor may not intend, and hence not expect, to default while the market contrarily believes that there is a positive probability of default, thus explaining the market discount. In that case the debtor government will believe it would gain from any debt relief, whereas the creditors—selling their debt voluntarily on the market (and assuming no subordination)—will not expect to lose. If the facility paid the banks a price above the initial market price—still with a discount—the banks may believe that they would actually gain, even though, if the debtor government's expectations were correct, the banks would actually have lost by selling.

A scheme could conceivably be worked out whereby the facility pays, for example, $400 for debt with a contractual value of $500 and marks that debt down to only $450, with the margin of $50 adequately compensating the facility for the risk it incurs so that it neither gains nor loses. In this case the creditors believe that they gain through the market price effect, the debtor government believes that it gains because there is some reduction in the contractual price, and the facility neither gains nor loses.

This scheme leads into the second possibility, whereby the facility actually makes a profit or at least is expected to do so by its owners or managers. The market may have an unduly pessimistic view of the debtor's prospects, and hence there may be a large market discount. But the facility only marks the debt down by a little, so that the contractual value of the marked-down debt it holds stays well above the cost price and there is a high degree of certainty that there will be low or zero default. All this depends on confidence in the ability to get the debtor's policies improved sufficiently to disprove the market's pessimistic expectations.

Finally, it has been argued in the main analysis here that the market price effect represents a benefit for the banks, at least relative to the situation after the debt crisis and the discount developed. But there may be some holders of debt who do not sell to the facility because—contrary to the expectations of marginal holders—they do not believe that the probability of default is high at all. They may value the debt they hold at the contractual value, not near the market price. They may have made a more optimistic assessment of capacity or willingness to pay. If they feel assured that there will be full repayment in any case, it would make no difference to them if the total contractual claims are reduced through the operation of the facility. But if they really believed that the debt is worth more than its market price, the question then arises why they did not buy up the debt held by others and so bring the price up to their optimistic expectations. The argument assumes that the market is, in some sense, imperfect.

VIII. Would New Investment Increase as a Result of the Facility?

There are three parts to the answer to this question. If the debt of the facility is given senior rights the answer is not clear; it is possible that new investment would actually be discouraged.

First, the analysis has shown that for various reasons there may be an actual reduction in resource transfer from the debtor country as a result of the facility—that is, the debtor country may actually gain something. Indeed, in the view of some this is the primary objective of the exercise. An expectation of such a gain would lead also to an expectation of lower taxation than otherwise—including taxation of profits and capital—and this may well encourage new investment.

Second, if the debt held by the facility does not acquire senior rights, so that the discount in the market falls as described earlier, there should indeed be a tendency for investment inflows to resume or to increase. The facility will have assumed some of the burden of potential default on the existing debt, and new investors will have a lesser burden to bear than before.

Finally, the matter is not so simple if the existing debt is subordinated to the facility's debt. The question then is whether new debt incurred in the market would also be subordinated, or whether it would acquire seniority over the facility's debt. The reasonable assumption is that the facility would enjoy complete seniority. As noted above, in the absence of increased certainty, subordination would actually reduce the market price (raise the discount) owing to the "ceiling effect"; hence new investment would be further discouraged. If all old debt had been sold to the facility, in effect new debt would then be subordinated to old debt completely.

IX. Is There Really Need for an International Facility?

A central question remains. One might grant the desirability of a reduction in the contractual value of the debt but still wonder why an intermediary in the form of a facility along the lines proposed would be needed.

Although banks can sell the developing countries' debts in the market at a discount, bank managements may not feel free to grant outright relief in the form of reduction of the contractual value, possibly because of legal obstacles. In practice, however, relief in the form of long-term debt rescheduling and various debt transformations can be and has been granted—although such arrangements are different from reducing contractual value. One could also argue that there is no incentive for any private holder to grant relief because of the ceiling effect. There is always the possibility that the full contractual value will be repaid, so why forgo this possibility? Incentive for relief may, however, be created by the threat of more severe default.

One can think of three arguments in favor of the establishment of a facility from the points of view of the banks and the debtor countries involved.

A Channel for Resource Transfer

The most obvious argument from the point of view of both parties is that the facility could act as a channel for the transfer of current resources (that is, aid) from the countries that underwrite it, or for the possible transfer of future resources if some default risk is perceived. This, of course, is also an argument *against* a facility from the point of view of its potential owners if they are not interested in providing aid either in general or specifically to the debtor countries. This point will be taken up again below.

If foreign aid to the debtor countries is indeed intended, one alternative could be for the parties to negotiate debt relief contracts bilaterally and then for some or all of the industrial countries to guarantee the marked-down debts in part or in full. This arrangement would give particular industrial countries an opportunity to help those debtors that are of special interest to them. The familiar difficulty here is that the banks are not a single "party," as the problems of organizing concerted lending have shown.

For the debtor countries the other alternative is to receive direct bilateral aid. The aid could be used by the debtor country to buy back some of its own debt. Again, there would be an opportunity for industrial countries to discriminate in favor of particular debtor countries. But the fundamental question is highlighted in that case: whether funds received in aid are best spent in buying back debt. They could perhaps be better used to finance extra investment.

A More Orderly Process

It could be argued that, if world economic conditions turned adverse, the alternative to the operation of such a facility would be a decentralized process of debt restructuring with relief. In that situation numerous bilateral arrangements—with the banks represented by committees that have difficulty in getting support from sufficient banks—could get rather disorderly. The facility could be an intermediary that would bring more orderliness to the process. An element of automaticity and consistency across countries and kinds of debt in the choice of purchase prices, the extent of relief, and so on, could smooth the restructuring and debt relief process. The facility might thus avoid default crises that could lead to political difficulties and disruption of trade flows.

Greater Realism and Certainty

A key feature of such proposals is that very uncertain obligations, with contractual values well above what is expected to be paid on a probability basis, would be replaced by more realistically valued debt that (in the view of its proponents) would be more certain to be repaid and, ideally, would be free of serious default risk.

It might be argued that the increase in certainty (if it could be obtained) is in general desirable even though it does, to an extent at least, shift the burden of exogenous uncertainty (for example, in the terms of trade) back toward the debtor countries. This is possibly a gain because some uncertainty is believed to be endogenous—a result of the lack of firm political will by debtor governments rather than capacity-to-pay uncertainty. Then there is a role for conditionality and, hence, for the Fund or the World Bank. This does not necessarily mean that the two institutions, or their owners, should, through the facility, take on the remaining risks.

One negative point is also important. It refers not to the actual operation of a facility but to the effects of expectations that it might come into operation. It concerns a moral hazard problem. If the banks and the debtor countries believe that there is some chance that an institution such as the facility might be established to take over some of the risks, they will have less incentive to arrive at debt relief agreements directly or without disruption. The threat of disruption, particularly of trade flows, could be an inducement leading the international community to establish such a facility. But if such an institution were never seen as being even a possibility, the parties directly involved would have an incentive to arrive at agreements. They would try to avoid prolonged uncertainty and disruption because it is damaging to them all.

X. Is Any Compulsion Involved?

To what extent would such a scheme be voluntary? I first consider the debtor country and then the creditors.

On the Debtor

On the one hand, if conditionality were not involved, a debtor country would have nothing to lose in the short run from debt relief through the medium of the facility. But in the long run it might lose some credit-worthiness, since future creditors may well think that what has happened once can happen again. Therefore a debtor government, confident that it will be able to repay the full contractual value of its debt and wanting to take a long view, may benefit from staying out of the scheme. This is true even though there may be a market discount on its debt that suggests that, so far, the debtor country has not been able to convey its confidence to the market.

On the other hand, if conditionality were part of the scheme, then each debtor country could decide whether it preferred to accept the burdens of conditionality and get debt relief through the facility, or whether it preferred to stay out. There would not need to be any compulsion.

On the Creditor

Each bank could be free to sell or to keep as much as it liked of the debt it holds at present. Sales of debt need not be compulsory. As described here, the facility would operate in the market, even though this is not a feature of all proposals. But this freedom of the banks to sell or not to sell could be somewhat illusory. The willingness to sell will be influenced by the debtors' actions. A decision by the debtor government to subordinate debt that is not sold would lower the market price—as would threats of, or actual, default. Furthermore, changes in bank regulations in creditor countries that reduced the attractiveness to banks of holding on to debt could also increase the willingness to sell to the facility.

XI. Concluding Remarks

From the viewpoint, first, of a debtor country, the availability of an international debt facility cannot be harmful to it because it cannot be compelled to participate and, if use of the facility is associated with conditionality, as is usually proposed, it may choose not to. But, for the reasons given in Section VI, a debtor country is quite likely to gain from participation.

From the viewpoint of creditors, the banks would gain if sales of debt to the facility were truly voluntary, if there were no subordination of debt that is not sold to the facility, and if the moral hazard problems discussed in Section VI were overcome. Otherwise the banks could lose. It has been noted that the moral hazard problem might be overcome by determining purchase prices of debt on some objective basis or on the basis of market prices at an early "cut-off" point. But this can present some of the most difficult practical problems involved with the establishment of a debt facility.

Finally, and most crucial, there are the interests of the potential owners or underwriters of the facility to consider. If the facility would purchase a significant part of the commercial debt of all the developing countries that currently have problems—as is suggested in many of the proposals—a large transfer of risk internationally from private banks to the underwriting governments or multilateral institutions would take place. The extent of the transfers would depend on the detailed arrangements that have been discussed here. Of course a facility could operate on a small scale, but then it would only make a small impact on the world debt situation.

The potential owners may see some benefit in increasing certainty (which might be brought about by the debt relief process combined with conditionality) and in avoiding a disorderly process of debt restructuring, default, and so on (as discussed in Section IX). Furthermore, the owners may wish to provide aid to particular debtors or assistance to particular banks, although a generalized facility is not the best way of doing this. But it is inevitable that, by underwriting the obligations that the facility issues, the owner governments would assume some risk even when the debt not sold to the facility is subordinated to that held by the facility, and even more so without subordination.

REFERENCES

Feldstein, Martin, and others, "Restoring Growth in the Debt-Laden Third World: A Task Force Report to the Trilateral Commission," Triangle Papers, Report 33 (New York: The Trilateral Commission, April 1987).

Krugman, Paul R., "International Debt Strategies in an Uncertain World," in *International Debt and the Developing Countries,* ed. by Gordon Smith and John Cuddington (Washington: World Bank, 1985), pp. 79–100.

Sachs, Jeffrey, and Harry Huizinga, "U.S. Commercial Banks and the Developing-Country Crisis," *Brookings Papers on Economic Activity: 2* (1987), The Brookings Institution (Washington), pp. 555–601.

A Delicate Equilibrium: Debt Relief and Default Penalties in an International Context

GUILLERMO A. CALVO*

Debt relief and penalties are discussed in connection with sovereign-country loans. The paper focuses on conditions for the existence of penalties that are too low for ensuring Pareto efficiency and shows the possible time inconsistency of optimal debt contracts. A methodology for ascertaining debt relief implicit in international loans is outlined.

T‍HIS PAPER DISCUSSES two issues central to debt contracts: default penalties and debt relief. Both topics have received considerable attention in the economics literature, although the terminology used in discussing them varies from paper to paper.

Take, for example, the concept of debt relief. In standard general equilibrium models with complete markets, individuals and firms are assumed to engage in different types of trade contracts. Contracts involving trading present goods, say, for future goods correspond to contracts in which the buyer of present goods borrows from the seller and, in exchange, promises to deliver future goods. If uncertainty exists, these contracts are made contingent on the "state of nature," such that repayment becomes a function of the outcome of the associated random process. Thus, conceivably, full repayment would occur if things turn out to be "good" for the borrower, but a "cut" would be granted if the

* Mr. Calvo is a Senior Advisor in the Research Department and is on leave from the University of Pennsylvania, where he is Professor of Economics and Co-Director of the International Economics Research Center. He holds a Ph.D. from Yale University.

This paper benefited from many useful comments on a previous version. The author would like to thank, without implications, Eduardo Borensztein, Max Corden, Michael Dooley, Sara Guerschanik-Calvo, and Ken Rogoff.

172

borrower is hit by a "bad" shock. Thus, general equilibrium theory—the bread-and-butter of modern economics—contemplates and explains the possibility of a debt relief.

The above standard theory of debt relief assumes that both borrower and lender will always honor the debt contract. To honor the contract implies that the borrower will repay the contracted amount even when it may be to his advantage to pay less, and, conversely, it also means that the lender will not claim that the borrower owes him more than what is specified in the contract even when the terms of the latter are not fully specified (i.e., even when portions of the contract are implicit). These assumptions are, of course, highly unrealistic, particularly when debt contracts involve sovereign countries whose decision to repay may be partly determined, for example, by a democratic process in which considerations having to do with the welfare of the state may override moral principles.[1]

Economic theory has not been slow to respond to the challenge. As a matter of fact, the economics of "moral hazard"—as this branch of the literature is generically called—date back at least to the pioneering work of Kenneth Arrow (1968).[2] This approach, however, came to full bloom only in the 1970s (see, for example, the collection of papers in Diamond and Rothschild (1978)) and was formally introduced in the field of international finance by Eaton and Gersovitz (see the useful survey by Eaton, Gersovitz, and Stiglitz (1986)).[3]

In a moral-hazard model it is typically assumed that the debtor will comply with the (explicit or implicit) letter of the contract if, and only if, the costs associated with paying less exceed the associated benefits. These costs are usually assumed to be penalties that creditors can impose on debtors. Thus, for example, in case of default, creditors could block the country from receiving trade credit and, hence, cause it to lose some of its "gains from trade" (see Aizenman (this volume), and Borensztein and Ghosh (1989)). Naturally, the larger the penalty, the less likely it is for the borrower to default. Conceivably, too, the penalty could be so large that the borrower would always find it to his advantage to comply with the contract. In that case, therefore, the outcome of debt contracts

---

[1] In some cases moral principles are themselves quite blurry, as, for example, when the debt is originally contracted by a de facto government rejected by the mass of citizens.

[2] The term "moral hazard" has apparently been taken from insurance literature. It refers to situations in which one of the parties could misrepresent the facts.

[3] This type of research appeared in working-paper form even before we heard the first squeaks about the current "debt crisis."

would coincide with that of "naive" general equilibrium theory in which moral hazard problems are assumed away.

This last observation gives us an important insight into the new theory of lending with default risk and also reveals one of its weaknesses (or, more appropriately, one piece of "unfinished business"). It turns out to be to the advantage of both borrowers and lenders to be able to write contracts that are free from moral hazard problems. The penalty must be large, but that has no negative welfare effects, because the penalty is paid only if the country decides to default. Hence, since a big penalty implies no default, the penalty is never paid. In practice, however, as penalties do not appear to be very big and default is not unheard of (see Kaletsky (1985), Eichengreen and Portes (1986)), it looks as if the theory has to be extended to explain why penalties are not effective enough to achieve moral-hazard-free equilibria.

The following section of the paper takes a closer look at the theory of penalties. There and in the subsequent sections we take the "optimal contracts" approach, which amounts to assuming inter alia that debt contracts are Pareto Optimal, that is, they cannot be modified without reducing the welfare of at least one of the parties to the loan contract.[4] We conduct our discussion in terms of a two-period framework, in which the loan is granted in the first period and repaid in the second. Two independent explanations for the existence of relatively small penalties are presented there. The first is that if the penalty has to be imposed after the borrower defaults, the lender may have no incentive to impose it. This would be so, for example, if carrying out the penalty is costly to the lender, as when the lender is also hurt by a cut in trade credits. Under these circumstances, the lender has no hope of recovering what is owed to him and would get only the cost of imposing the penalty. Consequently, costly penalties are not likely to be carried out, which puts a natural upper bound on observed penalties (this argument is in line with the points made in Kaletsky (1985)).

Penalties could, however, be part of the lending process. To bring this point home, we examine the case in which loans are closely monitored and a penalty is automatically incurred if the country's loan application (or rescheduling) is turned down. Here, again, large penalties would be the optimal solution if monitoring is perfect. However, in our second explanation for relatively low penalties, we show that an upper bound could emerge if monitoring is less than perfect and, say, good loan pros-

---

[4] Notice that this way of looking at the problem abstracts from the coordination issues among creditors that has played such a prominent role in the debt-forgiveness literature (see, for example, Sachs (1988), Corden (1988), as well as the papers by Helpman and Krugman in this volume).

pects have a positive probability of being rejected. The reason for this is that the penalty could now fall upon an "innocent" borrower; hence a contract that specifies large penalties may end up imposing them even when the borrower is well behaved.

Perhaps the most interesting implication of the above model is that lenders may be tempted to increase the penalty after the borrower has accepted the loan because penalties could be less expensive than a careful monitoring. This potential "time inconsistency" of optimal penalties suggests that future innovations facilitating penalties may induce lenders to adopt them. This has a direct implication for after-debt-crisis arrangements through which banks are cartelized and are thereby able to impose bigger penalties on problem debtors. We argue that if this cartelization was anticipated in original contracts, then bank cartels could just be a way of implementing those contracts. However, a major insight of this section of the paper is that the sudden (i.e., largely unanticipated) presence of outside parties in the debt renegotiation process, particularly when bigger penalties are involved, may, in fact, help enforce a contract that was not intended by any of the parties. In our example, lenders end up getting the lion's share.

Section III of the paper is independent of the previous one and is concerned with debt relief. It discusses a methodology that relates risk premia to probabilities of default. In a tentative exercise the methodology is applied to the case of Argentina and it is shown that debt relief cannot be ruled out as the outcome of an optimal contract. In essence, this methodology suggests estimating the implicit probability of default from actual debt contracts and to calculating the probability distribution of current macroeconomic variables from the perspective of the time at which the loans were granted. If current macroeconomic variables are unfavorable to the borrower and fall into a region which, according to the probability distribution alluded to before, has a probability smaller than the probability of default implicit in debt contracts, then we will argue that a prima facie case could be made for debt relief. Under those circumstances debt relief might be thought of as the outcome of an actuarially fair insurance contract.

I. A Theory of Penalties, Monitoring, and Default

The central points of this section can be made in terms of a simple model. We will assume that the country can borrow from a large set of competitive "banks." The opportunity cost of funds for banks is exogenous with respect to the loans funneled toward this particular country (small-country assumption) and is denoted by ρ. We assume that the country can use the borrowed funds either in "legitimate" or in "illegitimate" activities. If funds are applied to a legitimate activity, their marginal productivity is α (not necessarily a constant), while, if they are used in an illegitimate activity, their marginal productivity is θα, where θ is a nonnegative constant and θ ≤ 1. Thus, the illegitimate activity never dominates the legitimate one from a technological point of view. The advantage of the illegitimate activity, however, stems from the existence of informational asymmetries. In this respect, we assume that if the country invests in the legitimate activity, everybody is able to observe it, and, if solvent, the country is thus obliged to pay back $(1 + \rho)$ "next period" per unit of borrowed funds.[5] On the other hand, if funds are invested in the illegitimate activity,[6] then the borrower is unable to detect any marginal output, the country could declare itself insolvent and pay nothing to the lender.[7]

Consequently, marginal profit associated with legitimate investments is given by

$$\alpha - (1 + \rho). \tag{1}$$

Moreover, marginal profit of investing in an illegitimate activity would be

$$\theta\alpha. \tag{2}$$

Under the present circumstances, if expression (2) is larger than expression (1), funds are channeled to illegitimate activities (at the margin), the lender gets nothing in return, and consequently the country is unable to borrow the marginal funds.[8] Borrowing, however, would exist if there was a level of investment for which the opposite inequality prevails, that is,

$$\alpha - (1 + \rho) \geq \theta\alpha. \tag{3}$$

Equation (3) illustrates the point, well known since the pioneering work of Eaton and Gersovitz (1981), that, contrary to pure neoclassical theory, investment will stop short of the level at which the gross marginal

---

[5] For the present discussion it is enough to divide time into "present" and "future." "Next period," then, corresponds to the future.

[6] Legitimate and illegitimate are just labels. A possible interpretation for a legitimate investment could be just regular investment, while illegitimate investments could be thought as consumption. The latter is obviously much harder to attach than the former.

[7] In reality there are always some assets that could be attached by the lender. Extensions to this case, however, would complicate the analysis with no appreciable gain in economic insight.

[8] In case of a tie we assume the country chooses the legitimate activity.

productivity of capital equals the interest factor, $1 + \rho$, even though the country has unlimited access to international capital mobility. Thus, in the present context, neoclassical theory would give the right answer only in the special case where the illegitimate use of funds yields no return, that is, $\theta = 0$. The intuition behind this result is quite straightforward. If the marginal profit from legitimate investments is zero, while that of illegitimate ones is positive, it would obviously pay the country to choose the second course of action. Thus, marginal profits in the legitimate activity could be zero in equilibrium (the neoclassical implication) only if the marginal product of illegitimate investments is also zero.

In the interesting case in which the country gets a positive return from illegitimate investments (i.e., $\theta > 0$), the above argument shows that there will be less international investment in this country than what is called for by considerations of pure efficiency. There exists, therefore, room for improving worldwide welfare by devising a system that reduces the incentives to cheat. One such device could be default penalties.

Consider, for example, the case in which there is a default penalty P per unit of debt that is not repaid, if less than total debt is repaid. Clearly, the repayment condition (3) now becomes

$$\alpha - (1 + \rho) \geq \theta\alpha - P, \tag{4}$$

or

$$\alpha \geq (1 + \rho - P)/(1 - \theta). \tag{5}$$

Obviously, therefore, we could eliminate all incentives to cheat by setting P large enough. Equation (5) shows how central is the existence of relatively small default penalties for default cum solvency to be a real possibility. Notice, also, that under present assumptions the borrower will always agree to higher default penalties at the time of signing the loan contract. This is so because penalties give a way for the borrower to close the gap between the marginal productivity of capital and the international interest rate factor, thus increasing ex-ante expected income. Furthermore, under perfect foresight (or perfectly contingent contracts) the penalty is never imposed, so its being large serves only as a deterrent, but costs the borrower nothing—it just makes him more credible. So, the question arises, why are penalties not big enough to deter solvent defaults at full efficiency (i.e., $\rho = \alpha$)?

Suppose that penalties are costly to the lender, and let the cost be βP, where $\beta > 0$. Since, as argued above, in equilibrium the penalty is never imposed because the country never defaults,[9] the competitive rate of interest charged to this country is still ρ. Thus, if P is credible, conditions (4) or (5) would still hold. The problem here is, however, that P will not be credible unless the lender can precommit P by, for example, pre-arranging for some outside institution to carry out the penalty for him. This is so because the borrowing country knows that if it defaults the lender would have no incentive to impose the penalty, for the latter will only increase the lender's cost. In equilibrium, therefore, the situation is equivalent to there being no penalty, and we revert to condition (3). This shows how sensitive the equilibrium solution may be to changes in the credibility of penalties, and it provides a rationale for relatively small penalties at equilibrium.

Another mechanism to improve the efficiency of the loan market is loan monitoring (see Diamond (1984), Townsend (1979)). By definition, monitoring is an activity that occurs before or simultaneously with the disbursement of funds. Thus, the lender could, in principle, ensure that the loan is used for a legitimate activity. In practice, however, monitoring has two problems: it is costly, and it is imperfect, that is, there is a positive probability that it gives inaccurate information.

Suppose monitoring is costly but perfect, and let the cost per unit of loan be γ. In this case, the borrowing country being monitored knows that, if it chooses the illegitimate activity, no funds will be available. Hence, its only realistic option is to use the funds for legitimate invest-ments. Since the cost to the lender has now risen to $\gamma + \rho$, loans will flow into the country as long as

$$\alpha - (1 + \rho + \gamma) \geq 0. \tag{6}$$

Clearly, this could represent a significant efficiency improvement if γ is relatively small. Since monitoring is likely to be subject to increasing returns to scale, γ could be significantly reduced by pooling loans from different banks. This suggests, incidentally, that the emergence of bank syndicates in the 1970s may have led to substantially smaller γ's, which may help to explain the relatively small "risk premia" on those loans and the extraordinarily large flow of funds that were channelled that way (see Folkerts-Landau (1985)).[10]

To simplify the discussion, but without loss of generality, we will further assume that without credible penalties or monitoring the country will always have incentives to choose illegitimate investments (i.e., in-equality (3) is never satisfied). In this case monitoring would be credible

---

[10] This effect must be distinguished from the possible higher penalties that may be involved if each participant in the bank syndicate credibly vowed to exclude a default country from future lending.

because in its absence the borrower will always choose the illegitimate activity.

Let us now consider the case in which monitoring is imperfect. This situation could arise if, owing to imperfect information, a "good" borrower could be mistaken by a "bad" one. An interesting instance occurs when the lender employs a wrong or incomplete model, as when a country is denied credit because one of its neighbors declared a debt-service moratorium, even when the country has no intention to default.

We will denote by q the probability that monitoring transmits the right signal (legitimate if legitimate, and so forth). Thus, $(1 - q)$ is the probability of getting the wrong signal (i.e., illegitimate if legitimate, and so forth). Without loss of generality we assume $q \geq 1/2$. If the borrowing country is monitored and considered unreliable, then no loan (at the margin) will be forthcoming. As a result no marginal investment occurs and the country incurs a marginal cost C. Hence, if the borrower's investment is legitimate his payoff will be given by equation (6) with probability q and $(-C)$ with probability $1 - q$.[11] Thus, his expected profit will be

$$[\alpha - (1 + \rho + \gamma)]q - (1 - q)C. \tag{7}$$

On the other hand, if his choice is illegitimate, then his expected profit would be

$$\theta\alpha(1 - q) - Cq. \tag{8}$$

Consequently, the legitimate activity will be selected if (8) does not exceed (7), which implies

$$[\alpha - (1 + \rho + \gamma)]q + (2q - 1)C \geq \alpha\theta(1 - q). \tag{9}$$

Clearly, if, as in the above simple case, $q = 1$ and $C = 0$ (perfect monitoring and no side effects from choosing an illegitimate investment), then inequality (9) boils down to (6). Moreover, if $C = 0$ and $q = 1/2$ then

$$\alpha - (1 + \rho + \gamma) \geq \alpha\theta, \tag{10}$$

which can never hold true because we assumed that inequality (3) never holds. This shows that (a) if perfect monitoring succeeds in bringing some loanable funds to the country (i.e., inequality (6) holds for some level of foreign loans), and (b) no loan would be possible if no monitor-

---

[11] We are implicitly assuming that the marginal cost of credit is $1 + \rho + \gamma$. This is correct in the present example because, in equilibrium, there will be no default.

ing or penalties exist (i.e., inequality (3) never holds), then there exists some sufficiently low critical level of monitoring accuracy, $q^c > 1/2$, such that monitoring becomes ineffective for improving the capital market for all $q < q^c$.

A look at equation (9) quickly reveals that marginal costs incurred by the borrower when he is deemed not creditworthy, C, help ensuring that legitimate investments are undertaken if $q > 1/2$ (a very mild constraint). However, the marginal impact of C on the left-hand side of inequality (9) is just

$$2q - 1 < 1, \text{ unless } q = 1. \tag{11}$$

Thus, the effectiveness of an increase in credit-rejection costs to induce legitimate investments is an increasing function of the accuracy of monitoring.[12]

From a formal point of view, C plays very much the same role as penalties, P, in our previous examples. Thus, if C is costly to the lender we would, once again, face the problem of its credibility. We have in mind, however, a situation where C is an essential part of the monitoring process. It could stand, for example, for the "time lost" if the country is not considered creditworthy. The cost is, however, dependent on institutional arrangements, such as when banks wait for a "green light" from the International Monetary Fund before extending new credit. In this context, not reaching an agreement with the Fund may imply losing the marginal productivity of capital net of the associated interest payments times the new capital that would otherwise have flowed in. Notice, incidentally, that these costs could therefore be modified by the granting of so-called bridge loans.

As a matter of fact, the country itself could modify the costs of not getting credit by changing the sectoral allocation of capital. This is a subject that has been extensively explored by Aizenman (see his paper in this volume) and Borensztein and Ghosh (1989) under the assumption of non-stochastic penalties. They show that in the quest to increase their access to international credit, countries may tend to follow trade-

---

[12] Notice that in equilibrium the borrower always chooses legitimate investments and yet, under imperfect monitoring, some loan applications are rejected *even when the lender knows that the borrower is perfectly reliable.* Thus, if the lender was free to revise the rule, he would accept all loans. This is another example of potential time inconsistency. If the borrower anticipated such revision of the rule, however, it would always pay him to cheat, and no loans would occur in equilibrium. In a more realistic scenario with heterogeneous borrowers, there will be some role for ex-post monitoring since the penalty may not be enough to deter everybody from cheating. This will allow the capital market to function even when lenders are free to change the rules ex post.

oriented policies beyond the point dictated by comparative advantage. This is an intriguing result, because although it helps to explain the newly industrializing economies' export-oriented policy, it does not seem compatible with the record of several heavily indebted countries, which, to the contrary, appear to have followed inward-looking industrial policies (before the present debt crisis episode). As the following arguments show, however, the existence of inaccurate monitoring places a natural upper bound to credit-rejection costs, C, and could thus be employed to argue that the optimal degree of openness is less than that suggested by the Aizenman-Borensztein-Ghosh analysis.

To simplify the exposition, let us further assume that α is a constant. Therefore, in equilibrium, the country's net income from borrowing is expression (7) times total borrowed funds (the upper limit of which will, without loss of generality, remain exogenous for the present discussion). Hence, if monitoring is imperfect (i.e., $q < 1$), then net expected income is a decreasing function of C. This is so because under imperfect monitoring a country could incur credit-rejection costs even when it chooses legitimate investment projects. On the other hand, if credit is to become available to this country, the incentive-compatibility constraint (9) must hold. This implies that the net-income-maximizing C is the lowest possible value of C that is consistent with inequality (9). This implies, of course, that optimal C, C^* satisfies (9) with equality. Hence,

$$C^* = \{\alpha\theta(1 - q) - [\alpha - (1 + \rho + \gamma)] q\}/(2q - 1). \tag{12}$$

Thus, in the relevant region where C^* is nonnegative, one can readily verify that C^* is a decreasing function of monitoring accuracy and the marginal productivity of capital, q and α, and an increasing function of monitoring and interest costs, γ and ρ, and of the productivity of illegitimate projects, θ.

In a competitive banking environment, in which banks compete in terms of both interest charges and monitoring cum credible penalties, it is not possible that C exceeds C^* at equilibrium; for, as one can easily verify, if that were the case, an individual bank could get nonzero profits and increase the country's expected income by offering lower penalties coupled with a rate of interest higher than $(\rho + \gamma)$. Hence, the competitive solution coincides with the net-income-maximizing solution discussed above.

Thus far, our discussion is predicated on the assumption that the country takes the loan. Loans will be taken, however, only if they are profitable, that is, if expression (7) is nonnegative. This fact can be used to show that in the present context penalties may not be able to ensure moral-hazard-free equilibria, even in the polar case in which monitoring costs are zero (i.e., $\gamma = 0$). The proof is simple. Let us assume $\alpha = 1 + \rho$ and $\gamma = 0$; then, by (12), $C^* > 0$ and, hence, expression (7) is negative (i.e., profits are negative). Thus, loans are not profitable and will not be taken. The intuition for the result is also very straightforward. We are examining a situation in which the marginal cost of funds is equal to their marginal product. Thus, in a moral-hazard-free world, funds would flow into the country at no risk for borrowers or lenders. In our setup, on the other hand, penalties are designed to discourage cheating and are therefore positive. Hence, if a borrower can be found, the loan would be riskless from the point of view of the lender. However, the borrower would not be willing to take the loan, because (a) marginal cost = marginal product, but (b) there is a positive probability of being (unjustly) punished. So net revenue is negative.

The assumption $\alpha = 1 + \rho$ is extreme and was only made to simplify the exposition. It should be clear, however, that the imperfect-monitoring model could be employed to show that the risk of being punished for the wrong crimes prevents a country from fully exploiting its intertemporal gains from trade, even though the size of penalty could be (credibly) written into the loan contract.

In the first model of this section equilibrium penalties were shown to be small because of lack of credibility. In the second model, where credibility was taken for granted (i.e., C is predetermined, and cannot be changed ex post), penalties are small because of imperfect monitoring. Thus, the next natural step is to examine the credibility of penalties in the context of the imperfect-monitoring model.

Penalty credibility is a very delicate matter. We have shown that if penalties are costly to the lender, their credibility could be greatly impaired. We have also argued, however, that their credibility could be enhanced if penalties are made an essential part of the monitoring process. Interestingly, in discussing the credibility of C^* we may actually face the opposite problem. Since C^* is smaller than the monitoring-related maximum, it would be tempting for the lender to increase penalties ex post, that is, when the loan is already in process and the country is "hooked" to this particular lender (or lenders), and adopt a less costly and hence more imperfect monitoring.[13] How feasible this is in practice is an open question; but this is another example where, once again,

---

[13] This falls outside the model, but easy extensions would yield this kind of result. For example, we could assume that the lender can choose monitoring accuracy, q, at a cost. Thus, the optimal ex ante contract will endogenize q and C. Ex post, however, once the borrower has taken the loan, incentives change. If C is costless, for example, the lender will be tempted to rely entirely on high C.

lenders would welcome the intervention of a third party that helps to increase the penalty after the contract has been signed. If the third party was not anticipated in the contract, though, its presence ex post may in fact enforce the wrong contract, not the one that lenders and borrowers intended to sign.

Thus far, we have no story to justify default or debt relief. Fortunately, the latter can be easily remedied by a straightforward extension of the model(s). Suppose there are two possible states of nature: the good and the bad. In the good state the marginal productivity of capital is $\bar{\alpha} > 0$, while in the bad state it is 0. We assume that in the bad state it is impossible for the country to pay back its debts. In order to be able to use the former apparatus, we will now identify α with the expected marginal   productivity of capital. Thus, by definition,

$$\alpha = \bar{\alpha}g, \tag{13}$$

where g is the probability of the good state.

Furthermore, let us now denote the international rate of interest by ρ^*, and let ρ stand for the interest charged to this particular country. Hence, recalling that lenders are assumed to be risk neutral, if the only state in which the country defaults is the bad state, then in equilibrium we have

$$\rho = \rho^*/g. \tag{14}$$

Since the incentive-compatibility constraint is relevant for the good state of nature only, it is quite clear that all of the above results remain the same when α and ρ satisfy (13) and (14). Consequently, the borrower will not pay back its debts with probability $(1 - g)$ and the country-specific interest rate, ρ, will be correspondingly larger to compensate banks for this, possibly unlikely, event. If this arrangement is legally binding and well understood by everybody concerned, then cessation of payment in the bad state would carry no stigma. The problem in practice, however, is that although loan contracts normally contain positive risk premia, conditions for default are unlikely to be fully specified. Therefore, a long negotiation process could be set in motion.[14] The latter, incidentally, could be costly to the debtor and could operate, therefore, very much like penalties. If the process ensuing a default is well under-

---

[14] This does not apply to our overly simple example in which the borrower has no attachable wealth in the "bad" state, but, as the reader can verify, it would be a feature of more realistic models where some assets can be attached by the lender.

stood, the penalty itself would have been taken into account in the original (implicit) contract. Once again, however, it is not clear that bringing new players into the picture is desirable, unless their eventual participation was taken into account in the original contract.

II. Debt Relief

Previous remarks have made it abundantly clear that optimal ex-ante loan contracts are bound to be time inconsistent, that is, lenders, and borrowers as well, may have incentives to pretend, ex post, that the terms of the contract were different from those agreed upon ex ante. In this respect, we discussed the possibility that the lender or lenders be tempted to increase penalties ex post. In practice this may take the form of banks forming coalitions to increase penalties directly or to seek support from the international community.

Another aspect that may tend to be misrepresented ex post is ex-ante arrangements for partial or total default in the "bad" states of nature. This is obviously more likely to be so if the conditions for default are not fully specified in the original contract, that is, if some default conditions are "implicit" in the loan contract.

A relevant question in this respect is: Does the above imperfect-enforceability scenario justify some kind of outside intervention? Our previous discussion suggests that the question has a rather subtle answer. If lender and borrower are fully aware of the ex-post situation, and none of them expected outside intervention, then there is no obvious reason to justify ex-post intervention. However, this type of equilibrium is not Pareto optimal because the contract was signed under the assumption that some of its terms could not be enforced ex post. Therefore, there is room for outside intervention ex ante. For example, an outsider could be asked to participate in the loan contract so as to ensure the ex-post enforcement of the contract. The point to keep in mind, however, is that if the objective is to ensure the validation of ex-ante implicit contracts, then for outside intervention to be justified ex post, it is necessary that this kind of intervention be well understood ex ante by both parties to a loan contract, to such an extent that the contract would not, or could not, be carried out in the absence of such participation.

Did international loan contracts during the 1970s anticipate the participation of outside parties? According to the above discussion this is the acid test that any such participation has to pass in order to be justifiable. Unfortunately, however, such a test is likely to be very hard to carry out in practice, because most international contracts do not explicitly mention that the parties will resort to international financial institutions in order to resolve the debt problems.

There is, however, a related question that may be somewhat easier to handle. Suppose that outside intervention can be taken for granted, and that, therefore, outside parties are (at least implicitly) obliged to adjudicate on this issue, is there anything that one could infer from explicit contracts about implicit penalties and partial default? The remainder of this section will be devoted to discuss a possible methodology to answer only a part of the latter question, namely, whether implicit contracts accounted for the possibility of partial debt relief.

Most international loan contracts specify an interest rate above LIBOR. In a competitive market (which we assume) this may reflect transaction costs (e.g., monitoring costs, γ, in our previous discussion), risk aversion, or the possibility that the debt will not be paid in full. Given that a good portion of total official loans was made through bank syndicates (see Folkerts-Landau (1985)), we could perhaps assume, as a first approximation, that transaction costs are nearly zero and, as in our previous analysis, that lenders are risk neutral. This leaves us with only one factor: default risk.

Consider a one-period loan with interest rate $i + k$, where i is the LIBOR interest rate, and k is the risk premium. Let us further assume that p is the probability that the country will pay less than 100 percent of its debt, and, for simplicity, let σ be the share of the debt that will be repaid in case of default.[15] Hence, the expected return from a one-period loan would be:

$$(1 + i + k)(1 - p + p\sigma). \tag{15}$$

By definition, $(1 + i + k)$ is contractual repayment at the end of the period per unit of loan; $(1 - p)$ is the probability of full repayment, and p the probability that only a share σ will be repaid. Adding up yields (15).

A bank, however, has the option of investing in the interbank loan market and get

$$1 + i, \tag{16}$$

at the end of the period. Thus, since in competitive equilibrium banks should be indifferent between those two alternatives, we have, equating (15) and (16),

---

[15] A richer scenario would specify a range of repayment shares with different probabilities. However, the present assumption is enough to illustrate the basic point, and, given the complexity involved in actual defaults, the two-options assumption may even be "realistic."

$$p = \left(1 - \frac{1+i}{1+i+k}\right)\bigg/(1-\sigma). \tag{17}$$

The last equation could be used to calculate the default probability given σ. For example, if we were interested in estimating a plausible lower bound for p given σ, we should choose realistically high i and low k. For example, for one-year contracts we could set $i = 20$ percent and $k = 1$ percent. Table 1 shows the results. Thus, if the country was expected to pay 50 percent of its debt in case of default, the implicit probability of default could not have (realistically) been smaller than 1.65 percent.

The next important issue is to determine the set of debt-relief-triggering indicators. This is, of course, a very hard problem. Fortunately, however, we can get some clues from the theory of optimal implicit contracts. Thus, if, as is widely accepted, a nation's welfare is closely linked to its sustainable (or "permanent") consumption level, and the latter is tightly linked to its net permanent income (i.e., net of loan repayments), then, conceivably, an optimal loan contract would aim at insulating net permanent income from random fluctuations (particularly, if the country exhibits risk aversion, and lenders are risk neutral). This suggests that (optimal) loan repayment would tend to increase with positive shocks to permanent income, and to decrease when shocks are negative (recall last part of Section I). An implication of the latter statement is that debt relief is more likely to be exhibited in an optimal implicit contract as the negative shocks to permanent income are larger. Consequently, looking at Table 1, it could be argued that *some* debt relief would be called for if permanent income fell into a range that had probability smaller than 0.83 percent at the time of signing the contract.

Table 1. *Default Probabilities*

$\sigma \times 100$	$p \times 100$
00	0.83
10	0.91
20	1.03
30	1.18
40	1.38
50	1.65
60	2.07
70	2.75
80	4.13
90	8.26

Table 2. *Forecast Errors*

Year	Standard Deviations Below Forecast
1981	2.55
1982	3.98
1983	4.17
1984	4.18
1985	5.81
1986	5.20

The case of Argentina is very interesting in this respect. A regression of annual GDP on a time trend for the period 1957–80 yields:[16]

$$y = 9.32 + 0.029 \ T, \tag{18}$$
$$(297) \quad (21)$$

where y is the logarithm of GDP and T is calendar time. This implies, of course, that the country grew, on average, at the rate of 2.9 percent per year. More interestingly, the Durbin-Watson statistic is 1.5, which means that serial correlation of equation's residuals does not seem to be a major problem. In economic terms, this type of result suggests that the country does not seem to have gone through extended periods of recession or expansion with respect to trends.[17] Furthermore, it suggests that lenders might have used a trend line like (18) to forecast GDP in the 1980s. What would be the implications if they actually did so?

The standard error associated with equation (18) is 4.71 percent. The latter could be used as an estimate of the standard deviation of the error term in equation (18), and, thus, to calculate the distance of each observation from its corresponding forecast in terms of standard deviations. These results are shown in Table 2 (see also Figure 1). Interestingly, all of these observations fall into a range that has probability less than 0.7 percent, which is smaller than the 0.83 percent mark discussed in connection with Table 1. This could thus be conceivably utilized to build up a case for debt relief.

[16] Data was taken from line 99b.p, of the treatment of Argentina in International Monetary Fund, *International Financial Statistics,* various issues; t-statistics are in parenthesis.

[17] This is, incidentally, quite remarkable because one-to-three year GDP cycles are common in industrial and other Latin American countries. Similar regressions for other countries yield a Durbin-Watson statistic of 0.25 for the United States and Colombia, 0.85 for Mexico, 0.34 for Chile, 0.39 for Venezuela, and 0.19 for the Philippines. Brazil, on the other hand, comes closer to Argentina with a Durbin Watson of 1.32.

Figure 1. *Gross Domestic Product: Argentina*
(Log Scale)

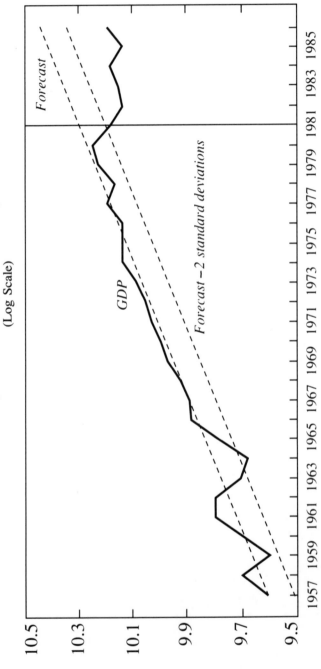

The above remarks are just suggestive. A more serious attack on the issue should be able to grapple with at least the following two queries. First, has income suffered a permanent or just a temporary shock? Second, since income is a variable that reflects, among other things, internal policy, shouldn't we thus try to isolate domestic factors—which are controllable by the country's policymakers—from those that are mostly exogenous (such as the price of copper for Chile, or that of wheat for Argentina)?

We will not attempt to give a full answer to these queries. I would like to point out, however, that there is some ongoing research (e.g., Baxter (1988) and Kaminsky (1988)) on detecting permanent regime changes that ought to be useful in the present context.[18] At any event, however, our analysis suggests that the objective is not necessarily to look for more sophisticated empirical methods, but rather to use models similar to those employed by lenders. This calls for studying the technical memoranda that served as a basis for granting those loans.

The second query has to do with the issue of moral hazard. Suppose that permanent income can be manipulated by policymakers, and loan repayment decreases with negative shocks to permanent income. Hence, if debt relief as a function of permanent income loss is generous enough, policymakers may find it to their advantage to engineer a negative shock (by, for example, failing to implement an adjustment program, or generating policy uncertainty). An alternative would be to write contracts that take into account only fully exogenous variables such as terms of trade. However, an important disadvantage of this approach is that variables such as terms of trade, cannot capture such important random shocks as those associated with political uncertainty and trade-union policies. These shocks are not easy to manipulate by a finance minister, and are hard to write into a contract, either explicitly or implicitly. Going back to the case of Argentina, for example, part of the output loss during the 1980s could possibly be traced to the associated political cost of a return to democracy. This is an interesting case study because it shows an instance in which output contains information that would be difficult to take account of by means of other exogenous variables.[19]

---

[18] Mauro Mecagni of the International Monetary Fund performed some more sophisticated time-series analysis on the Argentine GDP data. He was able to reduce the forecast error somewhat by exploiting the slight serial correlation of the series, but he also found that the distance between actual and forecast GDP during the 1980s exceeded two standard deviations.

[19] It should be remembered that we are talking about contracts that, by definition, are written before the relevant events are known. Thus, although it may be relatively easy to argue after the fact that certain events have occurred (e.g., a return to democracy), the point that I am trying to make is that it may still be very difficult to account for them ex ante by means of variables other than income or some related macroeconomic measures.

Suppose, however, that output was manipulable within certain bounds, but, since output is a good proxy for permanent income, it is nevertheless employed by lenders and borrowers as a sufficient statistic for debt relief. Clearly, under these circumstances, the contract should make sure that an output loss is not accompanied by such a big debt relief that it induces policymakers to provoke a fall in output in order to increase social welfare. In other words, the contract must be "incentive compatible." Interestingly, these types of constraints may make some of the (σ, p) combinations of Table 1 infeasible because not all of them do necessarily satisfy that kind of incentive compatibility; consequently, this may allow us to narrow down even further the possible set of optimal ex-ante implicit loan contracts, which, from our Sherlock Holmes perspective, is "good" news.

III. Conclusions

This paper is motivated by the need to understand the origin and incentives behind the debt contracts that were written during the 1970s in order to shed some light on the principles behind the granting of debt relief or the enforcing of default penalties.

We have argued that a loan contract may contain clauses that are not necessarily expressed in the written document. For example, we suggested that the existence of a positive risk premium shows that contracts may not have ruled out debt relief. The premium was undoubtedly small but still could be consistent with at least a 0.8 percent probability of (some kind of) debt relief. The relevance of these numbers was tested for Argentina. It was argued that Argentina's GDP levels for the 1980s, based on the experience in the period 1957–80, appears to be a low-probability event. In fact, the econometric exercise suggests that the probability of those events, given the track record for the period from 1957–80, could be smaller than 0.7 percent. These results suggest that some countries could be in the position of someone who bought car insurance and had an accident. Everyone would agree that the car owner has the right to collect from the insurance company. The same logic applies to debt relief. It could be argued that borrowers paid a "risk premium" in case a bad, and unlikely, event happened. If one could then prove that a given country has actually been involved in an accident, it follows that, like the car owner, this country would have the right to receive some compensation. One form that the latter can take is debt relief.

The paper, however, stops short of recommending debt relief. The analysis is still too preliminary and incomplete. Its main contribution, however, is to show that one can in principle discuss thorny issues like debt relief on the basis of solid economic concepts, many of which have been in the toolbox of economists for many years. There is always going to be room for disagreement, but an effort should be made to find a common ground.

A related issue that the paper focused on is penalties. This issue is important because debt crises tend to polarize the world between problem debtors and creditors. It could, therefore, be misleading to discuss policy issues under the assumption of perfect competition in the capital market (for problem debtors, at least). Creditors and international institutions are likely to be engaged in a game in which a lot of power can be exercised over problem debtors. This power could be used to threaten them with big default penalties or to reach an agreement whereby less that 100 percent of the debt is repaid.

The paper contributes to understanding these issues by looking at examples in which the penalty is one of the contract's variables. It is shown that although at the time of writing the contract, lenders may find it to their advantage to agree to relatively low penalties, their incentives could be quite different after the contract has been signed. If they could revise penalties they may have incentives to make them bigger. The situation is not very different from the one faced by an individual who borrows from a bank. He may be first enticed to the bank by "low rates" and by appealing commercials whose emphasis is on how well he will be treated when applying for a loan. Afterwards, however, at the slightest indication of insolvency the bank might be tempted to hire a nasty private company to fill the borrower with apocalyptic terror. The paper discusses the rationale for this to happen, and, more important, it strongly suggests that extreme caution should be taken if one is called in to reinforce the contract's penalties.

Our analysis gives strong support to the case-by-case approach to the debt problem. According to the above discussion, its resolution hinges upon being able to understand the nature of the original loan contracts. Contracts and objective situations are clearly not identical across countries, so there is no reason to expect that all countries should be subject to the same debt relief and default penalties.

This paper represents a very tentative attempt to deal with the debt problem on the basis of standard economic theory. There is a long way to travel before we arrive at a reasonably interesting destination. Nevertheless, it shows that there is hope that a serious economic analysis can considerably enhance the possibilities of narrowing the band of disagreement between borrowers and lenders. Furthermore, a resolution of the debt problem along the lines suggested here has the added attraction that it does not call for a breach of (implicit) contracts. On the contrary, a successful application of these methods should enable the spirit of the original contracts to be implemented, and, therefore, should cause minimal damage to the fabric of international financial relations.

There are several important issues that the paper has not covered. In particular, it has nothing to say about the possibility that debt relief may improve the welfare of both lenders and borrowers through coordination among creditors (see Corden (1988), Sachs (1988), Froot (forthcoming), Helpman, and Krugman (this volume), for example). This is so because, by definition, under optimal contracts there is no room for Pareto improvements.[20]

References

Arrow, Kenneth J., "Uncertainty and the Welfare Economics of Medical Care," *American Economic Review* (Nashville, Tennessee) Vol. 53 (1968), pp. 941–73.

Baxter, Marianne, "Rational Response to Unprecedented Policies: The 1979 Change in Federal Reserve Operating Procedures" (unpublished; Rochester, New York: University of Rochester, October 1988).

Borensztein, Eduardo and Atish Rex Ghosh, "Foreign Borrowing and Export Promotion Policies," IMF Working Paper WP/89/16 (unpublished; Washington: International Monetary Fund, February 1989).

Corden, W. Max, "Is Debt Relief in the Interest of the Creditors?" IMF Working Paper WP/88/72 (unpublished; Washington: International Monetary Fund, October 1988).

Diamond, Douglas W., "Financial Intermediation and Delegated Monitoring," *Review of Economic Studies* (Edinburgh) Vol. 51 (July 1984), pp. 393–414.

Diamond, Peter and Michael Rothschild, *Uncertainty in Economics: Readings and Excercises* (New York, Academic Press, 1978).

Eaton, Jonathan and Mark Gersovitz, "Debt with Potential Repudiation: Theoretical and Empirical Analysis," *Review of Economic Studies* (Edinburgh), Vol. 48 (1981), pp. 289–309.

Eaton, Jonathan, Mark Gersovitz and Joseph E. Stiglitz, "The Pure Theory LLof Country Risk" *European Economic Review* (Amsterdam), Vol. 30, (1986), pp. 481–513.

Eichengreen, Barry, and Richard Portes, "Debt and Default in the 1930s: Causes and Consequences," *European Economic Review* (Amsterdam), Vol. 30 (1986), pp. 559–640.

[20] This implies, of course, that our arguments for debt relief are entirely independent of the ones given by the above-mentioned literature.

Folkerts-Landau, David, "The Changing Role of International Bank Lending in Development Finance," International Monetary Fund, *Staff Papers* (Washington), Vol. 32 (June 1985), pp. 317–63.

Froot, Kenneth, "Buybacks, Exit Bonds, and the Optimality of Debt and Liquidity Relief," *International Economic Review* (Philadelphia), forthcoming.

International Monetary Fund, *International Financial Statistics* (various issues).

Kaletsky, Anatole, *The Costs of Default* (New York: Twentieth Century Fund, 1985).

Kaminsky, Graciela, "The Peso Problem and the Behavior of the Exchange Rate. The Dollar Pound Exchange Rate: 1976–1987" (unpublished; San Diego: University of California, November 1988).

Sachs, Jeffrey D., "New Approaches to the Latin American Debt Crisis" (unpublished; Cambridge, Massachusetts: Harvard University, September 1988.

Townsend, Robert M., "Optimal Contracts and Competitive Markets with Costly State Verification," *Journal of Economic Theory* (New York), Vol. 21 (October 1979), pp. 265–93.

Multilateral Negotiations for Rescheduling Developing Country Debt

A Bargaining-Theoretic Framework

JEREMY BULOW and KENNETH ROGOFF*

A dynamic bargaining-theoretic framework is used to analyze multilateral negotiations for rescheduling sovereign debt. The analysis illustrates how various factors, such as the debtor's gains from trade and the level of world interest rates, affect the relative bargaining power of various parties to a rescheduling agreement. If creditor-country taxpayers have a vested interest in maintaining normal levels of trade with debtor countries, then they can sometimes be bargained into making sidepayments. The benefits from unanticipated creditor-country sidepayments accrue to both lenders and borrowers. But the benefits from perfectly anticipated sidepayments accrue entirely to borrowers.

IN SOVEREIGN DEBT contracts, borrowers are unable to offer collateral in the traditional sense. Instead, lenders must rely on the sovereign country's desire to maintain unfettered access to world capital and goods markets. But although the costs of being forced into economic autarky are almost certainly enormous for most debtor countries, the bargaining over debt repayments is not entirely one-sided. Debtor countries have some leverage because foreign lenders do not directly benefit by cutting them off from world markets. Moreover, in punishing a debtor who

* Mr. Bulow is a Professor in the Graduate School of Business at Stanford University.

Mr. Rogoff is a Professor of Economics at the University of Wisconsin, Madison. This paper was prepared while he was a visiting scholar in the Research Department of the Fund.

repudiates, lenders may also be inflicting damage on their own compatriots. In particular, they will be hurting any creditor-country citizens who benefit from trade with the debtor. A conflict of interest can arise among different groups in the creditor countries, pitting investors who want to enforce maximum repayments against consumers and exporters who want to maintain normal trade relations.

This paper attempts to develop a formal bargaining-theoretic model that takes into account the multilateral dimensions of developing country debt reschedulings. Previous efforts to model sovereign debt contracts have typically focused only on the bilateral relationship between the debtor nation and its foreign private creditors, taking the behavior of creditor-country governments as exogenous.[1] Because it would be rather difficult to develop a complete general equilibrium, game-theoretic model of international economic relations, we do need to treat some aspects of creditor-country policy as exogenous. In particular, we take the creditor nations' political and legal systems as given. Nevertheless, our analysis yields some insights that we believe would hold up in a richer model.

Our central result is that if creditor-country citizens enjoy sufficiently large gains from trade with the debtor country, they may be induced to facilitate rescheduling agreements by contributing money or by consenting to policy changes that would be favorable to the debtor country or the banks (that is, by making "sidepayments"). They may be induced to make sidepayments even though all parties have a common interest in avoiding trade disruptions. But there is an important distinction between anticipated and unanticipated sidepayments. Unanticipated sidepayments benefit both debtors and bank stockholders. If, however, lenders anticipate receiving third-party sidepayments, they will be willing to lend more at any given interest rate. With competitive loan markets, the borrowing country is thereby able to extract the entire surplus.

I. Sovereign Debt Contracts Versus Domestic Debt Contracts

To motivate our bargaining-theoretic approach to analyzing developing country debt rescheduling negotiations, it is helpful to review why sovereign debt contracts work somewhat differently from domestic lending contracts.

---

[1] For an analysis of the case where bargaining is bilateral, see Bulow and Rogoff (1989a). See Eaton, Gersovitz, and Stiglitz (1986) for a discussion of the early literature, in which creditors are implicitly assumed to have all the bargaining power.

If a supranational legal authority capable of enforcing contracts across borders existed, there would be nothing unique about international debt contracts. One could, in principle, include the same clauses and covenants in international loan contracts that are typically built into domestic contracts, and one could have international bankruptcy courts parallel to domestic ones. There might still be frictions in international capital markets—that is, reasons for departure from the Arrow-Debreu world of complete (perfect) capital markets. Having a world legal authority does not eliminate adverse-selection and moral hazard problems.[2]

In practice, of course, cross-border contract enforcement is generally limited. Indeed, the real question is why foreign investors are willing to trust sovereign debtors at all. If there were no direct or indirect costs to default, sovereigns would have no incentives to pay. Since one actually observes sovereign loans, there must be some costs to default, but what are they? Though foreign creditors may not always be successful in pressing their claims in debtor-country courts, they do in general have meaningful rights within their own countries.[3] Creditors' rights depend in part on their political influence at home, but also on their ability to employ the creditor-country legal system. Through the legal system, creditors can make it difficult for their fellow citizens to transact with any sovereign that stands in default. A recalcitrant debtor will thus have problems holding assets abroad, employing bank intermediaries to conduct trade, and even exporting and importing.[4] These inconveniences may appear minor, since gains from trade (in goods and financial assets) are a *flow*, and the flow is typically small relative to the *stock* of a borrower's debt. But if one recognizes that a repudiating country may suffer reduced gains from trade for an extended period, it is clear that the cumulative losses can be enormous.

Whereas a country's gains from trade are in some sense a form of collateral, three key differences serve to strengthen the negotiating position of a defaulting borrower relative to the standard domestic case. First, a sovereign debtor has considerable potential to reduce tempo-

---

[2] Even if no special problems enforcing contracts across national borders existed, one still could not index legal contracts to variables that are only observed by one of the two contracting parties, or to variables that both parties observe but that are prohibitively expensive for a third party (for example, a court) to verify.

[3] An alternative view holds that sovereign debtors repay mainly to preserve their reputation for repayment in world capital markets. For a skeptical assessment of this view, see Bulow and Rogoff (1989b).

[4] For a discussion of the empirical evidence on lenders' ability to punish borrowers, and of some of the underlying legal issues, see Alexander (1987) or the Appendix to Bulow and Rogoff (1989a).

rarily its exposure to penalties while bargaining with its lenders. For example, a debtor can use circuitous, and presumably more costly, trade routes and trade mechanisms to avoid seizure of its property during negotiations. Second, most of the penalties at the disposal of lenders involve large deadweight costs. In the case of a domestic bankruptcy, creditors can, in principle, simply carve up and sell a firm's productive assets.[5] Lenders gain no such direct benefit by forcing a country into economic autarky. On the contrary, creditors may have to bear significant legal and lobbying costs. Third, the punishments inflicted by lenders on sovereign debtors may also harm other creditor-country citizens. If lenders are successful in stemming a debtor's trade flows, exporters and importers in creditor countries also lose. This externality gives both creditors and debtors a certain amount of bargaining power in relation to other citizens in the creditor country.

For all the reasons discussed above, bargaining issues seem particularly central to developing country debt contracts.

II. Bilateral Rescheduling Negotiations: The Basic Model

Before turning to multilateral debt rescheduling negotiations, we first review the bilateral case in which the behavior of creditor-country governments is treated as exogenous. We will deliberately try to keep the underlying macroeconomic model quite simple, in order to focus on bargaining factors.[6]

Consider a small country facing an exogenously given world interest rate r; initially it has no foreign debt. The country's utility function is given by

$$\Lambda_t = \sum_{i=0}^{\infty} C_{t+hi}/(1 + \delta h)^i, \qquad C \geq 0, \tag{1}$$

where C is domestic consumption of an imported good, $\delta(>r)$ is the country's discount rate, and h is the length of each period.[7]

Note that the country's utility function is linear in C. The assumption of risk neutrality greatly simplifies our later analysis of the dynamics of debt rescheduling negotiations. However, because the country is risk

---

[5] We are somewhat overstating the differences between domestic and international contracts here. Indeed, many of the bargaining issues analyzed here are present in the domestic setting, albeit in less acute form.

[6] The discussion of bilateral bargaining here is based on our earlier paper (Bulow and Rogoff (1989a)).

[7] Allowing the time interval to be of arbitrary length h will make it easier later to consider the limiting case of continuous bargaining.

neutral, it is not concerned with smoothing out its consumption over time. Consequently, the country's sole motive for borrowing is that its discount rate, δ, is greater than the world interest rate, r.

Each period, the country produces yh units of an export good. Production is exogenous; there is no investment. Each unit of the export good can be traded abroad for P units of the imported consumption good. Thus, the country's consumption in period t is given by

$$C_t = PT_t, \tag{2}$$

where T_t denotes exports in period t. If, however, the country stands in default on its foreign debt and has not yet reached a rescheduling agreement, creditors can prevent the country from trading. This assumption is extreme, but very similar results would obtain if the creditors were able to forestall only a fraction of the country's shipments. Although the country is unable to trade after repudiating its debt, it can store its export good while it negotiates. The storage technology is such that

$$S_{t+1} = (1 - \gamma h)S_t + yh - T_t, \qquad \gamma h < 1, \tag{3}$$

where S_t is the amount of the export good the country has in storage when entering period t, and γh is the depreciation rate. That is, the amount of the export good the country has in storage when entering period $t + 1$ is equal to the amount of the good it had in storage when entering period t, plus production of the good during period t, yh, less depreciation and less any amount traded abroad, T. The country need not be able to store its export good for extended periods. The good has to be kept in storage only long enough for the country to be able to exchange offers and counteroffers with its creditors.

We must now be more precise about our specification of international loan markets. When the country goes to borrow in the initial period, it can approach any one of a large number of competitive risk-neutral banking consortia. These consortia are willing to lend money as long as they anticipate receiving at least the market rate of return. We assume that, through cross-default clauses, a consortium can deal with the country as a unified entity. The type of bargaining model employed here is actually quite useful for analyzing the effects of conflicting interests among lenders, but these issues are not considered here.[8]

As we have already explained, the debtor country cannot offer collateral on loans, but it can sign legal contracts valid in lender-country

---

[8] The model here may be thought of as holding constant the aggregate bargaining power of the banks relative to the country. In the bargaining analysis below, this is tantamount to saying that the banks' share of the offers is fixed.

courts. These contracts allow lenders to seize the debtor's assets abroad in the event of repudiation (that is, if the country fails to fulfill its interest obligations and does not reach a rescheduling agreement).[9] There may be large deadweight costs associated with seizure (for example, legal fees), so that the value that lenders receive is less than the value that the debtor loses. We will assume that lenders do not benefit directly from interfering with the country's trade (only the lawyers benefit). None of the results below hinges on this assumption. The country's bargaining power actually derives from its ability to store its export good at home and avoid seizure while negotiating a rescheduling agreement. In practice, the ability to circumvent seizure is not the country's only source of bargaining power, but, for analytical purposes, the paradigm is a convenient one.

III. Equilibrium Under Bilateral Bargaining

Because there is no uncertainty in the model, the country's lending limit is determined simply by the maximum amount lenders can bargain it into repaying.[10] If rescheduling negotiations were completely one-sided, lenders could extract repayments each period up to the full value of the country's output. In this case the country's borrowing ceiling would simply be (in the limit as $h \rightarrow 0$)

$$\Re = Py/r, \tag{4}$$

or, in words, the world market value of a claim on the country's entire future income. Of course, if the country has any bargaining power, lenders will realize that it cannot be forced into paying over its full gains from trade, and the country's true lending limit will be lower than the amount given by equation (4). To model the bargaining over rescheduling as two-sided, we adopt the alternating-offer framework first proposed by Rubinstein (1982) in his classic paper on bargaining. The debtor and the creditor take turns each period at making offers on how much the country has to pay to be allowed to trade freely its current production and any of the export good it has in storage. Whenever an agreement is reached, the banks sign a rescheduling agreement that

---

[9] The banking consortium typically includes representatives from all the borrower's major industrial country trading partners; this situation maximizes lenders' legal rights in the event of default.

[10] As Bulow and Rogoff (1989a) show, it is not difficult to allow for uncertainty in this framework. The focus here is on the extension to multilateral bargaining; our main results do not depend on the assumption of perfect foresight.

places the country in good standing on its debts until the next period. This agreement allows the country to trade freely provided that it makes the current payment specified in the rescheduling agreement.[11] If no agreement is reached, because the banks reject the country's offer or vice versa, the country places its production in storage to await further negotiations. The country's borrowing limit is then determined by the maximum amount creditors believe they can induce the country to repay through bargaining. It should be emphasized that the present problem differs from Rubinstein's problem in that here no agreement can be final. The debtor always retains the option of reopening negotiations at a later date.

Note that if lenders could really anticipate the outcome of this bargaining, they would know exactly how much they could lend the country without being forced to reschedule later. If uncertainty was introduced, of course, reschedulings would occur unless debt contracts were perfectly indexed to all disturbances. Reschedulings can also be explained by the desire to induce third-party sidepayments, as in the analysis in Section IV.

We do not present here all the intermediate steps required to solve formally for a bargaining equilibrium; we will present the essential details for the multilateral case later. Besides, the most important result for our later discussion can be deduced just by noting that there is no private information in this model. (This assumption is equivalent to specifying that all agents have equal knowledge about all the parameters of the model.) It is well known (see Sutton (1986)) that in Rubinstein-type bargaining models an agreement will always be reached without delay under symmetric information for two reasons: because both sides can calculate what will happen if they continue to bargain and, because both sides know that they will not be believed if they make outrageous threats. Thus, banks would disregard any country that said "give me almost everything or I'll stop negotiating." Banks can refuse the offer because they know the country must eventually return to the bargaining table. Because both the country and the banks are impatient to come to an agreement, it is not worthwhile for either to make offers that will surely be refused.[12] The equilibrium division of the gains from trade can be

---

[11] In practical terms, it is best to think of this payment as the net resource transfer from the country to its creditors. The net resource transfer is essentially the country's current interest payment minus any so-called new money loans.

[12] Although we do not stress it here, there is actually a fundamental difference between our model and Rubinstein's. In Rubinstein's model, once an agreement is reached, it cannot be renegotiated. Here, the country always has the option of asking for rescheduling of the agreement. To solve this problem in general is quite difficult, but it is possible to solve the model for the risk-neutral case considered here.

shown to depend on the relative rates of impatience of the two parties. Denoting q as the banks' share of the country's output, Py, one can derive

$$q = (\delta + \gamma)/(\delta + r + 2\gamma). \tag{5}$$

The numerator in equation (5), $\delta + \gamma$, is the sum of the country's rate of time preference, δ, and the rate at which the goods depreciate in storage, γ. This sum may be thought of as the country's effective discount rate. Similarly, the banks' effective discount rate is $r + \gamma$, so that each party's share is inversely proportional to its rate of time preference. Having solved for q, we can then write the country's lending ceiling as

$$\Re = qPy/r; \tag{6}$$

that is, the present discounted value of the maximum repayments banks can bargain the debtor country into making.

The case of symmetric information is certainly not completely realistic, and it is necessary to relax this assumption to explain delays in reaching agreements. The present analysis, however, still yields some useful insights; in addition, one might argue that this case helps to explain why international lending negotiations do not break down more often.

IV. Rescheduling Negotiations Involving Creditor-Country Taxpayers

The preceding analysis is based on the implicit assumption that creditor-country taxpayers can precommit to staying out of any rescheduling negotiations, even if they would be hurt by a disruption of trade with the debtor. Here we show that, although creditor-country taxpayers might benefit from such a commitment, the taxpayers may not be able to make the commitment credible. This can be the case even if all the relevant parties believe that the debtor country and the banks would come to an immediate agreement without third-party involvement. The key parameter governing sidepayments is the relative magnitude of the two countries' gains from bilateral trade. On the one hand, if the creditor country enjoys gains from bilateral trade on the same order of magnitude as the debtor country, then the creditor country may be induced to make sidepayments to both the debtor and the banks. On the other hand, if the debtor's gains from trade are much larger, then it may be the debtor that has to make sidepayments to the creditor. (Obviously, political and strategic factors can also affect the benefits calculus, but we do not explicitly incorporate them here.)

Although we allow for creditor-country government participation in rescheduling negotiations, we continue to assume that the creditor-country legal system is constitutionally immutable and not subject to manipulation by the legislative or executive branches. Hence, borrowers can still sign contracts that give creditors meaningful legal rights in the event of default. Implicitly, the creditor country is assumed to be unwilling to undermine its valuable legal system just to improve its negotiating position in relation to a relatively small debtor. This assumption may be too extreme; in practice, creditor-country governments appear to exercise a considerable degree of latitude over the intensity of enforcement of sovereign debt contracts. Nevertheless, it might be very costly for the executive branch to avoid enforcing the contracts entirely, and this weaker assumption is all that is really necessary for our results.

Thus far we have been describing the debtor country as small, and we will continue to assume that it is small in world capital markets. But we will now also assume that the debtor is large in the sense that the creditor country gains from their bilateral trade. There are two possible rationales for this assumption, and either can be used to motivate the multilateral bargaining analysis. The most straightforward assumption is that the debtor is large in the market for the good it produces. An alternative assumption, which turns out to be considerably more convenient here, is to posit that the debtor is one of a large number of suppliers of a good that the creditor country consumes heavily but does not produce. When the debtor reduces its exports, the price of the good rises. The benefits of the price rise are spread across a large number of producers, so that, to a first approximation, the debtor views its marginal revenue as equal to the price of its export good, P. The creditor country, in contrast, is the main consumer of the good, and the burden of the price rise therefore falls primarily on its citizens.

The objective function of the creditor country is to maximize the present discounted value of consumer surplus:[13]

$$\Psi_t = \sum_{i=0}^{\infty} (zPT_{t+hi} - B_{t+hi})/(1 + rh)^i, \qquad (7)$$

where T represents imports from the debtor country, B represents side-payments to the banks and the debtor country (which can be negative), and zP represents the creditor country's gain in consumer surplus per

---

[13] Note that we are assuming that the profits of bank investors do not enter into the creditor-country government's utility function. Similar results obtain as long as the creditor-country government values an extra dollar of bank profits less than an extra dollar of government surplus.

unit of imports from the debtor. The creditor government's interest rate is taken as equal to the world interest rate r, but this assumption is easily modified.

The objective functions of the debtor country and the banks remain as described in Section II above, but to simplify the exposition we will assume that $\gamma = 0$, so that the good does not depreciate in storage. To close the model, it is still necessary to provide some details about the three-way bargaining process that governs debt rescheduling negotiations. We will again adopt a variant of the Rubinstein alternating-offer framework, but since three-player bargaining models have not been studied previously in the literature on sovereign debt, more detail is necessary here.

To calculate the borrower's debt ceiling, it is useful to assume initially that the debtor country owes an *infinite* amount, so that no trade can ever take place without a rescheduling agreement. The borrower's debt ceiling is then given by the present discounted value of the banks' receipts. In a nonstochastic model such as the present one, marginal increases in the face value of a borrower's obligations are meaningless once the debt ceiling is reached.

Any rescheduling agreement must be signed by both the banks and the debtor country. The creditor-country government's consent is required only if the agreement calls on it to make positive sidepayments.[14] (If the creditor country's gains from trade are small enough, it may actually receive sidepayments outside the context of the rescheduling negotiations; we consider this issue below.) In three-way rescheduling negotiations, each of the three parties takes turns making offers on how to divide the total gains from trade for the current period. An agreement is reached only when all three parties consent. If no agreement is reached, the debtor country adds current production to its stockpile, and all sides await the next round of offers.[15]

In any period t, the total surplus to be divided among the three parties is the sum of the creditor's gains from trade zPv_t, plus the debtor's gains from trade Pv_t. The term v_t denotes the total amount of debtor-country production available for current trade (including quantities of the good from storage). Our notation for describing the negotiation process under

---

[14] Note that the creditor-country's sidepayments can take many forms other than cash payments: military assistance, a lowering of tariffs, changes in immigration laws, and so forth.

[15] The analysis would be similar if the creditor country also could store some of its own export good. The key assumption here is that both sides' gains from trade are linear in the level of bilateral trade; the model is much easier to solve in the linear case.

alternating offers is as follows. When it is the banks' turn to make an offer, they offer themselves $100q$ percent of the total gains from trade, $Pv_t(1+z)$, and they offer the creditor-country government $100w$ percent. Thus, if the banks' offer is accepted, the debtor country would receive $100(1-q-w)$ percent. When it is the debtor's turn to make an offer, it offers the banks $100q'$ percent of the surplus, and it offers the creditor-country government $100w'$ percent. When it is the creditor-country government's turn, it offers the debtor $100(1-q''-w'')$ percent of the surplus, and it offers the banks $100q''$ percent. When an agreement is reached, the debtor country exports, the gains from trade are divided according to the agreement, and negotiation begins immediately on the gains from trade for the next period.

Having fully specified the model, it is straightforward to show that the following conditions must hold in any perfect equilibrium for all $s \geq 0$, where s is a multiple of 3:[16]

$$1 - q_s - w_s = [1 - q'_{s+1} - w'_{s+1}]/(1 + \delta h), \tag{8a}$$

$$w_s = \min[w'_{s+1}/(1 + rh), \quad z/(1 + z)], \tag{8b}$$

$$q'_{s+1} = q''_{s+2}/(1 + rh), \tag{8c}$$

$$w'_{s+1} = \min[w''_{s+2}/(1 + rh), \quad z/(1 + z)], \tag{8d}$$

$$1 - q''_{s+2} - w''_{s+2} = [1 - q_{s+3} - w_{s+3}]/(1 + \delta h), \tag{8e}$$

$$q''_{s+2} = q_{s+3}/(1 + rh). \tag{8f}$$

The intuitive interpretation of equations (8a)–(8f) is also straightforward. Equations (8a) and (8b), for example, state that when it is the banks' turn to make an offer, they will craft the offer such that both the other players are just indifferent between accepting the offer and waiting until the next period (when it will be the debtor country's turn to make an offer). The left-hand side of equation (8a) gives the value to the debtor country of accepting immediately, whereas the right-hand side gives the present discounted value to the debtor of reaching an agree-

---

[16] The derivation of equations (8) follows the same algorithm presented in Bulow and Rogoff (1989a) for the bilateral case. In deriving the conditions for an equilibrium bargain, we have not allowed for history-dependent strategies. One can show, however, that the equilibrium considered in the text is the unique equilibrium of the limiting finite-horizon game, and it is also the unique equilibrium when strategies are continuous in the history of the game; see Sutton (1986).

ment in the next period (when it will be the debtor's turn to make an offer). The debtor country discounts the share it would receive from a deal in the next period by $1/(1 + \delta h)$. Similarly, the left-hand side of equation (8b) gives the value to the creditor country of accepting the banks' offer, and the right-hand side gives the value to the creditor country of waiting for the next round; note that the discount rate it uses is $1/(1 + rh)$. The creditor-country's payoff is written as $\min[\cdot]$ because we are assuming that the creditor country has to sign the agreement only if it is called on to make positive sidepayments. So if the creditor country's share from participating in rescheduling negotiations exceeds its own gains from trade, its commitment not to make sidepayments becomes credible, and the analysis is then the same as in the bilateral case. (There is even the possibility that the creditor country might be able to *extract* sidepayments from the debtor; we return to this question below.)

Formally, equations (8a)–(8f) comprise a system of first-order difference equations in which all the roots lie outside the unit circle. (In macroeconomic jargon, the system is saddle-point stable.) The unique equilibrium (in the limit of continuous bargaining as $h \rightarrow 0+$) is given by

$$q = q' = q'' = \delta/(2\delta + r), \tag{9a}$$

$$w = w' = w'' = \delta/(2\delta + r), \tag{9b}$$

$$(1 - q - w) = (1 - q' - w') = (1 - q'' - w'') = r/(2\delta + r). \tag{9c}$$

As in the case of bilateral bargaining, an agreement is reached immediately, and each party's share depends inversely on its discount rate (recall that we have set γ to zero here). A more patient player has greater capacity to threaten credibly to wait and therefore can demand a better offer.

We will focus first on the case in which the creditor's gains from trade are greater than its share of a three-way bargain, so that

$$zPy - Py\delta(1 + z)/(2\delta + r) > 0. \tag{10}$$

If the creditor country is making positive sidepayments in equilibrium, then both the banks and the debtor country get a larger payoff than in the absence of creditor-country participation:

$$Py\delta(1 + z)/(2\delta + r) - Py\delta/(\delta + r) > 0, \tag{11a}$$

$$Pyr(1 + z)/(2\delta + r) - Pyr/(\delta + r) > 0. \tag{11b}$$

The second term on the right-hand side of equation (11a) is the payoff to banks under bilateral bargaining (see equation (5), and recall that

$\gamma = 0$). The first term is the payoff under three-way bargaining. Thus no conflict of interest arises between the banks and the debtor country about whether to bring in the third party.

If creditor-country sidepayments are anticipated at the time of borrowing, the debtor country will be able to obtain a larger loan. The size of the maximum loan, $\Re$, depends on the present discounted value of the banks' share in any rescheduling agreement, so that

$$\Re = qPy(1 + z)/r. \tag{12}$$

There is an important distinction between anticipated and unanticipated creditor-country sidepayments. Unanticipated sidepayments benefit both the banks and the debtor country. The benefits of perfectly anticipated sidepayments, however, accrue entirely to the debtor country. Lenders are competitive, and thus earn zero profits on the loan (if there are no surprises). Therefore, the anticipation of creditor-country sidepayments just means that the borrowing country can take out a larger loan, with the creditor country effectively making the additional payments. As a detail, note that the amount by which the right-hand side of equation (12) exceeds the right-hand side of equation (6) does not quite equal the full discounted value of the creditor-country sidepayments, because the banks anticipate that the debtor country will be able to retain a larger share of its gains from trade when the creditor country becomes involved in negotiations.

How can the creditor-country taxpayers be induced to make sidepayments when they know that the banks and the debtor country would immediately arrive at a rescheduling agreement without their participation and, moreover, that this agreement would fully protect their gains from trade? The problem faced by the creditor-country taxpayers is that when their gains from trade are large enough, they cannot *credibly* refuse to bargain. The creditor country could, of course, avoid making sidepayments by abrogating the legal contracts between the banks and the debtor, thereby preventing the banks from impeding trade. We have assumed that the creditor country is unwilling to take this course, because the potential benefits are outweighed by the long-term damage to its legal system. Of course, if the creditor country planned on giving foreign aid to the debtor country anyway (aid in excess of the sidepayments it has to make in any rescheduling negotiations), the advent of debt merely converts a voluntary gift into a coerced contribution.

Thus far, we have focused on the case in which it is the creditor country that is called on to make sidepayments. If the inequality in equation (10) is reversed, then the creditor country's gains from trade are small enough for it to credibly commit to not making payments; with less to lose it can just outwait the other parties. It is even possible that the creditor country will be able to extract sidepayments from the debtor in order to allow bilateral trade. Nevertheless, the debtor could still use bank loans to reduce the discounted value of the sidepayments it has to make. Bringing in the banks may actually enhance the bargaining power of the debtor, as in the case considered above. The critical question, again, is whether the creditor country is able to abrogate easily the banks' lending contracts and undermine their bargaining position.

V. Concluding Remarks

This paper has provided a general bargaining-theoretic framework for analyzing multilateral debt rescheduling negotiations. Because our main results were summarized in the introduction, we conclude by observing that our approach to international trade negotiations differs sharply from the traditional literature on tariff wars (for example, Johnson (1954)). Our analysis predicts that all efficient *contemporaneous* trades are made. Although both sides may make threats, these threats are never executed in equilibrium. Threats do govern the distribution of the gains from trade, but only credible threats matter; that is, threats that the bargainer would carry out if called on to do so. The debtor country's inability to commit not to bargain over repayments does, however, lead to distortions in *intertemporal* trade.

REFERENCES

Alexander, Lewis S., "The Legal Consequences of Sovereign Default," (unpublished; Washington: Board of Governors of the Federal Reserve System, 1987).

Bulow, Jeremy, and Kenneth Rogoff (1989a), "A Constant Recontracting Model of Sovereign Debt," *Journal of Political Economy* (Chicago), Vol. 97 (February, forthcoming).

――― (1989b), "Sovereign Debt: Is to Forgive to Forget?" *American Economic Review* (Nashville, Tennessee), Vol. 79 (March, forthcoming).

Eaton, Jonathan, Mark Gersovitz, and Joseph E. Stiglitz, "The Pure Theory of Country Risk," *European Economic Review* (Amsterdam), Vol. 30 (June 1986), pp. 481–513.

Johnson, Harry G., "Optimum Tariffs and Retaliation," *Review of Economic Studies* (Edinburgh), Vol. 21 (1954), pp. 142–53.

Rubinstein, Ariel, "Perfect Equilibrium in a Bargaining Model," *Econometrica* (Evanston, Illinois), Vol. 50 (January 1982), pp. 97–109.

Sutton, John, "Non-Cooperative Bargaining Theory: An Introduction," *Review of Economic Studies* (Edinburgh), Vol. 53 (October 1986), pp. 709–24.

Sovereign Debt Renegotiation Under Asymmetric Information

KENNETH M. KLETZER*

This paper analyzes equilibrium debt contracts under potential renegotiation in the presence of sovereign risk. A simple model of borrowing from abroad to smooth consumption with stochastic national income is studied. Borrowers can choose to repudiate their debt obligations but face sanctions for doing so. With free entry in loan contracts, equilibrium debt renegotiations take the form of reductions in current debt service obligations with a new equilibrium market debt-contract. Under symmetric information, net inflows of funds are never provided in a renegotiation to a recalcitrant debtor. This contradicts part of the rationale given in the literature for a strategy of "defensive lending" to problem debtors. Asymmetric information about some debtor characteristics is introduced, and renegotiation of existing debt service obligations is shown to give rise to separating equilibria. Because of the presence of private information, new net inflows may occur along with significant increases in future debt obligations in the event of renegotiation. The implications of these results for the dynamics of debt-service obligations and several extensions of the simple model are discussed.

T HIS PAPER presents a theoretical analysis of the negotiation of the terms of contracts between private lenders and sovereign debtors. Credit market equilibrium when debt contracts are subject to renegotiation is studied in a framework which emphasizes the ability of a sovereign to repudiate its debt obligations. Our objective is to examine the consequences of contract renegotiation for new capital inflows to a country

* Kenneth Kletzer is Associate Professor of Economics at Yale University and holds a Ph.D. from the University of California at Berkeley.

and the growth of its external debt burden. Some of the results suggest that private negotiations lead to socially inefficient outcomes.

Several authors have discussed the potential of new loans to problem debtor nations for increasing the present value of existing external debt. Two issues need to be distinguished. The first of these, which is addressed in this paper, is the hypothesis that additional funds provided to a currently recalcitrant sovereign debtor form part of an optimal strategy for creditors as a whole. Cline (1984), Krugman (1985 and 1987), Sachs (1984), and others argue that additional funds reduce the probability of default on outstanding debt. Cline, in particular, merely assumes that new loans reduce the likelihood of default, so that additional loans which taken by themselves achieve negative expected profits provide the benefit of raising total expected repayments of outstanding debt. Therefore, the total return on the incremental loans to all creditors exceeds their opportunity cost. The second issue is that private lenders do not provide additional funds which increase the expected present value of all existing debt because existing creditors may be unable to internalize all the benefits due to the public-goods aspect of the new loans.

The characteristics of equilibrium loan contracts subject to subsequent renegotiation are discussed in a simple model of borrowing from abroad to smooth consumption when national income is stochastic, following the approach of Eaton and Gersovitz (1981). Borrowers have the ability to repudiate their obligations, but face sanctions for doing so. Lenders are assumed to be risk neutral and there is free entry in loan contracts, so that new creditors will provide any debt contract which assures them non-negative expected profits given existing debt service obligations. When a debtor suffers a low income state, repudiation with consequent penalization can be superior to meeting debt service obligations as originally contracted and choosing a new debt contract that provides zero expected profits to lenders.

In this case, existing creditors have an incentive to reduce the repayment obligations and refrain from declaring a default. A breach of contract does not automatically lead to declaration of default, because this is a subsequent option available to creditors and need not be exercised.

Equilibrium contract renegotiations are first examined for the case in which the debtor's current state is common knowledge. Optimal second-best renegotiations for the creditor in the presence of free entry in new debt contracts are shown to result in a reduction in existing debt service with no concurrent net inflow of funds to debtors. Furthermore, simple relending of funds to cover existing debt service payments in order to obtain an option on even larger future repayments is not, in general, optimal behavior for a creditor. The rationality for lenders of such "defensive" lending and debt reschedulings (suggested, for example, by Cline (1984) and Krugman (1985 and 1987)) is put into question by these results. The first section of this paper shows that when the debtor prefers the penalties that accompany repudiation to repaying its current debt and taking a new loan contract that assures non-negative expected profits to a new lender, then the old creditors' best actions are equivalent to reducing current debt service payments followed by a new market debt contract. Lindert (1986) makes a similar argument in a model without repayment renegotiations, in which the debtor can choose only full repayment or repudiation.

The section concludes by comparing debt contracts with subsequent renegotiation to equilibrium complete state-contingent loan contracts, constrained by the possibility of repudiation. Under free entry, ex post renegotiation of standard debt contracts does not lead to the same outcome as lending with ex ante specification of state-contingent repayment schedules.

The next section of the paper introduces asymmetric information about the debtor's state; this motivates the use of debt contracts in place of state-contingent claims. Equilibrium renegotiations in this extension of the simple model of sovereign borrowing may entail debt reschedulings and new capital inflows in order to satisfy a set of incentive compatibility constraints. These alternatives to debt write-downs will separate borrowers according to their current state, which is not observable directly by creditors. By inducing self-selection by borrowers, equilibrium debt renegotiation offers induce revelation of the debtor's private information. The introduction of private information qualifies the argument made in the perfect information model, but for very different reasons than those given by proponents of defensive lending. Debt renegotiation in this model leads to a dynamic behavior of net capital flows and debt service obligations that may be of some interest. Poor states of the world for debtors lead to large increases in debt burdens although the net inflow of capital is negative or small. The marginal rate of interest for rescheduled debt can become very large as a consequence of the asymmetry in information.

A natural extension of the analysis of these two sections is the introduction of bilateral bargaining ex post, to give debtors more market power than simply access to new lenders. The adoption of the non-cooperative strategic approach to the Nash bargaining problem in the complete and perfect information model will not affect qualitatively the outcomes of debt renegotiation. Under incomplete information about debtor characteristics, separation of different types of borrowers occurs through strategic delay rather than choice over a number of simultaneous offers made by creditors. The third section presents an approach to extending the analysis under asymmetric information to a strategic Nash bargaining framework. Both separating and pooling equilibria are possible outcomes. The model outlined includes capital accumulation, so that depreciation of the per capita physical capital stock is part of the social cost of delaying agreement in debt renegotiations.

The fourth section briefly summarizes a multi-period contracting approach when the debtor has sovereign immunity and lenders can credibly enter into contractual obligations binding on them which are enforceable in creditor nation courts. An application of such contracts, which incorporate, explicitly or implicitly, the possibility of revision, is the self-enforcement of restrictions on debt-dilution and provisions for debt-seniority. Contracts providing access to future loans on favorable terms provide an incentive for performance contingent on future events; repayment terms for early periods compensate lenders for the expected loss on these future contract options.

An alternative to the two extreme information assumptions is also discussed. A more realistic assumption may be that the debtor's current state is observable by creditors, but that policies (for example, those affecting investment levels) chosen by debtors are unobserved by lenders. In this case, the pattern of capital flows over time induces debtors to choose certain policies, but contracts cannot be written or renegotiated contingent upon the choice of policy. Capital flows can, at best, depend only on the history of borrower income in a stochastic model. The principal-agent approach to the repeated moral hazard problem can be extended to the sovereign borrowing case under a number of restrictive assumptions to yield a characterization of constrained optimal capital flows contingent on income. With the violation of the validity of a major assumption a distinct possibility arises that a complementarity between the collective actions of lenders and borrower policy choices can lead to inferior outcomes. This is especially likely when the policy instruments available for transferring resources from the private sector to the government for debt service are distortionary. Equilibria can exist that involve periods of large capital outflows requiring policies creating significant deadweight losses. At the margin, no additional loan will achieve non-negative profits, but the burden of distortionary policy can lead to a fundamental non-convexity. A large reduction in the current trade surplus may lead to an adequate shift in the marginal productivity of new loans to support the lower current debt service requirement. Since this requires lending by creditors with concurrent domestic policy revision by debtors, coordination can be a significant problem.

The last section offers concluding remarks and discusses implications of the asymmetric information case for the dynamics of debt service obligations. These suggest a significant social inefficiency reflected in the onset of repayment difficulties.

I. Debt Renegotiation in a Principal-Agent Model

This section discusses the renegotiation of debt service obligations in a version of the familiar Eaton-Gersovitz (1981) model. The sovereign debtor always has the option to repudiate its obligations outright and suffer consequent sanctions. The reduction in social welfare for the debtor country that sanctions can cause is limited, so that the borrower has limited liability for debt obligations. We assume that the threat of penalization for repudiation is credible and that creditors receive nothing by imposing sanctions. The behavior of the borrower is derived by maximizing a discounted stream of felicity of current consumption subject to a set of constraints. This represents a decisionmaker's social welfare function. A single good is produced and consumed. For simplicity, we ignore investment, so that output is an exogenous random variable. Under the informational assumptions of this section and the next, investment plays no essential qualitative role.

If the debtor chooses to repudiate, it receives a level of utility, $\overline{V}$, which depends on the current realization of output, y, and possibly on the value of the outstanding debt service obligations, R. That is, the repudiation level of utility depends on the debtor's current state, (y, R). The borrower's felicity function, $U(c)$, is concave, displays positive marginal felicity of current consumption, c, and is continuous. In equilibrium, the borrower will face a set of debt-contract offers in the event it chooses to pay current debt service and another set of offers if it seeks to renegotiate current contractual obligations. Because we assume a stationary environment (output is identically and independently distributed each period), the borrower can always select the same debt contract each period by paying the interest obligation on the constant principal every period. Since the realized level of output is observed before current consumption and the new loan are chosen, the borrower will select different contracts (or repudiation), including a possible request to renegotiate, depending upon the current state, (y, R).

An important assumption is that there is free entry in debt contracts— any expected profitable contract will be offered by a pool of potential lenders. If a loan providing non-negative expected profits will be accepted by a borrower, then it will be offered by some creditor. When a debtor prefers repudiation to repayment and selection of a new debt contract from this pool of potential lenders, existing creditors have an incentive to offer combinations of net current payments and new debt service obligations that cannot be obtained from the market. We model such renegotiations in a setting in which current creditors make offers to their debtors who choose to accept or reject these offers, but do not make counteroffers. This corresponds to a principal-agent setting in which the market power of existing creditors is limited by the potential entry of new creditors.

The utility maximization problem for debtors is first described. This provides constraints for the creditor's maximization problem. A debt contract is a pair (l_t, R_{t+1}), where l_t is the principal provided at time t and R_{t+1} is the total debt service obligation due at time $t + 1$, or, equivalently, the time $t + 1$ present value of the contracted repayment obligations.

In the event of full repayment, the borrower's value is given by:

$$V'(y_t, R_t) = \max \ U[y_t + l_t - R_t) + \beta EV(y_{t+1}, R_{t+1}], \tag{1}$$

with respect to l_t and R_{t+1} subject to $(l_t, R_{t+1}) \in S$, where the set S is independent of (y_t, R_t). The expectation is taken with respect to y_{t+1}; $V(\cdot, \cdot)$ will be defined below. The set S is the equilibrium set of debt contracts providing non-negative expected profits. The difference, $(l_t - R_t)$, is the net inflow of funds at time t. The discount factor, β, is between 0 and 1.

Let the debtor's repudiation value under limited liability be given by $\overline{V}(y_t, R_t)$ which is increasing in y_t and non-increasing in R_t. In the event of renegotiation, the debtor will choose a contract from a set of debt contracts that depend on the information available to creditors. We assume that this always includes R_t and discuss the case in which y_t is common knowledge in this section. In the next section, it is debtor private information. Define:

$$V^{re}(y_t, R_t) = \max \ [U(y_t + l_t - R_t) + \beta EV(y_{t+1}, R_{t+1})], \tag{2}$$

subject to $(l_t, R_{t+1}) \in S(y_t, R_t)$.

This latter set contains S and will include additional contracts if $V'(y_t, R_t)$ is less than $\overline{V}(y_t, R_t)$. The value of the debtor's optimal program is just

$$V(y_t, R_t) = \max \ [V^{re}(y_t, R_t), \overline{V}(y_t, R_t)], \tag{3}$$

since $V^{re}(y_t, R_t)$ is at least as great as $V'(y_t, R_t)$.

The distribution for output is assumed to have compact support. The expectation of V is taken with respect to y_t. We use the shorter notation $EV(R)$ for the remainder.

Creditors are assumed to be risk neutral (therefore, expected profit maximizers) and face an opportunity cost of loans given by a discount factor, ρ. A one-period debt contract provides expected profits given by

$$E\pi(l_t, R_{t+1}) = -l_t + \rho E(R|R_{t+1}), \tag{4}$$

where the expectation, taken with respect to the distribution of output, is of the actual period $t + 1$ present value of debt service payments conditional on the contractual obligation, R_{t+1}.

The legal status of existing debt service obligations within or between creditor nations will be crucial for determining the set of offered contracts. For example, while loan covenants binding on debtor behavior may not be credibly enforceable, seniority provisions binding on subsequent lenders may be enforceable in creditor nation courts. A senior creditor may be able to recover fully any payments made to successor lenders in its home country up to its contractual claim. On the other hand, if all claims have equal priority, creditors will share according to some proportions in actual settlements.

Suppose that the variable x denotes the surplus available for meeting debt service paid in an equilibrium settlement of obligations and that x is distributed according to the cumulative distribution function $F(x)$. This distribution depends upon the distribution of y and is conditional on R, in the general case. With strict seniority, the senior creditor obtains expected profits

$$E\pi(l, R) = -l + \rho\left[\int_0^R xdF(x) + R\int_R^M dF(x)\right], \tag{5}$$

where M is the maximum total settlement possible.

A second creditor will obtain

$$E\pi(\bar{l}, \bar{R}; R) = -\bar{l} + \rho\left[\int_R^{\bar{R}} (x - R)dF(x) + \bar{R}\int_{\bar{R}}^M dF\right]$$

with contract $(\bar{l}, \bar{R})$ given prior commitments R. In such an instance, the set of new debt contracts available to a borrower will be identical for any number of concurrent loans taken. The debtor can do no better than to accept a zero-expected profit contract from a single source.

If lenders share in payments according to the portion of their claims in total claims, then each lender attains expected profits

$$E\pi(l_i, R_i; R) = -l + \rho\left[(R_i/R)\int_0^R x \, dF(x) + R_i\int_R^M dF(x)\right],$$

where $R = \sum_i R_i$.

In this case, in an equilibrium debt contract, each lender correctly anticipates subsequent contract offers so that expected profits for every creditor are non-negative. The set of total debt contracts that attain non-negative expected profits is the same whenever obligations to new lenders do not take precedence over existing debt, since the conditional distribution of x is unaffected. However, the equilibrium debt contract will not be the same. Under strict seniority, the choice of contract made in equation (1) will be the best zero-expected profit contract for the debtor (equivalent to the Nash equilibrium contract under observability defined in Kletzer (1984)). In the absence of seniority provisions (for example, the neutral case above), the equilibrium contract will be an interest-rate taking zero-profit contract, as defined in Kletzer (1984) (equivalently, in Gale and Hellwig (1985)). This type of contract is socially inefficient, in that it is dominated for the debtor by the strict seniority outcome. For now, we assume that seniority provisions enforceable between creditors in their home courts are credible.

The initial description of equilibrium debt renegotiations in this standard approach will be made assuming that the debtor always has the option to pay contractual debt service and select a new debt contract that will realize a non-negative expected profit. However, a new debt contract may not be offered if existing obligations are not met, because new creditors' claims are junior to existing claims. If new funds are offered when old debts are not being serviced, in the absence of a negotiated settlement, the debt service obligations on these new funds are at least as great as they would be for incremental funds taken in addition to the original contract (that is, the additional debt service that would be incurred to obtain a larger original contract). The additional debt service obligations will be even greater if the old creditors can claim additional interest from payments made to the new suppliers.

Free entry in debt contracts and the limited liability of debtors impose limitations on the outcomes attainable by creditors in debt service renegotiations. Constrained contract renegotiations for the lender can be described using a principal-agent framework in which the creditor offers contract revisions to the debtor. We first assume that the borrowers' current output, y, is common knowledge (throughout, we assume that the debtor's utility function is common knowledge). In this setting, a first-best contract may not be a standard debt contract with ex post renegotiation of debt service because additional risk sharing may be provided by state-contingent contracts. We first discuss renegotiation of debt contracts because this corresponds more closely to the framework in which the case for defensive lending has been argued. The structure of equilibrium state-contingent contracts in this approach is discussed at the end of this section.

Because the equilibrium set of debt contracts offered will be bounded from above in l, there exist states such that the borrower prefers repudiation to full repayment. These states can be shown to occur with positive probability. Because creditors lose the entire opportunity cost of their loans in a repudiation, any settlement that provides some current repayment or net expected future payment will be preferred by the creditor. The borrower's alternative of choosing a zero-expected profit contract (but junior claim) from another lender without repaying will, at the worst, result in a loss to the current creditors of the opportunity interest on the maximum settlement they would obtain in the current state. If we assume, for simplicity, that no additional interest is attainable, then the debtor prefers to repudiate if

$$\overline{V}(y, R) > \max\{\max\ [U(y + \overline{l}) + \beta EV\ (R + \overline{R})],\ V'(y, R)\}, \qquad (6)$$

$$(\overline{l}, \overline{R} + R) \in S.$$

Modification for imperfectly enforceable seniority clauses or enforceable contracts specifying overdue interest charges is straightforward.

Whenever (6) obtains, creditors will select contracts that provide the debtor with utility at least equal to the repudiation level. These offers will depend only on the debtor's current state. If we make the simplification that $\overline{V}(y, R) = \overline{V}(y)$, then the equilibrium expected profits for debt contracts is given by (5), where $F(x)$ depends on the level of debt service obligations and the distribution of y. The set S is given by

$$S = [(l, R) \,|\, E\pi\ (l, R) \geq 0]$$

When only the lender makes offers that the debtor accepts or rejects (in the presence of free entry of new creditors under our seniority assumption), the equilibrium renegotiated offers satisfy

$$\max\left[R - l(y_t) + \rho \int_0^{R(y_t)} x dF(x) + \rho\ R(y_t) \int_{R(y_t)}^M\ dF(x)\right] \qquad (7)$$

with respect to $l(y_t)$, $R(y_t)$

s.t. $\overline{V}\ (y_t) \leq U[y_t + l(y_t) - R] + \beta EV[R(y_t)].$

Note that any solution cannot be contained in S since (6) holds. The solution to this problem is identical to the solution to the problem:

max R

s.t. $\overline{V}(y_t) \leq \max\ [U(y_t + l' - R) + \beta EV(R')],$

with respect to $(l', R') \in S.$

The profit-maximizing lender will never choose to make an offer of a net flow of funds to or from a debtor that involves an incremental loan providing negative expected profits. Any creditor-optimal renegotiation is equivalent to a simple reduction in current debt service (in expected present value terms) plus a new loan attainable from any potential entrant. The creditor should be indifferent between offering a current net payment with a new debt service obligation and offering a reduction in the current debt service just enough that a new creditor will take over the debt and the borrower will not choose to repudiate. Because the debtor always has the option to repudiate, the expected value of continuation in (1)–(3) must be at least as great as the expected value under repudiation. Therefore, whenever (6) obtains, contractual performance must require a net outflow of output from the debtor. A solution to problem (7) never entails a new inflow of funds to the borrower.

A common argument (for example, Krugman (1985)) is that the relending of contractual debt service obligations when a debtor is unwilling to meet them currently is a preferred action for lenders because the option on higher future payments is obtained at no cost in new capital. The above discussion lends considerable doubt to this commonsense proposition. Relending old debt service with interest and a zero current net flow of funds is not generally the optimal ex post contract for the creditor. The maximum expected present value of a renegotiated contract is attained by reducing debt obligations by just enough so that the debtor can achieve its repudiation level of utility by selecting its optimal new zero-expected profit debt contract. This debtor action (or its equivalent, in which current creditors are also the new providers of the zero-expected profit loan) extracts all the debtor's surplus; therefore, no other contract renegotiation is superior for the current creditors. The option on new debt repayments under the rollover scheme has a positive opportunity cost; starting at the creditor-optimal revised contract devised above, a negative expected profit loan must be made implicitly to provide the rescheduled loan that gives the debtor utility equal to its repudiation utility.

Figure 1 depicts the set of new debt contracts, S, and indifference curves for the debtor for the more general case of the repudiation utility depending on both y and R. The horizontal axis measures the net inflow of resources to the debtor. The set S is not bounded from above in contractual obligations in the presence of equilibrium renegotiations. The maximum expected present value of a renegotiation attainable by creditors can be seen to be the greatest value of $-R$ such that the set S intersects the repudiation indifference curve.

Because the debtor has limited liability for debt obligations in this framework, the utility attained with a current zero net flow of resources is always at least as great as the level of utility received by repudiating. Therefore, no new flows from lenders are required to avoid repudiation.

Figure 1.

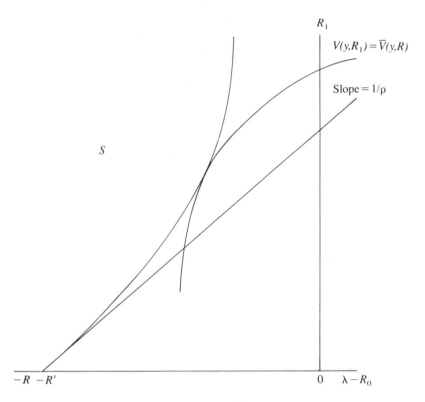

The presence of debt service obligations as a state variable introduces a simple history dependence in the expected utility of debtors and the renegotiation offers made available. Past realizations of income affect current choices of debtors and, in the event of renegotiation, existing creditors. In this simple Markov model, however, the set of new debt contracts, S, is unaffected. In equilibrium, only partial risk sharing between risk-neutral lenders and risk-averse borrowers is achieved through debt contracts with renegotiation. This occurs because creditors are limited in their abilities to obtain large payments in the best income states of nature.

An alternative approach to the problem of lending with potential repudiation under complete and perfect information is to derive the first-best type of contract (constrained by the threat of repudiation) that will be state contingent. The problem of characterizing such contracts in our setting can be posed as a simple static constrained maximization problem by recognizing that the future utility of the debtor will be determined completely by the difference between income and debt service obligations, $[y_{t+1} - R(y_{t+1})]$, since repudiation will never occur (if creditors receive nothing in that event).

The first-best problem with free entry in loan contracts is given by (assuming $\overline{V}$ is only a function of y):

$$\max V(y_t - R_t) = U(y_t + l_t - R_t) + \beta EV[y_{t+1} - R(y_{t+1})],$$

with respect to l_t and $R(y_{t+1})$,

subject to $V[y_{t+1} - R(y_{t+1})] \geq \overline{V}(y_{t+1})$

and $-l_t + \rho E[R(y_{t+1})] = 0$.

The solution to this problem is straightforward and entails constant consumption for a subset of the output states, if ρ equals β. The states for which utility may be held to the repudiation level will be the high output states, not the low ones. Consumption is imperfectly smoothed if repudiation is superior in some (high output) state to consumption of mean output. This contrasts sharply with the second-best renegotiation case. If ρ exceeds β (the borrower is more impatient than the lender), then a sequence of one-period loan contracts may smooth income for early periods, but after the repudiation constraint becomes binding in the best output state, consumption will continue to decline and will not be smoothed thereafter in the framework used above. Worrall (1987) adopts a trigger-strategy penalty mechanism for competitive lenders and shows that long-run consumption smoothing can result.

In the perfect information setting, first-best contracts are fully state contingent. Such contracts cannot be replicated by simple debt contracts with ex post renegotiation in the presence of free entry of new creditors. The latter type of contracts may arise as first-best outcomes when debtors' current states are observable by creditors only at a cost (for example, see Gale and Hellwig (1985)).

II. Private Information and Separating Equilibria

In this section, debtors are assumed to possess private information about the utility they receive by accepting various debt contracts. Therefore they have an incentive to report incorrectly their willingness to repudiate to obtain a reduction in debt service payments. Whenever lenders perceive a positive probability, given current debt obligations, that a borrower would prefer repudiation to the selection of a new debt contract with repayment, the borrower may be able to misrepresent its private information. If creditors are unable to observe the realized value of output, under the equilibrium renegotiation scheme of the previous section in every output state the debtor will claim willingness to repudiate. Some contract with debt service reduction chosen in a low output state will be preferred in a high output state to repayment. Creditors will seek to design the offers they make in debt renegotiations to induce correct revelation of the private information. Lenders will want to offer debt renegotiation packages which will be chosen over repudiation in poor events but which are inferior to repayment in favorable outcomes.

The private information possessed by debtors can be anything that affects the social welfare attained by choosing different debt contracts. For example, national leadership may be better informed about factors determining the social costs of achieving given levels of trade surplus than are foreign creditors. For expositional simplicity, let the realized value of output be unobservable by creditors, although we intend it to be a proxy for some measure of debtor country surplus. The distribution of output is assumed to be common knowledge, as are all other characteristics of the borrower. Also, suppose that output, y, can only take a finite number of values with positive probability. These are given by $y_1, y_2, \ldots, y_n$ in increasing order. The random variable, y, can be thought of as parameterizing a class of utility functions for the national leadership. Creditors do not know what type of decisionmaker they face at each date. Each period a new type is drawn from the common distribution. In this interpretation, the period length is the time a particular type is in power. Again, the identification of y with output is not intended to be literal.

The creditors' problem is to choose a set of contracts to offer in the event of renegotiation requests such that their ex ante expected profit is maximized, when debtors ex post maximize utility over the set of contracts (including renegotiation packages) available. A contract renegotiation will be chosen only if it is the maximal contract in the realized state over the set of contracts offered for all states. The creditor's inability to observe output implies that debtor self-selection alone must be relied upon to assure the anticipated behavior in each output state. The creditor's problem is to design a contract set that induces truthful revelation. The equilibrium set of renegotiations offered will separate different output realizations through contract choice, so that ex post the private information is revealed.

The set of equilibrium offers under free entry in ex ante contracts, debtor-creditor relationships and debtor limited liability is characterized again using a principal-agent framework. Because simple reductions in debt service will be chosen by the borrower in either low or high output states, offered revisions of debt repayments under asymmetric information about output realizations must observe a self-selection constraint.

The contracts offered to assure non-repudiation in low output states must be inferior to other contracts available when the debtor realizes high output value. The addition of constraints assuring correct contract selection leads to a separating equilibrium. There will be n contracts available, with a different contract selected in each output realization. The contract intended to be selected in a particular state will provide the maximum utility to the debtor in that state over the set of offers. Some of these contracts will simply be the best choices over the set of new debt contracts available from any potential creditor. That is, the set of ex ante debt contracts will always be available with repayment of contractual debt service.

The set of ex ante debt contracts (those available from any new entrant creditor following repayment) will be found by first characterizing the set of ex post repayment revisions offered in equilibrium for a given current debt service obligation, R. Each member of the set of debt contracts offered by the current creditor will consist of a current net payment and a debt service obligation for the next period. These contracts will not be equivalent to the debt reductions derived in the previous section. Imposition of the self-selection contraints is found to result in lower ex post profit in each state than could be attained if the value of output were observed directly by the creditor. The equilibrium set of contracts involve higher levels of debt service for the next period for low output realizations than would arise with symmetric information.

The set of ex ante offers is derived using the solution to the creditor's ex post problem, as a perfect equilibrium. The set of initial non-negative expected profit contracts offered is a subset of what it would be without private information. Lenders are assured non-negative expected profits ex ante, so that ex ante debtor utility is lower than under symmetric information. In most states, however, debtors are better off ex post than if they could then report their output state before revised repayment offers are made. In states for which repudiation provides higher utility than full repayment, the debtor can receive higher utility under debt renegotiation than the repudiation level. Since under symmetric information, the debtor is always forced to either its repudiation utility level or its maximal utility over the set of new contracts with repayment (whichever is larger), direct reporting of the value of output before the choice of a contract ex post is incredible. Direct revelation only occurs with the selection of a separating equilibrium contract revision.

Given a level of existing debt service obligations, R, the existing creditor's problem is to find contracts, (l_i, R_i), for each i, to maximize expected profits. The set of zero expected profit debt contracts, S, will be found implicitly; however, we assume that it is non-empty and define a loan offer, l', for each next period debt service obligation, R_i. That is, $l'(R_i)$ is the size loan which repayment obligation R_i equals in expected present value for creditors. The present value loss to a creditor from offering the contract

(l_i, R_i), is $[l_i - l'(R_i)]$.

The existing creditor's problem is given by

$$\max \sum_{i=1}^{n} p_i[l_i'(R_i) - l_i] \tag{8}$$

with respect to $[(l_i, R_i)]$ for $i = 1, \ldots, n$, subject to, for all i,

(a) $U(y_i + l_i - R) + \beta EV(R_i) \geq \overline{V}(y_i, R)$

(b) $U(y_i + l_i - R) + \beta EV(R_i) \geq V'(y_i, R)$

(c) $U(y_i + l_i - R) + \beta EV(R_i) \geq U(y_i + l_j - R) + \beta EV(R_j)$,
for all $j \neq i$.

The probability of output y_i being realized is p_i. Constraint (a) is the restriction that repudiation is inferior to the debt contract offered for each value y_i, and (b) is the restriction on offers created by free entry in new contracts. The third is the self-selection constraint. The contract (l_i, R_i) is at least as good for the debtor in state i as every other offer. We assume that indifference for the debtor is resolved in the lender's favor to assure a solution.

The solution to this problem yields a set of n offers ex post such that debt repudiation never occurs. The contracts offered to the debtor which are taken in some states for which repudiation is superior to repayment on contracted terms can provide greater utility than outright repudiation. Likewise, in some states for which selection of a new ex ante debt contract (with full repayment) is preferred to repudiation, the debtor will attain even higher utility by taking a contract offered by the current creditor but not by new entrants. The self-selection constraints produce these possibilities by creating trade-offs between expected profit in different states. The equilibrium contracts are interrelated.

The following proposition summarizes the properties of the equilibrium set of debt renegotiations. Define $V(x_i, R_i) \equiv U(y_i + l_i - R) + \beta EV(R_i)$, where $x_i = l_i - R$.

Proposition: Given current debt service obligations, the lender's most preferred debt renegotiations satisfy:

a) x_i and R_i are both non-increasing in i.

b) $V_i(x_i, R_i)$ is non-decreasing in i.

c) If $\overline{V}(y_1, R) < V'(y_1, R)$, then $V_1(x_1, R_1) = \overline{V}(y_1, R)$.

(An analogous condition may hold for additional i.)

d) Whenever $V_i(x_i, R_i) > \max[\overline{V}(y_i, R), V'(y_i, R)]$, $V_i(x_i, R_i) = V_i(x_{i-1}, R_{i-1})$ holds.

e) If $V_i(x_i, R_i) = V'(y_i, R)$, then $(l_i, R_i) \in S, l_i = x_i + R$, and $(l_j, R_j) \in S$, for all $j > i$, so that $V_j(x_j, R_j) = V'(y_j, R)$, also.

The proof of this proposition and additional hypotheses are contained in the appendix. Sappington (1983) presents similar results to part of the above for a simpler limited liability principal-agent problem.

In equilibrium, utility is nondecreasing and the net payment by the debtor is nondecreasing in output, while the next period debt service obligation is nonincreasing in output. The set of debt renegotiations offered forces the debtor in the lowest output state, if repudiation is ever preferred to repayment, to its repudiation level of utility. This may also be true for higher states.

The debtor may choose contracts from the ex ante zero expected profit set (contracts new entrants offer) in some high output states. The equilibrium ex post contract in these states may provide even higher utility. If the debtor attains just $V'(y_i, R)$ in state y_i, then the existing creditor just offers the same set of debt contracts which any new entrant will offer, S. If the solution to the creditor's problem has the debtor choose repayment and a new zero expected profit contract in a state j, then the equilibrium choice in all higher states is also repayment as contracted. Result (d) states that the debtor is indifferent between the equilibrium debt contract for the realized state under renegotiation and the contract offered for the next lowest state, except, possibly, in two situations. The first occurs when the current state renegotiated debt contract provides just the repudiation level of utility for that state. The second occurs when the contract chosen in equilibrium involves full repayment for the present realization of output.

The continuous-state indifference property of result (d) and the above exceptions deserve explanation. If the debtor is offered a contract, (x_{i-1}, R_{i-1}), expected present value for the creditor in the next highest state can always be increased if the debtor's utility can be reduced in this next highest state. Therefore, unless utility cannot be reduced further in state i, the debtor is indifferent between the debt renegotiations for that state and for the next lower state. When the debtor achieves exactly the repudiation level of utility or the level assured by free entry in new debt contracts, this indifference may or may not hold. If the debtor chooses a new debt contract with full repayment in both the present state and next lower state, under concavity of felicity, this property does not hold.

Figure 2 shows a separating equilibrium set of debt renegotiations. The intertemporal marginal rate of substitution portrayed decreases with

Figure 2.

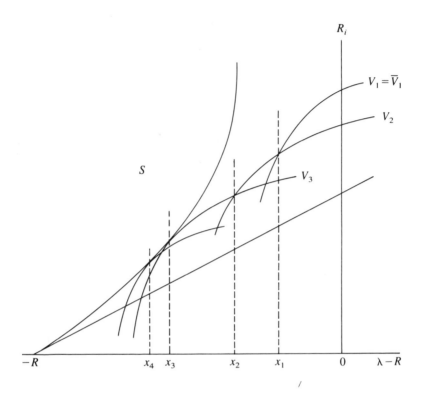

y for a given contract because $U(c)$ is strictly concave. Concavity is important for demonstrating the proposition; however, concavity of $U(c)$ does not imply that the derived indifference curves are convex everywhere. The relation between expected value and contractual debt service obligations depends on the entire set of equilibrium debt contracts. The indifference curves are drawn smooth in Figure 2 for simplicity; with a finite number of states, they will each contain kinks.

The equilibrium ex post contracts display a simple relationship between the intertemporal rate of substitution in contract terms along the boundary of S (zero expected profit contracts) and the intertemporal marginal rate of substitution. These are equal if full repayment occurs in equilibrium. If the debtor in state i is assigned contract (x_i, R_i), then the slope of the boundary of S at the contract $[l'(R_i), R_i]$ equals the intertemporal rate of substitution if the debtor is not indifferent in state $i + 1$ between this contract and (x_{i+1}, R_{i+1}). In the case of continuous state indifference, the rate of contract substitution equals a weighted sum of the marginal rate of substitution in state i and in state $i + 1$. The weight on the state $i + 1$ marginal rate of substitution is negative, but smaller in absolute value than the weight on the state i rate of substitution. This reflects the trade-off to ex post expected profit between lowering state i profit by revising R_i and x_i and increasing state $i + 1$ profit by reducing utility in state $i + 1$ (lowering x_{i+1}). The marginal rate of substitution of R_i for x_i in state i is less than the intertemporal rate of contract substitution. Therefore, state i profit alone is not maximized. The weights are implicitly given in the proof of the proposition; they depend upon the probability distribution of output and the marginal felicity of consumption in the two states.

Derivation of the set of initial loan contracts, S, remains. The ex ante expected profit is given by

$$E\pi = -l + \rho\{R + \sum_{i=1}^{n} p_i[l'(R_i) - l_i]\},$$

where (l_i, R_i) are solutions to the creditor's ex post optimization problem. The last term (summand) is the expected present value of the reduction in debt service received. Even if l_i exceeds $l'(R_i)$, the lender's return may exceed opportunity cost in some states. Maximization of expected profit will lead to a non-zero probability that the debtor is willing to repudiate. Risk neutrality of creditors allows risk-averse debtors to achieve some degree of insurance. As in the well-known principal-agent literature (for example, Holmstrom (1979), Harris and Raviv (1979)), risk sharing is incomplete owing to the need for equilibrium debt renegotiation to observe the self-selection constraints. Maximization of ex ante expected profit gives the set of non-negative expected profit contracts offered by new entrants. We assume that the utility function for the debtor, possible output states, and lender's discount factor are adequate to assure that the set is non-empty and potential debtors choose to borrow initially.

An important consequence of the proposition is that the maximal ex ante contractual debt service obligation is at least as great as the resulting ex post debt service for the succeeding period in the lowest output state. Any increase in debt obligations beyond this level will never be met. A corollary to the proposition is that this level of debt obligations is the maximum amount such that ex post, the debtor repays in full and selects a new zero expected profit contract in the highest output state. Figure 3 portrays this equilibrium. The indifference curves are vertical beyond R_1, as increases in R_i have no effect on the debtor because such incremental repayment obligations are never repaid.

In a separating equilibrium, the net capital outflow from the debtor

Figure 3.

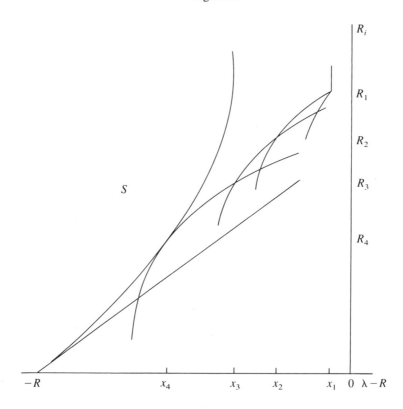

can be either positive or negative in a state for which repudiation dominates full repayment of existing debt service and choice of a new ex ante
debt contract. This contrasts with the equilibrium outcome under symmetric information. The possibility that the lender provides additional
inflows to a recalcitrant debtor arises when the repudiation level of
utility depends upon the debt service obligations that are repudiated.
Contracts that satisfy the necessary conditions for expected profit maximization in low states may involve positive values of x, because the
intertemporal marginal rate of substitution is finite for the repudiation
level of utility at contracts with zero net outflows (x equal to zero). This
possibility does not arise if the cost of repudiation depends only on the
current value of output. In this case, the debtor will always prefer a
contract with zero net outflow to repudiation, regardless of the next-
period repayment obligation. Therefore, in the lowest state, a net
payment to the existing creditor is made under debt renegotiation.

Two properties of the solution to the creditors' two-stage optimization problem are notable. The first is that there may be many equilibria; nothing in this framework rules them out. Multiple equilibria are likely to occur when repudiation costs depend upon current debt service obligations. The second is that there is no reason that an ex ante state-contingent contract not be written. Such contracts can specify the same equilibrium set of contracts as derived in the revision problem. Ex post, the debtor reveals its private information by selecting the net payment and contract for the next period we characterized above. Because the sovereign debtor always can choose to accept none of the contracted payments and next period obligations and select a new ex ante contract if utility is higher by doing so, such state-contingent contracts will be solutions to an identical two-stage problem. The only difference is in interpretation. We have solved the problem of contract selection by creditors when the debtor has limited liability, and there is always free entry in new debtor-creditor relationships. That is, the equilibrium state-contingent contract will assure the debtor at least as much utility in the highest state as it attains by meeting the current obligation and choosing a new creditor.

While we have represented the solution as formed by an initial debt contract followed by debt renegotiation offers by the current creditor, when both sides place positive probabilities on all possible subsequent events, a more complex state-contingent contract would suffice. There is no need for renegotiation. If an event occurs upon which one of the parties to the contract placed zero probability, however, a contract renegotiation can be mutually beneficial. For example, if there is an unanticipated change in the world interest rate (creditors' discount rate), the creditor may wish to revise the set of ex post contracts offered. If a full state-contingent contract binding on the creditor is in force, then only changes favoring the debtor can be acceptable. With private information, both the existing separating contracts and any new offers can be selected by the debtor. If, instead, the ex ante contract specifies only the loan principal and debt service obligation, then the ex post contracts can be offered by the creditor after observation of the interest rate shift. The creditors can offer initial relationships that specify contracts for each output state in every possible realization of the world interest rate. Because the world interest rate is public information, such contingent debt contracts can provide welfare gains when the creditor is risk neutral and debtor risk averse. If the creditor's discount rate is private information (for example, depending upon the remainder of its loan portfolio), then debt contracts with subsequent renegotiation possibilities can arise in equilibrium. We can also appeal to the costs of writing or resolving disputes over complex state-contingent contracts to support the assumption of renegotiation and to rule out interest rate contingencies.

The effects of an interest rate shock (realization of ρ anticipated with zero probability) on the set of ex post separating contracts is ambiguous. An increase in creditors' discount rates causes a reduction in the set of ex ante contracts. In states for which repayment is preferred to repudiation (although the equilibrium debt renegotiation is not necessarily in S), there is a tendency for x_i to fall and R_i to increase (therefore, utility must decrease). For states in which repudiation is superior, however, the change in contract is ambiguous. The interest rate increase will lead to a reduction in debtor expected utility and a reduction in the present value of the contract for the creditor.

III. Separation Through Costly Delay in Bargaining

The principal-agent framework used in the previous two sections provides insight into the nature of debt renegotiation outcomes when borrowers have more bargaining power than just the options to return to the loan market or repudiate. If we allow output in any given period to be storable for some positive length of time (however short, or with arbitrarily large but finite rate of depreciation), then the equilibria derived in both the perfect and imperfect information cases are equilibria for a strategic bargaining game in which the creditor makes all offers (see Sobel and Takahashi (1983)). For a strategic bargaining game, with alternating offers, debtors will achieve better outcomes ex post than were attained in the preceding solutions. Nevertheless, the ex ante contract offers will adjust to account for the ex post divisions of surplus in any subgame perfect equilibrium.

Bulow and Rogoff (1989) adopt the strategic approach to Nash bargaining games under complete information, owing to Rubinstein (1982), to sovereign debt negotiations. The creditor who acquires the right to impose sanctions by making an initial loan sells a promise not to impose sanctions each period to the debtor. The amount paid in the subgame perfect equilibrium each period for this property right is just the debt service payment. The discounted stream of these prices is equal to the amount initially lent under perfect competition among lenders. The perfect equilibrium is unique if penalization benefits creditors an arbitrarily small amount. The complete information model presented earlier in this paper needs minor additional assumptions to fit the Rubinstein (1982) framework: let output be storable and let the debtor be risk neutral. In this setting, renegotiations will never result in new inflows unless a new creditor will also supply them. Under risk aversion, access to new credit in the presence of seniority provisions can become the object bargained over, but the characterization of renegotiations will not be affected. In the complete information bargaining approach, there is no particular reason why the initial contract does not simply specify the perfect equilibrium debt service payments. If it does, then no bargaining actually takes place.

The asymmetric information model can also be extended to a bargaining framework. Delays to agreement can lead to separation of debtors by type in an alternating offers bargaining game. Simultaneously offered contracts by the creditor no longer serve the purpose of inducing truthful revelation. Incomplete information can be introduced, as before, through asymmetric observability of output, or through private information about rates of time preference. Delaying agreement can arise strategically to separate borrowers with different realizations of privately observed random variables, or of different social preferences, which are unobserved by creditors. Delay can also arise because one or both parties find that waiting for publicly observed information to arrive is individually rational. This case may be important when creditors, as well as debtors, have limited liability and are therefore risk loving.

This section outlines an approach to modeling socially costly delays to a resolution of debt repayment problems. The impasse in the current repayments crisis and the consequent lack of funds to finance capital formation have been discussed widely. In noncooperative Nash bargaining models, equilibrium delay to agreement has been shown to arise in the presence of incomplete information by a large number of authors. We discuss one source of delay: strategic delay necessary to convey the debtor's private information.

Our approach is to adopt the bargaining model with one-sided incomplete information of Admati and Perry (1987), which has equilibrium paths displaying strategic delay to external borrowing by a growing economy. Following Bulow and Rogoff, we assume that by lending the creditor purchases a right to impose sanctions; the promise not to exercise this right is then sold to the debtor at the subgame-perfect price and time. Unlike their model, agreement need not occur immediately here. A major cost of delay to agreement will be the absence of new credit. New creditors may not provide additional funds to a growing debtor in the presence of unresolved existing claims. The reason is that the net inflow of resources will affect the bargaining game between old creditors and the debtor and therefore the investment undertaken by the borrower. The future flow of output following a given loan will, in general, be less if existing claims need to be resolved.

Several possible approaches can motivate the adoption of the strategic delay model. The debtor is assumed to have private information about the value it places on avoiding sanctions. Sanctions are assumed to lead to lower levels of per capita consumption than are attainable along an equilibrium path for the bargaining game, so that debt repudiation will never occur in equilibrium. Capital accumulation is possible, and either the labor force grows at a constant proportional rate or physical capital depreciates. Foreign borrowing can be motivated by assuming that either the planner's discount rate or the marginal productivity of capital exceed the world rate of interest. A simple model is one in which output, which depreciates in storage, is traded for capital goods which are noncompetitive imports. During an impasse, the per capita capital stock declines.

The private information of the debtor is about the surplus available to pay creditors. This can be the current realized value of output in a stochastic model, as in previous sections, or it can be the minimum level of per capita consumption politically acceptable in a renegotiation, or other debtor characteristics. Suppose that whenever per capita consumption falls below some level, $\bar{c}$, political leadership is replaced immediately (through either parliamentary or nondemocratic means). Then the surplus available to service debt obligations, that is, the value placed on purchasing the promise not to impose sanctions, is the amount of current resources exceeding those needed to sustain $\bar{c}$ along a perfect equilibrium path. The country's policymakers are likely to be more informed about $\bar{c}$, or, more generally, the social cost of generating given levels of trade surpluses (for example, the excess burden of indirect taxes).

We assume that output is produced using capital and labor according to a constant returns-to-scale technology. Output is storable (depreciation can occur, but need not) and is consumed or traded for investment goods, which are not produced at home. Let output be given by

$$y_t = f(k_t)$$

and let

$$\Delta k_t = k_{t+1} - k_t = i_t - nk_t.$$

Storage is given by s_t, so that

$$y_t = c_t + (\gamma s_{t-1} - s_t) - R_t,$$

where γ is the rate of depreciation of stored output and R_t is output exported.

The trade surplus is just

$$R_t - i_t.$$

We ignore sanctions by assuming that repudiations lead to consumption equal to or less than the minimum politically acceptable in a negotiated settlement. If lenders benefit from imposing sanctions, by any arbitrarily small positive amount, then no subgame-perfect equilibrium involves repudiation without consequent penalization (see Bulow and Rogoff). We simply assume that penalization for repudiation is a credible threat.

The policymaker's social welfare function is just

$$U = \sum_{t=0}^{\infty} \beta^t c_t.$$

The value of the optimal capital accumulation program along a subgame-perfect equilibrium path can be defined directly. We first need to note that once the debtor's private information is revealed, a complete information bargaining subgame follows for the model described here. The creditor's lack of information about the value of sanctions to the debtor derives from potential differences in the type of debtor, rather than imperfect information about its current state. This assumption allows us to look at a single episode, but the generalization is a formal exercise.

The debtor's type is characterized by the maximum surplus it can transfer to creditors in exchange for suspension of the threat of sanctions at a given time. Time matters both because the social discount rate is positive and the per capita capital stock declines during delays to agreement.

Suppose that the low $\bar{c}$ type repays at time 0. Then the surplus (denoted h_0) in a given state, k_0, is defined by the problem

$$V(k_0 \mid h) = \max_{k_1} [c_0 + \beta V(k_1)]$$

subject to

$$k_1 = k_0 + i - nk_0,$$

$$c_0 = f(k_0) - (h + i),$$

where $V(k_1)$ is the value of the debtor's utility along a subsequent equilibrium path. Let h_0 be the maximum value of h such that $c_0 \geq \bar{c}$.

We can derive the debtor's value in terms of the amount paid the creditor and the time at which settlement takes place by noting that if its type is revealed, then subsequent negotiations have the unique complete information bargaining solution, so that the value function is well defined. If a pooling equilibrium results (which is a possible outcome), then the game repeats. If the state variable, k_t, is observed by the creditor, however, the type can be inferred after one round with a pooling equilibrium outcome.

For given k_0, define the debtor's value of an agreement as

$S(h_t - R, t)$, for the low $\bar{c}$ type, and

$S(l_t - R, t)$, for the high $\bar{c}$ type,

where $l_t < h_t$ for an agreement which transfers an amount R at time t to creditors. $S(\cdot, \cdot)$ is increasing in the first argument and decreasing in the second. The approach of Admati and Perry (1987) can now be applied.

Suppose at time 0, the lender can make an offer to which the debtor replies at time 1. The debtor will never accept an offer that provides less value than the value of an offer it can make at time 1 that would be accepted by the lender. The discount factor for the lender is determined by the opportunity interest rate. The results of Admati and Perry can be directly applied to this model with algebraic modification. The high surplus type can refuse a current high offer and wait to receive an offer that the low surplus type would accept. In equilibrium, the low surplus debtor cannot offer at time 1 an amount which the high surplus type would prefer to wait and offer to taking the time 0 offer. The low surplus debtor must wait long enough to make a counteroffer to separate itself from the high surplus type when the creditor's first (time 0) offer is the equilibrium offer for the high type in the complete-information bargaining game.

Multiple equilibria emerge from this approach. Unique separating equilibria exist for large enough creditors' priors that the debtor is of the high surplus type. These involve offering the complete information game division for the high type at time 0. The low type offers its complete-information game equilibrium division after a time delay adequate to signal its type. Separation becomes costly by reducing the surplus obtained by the low value debtor and reducing through delay the available output that may be divided.

If the creditor's prior belief is that there is a low probability that the debtor is the high surplus type, both multiple separating and pooling equilibria are possible. For low priors, there exists only a unique pooling equilibrium in which no delay occurs. This latter equilibrium involves lenders offering the complete information equilibrium repayment for the low surplus type in time 0. Either type accepts this offer.

One consequence of introducing capital stock depreciation as a cost of delay is to increase the possibilities for pooling equilibria to arise. Another is that the cost of delay to the high surplus type can, in general, be lower than the cost for the low surplus type. Of course, the depreciation of the capital stock also increases the effective discount factor for the lenders. Resulting separating equilibria may entail even longer delays with capital decumulation when the cost of delay is lower for high surplus types. If there are many possible types of debtors (as noted above), a separating equilibrium (or mixed pooling and separating equilibrium) must entail a delay between counteroffers made by each possible type of debtor, in declining order of surplus. Because this type of delay does not disappear as the length of time between possible offers shrinks to zero, significant costly delays to agreement can arise.

IV. Possible Extensions

Multi-Period Contracting

In the simple stationary consumption-smoothing model with potential repudiation, multi-period debt contracts serve no additional purpose if seniority provisions are enforceable. If every creditor claims on an equal footing renegotiation proceeds, then multi-period contracts with renegotiation may arise in equilibrium. Creditors offering zero-expected profit loans recognize that an entrant will offer an additional loan on terms preferred by the debtor to those that would not reduce the value of earlier creditors' claims. A two-period contract may be profitable that reduces the debtor's incentive to borrow additional amounts. Such contracts can increase the ex ante utility of the debtor in equilibrium by moving the chosen contract away from the interest-rate-taking one toward the constrained first-best one (Kletzer (1984)). Because renegotiation is possible, such a contract offers the debtor an option to choose a particular second-period loan that, in events in which it would be taken, new lenders would not offer.

An example of such contracts is one offering a loan that, taken by itself, is expected to be profitable for the first period. A clause is included which obligates the lender to provide a new loan during the second period, which entrants would not offer if performance criteria are met by the debtor. If these covenants are not fulfilled, the lender can choose to declare a default and not provide the second loan. A restriction on debt dilution in the first period is a potential covenant; this type of contract can be self-enforcing for the sovereign debtor. In the case of sovereign loans, creditors may be subject to third-party enforcement of their obligation if the debtor does not breach the contract, which can specify that disputes be brought to the home court of the creditor. The debtor will generally choose not to breach the contract through first-period debt dilution. Because the debtor can choose to exercise the second-period option or select another debt contract in the absence of renegotiation, the debtor's expected utility during the second period is increased, inducing first-period performance (if output in the first period is private information, then contract breach may occur in equilibrium). These two-period loans may provide access to debt contracts in the second period that the debtor desires in poor output states over market contracts and chooses not to accept in high output states. Because of the debtor's limited liability (and consequent market imperfection), these loans offer insurance possibilities that a sequence of one-period loans with renegotiation do not. In the event of a demanded second-period revision of debt service obligations (which may become less probable), the obligations of the creditor to supply a second loan can be voided by a contract clause. Therefore, in the event of a renegotiation of debt service, the multi-period contracts have no effects.

The creditor's two-period lending problem is to maximize the expected two-period profit with respect to the choice of contract terms while deciding whether or not to declare a subsequent default in the event of contract breach subject to a series of constraints. These constraints include the debtor's choice of accepting the contract over other contracts available and the equilibrium choices in each output state at each of the two future dates of the debtor. That is, the creditor correctly values the repayment streams along each equilibrium path for the subsequent subgames. In the absence of creditor observability of the debtor's output, the incentive compatibility constraints employed in the previous section are imposed at each date.

If the opportunity cost to creditors is a random variable, then an additional motive arises for multi-period contracts. Since the set of offered contracts shrinks with an increase in the world rate of interest, the second-period loan option will provide desirable insurance opportunities to the debtor; if the lenders' opportunity cost of funds falls, then the second-period (or later) debt contract can be revised. In equilibrium, in these events the resulting debt contract will be the debtor's best contract from among those offered by other lenders. While risk-neutral lenders will offer multi-period contracts providing higher utility to borrowers than equilibrium single-period loans, interest rate increases benefit borrowers ex post and interest rate declines lead to contract revision ex post. Therefore, the length of multi-period contracts in equilibrium is limited by the ex ante expected profitability of debtor welfare-improving contracts. Such contracts exist at all because the limited liability of debtors leads to equilibrium contractual marginal rates of interest exceeding average rates of interest on their debts.

Unobservable Debtor Policy Choices

The supposition that debtor income is unobservable by creditors may strike readers as peculiarly unrealistic. The natural alternative is to suppose that income is publicly observable while policy choices by the debtor affecting the distribution of income are unobserved by creditors. In a stochastic environment, moral hazard in policy selection arises if policies enhancing the probability of favorable outcomes for creditors (that is, if they raise anticipated debt repayments) are costly to debtors. The choice between investment and current consumption is a standard example.

The first-best contracts for simple principal-agent problems have been characterized as occurring when output is publicly observable, while the agent's choice of an action affecting the distribution of output is known only to the agent (Holmstrom (1979) and Rogerson (1985)). These contracts specify divisions of output as functions of the observable quantity, output alone. In the repeated principal-agent problem, the first-best contract depends upon the entire past history of output, as well as current output. The extent of risk sharing between a risk-neutral principal and risk-averse agent is limited by the necessity that the output-contingent contract provide incentives for the agent to choose output-increasing actions.

In the model used in this paper, assume that debtor income is observed by lenders, but that the distribution of income realizations depends upon a set of current policies selected by the debtor, which cannot be observed directly by creditors. Let the distribution of income conditional on policy choice be stationary, and assume that current-period felicity depends positively on current consumption and negatively on some measure of policy choice (for example, investment).

Constrained first-best capital flows can be characterized under a number of special assumptions for the problem of maximizing debtor utility subject to the constraints that repudiation is never chosen in equilibrium, expected profits are zero in every period, and the contract is incentive compatible in the choice of policy. In a nontrivial step, this problem can be reduced to a static maximization problem using Bellman's equation when the incentive compatibility constraint can be written as a first-order condition (Spear and Srivastava (1987)). The pattern of capital flows between lenders and borrowers over time (as a function of the history of income) can be characterized if additional assumptions are made about the nature of the conditional distribution of income.

Suppose that the only policy instruments available to the debtor government for transferring resources from the private sector to service debt create distortions in the domestic economy (for example, commodity taxes). In this case, the contracts that satisfy the first-order incentive compatibility condition (that is, are locally maximal for lenders) will tend not to lead to the optimal pattern of capital flows (constrained by the asymmetry of information). In such a model, a serious coordination problem can arise between creditors and debtors because complementarities between policy choices and external capital flows can arise. Large net capital outflows may be compatible with distortionary policies that reduce the expected return to new loans. The possibility that unsatisfactory equilibria arise when the policies required to meet large debt service obligations are distortionary can create a significant international public policy problem. While the public goods problem of cooperation between lenders suggested by others (for example, Sachs (1984), Krugman (1985, 1987)) may not be severe in light of the possibilities for coordination between creditors, a problem of coordination between debtor-government policy selection and creditor lending choices would tend to be particularly difficult to address.

The derivation of a first-best contract solution for the model with privately observed investment levels but publicly observed output is possible given strong assumptions. However, the introduction of explicit debt-contracts with ex post renegotiation into this framework makes for a very difficult theoretical problem. Second-best contracting with renegotiations should involve outcomes (new flows of capital) that depend upon the entire past history of output.

V. Conclusions

The principal-agent framework adopted in this paper has implications for evaluating the argument for "defensive" lending to recalcitrant debtors. Under perfect information, a debt renegotiation never entails new concurrent flows of funds to the debtor and always involves a contract equivalent to a debt write-down combined with a new zero-expected profit loan. The "rescheduling" of willingly unmet debt service obligations in the form of a new loan does not occur in equilibrium in the model of this paper. The present value of the option on potential future repayments is less than its opportunity cost to the creditor at the margin in the stationary stochastic environment.

In the presence of informational asymmetries, equilibrium for the creditor-debtor renegotiation problem is a separating type. In lower output states, smaller current payments are made with larger debt service obligations carried forward. A debtor unwilling to meet current debt service may obtain new net inflows in a constrained optimal response by creditors only in the version of the model in which the penalties for repudiation increase with the debt service repudiated. This follows because a debtor may prefer to repudiate now with R relatively low to simply consuming current output while incurring larger future debt service obligations with the consequent reduction in expected utility.

The separating nature of equilibria derived in the imperfect information case may have implications for the evaluation of the (stochastic) debt service burden. Subsequent poor output realizations may lead in only a few steps to the maximal level of debt service obligations possible with net outflows or only minor net inflows of capital along the way. This might be the most significant cost of the informational imperfection. Such an expansion of debt service burden does not occur in equilibrium under symmetric information. In the first model, the debt service obligations have a stationary unconditional long-run distribution; under asymmetric information, they follow a simple Markov process instead.

Our model stands in contrast to an important paper on indeterminancy in lending under possible bankruptcy by Hellwig (1977). In that paper, the creditor sets a credit limit, which is optimal ex post to relax when it is reached by the debtor. If it is not relaxed, bankruptcy occurs automatically and the lender receives nothing. Additional loans are expected to be profitable because they raise the value of existing loans; no new creditor will provide them, but an existing creditor should. This is exactly "defensive" lending. However, the interest schedule is given to the creditor and the creditor's policies are restricted to setting limits on the stock of debt (so that time inconsistency arises). We have relaxed two constraints imposed by Hellwig: default need not be declared following a breach of contract, and the interest charged in a renegotiation of debt is a choice variable for the existing creditors. Current lenders have access to a richer set of policies. Hellwig uses a hazard process for income, while we adopt a stationary one. It is not clear if this is essential.

Appendix

Outline of proof of proposition:

To show that x_i is non-increasing in i, we use the self-selection constraint

$$U(y_i + x_i) + \beta EV(R_i) \geq U(y_i + x_j) + \beta EV(R_j).$$

Let $i > j$, then $U(y_j + x_i) + \beta EV(R_i) > U(y_j + x_j) + \beta EV(R_j)$, if $x_i > x_j$, because $U(c)$ is strictly concave. This violates the self-selection constraint for state j.

Therefore, $x_i \le x_j$. Monotonicity of $EV(R)$ in R implies that $R_i \le R_j$, again using the state i self-selection constraint.

$V_i(x_i,R_i) \equiv U(y_i + x_i) + \beta EV(R_i)$ is non-decreasing in i by

$$U(y_i + x_i) + \beta EV(R_i) \ge U(y_i + x_j) + \beta EV(R_j)$$
$$> U(y_j + x_j) + \beta EV(R_j),$$

since $y_i > y_j$.

The Lagrangian for the creditor's optimization problem is

$$L = \sum_{i=1}^{n} p_i \, (l'(R_i) - l_i) + \sum_{i=1}^{n} \sum_{j \ne i} \alpha_{ij}(V_i(x_i, R_i) - V_i(x_j, R_j))$$
$$+ \sum_{i=1}^{n} \delta_i(V_i(x_i, R_i) - V'(y_i, R)) + \sum_{i=1}^{n} \gamma_i(V_i(x_i, R_i) - \overline{V}(y_i, R)).$$

Necessary conditions for a maximum are

$$p_i = ((\delta_i + \gamma_i) + \sum_{j \ne i} \alpha_{ij}) \, U'(y_i + x_i) - \sum_{j \ne i} \alpha_{ji} \, U'(y_j + x_i)$$
$$p_i \cdot (dl'/dR_i) = ((\delta_i + \gamma_i) + \sum_{j \ne i} (\alpha_{ij} - \alpha_{ji}))(-\beta EV'(R_i)).$$

Because the derivative of l_i with respect to R_i may not be well defined for discrete values of y, (2) should be interpreted as the appropriate weak inequalities for right and left derivatives. The function $l_i'(R_i)$ can be shown to be continuous.

Following Sappington (1983), $\alpha_{ij} = 0$ for $j > i + 1$ and for $j < i - 1$. Using the fact that $x_j < x_{i+1}$ if $j > i + 1$, suppose the converse. Then, the i self-selection constraint implies

$$U(y_i + x_j) + \beta EV(R_j) \ge U(y_i + x_{i+1}) + \beta EV(R_{i+1}).$$

Concavity of $U(c)$ implies

$$U(y_{i+1} + x_j) + \beta EV(R_j) > U(y_{i+1} + x_{i+1}) + \beta EV(R_{i+1}),$$

which contradicts the $(i + 1)$ self-selection constraint. A similar argument holds for $j < i - 1$. Therefore, only $\alpha_{i\,i+1}$, $\alpha_{i\,i-1}$ can be non-zero for any i. Further, note that if $\alpha_{i\,i-1} > 0$, then

$$U(y_i + x_i) + \beta EV(R_i) = U(y_i + x_{i-1}) + \beta EV(R_{i-1}) \text{ and}$$

strict concavity of $U(c)$ and $x_i < x_{i-1}$ imply that

$$U(y_{i-1} + x_i) + \beta EV(R_i) < U(y_{i-1} + x_{i-1}) + \beta EV(R_{i-1}).$$

Therefore, if $\alpha_{i\,i-1} > 0$, $\alpha_{i-1\,i} = 0$, and conversely.

Similarly, for $\alpha_{i\,i+1}$ and $\alpha_{i+1\,i}$. S is convex, since $R + \sum_{i=1}^{n} p_i(l'(R_i) - l_i)$ is non-decreasing in R. The following arguments assume that dl'/dR_i is continuous in R_i. Rewriting (1):

$$p_n = (\delta_n + \alpha_{n\,n-1}) \, U'(y_n + x_n) - \alpha_{n-1\,n} \, U'(y_{n-1} + x_n)$$

If $\delta_n > 0$, then $\alpha_{n-1\,n}$ must be zero. Otherwise, either

$$V_n(x_n, R_n) < V'(y_n, R), \text{ or}$$
$$V_{n-1}(x_n, R_n) < V'(y_{n-1}, R).$$

This follows by simply increasing x_n by ϵ and R_n by δ such that expected profit remains zero. If $\delta_{n-1} > 0$, then $\alpha_{n\,n-1} = 0$ by the same argument.

Let k be the minimum value for i such that $\delta_k > 0$. Note that $\delta_k > 0$ implies that $\delta_{k+1} > 0$, because $\alpha_{k+1\,k}$ and $\alpha_{k\,k+1}$ are both zero. Also, whenever $\gamma_i > 0$, $V_i(x_i, R_i) = \overline{V}(y_i, R)$ which implies that $\overline{V}(y_i, R) \geq V'(y_i, R)$.

In case of equality, $\gamma_i + \delta_i > 0$, and with inequality, $\delta_i = 0$. We can let $\delta_i = 0$ whenever $\gamma_i > 0$. Let l be the maximum value of i such that $\gamma_i > 0$. (1) implies:

$$p_n = \delta_n U'(y_n + x_n)$$

$$\cdot$$
$$\cdot$$
$$\cdot$$

$$p_{k+1} = \delta_{k+1} U'(y_{k+1} + x_{k+1})$$

$$p_k = (\delta_k + \alpha_{k\,k-1})\, U'(y_k + x_k)$$

$$p_j = (\gamma_j + \alpha_{j\,j-1} + \alpha_{j\,j+1})\, U'(y_j + x_j)$$
$$- \alpha_{j-1\,j}\, U'(y_{j-1} + x_j)$$
$$- \alpha_{j+1\,j}\, U'(y_{j+1} + x_j),$$

for all $j < k$, and

$$p_1 = (\gamma_1 + \alpha_{1\,2})\, U'(y_1 + x_1) - \alpha_{2\,1}\, U'(y_2 + x_1)$$

Suppose γ_1 is zero, then $\alpha_{1\,2} > 0$; using both (1) and (2), this implies that $(l'(R_i) - l_i)$ must increase if (x_1, R_1) is changed so that $V_1(x_1, R_1)$ falls until $\gamma_1 > 0$. If $\alpha_{1\,2} > 0$, then the quotient of (1) and (2) for $i = 2$ implies that reduction of (x_2, R_2) along V_2 constant increases expected profit. Therefore, $\alpha_{1\,2} = 0$ and $\gamma_1 > 0$. Note, if $l'(R_i)$ has unequal right and left derivatives, then $\alpha_{k-1\,k} = 0$ because S is convex, but $\alpha_{j\,j+1}$ need not be zero for $j \geq k$.

Summing (1) over all i gives

$$\sum_{i=1}^{n} p_i = 1 = \sum_{i=k}^{n} \delta_i U'(y_i + x_i) + \sum_{i=2}^{k} \alpha_{i\,i-1}(U'(y_i + x_i) - U'(y_i + x_{i-1}))$$
$$- \sum_{i=2}^{k} \alpha_{i-1\,i}(U'(y_{i-1} + x_i) - U'(y_{i-1} + x_{i-1})) + \sum_{i=1}^{l} \gamma_i U'(y_i + x_i).$$

The arguments above can be used to imply that $\alpha_{i-1\,i} = 0$. Whenever $(\delta_{i-1} + \gamma_{i-1}) > 0$, $\alpha_{i\,i-1} = 0$ is possible, but not necessary. If $(\delta_{i-1} + \gamma_{i-1}) = 0$, then $\alpha_{i\,i-1} > 0$.

The above properties can be used recursively to derive values for each multiplier. The quotient of (1) and (2) when $\alpha_{i\,i-1} = 0$ yields

$$dl'(R_i)/dR_i = (-\beta EV'(R_i))/(U'(y_i + x_i)),$$

and if $\alpha_{i\,i-1} > 0$,

$$dl'(R_i)/dR_i = \frac{-\beta EV'(R_i)\,(\delta_i + \gamma_i + \alpha_{i\,i-1} - \alpha_{i+1\,i})}{(\delta_i + \gamma_i + \alpha_{i\,i-1})\, U'(y_i + x_i) - (\alpha_{i+1\,i})\, U'(y_{i+1} + x_i)}$$

$$< \frac{-\beta EV'(R_i)}{U'(y_i + x_i)}.$$

REFERENCES

Admati, Anat R., and Motty Perry, "Strategic Delay in Bargaining," *Review of Economic Studies* (Edinburgh), Vol. 54 (July 1987), pp. 345–64.

Bulow, Jeremy, and Kenneth Rogoff, "A Constant Recontracting Model of Sovereign Debt," *Journal of Political Economy* (Chicago), Vol. 97 (February 1989), forthcoming.

Cline, William R., *International Debt: Systemic Risk and Policy Response* (Washington: Institute for International Economics, 1984).

Eaton, Jonathan, and Mark Gersovitz, "Debt with Potential Repudiation: Theoretical and Empirical Analysis," *Review of Economic Studies* (Edinburgh), Vol. 48 (April 1981), pp. 289–309.

Gale, Douglas, and Martin Hellwig, "Incentive-Compatible Debt Contracts: The One-Period Problem," *Review of Economic Studies* (Edinburgh), Vol. 52 (October 1985), pp. 647–63.

Harris, Milton, and Artur Raviv, "Optimal Incentive Contracts with Imperfect Information," *Journal of Economic Theory* (New York), Vol. 20 (April 1979), pp. 231–59.

Hellwig, Martin, "A Model of Borrowing and Lending with Bankruptcy," *Econometrica* (Evanston, Illinois), Vol. 45 (November 1977), pp. 1879–1906.

Holmstrom, Bengt, "Moral Hazard and Observability," *Bell Journal of Economics* (New York), Vol. 10 (Spring 1979), pp. 74–91.

Kletzer, Kenneth M., "Asymmetries of Information and LDC Borrowing with Sovereign Risk," *Economic Journal* (London), Vol. 94 (June 1984), pp. 287–307.

Krugman, Paul R., "International Debt Strategies in an Uncertain World," in *International Debt and the Developing Countries,* ed. by Gordon W. Smith and John T. Cuddington (Washington: World Bank, 1985), pp. 79–100.

———, "Private Capital Flows to Problem Debtors" (unpublished; presented at the NBER Conference on Developing Country Debt, Washington, 1987).

Lindert, Peter H., "Relending to Sovereign Debtors," Research Program in Applied Macroeconomics and Macroeconomic Policy Working Paper Series (Davis, California: University of California-Davis, 1986).

Rogerson, William P., "Repeated Moral Hazard," *Econometrica* (Evanston, Illinois), Vol. 53 (January 1985), pp. 69–76.

Rubinstein, Ariel, "Perfect Equilibrium in a Bargaining Model," *Econometrica* (Evanston, Illinois), Vol. 50 (January 1982), pp. 97–109.

Sachs, Jeffrey D., *Theoretical Issues in International Borrowing,* Princeton Studies in International Finance, No. 54 (Princeton, New Jersey: Princeton University, July 1984).

Sappington, David, "Limited Liability Contracts Between Principal and Agent," *Journal of Economic Theory* (New York), Vol. 29 (February 1983), pp. 1–21.

Sobel, Joel, and Ichiro Takahashi, "A Multi-Stage Model of Bargaining," *Review of Economic Studies* (Edinburgh), Vol. 50 (July 1983), pp. 411–26.

Spear, Stephen E., and Sanjay Srivastava, "On Repeated Moral Hazard with Discounting," *Review of Economic Studies* (Edinburgh), Vol. 54 (October 1987), pp. 599–617.

Worrall, T., "Debt with Potential Repudiation: Short-Run and Long-Run Contracts," University of Reading Discussion Papers in Economics, Series A, No. 186 (Reading: University of Reading, 1987).

Debt Relief and Adjustment Incentives

W. MAX CORDEN*

The argument that debt relief would increase the incentive of a debtor country to make an adjustment effort (to invest) and that for this reason creditors may benefit by granting relief is analyzed in this paper. It is shown that there are actually opposing incentive effects of debt relief and that the argument could be valid in particular circumstances. A distinction is made between exogenous and endogenous relief, the latter compelled by low capacity to pay caused by low investment earlier.

I T IS SOMETIMES argued that debt relief reduces the incentive of a debtor country to adjust, and at the limit, if it obtained full relief, the country would not need to adjust at all because it would not need to generate resources to make the transfer of interest and principal. Against this a contrary argument has been put, that a high debt burden reduces the adjustment incentive because all or most of the benefits from increased output would go to foreign creditors. There are thus two quite opposing views, and it is an interesting question how they can be reconciled and, indeed, whether there are not more than two aspects to this question. Thus, it has also been observed that the present and expected tax burdens implied by the government's debt service obligations are likely to have familiar disincentive effects. Finally, and most important,

* At the time he wrote this paper, Mr. Corden was Senior Advisor in the Research Department of the Fund, on leave from the Australian National University. He taught at Oxford University from 1967 to 1976. Beginning in 1989, he will be Professor of International Economics at the School of Advanced International Studies of The Johns Hopkins University. He is indebted for comments on this paper to colleagues in the Fund and to Paul Collier, Carlos Rodriguez, and Maurice Scott.

the question arises whether the possible incentive effects of debt relief provide some case for creditors to provide relief.[1]

I. A Simple Intertemporal Model

"Adjustment effort" presumably varies in response to changing incentives. This concept can be given various meanings, and writers in this field are not always clear as to what they mean, possibly having more than one idea in mind. A specific meaning concerned with consumption and investment will be given to the concept here, and all the main issues will be explored in terms of that meaning. A broader interpretation will be noted later.

There are three relevant periods. In period 1—the past—the country acquired a debt to finance extra consumption and investment, and this period is now at an end. Immediately ahead is period 2, when the country receives further loans and benefits from rescheduling so as to finance its inherited debt service obligations. Hence, it will not make any net transfers of resources on account of debt, and on a net basis it is not really servicing the debt. Rather it is expected to invest appropriately so that it will be able to service the debt (including new debt incurred in period 2) in the following period 3.[2]

The contractual debt obligation in period 3 consists of a stream of interest and principal repayments, which is the equivalent of a stream of lump-sum taxes payable by the country to foreign creditors. In practice, the real value of this stream depends on world real interest rates, since most of the debt has been floating-rate debt, but in the main analysis real interest rates are assumed to be constant. (This assumption will be removed at the end.) Because the concern here is with sovereign debt, the stream is equivalent to taxes levied by foreign creditors on the government of the debtor country. The taxes will be payable out of the country's output stream in period 3, which will have been increased by investment that took place both in the past period 1 and in period 2.

---

[1] The argument that the incentive effect of debt relief (called the *pro-incentive effect* in this paper) provides a justification for creditors to provide relief has been put by Jeffrey Sachs in several papers. See, for example, Sachs and Huizinga (1987, pp. 594–95). In addition, the implications for various debt reduction schemes of the favorable incentive effects of debt relief are analyzed by Krugman in a model with uncertainty, in his paper in this volume.

[2] It is simplest to assume that there is no private capital inflow or capital outflow (capital flight) during periods 2 or 3. This simplifying assumption, unrealistic for some countries, does not alter the main argument. Capital flows will be reconsidered at the end.

In Figure 1, the horizontal axis shows output, consumption, and investment in period 2. Output is $0A'$ and is influenced by how much investment took place in period 1. The central issue is how much will be consumed and how much invested in period 2. Consumption in period 2 is measured from the left-hand axis. The vertical axis shows expected output and consumption in period 3, the excess of output over consumption being debt service payments. The stream of expected output and debt service payments is collapsed into a single time period, so that the vertical axis shows the present value (as perceived at the beginning of period 2) of expected period 3 output, consumption, and debt payments. Any investment in period 3 designed to benefit a later period is

Figure 1. *Effect of Debt Service on Investment:*
Disincentive Effect of Debt Relief

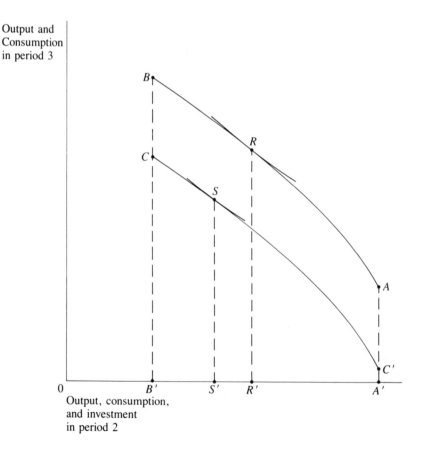

Output and
Consumption
in period 3

0

B'   S'   R'   A'

Output, consumption,
and investment
in period 2

ignored. It can be thought of as a fixed amount included in period 3 consumption.[3]

If investment in period 2 is zero, output in period 3 would be $A'A$. The curve AB shows how output in period 3 is expected to increase as investment in period 2 increases. It is assumed that there is a minimum level of consumption in period 2 so that consumption cannot fall below $0B'$. The debt service payment due in period 3—equivalent to a lump-sum tax on the country—is BC and the curve CC' is vertically below BA by the distance BC at every level of period 3 output. CC' represents the debtor country's absorption possibilities in period 3.

The next step is to imagine an intertemporal utility function for the debtor country's government, the arguments being only national consumption in period 2 and national consumption in period 3. The utility function is well behaved, with both goods normal, and can be represented by an indifference curve map. Two indifference curves are shown in Figure 1, one at R, tangential to AB, and the other at S, tangential to CC'.

If there is no debt service to be paid, equilibrium will be at R, investment in period 2 being $A'R'$. But when a lump-sum payment is to be made to foreign creditors in period 3, investment in period 2 will be higher, namely at $A'S'$. Thus the simple conclusion follows that debt service obligations in the future would increase investment now, and this can be interpreted to mean that current "adjustment effort" is increased. The debt service obligations involve a sacrifice in period 3, and the commonsense proposition is that it will be optimal for some of this sacrifice to be shifted to period 2.

It follows that debt relief would reduce investment and adjustment effort, this conclusion confirming one of the popular arguments referred to at the beginning of this paper. This is the *disincentive effect* of debt relief. In the diagram, complete debt relief would involve a movement from S to R and partial debt relief a movement to some point on SR between the two extreme cases.

The fuller macroeconomic implications of such debt relief might be noted. In period 2 investment falls, consumption rises, but net resource transfers abroad remain zero. In period 3, output falls relative to the situation in the absence of relief (because investment was lower in period 2), but resource transfers abroad decline so much that consumption

---

[3] One might allow explicitly for a period 4 when all inherited debt will have been paid off, but when the country may wish to borrow again, whether for consumption or investment, and for the sake of which it may wish to preserve its creditworthiness. But this fourth period does not enter the story directly here.

actually rises. Relative to the situation in period 2, one would expect the real exchange rate of period 3 to depreciate (to generate the appropriate switching of output toward tradables and demand away from them as required by the remaining resource transfer), but relative to the outcome without debt relief it would appreciate.

Various policies can bring about an increase in investment with an associated reduction in consumption—that is, a movement to the left in the diagram—and investment could be public or private. For example, increased public investment might be financed by reduced transfers, lower public sector wages, or higher taxes that reduce private consumption. Alternatively, increased bank credit might raise private investment, consumption being reduced at the same time through reduced government consumption spending, higher taxes, and so on. Of course, the form of investment will affect its productivity and hence the slope of the AB curve, a complication that is ignored here.[4]

In addition, the concept of investment might be defined more broadly if this analysis is to be relevant for current discussions. One might regard "economic reform" (for example, trade liberalization, an improvement in agricultural pricing policy, or a reform of parastatal organizations) as a form of investment that is expected to increase output and hence capacity to pay debt service in period 3. It imposes a current cost on the political system and on interest groups, which can be equated with a loss of current consumption. Hence, both an increase in investment as usually defined and "economic reform" in the broader sense represent increases in adjustment effort in period 2, and are represented in the diagram as an increase in investment—a movement to the left on the horizontal axis.

II. Capacity to Pay and Endogenous Debt Relief

The next step is to seek a formal basis for the argument that debt relief might increase adjustment effort—the *pro-incentive effect*. It will now be assumed that there is a minimum consumption level in period 3 and creditors will feel obliged to grant debt relief if it is needed for the country to attain this minimum level. This assumption is the crucial ingredient in the subsequent discussion. The alternative to debt relief is then default. The lower the debtor country's output in period 3, the more debt relief would have to be granted. Hence, a distinction must be made between exogenous debt relief that has been discussed so far, and which

---

[4] Investment might be defined as gross or net. If it were defined as *net*, output in period 3 resulting from zero investment in period 2 ($A'A$ in Figure 1) would presumably be equal to or greater than period-2 output $A'A$.

may be granted at the beginning of period 2, and endogenous debt relief, which may have to be granted in period 3.

"Capacity to pay"—a popular term in this field—can be defined as the excess of period-3 output over the minimum consumption level. It represents the maximum resource transfer (noninterest current account) that the country is capable of making. It is assumed here that the country would always meet its contractual debt service obligations up to the limits of capacity to pay. In other words, it would default only if default is unavoidable. There is no "willingness to pay" variable in this simple model. Endogenous debt relief is designed to avoid such default.

In Figure 2, the minimum consumption level in period 3 is 0L. If investment in period 2 had only been $A'K'$, output in period 3 would

Figure 2. *Minimum Consumption Level and Endogenous Debt Relief*

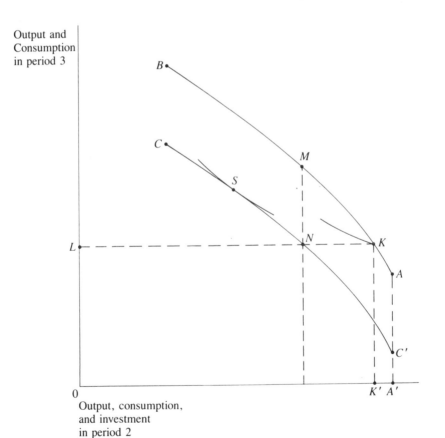

Output and
Consumption
in period 3

0

Output, consumption,
and investment
in period 2

have been just equal to this minimum level—at K. In other words, capacity to pay would be zero. The creditors would then feel obliged to grant 100 percent endogenous debt relief (or the country would completely default).

If investment in period 2 increased from that level, and hence output in period 3 increased, some endogenous relief would still need to be granted until M is reached when output would be sufficient for the full contractual debt service to be paid while the debtor country's period-3 consumption is at its minimum level. Capacity to pay is sufficient at M to meet the whole debt service. Capacity to pay is thus represented for each level of period-3 output (and hence investment in period 2) by the vertical distance between BK and LK.

The concept of a minimum consumption level is, of course, just a simplification for heuristic purposes. It expresses the general idea of a limit to the ability of a government to transfer resources out of an economy for any given real output level. The perceived minimum may well rise as the country's output and the before-tax incomes of its citizens rise, in which case a given increase in investment in period 2 would lead to a lesser increase in capacity to pay in period 3 than indicated in Figure 2 (that is, LK would slope negatively). The principal conclusions would stand although the analysis would become slightly more complicated.

If there were no debt relief of any kind, whether exogenous or endogenous, the debtor country's intertemporal consumption possibility frontier would be CC'. Assuming no exogenous relief but introducing endogenous relief based on the capacity to pay concept just described, the frontier becomes $CNKA$. Along CN there is full debt service. At N, the country is just able to make full payment given the need to sustain the minimum consumption level. Along NK, consumption stays constant at the minimum level and reductions in output are reflected in increasing endogenous relief until at K there has to be 100 percent endogenous relief. Output below K is insufficient to yield the minimum consumption level.

Given this new frontier, the country will presumably again choose to be on the highest indifference curve. This might, as before, be the curve at S (tangential to CN), but now there is also the possibility that it is the curve at K. If S is chosen, there will not be any endogenous debt relief. But if K is chosen, endogenous relief will be 100 percent.[5] The pro-incentive argument could be interpreted as saying that the country may

---

[5] One is tempted to draw an indifference curve *through* K (rather than *at* K), but, since there is a minimum consumption level, it should not go on below K or should become horizontal.

choose in period 2 to invest so little (engage in so little adjustment effort) that 100 percent endogenous relief becomes inevitable and, indeed, implicitly the country plans on that.

Any increase in output above K involves the payment of a 100 percent marginal tax rate to foreign creditors until M is reached, when the marginal tax rate becomes zero. Thus, it will pay the debtor country either to engage in no effort to get beyond K or so much as to reach S. The creditors will either get nothing, or they get all they are owed. The point K is the interesting one. If the country chooses this point, it is choosing an equilibrium resulting from low investment in period 2, leading to endogenous relief in period 3, when the creditors get nothing. This point will only be chosen if the indifference curve at K is higher than that through S. In other words, it is by no means inevitable that there is endogenous debt relief since the indifference curve through S could be higher.[6]

III. Possible Case for Exogenous Debt Relief

The final step in the argument is to show that it may be in the interests of the creditors to grant exogenous debt relief so as to avoid endogenous relief. Thus it may pay them to reduce the contractual value of the debt at the beginning of period 2 so as to avoid being forced to do so in period 3, in effect facing the alternative of default.

The key condition required is that, in the absence of exogenous relief, the point K would be chosen, at which creditors get nothing. As just noted, this is not inevitable, since S is also a possibility. This condition—that the creditors would get nothing unless there is exogenous relief—will now be assumed.

In Figure 3, exogenous relief can be represented by the CC' curve moving upward until it coincides with BA when there is 100 percent relief. If it does go that far, the debt service obligation has disappeared. Partial debt relief is represented by an upward movement of CC', but not so far as to make CC' coincide with BA. It might just go to the extent where the indifference curve through K becomes tangential to CC'. The

---

[6] This model yields an "all-or-nothing" result: either there is full payment of the debt service or there is 100 percent endogenous relief. It could be shown that if the minimum consumption level increased as output rose—so that LK was negatively sloped—there would no longer have to be an all-or-nothing result (corner solution). The country's optimal choice might then require a level of period-2 investment that led to partial endogenous relief in period 3. In that case an indifference curve in Figure 2 would be tangential to $CNKA$ somewhere within NK.

Figure 3. *Pro-incentive Effect of Debt Relief with a
Minimum Consumption Level*

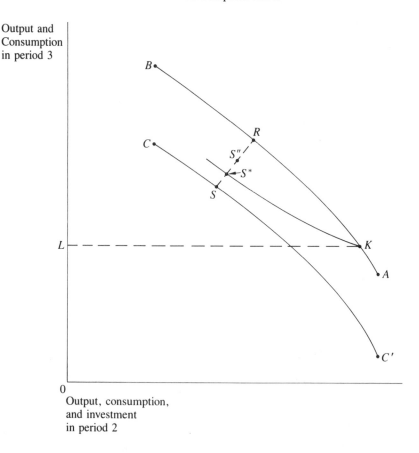

point of tangency is then S^*. In that case, the debtor country would be
indifferent between engaging in a big adjustment (investment) effort to
get to S^* and engaging in a low adjustment effort and so reaching K with
100 percent endogenous relief. At S^* it would be paying the full but
reduced value of the contractual debt service but its increased effort
would nevertheless yield it more consumption.

Slightly greater exogenous relief (moving CC' further up) would per-
suade the country to engage in extra investment. It might then get to the
new tangency point S'' where the indifference curve is slightly above that
through K and S^*. It would be marginally better off at S'' while the
creditors would be much better off.

Thus, exogenous debt relief, if it is sufficient, yields a Pareto improvement. Further relief would increase the gains for the debtor but would be at the expense of the creditors. Once endogenous relief is not chosen, further exogenous relief is not in the interests of the creditors. If full relief is granted (so that R is reached), all the gains would go to the debtor.

To summarize, until S'' is reached, exogenous debt relief has no effects. It is insufficient to induce the debtor country to forgo equilibrium at K—that is, a low investment or adjustment effort outcome in which there is endogenous relief. At S'', there is a gain to the creditors with only a marginal gain to the debtor. The creditors now obtain full payment of a reduced contractual debt service. This degree of relief maximizes the gains to the creditors. Further relief reduces the gain to the creditors and redistributes it to the debtor until at R, where the contractual debt has been reduced to zero owing to exogenous debt relief, all the gain goes to the debtor. The diagram shows that exogenous debt relief increases investment or adjustment effort if it is sufficient to bring equilibrium to S'', but further relief reduces investment at the margin (as indicated by the positive slope of $S''R$), though investment will still be greater with 100 percent relief than with no relief at all.

The practical message preached by advocates of exogenous relief based on the pro-incentive effect is that such relief may be in the interests of the creditors, since half a loaf is better than none. But there are judgments required. First, the starting point may not be K, so that there is no pro-incentive effect. Second, even if it is at K, relief could be too much from the point of view of creditors relative to the optimal extent of relief (to get to S'').

IV. Crucial Role of Expectations

The whole analysis really refers to expectations and not necessarily to actual events.

The debtor country makes its investment decision during period 2 on the basis of expectations about the marginal productivity of capital in period 3—in effect the slope of the BA curve—and other developments in period 3, which affect the position of that curve, as well as of the intertemporal utility function. An expected terms-of-trade improvement would shift the BA curve upward. The creditors make their decisions about whether to grant exogenous debt relief, and how much, at the beginning of period 2 and should base these on expectations of debtor behavior as well as exogenous developments, such as terms of trade changes, in both period 2 and period 3. This will be returned to in the next section.

One might ask why creditors would have agreed to certain levels of contractual debt in period 1 when, at the beginning of period 2, they perceive it to be optimal to grant some degree of exogenous relief. The answer is that expectations must have changed. On the basis of expectations in period 1 about debtor behavior in periods 2 and 3, it may have been rational to make loans involving particular contractual debt service obligations. But by the beginning of period 2 such contracts may no longer appear optimal.

In terms of Figure 3, the original expectation will have been that the indifference curve at K is lower than that through S, so that the debtor would not choose an equilibrium requiring endogenous debt relief in period 3. But by the beginning of period 2, a different configuration is expected by the creditors or by those who seek to advise them: the curve at K is expected to be higher. This may be because the minimum consumption level, $0L$, is now believed to be higher, because the marginal product of capital is expected to be less (possibly because of worse terms of trade) so that the BA curve is now flatter, or because the debtor is expected to discount the future more (the indifference curve at K is steeper). Of course, it is also possible that the creditors have not changed their expectations but that their expectations just happen to differ from those of the debt relief advocates who advance the pro-incentive argument.

One might also ask why debtors are not always expected to default in period 3. The standard answer is that there are two kinds of penalties.

The first kind would be imposed in period 3 and later: deprivation of trade credit, imposition of trade restrictions, seizure of assets, and so on. Threats of such penalties may, of course, not be credible because they also impose costs on creditors. But leaving this aside, the interesting aspect of our analysis is that when a country maintains a low level of investment in period 2 so that it fails to increase its capacity to pay in period 3 and thus compels endogenous debt relief, it is really doing much the same thing as when it is defaulting in circumstances when it does have capacity to pay. Capacity to pay in this model results from the debtor's own decisions. In effect, by investing less than is required to ensure adequate capacity to pay in period 3, the country is evading the penalties it would incur if it did have capacity to pay but did not actually pay. For the creditors, there is an information and enforcement problem.

The second kind of penalty concerns the effect of default on creditworthiness or reputation in later periods when the country may again wish to borrow. Of course, it is possible that its borrowing capacity later would not depend on reputation—there always being a risk of default in any case—but if it does, then the analysis here has an important implication. When the time for new borrowing comes the debtor country's reputation will surely depend not just on whether it defaulted or not but also on whether it engaged in behavior in period 2 that made endogenous debt relief unavoidable in period 3. Hence, the "reputation penalty" should provide a deterrent not only to default in period 3 but also to low investment or inadequate adjustment behavior in period 2 that leads to endogenous debt relief.

V. Uncertainty

In this model, the creditors must make their decisions about whether to grant exogenous debt relief, and how much, at the beginning of period 2 and must base these on their assessment of all the complex factors presented in this analysis and, above all, on their expectations about debtor behavior. Essentially they need to estimate the minimal degree of relief needed to avoid default in period 3 (that is, in Figure 3), to bring the CC' curve up to S'' but, if possible, no more. This degree of relief will be called minimal relief here, being in fact optimal from the point of view of the creditors. Assessments required to determine minimal relief will involve uncertainty, and this must therefore be brought into the analysis.

In Figure 4, the contractual value of the debt is shown along the horizontal axis. $0V (= VY)$ is the full value of the debt, that is, the value without any exogenous relief. The actual repayment that is expected in period 2 to be made in period 3, that is, the expected value that takes into account the expectation of endogenous relief, is shown along the vertical axis. Along $0Y$ the two are equal so that endogenous relief is zero. The extent of exogenous debt relief that will just avoid endogenous relief (that is, minimal relief) is LV, leaving a contractual debt of $0L (= KL)$. The creditors maximize the repayments they receive by granting this degree of relief and so obtaining KL. If they granted more relief, repayments would be reduced along $K0$. If they granted less relief they would get nothing. The possibilities open to them are thus represented by $0KLV$.

Allowance must now be made for uncertainty in the minds of the creditors as to the level of minimal relief. Let us suppose that they attach an equal chance that it is NV, LV, MV, and zero. If they granted zero relief, there is thus a 75 percent chance (as perceived by them) that they will get nothing (since relief would be insufficient) and a 25 percent

Figure 4. *Expected Value of Debt Resulting from Debt Relief with Uncertainty*

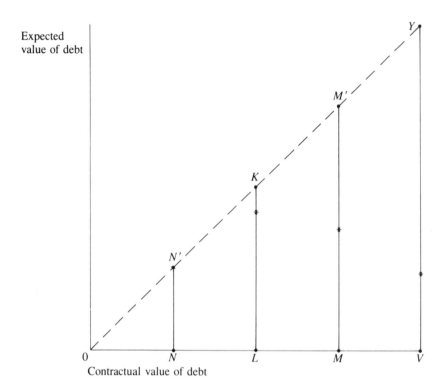

chance that they get *VY*. If they gave relief *MV*, there would be a 50 percent chance that they get *MM'* (that is, the full value of the reduced contractual debt) and a 50 percent chance that they get nothing. Relief *LV* would yield a 75 percent chance of getting *LK* and a 25 percent chance of nothing and, finally, relief of *NV* would give a 100 percent chance of getting the modest amount of *NN'*. Thus, for each level of relief, there is an expected value, represented by the stars in the diagram, and in this particular case the maximum expected value would result from relief *LV*. But, of course, it might actually turn out after the event that minimal relief had been more, in which case the creditors would get nothing.

The final step is to suppose that there are not just four probable cases, but that everything from almost complete relief to zero relief could be the minimal relief so that one would get a curve, rather than four points, tracing out expected values at different levels of relief. The result would be a "debt relief Laffer curve," as Krugman has called it in a slightly different model (in this volume). Given their expectations, it is then in the interests of the creditors to choose the degree of relief that yields the maximum expected value on the curve. In period 2, this is the optimal degree of relief based on the expectations then prevalent, though minimal relief may in period 3 actually turn out to be different.

VI. Extension and Variations

In this section the analysis is extended to consider changes in the real interest rate, the substitution effect, and capital flight.

Real Interest Rate Changes

In period 1, a particular (average) real interest rate was expected to prevail later, that is, in period 2, when more debt will be incurred to pay for debt service obligations falling due in that period, and in period 3 when interest payments and principal repayments must be made. Let us now suppose that, at the beginning of period 2, expectations change and the average real interest rate payable is expected to rise.

This means that the debt service obligation payable to creditors in period 3 is expected to increase: in terms of Figures 2 and 3, BC increases; that is, CC' shifts down. Hence S shifts down, and (with the position of K unchanged) it becomes more likely that the indifference curve at K is above that through S and that, in the absence of exogenous debt relief, there would have to be endogenous relief. There is then more likelihood that the pro-incentive argument for debt relief from the point of view of the creditors would apply. Thus a rise or expected rise in the real interest rate, like a deterioration in the terms of trade, may create a situation where it would be optimal for creditors to grant exogenous relief.

Substitution Effect

It has been assumed here that the intertemporal utility function is that of the debtor government. The debt service payment represents, in effect, a lump-sum tax obligation incurred by the government to foreign creditors. The obligation could be met by a reduction of government expenditure. Insofar as it is met by an increase in taxes on households or firms, further implications need to be allowed for.

It will now be assumed that the utility function is not that of the government but the representative function of households and that the debt service obligation of the government to external creditors is passed on to the domestic private sector through an increase in the tax rate on households, whether direct or indirect. Such tax increases will have familiar income and substitution effects since lump-sum taxes on households are not possible. The income effect is essentially the same as the effect of a lump-sum tax. The substitution effect needs to be introduced because it could have effects on the incentive to invest in period 2 and on output and work incentives in period 3.

The substitution effect represents various distortions, of which the distortion of the work-leisure choice is one. Of course, there are many sources of tax-induced distortions, all of which would reduce the productivity of the country and so shift down the *BA* curve. One set of distortions is produced by tax avoidance and evasion (which might be achieved by capital flight). Here one should note particularly the distortion of the work-leisure choice. The implication for the analysis of debt relief is that debt relief reduces the actual and expected tax burden on households. Hence, there would be a substitution from leisure to work: debt relief would thus have a pro-incentive effect additional to the one which has been so named in this paper.

Furthermore, an incentive effect on investment relates to the simple model of the paper. Expectations in period 2 of relief of the period-3 tax burden would (on account of the substitution effect in isolation) lead to more investment in period 2 and hence to more output in period 3. If output in period 3 is expected to be taxed less, there is more of an incentive to invest in period 2 in order to raise period-3 output rather than consuming now. In Figures 1 and 3, this means that the *SR* curve might be negatively sloped over a range.

Capital Flight

The assumption so far has been that there are no private capital imports or exports in periods 2 and 3. The question arises whether one could allow for private capital exports (so-called capital flight) in period 2 within the context of this model.

Capital flight might be given two alternative interpretations. One would be to treat it as a way in which the country (though not the government) pays off part of its foreign debt in period 2 rather than period 3. But since the debt we are considering is sovereign debt, one can hardly say that private investments abroad that are not within the reach of the debtor country's government pay off the government's debt.

Hence an alternative approach seems preferable. Capital flight is one way in which the private sector allocates its savings and possibly seeks to evade taxes. Instead of investing all savings at home, some of them are invested abroad. The vertical axis in our diagrams could then be re-interpreted to refer, not to national output in period 3, but rather to taxable income, whether resulting from investment at home in period 2 or from private investment abroad.[7] Anything that reduces the ability to collect taxes on the private sector, such as capital flight, will tend to shift the AB curve down and such a downward movement in the AB curve (and hence the CC' curve) would have the variety of implications that follow from the analysis in this paper.

VII. Conclusions

This paper has analyzed the pro-incentive argument for debt relief. It has been shown that the argument depends on the possibility of endog-enous relief or default, which in turn depends on there being some minimum consumption level and hence meaningful concept of "capacity to pay." If that is granted, one can conclude that in certain circumstances it may be advantageous for creditors to grant exogenous relief. Thus the paper has indeed provided a rigorous confirmation for the possible valid-ity of the argument. But the conditions required for it to be applicable have also been brought out and it cannot be automatically assumed that it is valid in particular cases, such as the current situation. There is also a disincentive effect of debt relief and, in addition, a substitution effect which provides an additional pro-incentive effect, though not a basis for a debt relief argument.

REFERENCE

Sachs, Jeffrey D., and Harry Huizinga, "U.S. Commercial Banks and the Devel-oping-Country Crisis," *Brookings Papers on Economic Activity: 2* (1987), The Brookings Institution (Washington), pp. 555–606.

[7] It would also include direct income of the government, out of which debt service payments could be financed. The horizontal axis would show consump-tion and domestic savings, and the latter could be invested at home or abroad. By contrast, in the main analysis, domestic savings and domestic investment were always equal.

Market-Based Debt-Reduction Schemes

PAUL R. KRUGMAN*

Recently much attention has been given to the idea of reducing the debt of developing countries through a "menu approach" of schemes that attempt to harness the discounts on debt in the secondary market. This paper, after reviewing the rationale for the orthodox strategy of concerted lending and the case for debt forgiveness, examines the logic behind several market-based debt-reduction schemes. It shows that such schemes will ordinarily benefit both debtor and creditor only when the debtor is on the wrong side of the "debt relief Laffer curve"—that is, when a reduction in nominal claims actually increases expected payment. This is, however, also the case in which unilateral debt forgiveness is in the interest of creditors in any case. The implication is that there is no magic in market-based debt reduction, as opposed to more straightforward approaches.

IN THE EARLY YEARS of the third-world debt problem, there was widespread consensus among creditors, international organizations, and the debtor countries themselves about the kind of solution that was needed. The basic post-1982 strategy was one of financing the debt overhang—that is, creditors were expected not only to reschedule debt but to engage in concerted, "involuntary" lending. This lending was intended to reduce the burden of outward resource transfer on debtor nations to levels compatible with economic recovery, while growth and inflation were expected to make a growing nominal debt consistent with

* Mr. Krugman is Professor of Economics at the Massachusetts Institute of Technology. He was on the staff of the Council of Economic Advisors in 1982–83 and is currently a member of the Group of Thirty.

declining indebtedness as measured by the ratio of debt to GNP or exports. The emergence of this strategy represented a remarkable turnabout from the market-oriented policies that the United States had been urging on the International Monetary Fund only months before the debt crisis broke. Suddenly the market mechanism for credit was discarded. Although the effort was intended to protect the property rights of existing creditors, new lending was expected to be provided as part of a collective decision process, and in an environment in which individual lenders acting independently would not have been willing to extend credit. Thus there was, as Carlos Diaz-Alejandro put it, an abrupt socialization of the international capital market.

More recently, the consensus in favor of financing the debt overhang has begun to erode. One challenge has come from advocates of debt forgiveness, who argue that instead of reducing current resource transfer burdens by providing new money, creditors should offer a once-for-all reduction in the future obligations of countries. This view is held not only by those who favor the interests of debtor countries over those of their creditors, but also by many who argue that such forgiveness would actually be in the creditors' interest, reducing debt to levels that are more realistic and thus more likely to be serviced. While the debt forgivers offer a very different prescription from those advocating the established strategy, both parties agree in their advocacy of collective action as opposed to laissez-faire.

A different kind of challenge, however, has come from the advocates of market-based solutions to the debt problem. A variety of schemes— debt buy-backs, securitization, debt-equity swaps—have emerged in the last few years in an effort to find a way out of the debt problem through voluntary actions on the part of creditors. The advocates of these schemes claim that through a "menu approach" of new financial arrangements, the exposure of banks and the liabilities of countries can be reduced without the need for collectively bargained new money or debt forgiveness. That is, market solutions are being offered as an alternative to the concerted-action strategy that has dominated the handling of the debt problem until now.

Can the market solve the debt problem? Despite the popularity of the new market-based schemes, there has been surprisingly little sensible discussion of their pros and cons. This paper provides a framework for thinking about market-based schemes for dealing with debt and compares these schemes with more orthodox strategies of financing and forgiveness.

The paper is in six parts. The first part reviews the rationale for the original strategy of rescheduling and concerted lending. The second considers the alternative case for debt forgiveness, with emphasis on the conditions under which forgiveness is in the interests of creditors as well as debtors (conditions that turn out to be crucial for the evaluation of market-based schemes). It then considers three kinds of market-based debt scheme: buy-backs, securitization, and debt-equity swaps. The final section of the paper offers some tentative evaluations.

I. Rationale for Concerted Lending

The defining feature of a problem debtor is its inability to attract voluntary lending—its lack of normal access to international capital markets. The essence of the concerted-lending strategy followed since 1982 has been to substitute nonmarket for normal sources of finance: to use a combination of official lending and involuntary lending from existing creditors to supply debtor nations with sufficient foreign exchange to service their debts. To many observers this strategy seems absurd. After all, what sense does it make to lend still more to countries that already owe more than they can repay? It is important as a starting point to understand the rationale for new lending to problem debtors.

This rationale is often stated in terms of the distinction between liquidity and solvency: a country is asserted to be worth lending to if it is solvent (i.e., is expected to be able to repay its debt eventually) but not liquid (lacks the cash to service its debt on a current basis). This distinction is, however, a misleading one for the debt crisis. If it is *known* to be solvent, a country can find voluntary lending, and there is no liquidity problem. The liquidity problem arises precisely because there is a possibility that the country will not be able fully to repay its debt— specifically, because nonpayment is sufficiently possible that the expected present value of repayment is less than the debt already outstanding (see Krugman (forthcoming)).

Why, then, should creditors lend still more to such a country? Because while incomplete payment is possible, it is not certain. Suppose that a country might be able eventually to make payments equal in present value to its outstanding debt, but that the risk of nonpayment is sufficiently large that it cannot find voluntary lenders. In the absence of concerted action by its creditors, the country will either have to meet its obligations out of current resources or, if this is impossible, default immediately. The latter will guarantee that creditors do not get all that they are owed, foreclosing the possibility of benefiting from any later good fortune on the part of the country. It may therefore be in creditors' interest to postpone at least part of a country's obligations, avoiding a current default and preserving at least the possibility of a favorable outcome later on.

A country's obligations to amortize debt can be postponed by a rescheduling of principal, which is a standard procedure. For heavily indebted countries this is not enough, however, since even the interest payments on debt exceed what they can reasonably be expected to pay out of current resources. Thus there is a need to postpone interest obligations as well. Such a postponement could be achieved directly, through interest capitalization, but this has so far been opposed strongly by creditors because it makes the process excessively automatic (and perhaps also excessively transparent). Instead, the method has been to round up existing creditors and require them to provide new loans that cover a fraction of interest payments, effectively deferring interest obligations. This is the process of "involuntary" or "concerted" lending.

The potential gains from concerted lending were argued strongly in the well-known study by Cline (1983) and have been demonstrated in formal models (see Sachs (1984), Krugman (1985)). The point may be seen informally if considered in terms of the subjective discount on debt—the percentage by which existing creditors expect the present value of actual repayments on debt to fall short of a country's legal obligations. Suppose that creditors believe that if no concerted lending is undertaken, a country will be forced into a disorderly default in which creditors will receive only a fraction $(1 - d)$ of the nominal value of their claims. Suppose also that they believe that a sufficiently large program of concerted lending—say lending L dollars—will reduce the expected loss from d to d^*. Then it is straightforward to see how such a program can produce a net gain. Each additional dollar lent as part of the concerted lending program is lent at an expected loss of d^*; however, the program increases the value of existing debt by $(d - d^*)D$, where D is the initial stock of debt outstanding. Thus the benefits of the program to creditors exceed its cost as long as $d^*L < (d - d^*)D$, or as long as $L/D < (d - d^*)/d^*$.

To take an example, suppose that, absent a program of concerted lending, the subjective discount would be 0.5—creditors would expect to get only half what they are owed—but that with a program avoiding immediate default the discount falls to 0.25. Then it is in the interest of creditors to pursue such a program as long as $L/D < 1$—that is, as long as the increase in their exposure is less than 100 percent.

This example clearly shows the fallacy of some common arguments against lending to problem debtors. It is not true, for example, that the existence of a secondary market discount on debt (presumably more or less equal to the subjective probability of nonpayment d) means that new money should not be put in. It only means that such new money will not be provided voluntarily—but that is by definition true of a problem debtor. It is also therefore not true that unwillingness of lenders other than the existing creditors to provide funds, or for that matter export of capital by domestic residents, are arguments against provision of new money by the creditors.

While thinking of the problem in this way makes the potential benefits of concerted lending clear, however, it also makes clear one of its problems. The gains from concerted lending are collective. They arise because by lending enough to avoid immediate default creditors raise the value of the claims they already have. Looked at in isolation, however, each new loan is made at a loss. Thus nobody who is not already a creditor of the problem country will be willing to lend, and even existing creditors will lack an individual incentive to lend. We therefore have the now-familiar free-rider problem, in which lending may be in everyone's collective interest but fails to take place because no individual finds it in his or her interest. The process of concerted lending, with creditors negotiating collectively, with pressure from creditor central banks and international agencies, and with the not-too-implicit threat by countries to declare moratorium if new money is not provided, is designed to overcome this free-rider problem. In practice, the problem remains serious—not just because it has been difficult to get agreements to provide new money, but because of capital flight that in effect rides free on the provision of new money by banks and official agencies.

Even aside from the free-rider problem, however, there are important objections to the strategy of concerted lending. The crude complaint against such a strategy is that it simply puts heavily indebted countries deeper into debt. Clearly this is not right. As many have emphasized, in a world in which countries can grow and there is still some inflation it is possible for nominal debt to grow yet for a country to become more creditworthy over time (Feldstein (1986)). In fact, however, problem debtor nations have grown much more slowly since the onset of the debt crisis than before, and, partly as a result, their debt indicators have improved little if at all. To at least some extent the slow growth can be attributed to the debt burden itself. This at least raises the possibility that the insistence of creditors on maintaining the full extent of their claims on debtor nations may be self-defeating, reducing their expected repayment below what might be achieved through a settlement that reduces countries' debt burden.

The possibility that less may be more—that a reduction in the debt burden of highly indebted countries, rather than financing that simply postpones debt repayment, might be to everyone's advantage—

underlies the case for a replacement of the strategy of financing debt with forgiving it.

II. Analytics of Debt Forgiveness

Why should creditors ever forgive debt rather than postpone repayment? If the stream of payments from the debtor were unaffected by the burden of the debt, it would always be preferable to maintain the nominal value of creditors' claims. After all, even the most seemingly hopeless debtor might conceivably discover a valuable mineral resource or experience an unexpected surge of economic growth, and it makes sense for the creditors to preserve the option of benefiting from such good fortune if it arises. If they reduce the obligations of a country, they have sacrificed this option.

Nevertheless, potential repayment by a country is not independent of its debt burden. When a country's obligations exceed the amount it is likely to be able to pay, these obligations act like a high marginal tax rate on the country: if it succeeds in doing better than expected, the main benefits will accrue not to the country but to its creditors. This discourages the country from doing well at two levels. First, the government of a country will be less willing to take painful or politically unpalatable measures to improve economic performance if the benefits are likely to go to foreign creditors in any case. Second, the burden of the national debt will fall on domestic residents through taxation, and importantly through taxation of capital; so the overhang of debt acts as a deterrent to investment.

Over and above these costs to potential repayment is the fact that no clean Chapter XI proceeding exists for sovereign debtors, and a confrontational and disorderly default may reduce the actual receipts to a creditor below what could have been obtained if debt had earlier been reduced to a level that could have been paid.

The upshot of these negative effects is that the higher is the external debt of a country, the larger the probability of nonpayment; and thus the greater the subjective discount on that debt. If debt is high enough, further increases in the level of debt may actually lead to a smaller expected value of payments.[1]

---

[1] If there is no uncertainty about the future, it is always in the interests of creditors to forgive debt down to the level at which it will be repaid. In this case any secondary discount would constitute a case for debt forgiveness. Unfortunately, this is not the case when the future is uncertain.

A useful way to think about the relationship between debt and expected repayment is in terms of the curve *CD* illustrated in Figure 1. On the horizontal axis is the nominal value of a country's debt; on the vertical axis the actual expected payments. At low levels of debt nominal claims may be expected to be fully repaid, so that the outcome lies along the 45 degree line. At higher levels of debt, however, the possibility of nonpayment grows, so that the expected payment traces out a curve that falls increasingly below the 45 degree line. At a point such as *L* the ratio of expected payment to nominal debt may be measured by the slope of a ray from the origin; ignoring risk and transaction costs, we may regard this as approximating the secondary-market price of debt.

Although increased levels of debt above point *C* will be associated with lower secondary-market prices, at first the total value of debt will still rise. At high enough debt levels, however, the disincentive effects discussed above may be large enough so that the curve actually turns down.

We may now ask: under what conditions will a reduction in nominal

Figure 1. *The Debt Relief Laffer Curve*

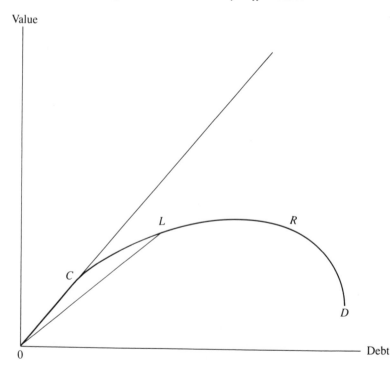

claims—that is, debt forgiveness—actually leave the creditors better off? Many authors have suggested that when debt sells at a discount on the secondary market creditors should "recognize reality" and reduce their claims on the country correspondingly. However, it is clear from Figure 1 that this is not necessarily right. At point L there is a secondary discount, but a reduction in the claims of creditors would still reduce what they expect to receive overall. The reason is implicit in the discussion of the previous section. Given the uncertainty about the future, a reduction in claims deprives creditors of the option value of sharing in good fortune. Only if this option value is outweighed by the improved incentives offered by a debt reduction do the creditors gain by passing on part of the secondary discount to the debtor. This is going to happen only if the debt burden is very large, so that these incentive effects predominate, at a point such as R.

The curve $DRLC$ should by now be a familiar sort of object. It is the *debt relief Laffer curve.* That is, just as governments may sometimes actually increase tax revenue by reducing tax rates, creditors may sometimes increase expected payment by forgiving part of a country's debt. In both cases the proposition that less is more depends on an initial extreme situation, whether of taxes that provide extreme disincentives or of a debt burden that is crippling in its effect on economic growth. Arguments that debt relief is in everyone's interest are, in effect, arguments that countries are on the wrong side of the debt relief Laffer curve.

Now of course in practice it is very difficult to ascertain which side of the curve a highly indebted country is on. A consensus holds that hugely indebted countries with weak governments, such as Bolivia, are on the wrong side, and this has led to granting of debt relief with few arguments. But for the major debtors the question is anybody's guess.

In spite of the difficulty of applying the concept of the $DRLC$ in practice, it remains useful as a way of organizing our thinking. For one thing, it is worth knowing what we don't know—Figure 1 makes it clear that both the confidence that secondary discounts can be freely passed on to debtors and the hard-line view that debt should never be forgiven are wrong in principle. Equally important, the $DRLC$ is useful as a way to think about the market-based schemes for debt reduction that have recently gained so much prominence. For it turns out that the prospects for success of these schemes are intimately tied to where on the debt relief Laffer curve we are.

The reason should be apparent. Market-based debt-reduction schemes, while they are sometimes aimed at producing other benefits, are in large part intended to "harness" the discount in the secondary market to the mutual benefit of debtors and creditors. As we have just seen, however, when concerted debt relief is considered, a secondary discount offers the possibility of mutual gain only when the debt is large enough to put the country on the wrong side of the curve. Can a market-based scheme harness the discount where collective action cannot? As we will see, it cannot—mutually beneficial debt reduction through market-based schemes is possible only under the same circumstances as mutually beneficial debt relief.

III. Debt Buy-Backs

Some of the problem debtors have accumulated substantial foreign exchange reserves, and others could possibly choose to run large enough trade surpluses to do the same. At the same time, the debts of these countries continue to trade at substantial discounts, reflecting doubts about the willingness or ability of the countries to continue to achieve such favorable trade performance. This raises an obvious possibility for reducing countries' debt through voluntary action rather than concerted debt forgiveness. Simply let them buy back their own debt on the secondary market, and the effect will be to reduce debt even net of foreign exchange reserves, because of the discount at which the debt sells. Is there anything wrong with this?[2]

Legally debtors are normally prohibited from repurchasing their own debt at a discount. The reason is twofold. First, there is the issue of seniority. Use of reserves to repurchase debt may impair the debtor's ability to repay the remaining debt, and existing creditors are entitled to first claim on whatever repayment the debtor is in fact able to make. In addition, there is a moral hazard problem: allowing debtors to buy back their debt at a discount rewards the least reliable, who therefore have the lowest secondary prices.

If it is decided that buy-backs are in the interest of both debtors and creditors, the moral hazard argument may be something that can be dealt with. For one thing, conditionality could be applied to the granting of permission for buy-backs. There are no doubt practical problems with this, but these may be left aside to focus instead on the question of whether it is in the interest of creditors to allow buy-backs.

To get some insight into this, it is useful to consider a simple numerical example, illustrated in Table 1. Here we imagine a hypothetical country that owes its creditors $100 billion and that has uncertain prospects of

---

[2] Debt buy-backs at a discount were actually quite common in the 1930s. See Portes (1987).

Table 1. *Effects of a Buy-Back*

	Bad State	Good State
Foreign exchange generated[1]	20	110
No buy-back		
Payments to creditors	25	100
Residual benefit to country	0	15
Reserves used for buy-back		
Payments to creditors who sell out	5	5
Payments to other creditors	20	90
Total payments	25	95
Residual benefit to country	0	20

[1] Country is assumed initially to have 5 in reserves.

repayment. Ignoring the question of when the country can make payments, we simply assume that there are two possibilities: a "bad" state in which the country can generate only $20 billion of foreign exchange, and a "good" state in which it can generate something more than $100 billion, say $110 billion. We also assume that the country starts with foreign exchange reserves of $5 billion. The probability of the bad state is 2/3, that of the good state 1/3.

Consider first what happens if there is no buy-back. In the bad state the creditors collect 25—the foreign exchange the country is able to earn, plus the reserves it has available. In the good state the country pays the 100 it owes. Thus the expected payments to creditors are $25*(2/3) + 100*(1/3) = 50$. Ignoring risk, the secondary market price on the country's debt will be 0.5.

Now suppose that the country uses its foreign exchange reserves to buy back part of its debt. Let us also initially suppose that the buy-back has no impact on the probability of a good outcome—which, as we will see, is crucial. At a secondary-market price of 0.5, the foreign exchange reserves can be used to buy back $10 billion of debt, reducing the outstanding debt to $90 billion.[3] Those creditors who sold out will receive $5 billion, whatever happens. Those who did not will receive $20 billion in the bad state (because the foreign exchange reserves are now gone) and $90 billion in the good state. Has the change hurt or helped the creditors?

[3] This is not quite right, because the secondary-market price of the debt will change as a result of the buy-back, and the amount purchased will depend on the post-buy-back equilibrium price, not the pre-buy-back one. For a marginal change, however, this makes no difference, and by focusing on the total returns to creditors we bypass the problem in any case.

The answer is that it has hurt them. The expected payments to the creditors are 5 in either state (the value of debt sold off in the secondary market) plus 20 in the bad state, plus 90 in the good state, implying expected payments of

$$5 + 20*(2/3) + 90*(1/3) = 48 \ 1/3.$$

That is, the buy-back reduces the expected total payment to the creditors. The effect of a buy-back in this case should be to lower the price of debt on the secondary market and make the creditors worse off.

The reason for this result is that the buy-back reduces the net contribution of the country in the good state, when it could repay its whole debt but now gets to pay less, while it has no effect in the bad state, when the country in any case pays all that it can. So the country gains at creditors' expense. It should be clear that this is a fairly general result. If a country's ability to pay is not affected by a buy-back, then the buy-back reduces the net payments by a country when it can pay and produces no gains for creditors when it cannot.

The only way that this result could be reversed is if the buy-back improves the country's ability to pay by a sufficient amount to offset this negative effect. The incentive effects indeed work in that direction. Consider the benefits to the country of having the good state occur. In the bad state the creditors take whatever the country can give. In the good state the country gets to keep any excess above its nominal debt. We have assumed that the country's foreign exchange earnings are 110 and its reserves 5, while its debt is only 100; so in the absence of a buy-back it gets to keep 15 in the good state. After a buy-back its reserves are gone, but its debt is reduced to 90, so in the good state it gets to keep 20. This greater gain in the good state should provide a greater incentive for the country to pursue adjustment policies, to invest, to do all those things that we think the country can do to increase its future ability to pay.

The creditors may, then, benefit from a buy-back, but only if the increased probability of the good state is enough to outweigh the loss of their rights to share in the good fortune if it comes. But this is exactly the condition that we saw was necessary for creditors to benefit from debt forgiveness. So in fact it is only in the interest of creditors to allow buy-backs of debt on the secondary market when the debtor country is on the wrong side of the debt relief Laffer curve.

We can see the equivalence precisely in the context of our numerical example. Suppose that instead of allowing the country to buy back part of its debt, the creditors had instead simply reduced the face value of outstanding claims from 100 to 95. Then the aggregate payments to creditors would be the same as in the buy-back case: 25 in the bad state, 95 in the good. Also, in the good state the country would have the same amount of foreign exchange left over: earnings of 110, less debt of 95, plus reserves of 5 = 20. Thus the incentive to increase the probability of the good state would be the same. It follows, then, that allowing buy-backs on the secondary market will benefit creditors if and only if debt forgiveness would do the same.

This suggests that creditors will not readily agree to buy-backs unless they are convinced that debt forgiveness is definitely desirable—which therefore also implies that debt buy-backs are not going to be in any meaningful sense an alternative to the collective-action strategies that were discussed in the first two sections of this paper.

IV. Securitization

Debt buy-backs are limited in their possible extent by the quantity of foreign exchange reserves available. Recently, however, investment bankers have proposed a way in which this limitation might be overcome. The idea of securitization is that a country issues new debt in the form of bonds that either are sold for cash that can then be used to repurchase debt on the secondary market, or are directly exchanged for debt (as in the recent Morgan-Mexico deal). If the new bonds sell at a smaller discount than existing debt, the effect will be to reduce the debt outstanding without any expenditure of foreign exchange reserves by the debtor.

What should be immediately clear—although it has been obscure in most practical discussions—is that such schemes will work only if the new debt is somehow made senior to the existing debt. If the new debt is not senior, it will face the same probability of nonpayment as the existing debt and should therefore sell at the same discount. This will mean that there will be no prospect for a reduction in net debt. Suppose, for example, that a country's existing debt sells at a 50 percent discount, and that the country attempts to reduce its debt through a securitization scheme involving the issue of $10 billion in face value of new bonds. If these are not senior to the existing debt, we can suppose that they will sell for only $5 billion; this will allow retirement of $10 billion of old debt, but the country will still end up exactly where it started. (This also confirms that the discount should not have changed.) So securitization depends on making the new debt senior to the old, with some perceived first claim on payments.

Such seniority is difficult to achieve. A sovereign debtor cannot make a truly credible commitment to service some of its debt more reliably than others, since any default puts it outside international law anyway. Nonetheless, it may be possible in some cases to establish de facto seniority. In the Morgan-Mexico plan the de facto seniority was supposed to come from the fact that the new debt took the form of bonds rather than bank loans. Since 1982 Mexican bonds have not been subject to reschedulings and new-money requests, essentially because of their relatively minor importance and the difficulty of achieving collective action from bondholders. So the Mexican Government claimed that the new bonds should be regarded as effectively senior to the existing bank debt. In practice they were only marginally successful in this: a few bonds were sold at a discount somewhat smaller than that on bank debt, but most of the offering went untaken.

Suppose, however, that it were indeed possible to establish the principle that new securities issued to retire part of existing debt are senior to the old debt remaining. Would such a securitization plan be in the mutual interest of debtors and creditors? We can show that the problem is exactly analogous to that of debt buy-backs, and that the answer once again depends on which side of the debt relief Laffer curve the debtor is on.

Table 2 shows an example that is designed to stress the parallel with the example we used to examine debt buy-backs. We consider a country that has an initial debt of $100 billion, and that in the "bad state" can pay 25, in the "good state" generates resources of 115. The probabilities of the two states are again 2/3 and 1/3, respectively, so that in the absence of a securitization plan the expected repayment is 50.

Now suppose that the country issues $5 billion of new bonds that are somehow guaranteed to be senior to the existing debt. These bonds will be fully repaid even in the bad state, so they will sell at full face value,

Table 2.　*Effects of Securitization*

	Bad State	Good State
Foreign exchange generated	25	115
No securitization		
Payments to creditors	25	100
Residual benefit to country	0	15
Senior bonds exchanged for part of debt		
Payments to new creditors	5	5
Payments to other creditors	20	90
Total payments	25	95
Residual benefit to country	0	20

and can therefore be used to buy back $10 billion of old debt.[4] The country's net debt will therefore be reduced to 95.

The parallel with the case of a buy-back should now be apparent. In the bad state the new creditors receive 5, the old creditors 20, for a total payment of 25. In the good state the new creditors also receive 5, the old creditors 90, for a total payment of 95. So if the probability of a good state has not been increased by the package, the total expected payments to creditors have been reduced to

$$(2/3)*25 + (1/3)*95 = 48 \ 1/3.$$

In order to make creditors better off, the probability of the good state must rise enough to compensate for creditors' loss of the option of benefiting as much from that state. The incentive for the country to increase the probability of the good state rises, just as in the buy-back case: before the debt reduction, the country gets to keep $115 - 100 = 15$ in that state; after the debt reduction it gets to keep $115 - 95 = 20$. Thus just as in the buy-back case, a debt reduction can benefit the creditors, but only if the debtor is on the wrong side of the debt relief Laffer curve.

It is also apparent that a straightforward debt forgiveness, reducing debt from 100 to 95, will have precisely the same effects as the securitization scheme.

V. Debt-Equity Swaps

The most publicized market-based scheme for debt reduction is the use of deals in which creditors sell debt at some discount in return for local currency that must be invested in equity. In some of the more enthusiastic descriptions of such swaps, the impression has been given that they solve all problems at once: that they could simultaneously provide a source of capital inflow and cancel countries' external obligations.

In fact, a debt-equity swap neither provides a capital inflow nor cancels a country's obligations. The foreign investor does not bring foreign exchange to the country since it is the country's own debt that is presented to the central bank; thus there is no capital inflow. The country's obligations are not cancelled; the foreigners acquire an equity claim on the country to replace their previous claim. What has really happened

---

[4] The same qualification as in footnote 3 applies: the price at which the bonds trade for old debt will be the post-securitization discount, which changes as a result of the action itself. But the analysis is exactly right for marginal changes, and the key point of total returns to creditors is correct.

is essentially the same as what happens in securitization. The country has exchanged a new kind of liability for some of its existing liabilities.

Now, a first question about this exchange is whether it can lead to a net reduction in the country's external obligations by harnessing the discount in the secondary market. The answer should be immediately clear when we realize that a debt-equity swap is a kind of securitization: the country can capture the secondary-market discount to the extent that the new claims are regarded as senior to the old. In the current political and economic climate it is widely expected that direct foreign investors will be allowed to repatriate earnings or use their profits as they wish within the debtor nations, even if these countries are failing to repay debts fully. This has allowed debt-equity swaps to capture part of the discount, though by no means all. Once one realizes, however, that the ability to reduce net obligations through debt-equity swaps depends on seniority of equity (which is itself a fairly weird idea), the limitations become apparent.

While debt-equity swaps are, at a fundamental level, a kind of securitization, the fact that the assets involved are so different introduces three other considerations that do not arise in securitization schemes involving issue of bonds. These are the effects of the swaps on the timing of payment, the possibility of "round-tripping" or other diversions of capital inflows, and the fiscal impacts.

In principle, exchanging a debt for equity should have a favorable effect on a country's timing of obligations. Where even a rescheduled debt requires a country to make a stream of payments that is flat in nominal terms, an equity claim on a country will normally provide a stream of repatriated earnings that rises over time with both growth and world inflation, and that is therefore lower at the beginning, higher later. Thus, converting debt to equity can serve the same purpose that concerted lending is supposed to serve, of postponing payment to a time when the country is presumed likely to be more able to afford it. An ideal debt-equity swap would clearly loosen the short-run liquidity constraint on a problem debtor.

In practice debt-equity swaps will not always be ideal, and it is unfortunately easy for them to worsen the immediate foreign exchange position of countries that allow them. The most extreme case is that of round-tripping: after swapping debt for equity, an investor then sells the equity and withdraws the proceeds from the country. In this case the debt-equity swap ends up being in effect a use of foreign exchange reserves to buy back debt on the secondary market, probably at less than the full discount. (Of course, if investors know they can get away with round-tripping, they will be prepared to pay the full discount for the right to carry out the transaction.)

Even if round-tripping does not occur, debt-equity swaps can still consume foreign exchange on net. Suppose that a foreign firm uses a debt-equity swap to carry out an investment that it would have undertaken anyway. Had it carried out the investment without a swap, it would have brought foreign exchange to the central bank to exchange for local currency with which to make the investment. If it does the swap instead, this foreign exchange inflow fails to occur. So in effect the central bank has used some of its own foreign exchange reserves to make a purchase of debt on the secondary market.

The net impact on foreign exchange reserves from a debt-equity swap is not, as many people continue to think, a trade-off between the capital inflow aspect and the diversion through round-tripping and substitution for alternative financing. At best, in the case of an ideal swap that represents 100 percent "additionality," there is a zero capital inflow; any round-tripping or substitution turns this into a net capital outflow. Since in practice there is bound to be some leakage, debt-equity swaps are realistically a mixture of securitization and buy-back.

In its fiscal effects, however, the securitization involved in debt-equity swaps is very different from straight securitization. In straight securitization the debtor government offers a new asset in exchange for old debt; in a debt-equity swap it offers assets belonging to the private sector. To make this offer, the government must provide the local currency with which to buy these assets; this currency issue will be inflationary unless offset by domestic borrowing. In the latter case the counterpart of the foreign investor's swap of debt for equity is a debtor swap of foreign for domestic debt.

So far so good; but many debtor governments have a domestic debt problem as well as a foreign debt problem. They have large budget deficits, so that anything that aggravates the budget deficit has a real cost; and, crucially, they pay much higher real interest rates on their internal debt than they do on their external debt—say 20 percent versus 5 percent. So even if a debt-equity swap does not have a large negative effect on foreign exchange reserves, it is virtually certain to aggravate a debtor country's fiscal problems.

As this discussion shows, debt-equity swaps are quite complex in their effects and difficult to evaluate even after the fact. They are in principle a kind of securitization that has the additional advantage of tilting the stream of payments away from the present and toward the future, but they are in practice likely to involve buy-back of debt at a higher effective price than the secondary price and will typically aggravate debtor fiscal problems.

Will creditors benefit from debt-equity swaps? To the extent that these swaps are a combination of buy-back and securitization, the answer depends as usual on the debtor's position on the debt relief Laffer curve. The financing aspect may improve the debtor's prospects as well, while the fiscal consequences will tend to reduce creditworthiness. There is also an important, though not too laudable, possibility for gain: that the countries may mishandle the swaps in such a way as to allow those who get the chance to make swaps to make substantial rents.

VI. Summary and Conclusions

The main conclusion of this paper may be stated bluntly: there is no magic in market-based schemes for debt reduction. The secondary-market discount on developing country debt does not automatically constitute a resource that can be harnessed to provide free debt relief; in many circumstances repurchase of debt on the secondary market, whether through reserve-financed buy-backs or through creation of new, senior securities, will hurt existing creditors. There is a mutual benefit from such repurchases only when a reduced debt burden strongly increases a country's likely ability to repay—the same situation in which unilateral debt forgiveness is in the interests of creditors in any case.

The most heavily advertised scheme for market-based debt reductions is the use of debt-equity swaps. This paper has argued that such swaps are in principle a kind of securitization; that round-tripping and other leakages tend to make them degenerate into buy-backs financed by reserves; and that they are likely both to be disappointing in terms of their ability to capture the secondary-market discount and costly in their effects on countries' fiscal positions. While there are potential advantages as well, the claims made for debt-equity swaps by their sponsors are clearly exaggerated.

Clearly, then, market-based debt reduction cannot serve as an alternative to the orthodox strategy of rescheduling and concerted lending. Schemes that benefit the debtor at the expense of the creditor—such as buy-backs and securitization for countries not on the wrong side of the debt relief Laffer curve—will be opposed by existing creditors when they become more than marginal. Schemes that benefit the creditors at the expense of the debtor—such as debt-equity swaps that fail to capture the secondary discount, while allowing firms to make investments they would have made in any case—will be opposed by the debtors as their effects become clear. Mutual agreement on schemes will come only when, as in the recent Bolivian case, there is more or less universal agreement that the debtor is so heavily indebted that a reduction in claims actually increases expected repayment.

APPENDIX

A Formal Model of Forgiveness, Buy-Backs, and Securitization

A key point in the text was that the condition under which it is in creditors' interest to allow buy-backs, whether financed out of foreign exchange reserves or by the issue of new, senior securities, is the same as that under which it is in their collective interest to reduce a country's debt obligations—namely, when the country is on the wrong side of the debt relief Laffer curve, so that a reduction in the country's nominal obligations actually increases its expected repayment. This point was suggested both in the text and with numerical examples; here I make the point with a simple formal model. The model is closely based on an earlier model of mine (Krugman (forthcoming)), but is even further simplified in order to allow market-based debt-reduction schemes to be introduced with a minimum of complication.

Consider, then, a country that may not be able to repay all its external debt. We assume for simplicity that there are only two possible states of the world: a bad state in which the country definitely cannot repay all its debt, and a good state in which the country definitely can. The maximum trade surplus that the country can run in each state is F_B, F_G. The actual payment made in each state is T_B, T_G.

Creditors are assumed to be able to make the country pay all that it can, up to the level of its debt obligations. In the bad state, this implies

$$T_B = F_B + R, \tag{1}$$

where R is the country's foreign exchange reserves. In the good state, the country simply pays what it owes:

$$T_G = D, \tag{2}$$

where D is the country's debt.

Let S be what the country has left over after paying its creditors—that is, the sum of feasible trade surplus and foreign exchange reserves, less actual payment. We have

$$S = F + R - T, \tag{3}$$

in each state.

Now a key element of any case for debt forgiveness must be an incentive effect from debt on a country's ability to repay. We introduce this by assuming that the probability of the good state depends on how hard the country tries, as measured by a variable we can call adjustment effort, A:

$$p_G = h(A). \tag{4}$$

The country is assumed to dislike making an adjustment effort, but to like receiving a surplus S; in particular, the country's objective function may be written[5]

$$U = S - V(A). \tag{5}$$

Since the country must make an adjustment effort before it knows whether the state will be good or bad, and since there is something left over for the country only if the state is good, we have an expected value of the country's objective function

$$EU = h(A)(F_G + R - D) - V(A), \tag{6}$$

where the term in brackets is what is left over to the country in the good state. Since the country will maximize this with respect to A, and since the country's choice of A determines the probability of a good state, we may write the outcome of the country's maximization as

$$p_G = p_G(F_G + R - D), \tag{7}$$

with $p_G' > 0$.

Next consider the expected receipts of the country's creditors. We can write the expected value of repayments as

$$ET = p_G D + (1 - p_G)(R + F_B). \tag{8}$$

And we can now ask: does a reduction of nominal debt raise or lower the expected repayment? Clearly,

$$\partial ET/\partial D = p_G - p_G'(D - R - F_B). \tag{9}$$

A reduction in debt will therefore increase expected repayment—that is, we are on the wrong side of the debt relief Laffer curve—whenever

$$p_G - p_G'(D - R - F_B) < 0.$$

The interpretation of this condition is that the positive incentive effects of the debt relief must outweigh the cost to creditors of the fact that they get paid less in the good state.

Now we consider what happens if a country is allowed to use part of its foreign exchange reserves to buy-back debt on the secondary market. We assume that the secondary market price of a dollar of debt is simply the expected payments on that debt, so that

$$\sigma = ET/D, \tag{10}$$

where σ is the secondary market price.

Suppose that a small quantity of reserves $- dR$ is used to repurchase debt on the secondary market. These reserves will buy back a larger nominal value of debt, so that

$$dD = \sigma^{-1} dR. \tag{11}$$

---

[5] The reason for assuming that the country's objective function is linear in S is in order to purge the problem of any risk-sharing aspects—not that these may not matter, but they do not seem central to the issue at hand.

The fact that debt falls by more than reserves means that the country will have more left over in the good state, so that it will have an incentive to do more adjustment, raising the probability of that state occurring:

$$dp_G = p'_G(dD - dR) = p'_G(1 - \sigma^{-1})dR. \tag{12}$$

The change in the secondary-market price reflects both any change in the expected payments and the fact of a smaller remaining debt:

$$d\sigma = D^{-1}(dET - \sigma dD) = D^{-1}(dET - dR). \tag{13}$$

But the change in expected repayment is

$$dET = (1-p_G)dR + p_G dD + (D-R-F_B)dp_G$$

$$= dR + p_G(\sigma^{-1}-1)dR - p'_G(D-R-F)(\sigma^{-1}-1)dR. \tag{14}$$

Substituting back into (13), we find

$$d\sigma = D^{-1}(\sigma^{-1}-1)[p_G-p'_G(D- R-F_B)]dR. \tag{15}$$

A buy-back that uses part of reserves ($dR < 0$) will therefore produce a rise in the secondary price, benefiting creditors, if and only if $p_G - p'_G(D - R - F_B) < 0$. This is precisely the condition for a reduction in debt to raise expected payment. So allowing a buy-back will benefit creditors only if the country is on the wrong side of the debt relief Laffer curve.

Next suppose that the debtor country is able to issue new debt in exchange for old, and that this new debt is somehow made effectively senior to the old, so that it receives first claim on available resources in the bad state. We will suppose that a small quantity of new debt dN is issued. Since the new debt is senior, it will trade at par, and can be used to retire old debt at the secondary-market price:

$$dD = -\sigma^{-1}dN. \tag{16}$$

In the bad state, the new debt gets served first, and old debt receives only what is left:

$$T_B = F_B + R - N. \tag{17}$$

As before, the incentive for a country adjustment effort depends on what is left over after paying both new and old debt; thus we can write

$$p_G = p_G(F_G + R - D - N). \tag{18}$$

Now consider the effect of issuing some new debt on the expected payments to the remaining creditors:

$$dET = -(1-p_G)dN - p_G\sigma^{-1}dN + p'_G(D-F_B-R)(\sigma^{-1}-1)dN$$

$$= -dN + [p_G - p'_G(D-F_B-R)](\sigma^{-1}-1)(-dN). \tag{19}$$

Substituting back into (13), this gives us the change in the secondary-market price

$$d\sigma = D^{-1}(\sigma^{-1}-1)[p_G - p'_G(D-F_B-R)](-dN). \tag{20}$$

As in the case of a buy-back using reserves, the value of the remaining debt increases if and only if $p_G - p_G'(D - R - F_B) < 0$—that is, if the country is on the wrong side of the debt relief Laffer curve.

REFERENCES

Cline, William R., *International Debt and the Stability of the World Economy,* Policy Analyses in International Economics, No. 4 (Washington: Institute for International Economics, September 1983).

Feldstein, Martin S., "International Debt Service and Economic Growth: Some Simple Analytics," NBER Working Paper 2138 (Cambridge, Massachusetts: National Bureau of Economic Research, November 1986).

Krugman, Paul R., "International Debt Strategies in an Uncertain World," in *International Debt and the Developing Countries,* ed. by Gordon W. Smith and John T. Cuddington (Washington: World Bank, 1985), pp. 79–100.

———, "Financing vs. Forgiving a Debt Overhang," *Journal of Development Economics* (Amsterdam), forthcoming.

Portes, Richard, "Debt and the Market" (unpublished; presented at the Group of Thirty Plenary Meeting, New York, September 1987).

Sachs, Jeffrey D., *Theoretical Issues in International Borrowing,* Princeton Studies in International Finance, No. 54 (Princeton, New Jersey: Princeton University, July 1984).

Voluntary Debt Reduction: Incentives and Welfare

ELHANAN HELPMAN*

In an economy with a debt overhang, investment depends on expected tax rates. On the other hand, expected tax rates depend on the debt's face value. Therefore investment depends on the face value of debt. The paper shows that this may lead to a positive or negative association between debt and investment depending on the degree of international capital mobility and attitudes toward risk. There may also exist multiple equilibria; with high and low investment levels. The paper explores the desirability of debt reduction in this environment. First, it characterizes circumstances in which debt reduction is desirable from the collective point of view of the creditors. Second, it formulates the forgiveness decision as a noncooperative game among creditors and explores the scope for debt reduction as an outcome of this game.

S IX YEARS of the international debt crisis have generated many proposals for its resolution. Some proposals involve pure financial engineering while others involve real economic change. The suggestions range from market-based debt reduction schemes to unilateral moratoria on debt. Prominent among them is a call for voluntary debt forgiveness. Proponents argue that forgiveness not only serves the interest of debtor countries but would also benefit the banks. High debt levels, it is

* Mr. Helpman is the Archie Sherman Professor of International Economic Relations at Tel Aviv University. He is a graduate of Tel Aviv University and Harvard University.

Part of this paper was written when the author was a visiting scholar in the Research Department of the International Monetary Fund and part when he was a visiting professor at the Massachusetts Institute of Technology. He thanks Michael Dooley, Rudiger Dornbusch, Jacob Frenkel, Gene Grossman, Paul Krugman, Assaf Razin, Jeffrey Sachs, and Lars Svensson for helpful comments and discussions.

claimed, bring about low incentives to adjust to the debt overhang. Low incentives to adjust lead in turn to a low capacity to service debt. If creditors were voluntarily to reduce the debt's face value, they would promote adjustment. The resulting greater capacity to service debt would more than compensate them for any initial losses (see Sachs (1988) for the original argument).

Two types of adjustment bear on the issue of debt relief: macroeconomic policies in general and the debtor country's investment level in particular. Better policies and more investment raise future income, thereby increasing the capacity to service debt. In order to deal rigorously with policy responses it is necessary to employ an explicit model of government behavior, but no accepted model is available for this purpose. For this reason I focus instead on market outcomes and investment-driven adjustments. My study is designed to explore in a systematic way the scope for voluntary debt reduction.

Among the many dimensions of the problem at hand I concentrate on three: the degree of international capital mobility, attitudes toward risk, and the degree of cooperation among creditors. These features prove to be important. I show, for example, that in the absence of international capital mobility and in the presence of high risk aversion in the debtor country the banks cannot gain from a voluntary write-down of debt. This result is independent of the degree of cooperation among the banks. In other cases forgiveness may or may not serve the interest of creditors. When it is in the collective interest of creditors to provide debt reduction, however, the prospects for forgiveness may hinge on the degree of cooperation among them.

The paper is structured as follows. In the next section I describe the debtor's repayment behavior as a function of its economic performance. Full repayment takes place as long as revenue raised by a tax on random output suffices to cover debt service without the tax rate exceeding a feasible maximal level. In other cases the tax rate ceiling determines repayment, which equals tax revenue. In Section II, I derive a formula for the valuation of these repayments on international financial markets, and use it to determine the value of debt on secondary markets as well as the secondary market price and discount. This information is then used to evaluate the effect on prices of a facility that purchases debt on secondary markets in order to forgive it. It is shown that the resulting price increases can be substantial even when investment does not change.

I explore the relationship between debt and investment in Section IV. This relationship is shown to depend on the degree of capital mobility and attitudes toward risk. In the absence of international capital flows and high risk aversion in the debtor country a larger debt is associated with more investment. In all other cases larger debts imply lower investment, and multiple equilibria may exist that differ in investment levels. With multiple equilibria small changes in debt may bring about sharp investment responses, because the economy may jump from one equilibrium to another.

Section V deals with welfare implications of debt reduction. I show that debtors gain from debt reduction. Creditors lose whenever debt reduction depresses investment. But creditors may lose or gain when relief stimulates investment. Gains by creditors are particularly likely if multiple equilibria exist and the debtor country is trapped in a low investment equilibrium. In this case debt reduction may force a switch to a Pareto-superior high investment equilibrium. This analysis identifies circumstances in which cooperating creditors would provide voluntary debt relief.

In Section VI, I consider the scope for debt reduction in the absence of cooperation. For this purpose I formulate a non-cooperative game in voluntary debt reductions. In the presence of a single investment equilibrium and where scope exists for collective debt relief, non-cooperative actions yield voluntary debt reductions if the initial debt is sufficiently large. In the presence of multiple investment equilibria the solution set of the non-cooperative game may contain an equilibrium with debt reduction together with an equilibrium without debt reduction. Some policy implications of these results are discussed in the closing section.

I. Repayment Structure

For the purpose of this study I employ a variant of the model developed in Helpman (1988). The entire future is collapsed into a single period. The debtor country's output in that period is a random variable given by $\tilde{\theta}E(I)$, where $\tilde{\theta}$ denotes a random productivity shock, I is the current period's investment level, and $E(\cdot)$ is an increasing concave function representing the country's activity level in production. In this section the investment level is predetermined. States of nature are identified with productivity shock levels; that is, $\tilde{\theta}$ obtains the value θ in state θ.

The government has an external debt D and its debt service payments are RD, where R is 1 plus the interest rate. All these variables are predetermined from the point of view of the current discussion. The government services debt from tax revenue. It can tax output at any desirable rate up to a ceiling $t \leq 1$. A debt problem prevails in the sense that states exist in which the highest possible tax revenue is insufficient to cover debt service payments. Namely, $Prob[t\bar{\theta}E(I) < RD] > 0$. Therefore there exists a critical state, defined by

$$\theta_c(D, I) = RD/tE(I), \tag{1}$$

such that debt is fully repaid in states $\theta \geq \theta_c(D, I)$ but cannot be fully repaid in states $\theta < \theta_c(D, I)$.

The government uses an income tax at the state-contingent rate $\tau(\theta; D, I)$ in order to raise revenue for debt service payments. It defaults on its payments only when they exceed its taxing capacity, but it pays in such states its maximum tax revenue. In other states it raises the precise revenue needed for debt service payments. This specification is the same as in Helpman (1988, Section IX). Therefore,

$$\tau(\theta; D, I) = \begin{bmatrix} t & \text{for} & \theta \leq \theta_c(D, I), \\ RD/\theta E(I) & \text{for} & \theta \geq \theta_c(D, I). \end{bmatrix} \tag{2}$$

Creditors receive state-contingent payments $\tau(\theta; D, I)\theta E(I)$, which are given by

$$T(\theta; D, I) = \begin{bmatrix} t\theta E(I) & \text{for} & \theta \leq \theta_c(D, I), \\ RD & \text{for} & \theta \geq \theta_c(D, I). \end{bmatrix} \tag{3}$$

This completes the description of payments in the single future period. The resulting repayment profile is depicted in Figure 1. As long as investment is constant, the same repayment profile arises when the government applies a state independent tax rate t and redistributes revenue in excess of debt service payments to the public in a lump-sum fashion. The tax system, however, affects investment incentives; a given debt level brings about different investment levels under different tax structures (see Helpman (1988, Section IX)). This point is further discussed in Section VI.

II. Debt Valuation[1]

In this section I discuss the valuation of debt on secondary markets. I assume that these markets are part of the international financial system and that debt repayments (3) are too small to affect state-contingent marginal valuations in this system. For simplicity let the marginal valuations be the same in all states, and let $R - 1$ be the real interest on safe loans. Then every uncertain future stream of payments is valued at its discounted expected value. In particular, the stream of payments by the debtor to its creditors has a market value of

[1] This and the next section follow closely Helpman (1988, Section VI).

Figure 1

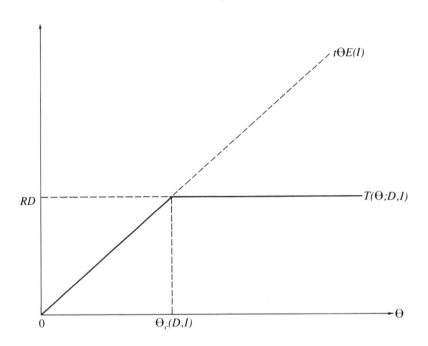

$$V(D, I) = R^{-1} \int_0^\infty T(\theta; D, I) dG(\theta), \tag{4}$$

where $G(\theta)$ is the probability distribution function over states. Using (3) this can be expressed as

$$V(D, I) = D - DG[\theta_c(D, I)] + \int_0^{\theta_c(D, I)} \theta[tE(I)/R]dG(\theta). \tag{5}$$

This function is increasing in both arguments, concave in debt, concave in invesment, $V(0, I) = 0$, and $V_D(0, I) = 1$, as depicted in Figure 2.

The price of a unit of debt in the secondary market is

$$p(D, I) = V(D, I)/D. \tag{6}$$

Using (5) it can also be expressed as

$$p(D, I) = \Pi(D, I) + [1 - \Pi(D, I)]E[t\bar\theta E/RD \mid \bar\theta < \theta_c(D, I)], \tag{7}$$

where $\Pi(D, I) \equiv 1 - G[\theta_c(D, I)]$ is the probability that $\bar\theta \geq \theta_c(D, I)$ and $E[\cdot]$ is the expected value of the repayment share $t\bar\theta E/RD$ conditional on the productivity shock being smaller than $\theta_c(D, I)$. Hence, the equilibrium price—equal to the mean repayment share—is a weighted average

Figure 2

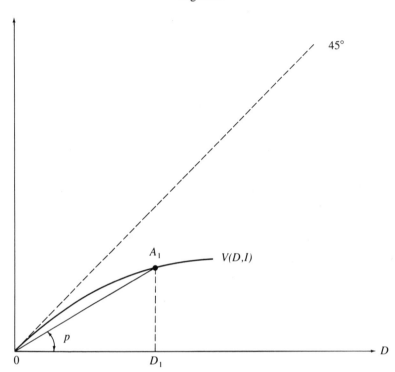

of 1 (full repayment) and the mean repayment share in the low productivity states in which debt is only partially repaid.

The price of a unit of debt on the secondary market is represented in Figure 2 by the slope of a ray through the origin (see (6)). Thus, for example, the slope of ray OA_1 represents the price when debt is D_1. The smaller the debt, the higher its price and the smaller its discount (the discount equals 1 minus the price). The price approaches 1 and the discount approaches zero as debt approaches zero. Higher debt levels lead to lower prices on the secondary market because the larger the debt the smaller the set of states in which debt is fully repaid and the lower repayment per-unit debt in states with partial repayment (the latter results from the fact that total payments in these states do not change with the level of debt; see Figure 1). In terms of (7) higher debt levels reduce the probability of full repayment as well as the conditional expected repayment share in states of partial repayment.

III. Price Effects of Debt Reduction

There exist several programs of debt forgiveness (see, for example, Cline (1987)). Some of them, such as Kenen's (1983), propose to establish an international facility that will buy debt on secondary markets and forgive it (see Corden, above in this volume, for a review). As pointed out by Dooley (below, in this volume), existing market discounts cannot be used to assess the cost of debt forgiveness, because the anticipation of forgiveness raises market prices. My model suggests that indeed the lower the outstanding debt, the higher its price on the secondary market. Rational expectations imply that in equilibrium the purchase price equals the post-purchase price on the secondary market. For suppose it is higher. Then every remaining holder of debt wants to sell for a somewhat lower price. And if it is lower, an owner of a unit of debt prefers to sell it after the reduction of debt. For these reasons, (6) or (7) can be used to calculate the purchase price for an international facility that intends to forgive debt. In this calculation D denotes the remaining debt.

Suppose, for example, that an international facility buys and forgives Δ of debt (it may buy more, but the following analysis depends only on the amount forgiven). Then our analysis suggests that $p(D - \Delta, I)$ describes the unit value of remaining debt. When the productivity shock is uniformly distributed on the interval $[0, 1]$ (7) yields (assuming that the critical values $\theta_c(\cdot)$ before and after the purchase are strictly between zero and 1)

$$p(D - \Delta, I) = 1 - \frac{1}{2}\,\theta_c\,(D - \Delta, I) = 1 - \frac{1}{2}\,\theta_c\,(D, I)\left(1 - \frac{\Delta}{D}\right). \quad (8)$$

Hence, if $\theta_c(D, I) = 0.8$ (the probability of full repayment is initially 20 percent), debt is valued at 60 cents to the dollar. And if the facility wants to buy 20 percent of the debt with an intention to forgive it (i.e., $\Delta/D = 0.2$), the price of debt goes up to 68 cents to the dollar. Thus, 20 percent forgiveness increases prices by close to 14 percent.

This calculation suggests that a great deal of the corporation's resources will go to the creditors, despite the facility's intention to help the debtor. This is in line with Dooley's argument. If, for example, debt is $100 billion and the facility buys back 20 percent, it spends $13.6 billion. The remaining claims of the creditors are worth $54.4 billion. Therefore, in order to reduce the value of claims by $5.6 billion the facility has to spend $13.6 billion. More generally, since $p(0, I) = 1$ (i.e., total debt forgiveness raises the price to its face value), the price goes up to as close as desired to 1 for sufficiently large debt forgiveness levels. Hence, if initially debt is traded at a high discount, say at 7 cents to the dollar (as some of Peru's debt was traded), a sufficiently high degree of debt forgiveness by an international facility that buys debt on the secondary market will bring about huge capital gains to the creditors with relatively little debt relief to the debtor. All this assumes constant investment. As I show below, however, the response of investment to debt reduction has important effects on secondary market values.

IV. Investment

I deal in this section with the effects of debt on investment. This analysis is of interest in its own right, but it also provides an essential ingredient in the following evaluation of the case for voluntary debt reduction. At this stage it is sufficient to observe that (5) implies that debt reduction does not help the creditors if it depresses investment or raises it only slightly (because the value of debt increases in both debt and investment). For this reason voluntary debt reduction requires a sufficiently strong investment stimulus. Naturally, in a broader context of adjustment there exist additional channels of influence. In this study, however, I deal only with investment.

In order to deal with these concerns we need to fill in additional details of the model. Assume that the debtor country's firms trade shares in a competitive stock market in the manner suggested by Diamond (1967). Using the terminology of Helpman and Razin (1978), $E(I)$ denotes the number of real equities. Given a real equity price q, the net value of firms is $qE(I) - I$. Firms choose investment to maximize their net value, which implies the first order condition $qE'(I) = 1$. Hence, the supply price of real equities is

$$q_s(I) \equiv 1/E'(I).$$ (9)

Higher investment levels lead to higher supply prices of real equities, as depicted in Figure 3. If we were to draw the supply price as a function of the stock of real equities rather than the investment level, it would represent a regular supply curve. However, since the stock of real equities increases with investment I refer to the plot of $q_s(I)$ in the figure as a supply curve.

In order to determine the level of investment we also need a demand curve. The nature of this curve depends on institutions, the distribution of the productivity shock, preferences, as well as additional features. In particular, it depends on the degree of international capital mobility

Figure 3

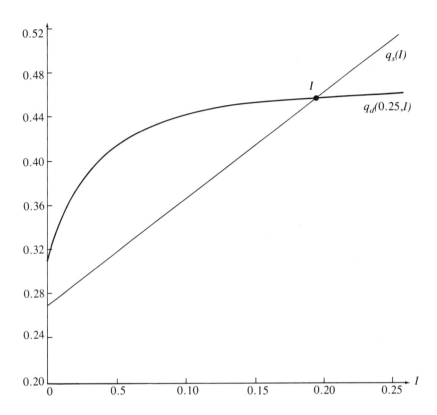

allowed by the debtor country. I will deal with two extreme cases; free capital mobility and a binding quantitative restriction on capital flows.

Free Capital Mobility

In the presence of free capital mobility the price of every asset is determined by its value on the international capital markets as the discounted expected present value of its future return. Thus, if $\eta(\theta; D, I)$ represents an asset's state contingent return, the market prices the asset according to

$$q_d(D, I) \equiv R^{-1} \int_0^\infty \eta(\theta; D, I)dG(\theta). \tag{10}$$

This representation underlines the dependence of the asset price on debt and investment, which is the subject of this study. Naturally, there exist many assets whose return structure does not depend on debt or investment; their price does not depend on these variables either. The return on a unit of real equity equals the after-tax value of θ. Therefore for real equities

$$\eta(\theta; D, I) \equiv [1 - \tau(\theta; D, I)]\theta. \tag{11}$$

Equation (11) applies to every state contingent tax structure. For the particular structure given in (2) we can combine (2), (10), and (11) to obtain

$$q_d(D, I) = R^{-1}\bar{\theta} - R^{-1}t \int_0^{\theta_c(D, I)} \theta dG(\theta)$$
$$- \{1 - G[\theta_c(D, I)]\}D/E(I), \tag{12}$$

where $\bar{\theta}$ denotes the mean of θ. This price declines in debt and increases in investment. It declines in debt because the larger the debt level the higher the tax rates in states with full repayment and the lower the after-tax return on equity. Higher debt also reduces the set of states in which there is full repayment, but this has a second order effect. The demand price increases in investment because the larger the investment level the larger the tax base and the lower the tax rates in states of full repayment. Hence, for positive debt levels the demand price rises with investment, as depicted in Figure 3 (changes in the set of states with full repayment have again second order effects). The demand price function also satisfies

$$q_d(0, I) = R^{-1}\bar{\theta},$$

and

$$\lim_{I \to +\infty} q_d(D, I) = R^{-1}\bar{\theta}, \text{ whenever } \lim_{I \to +\infty} G[\theta_c(D, I)] = 0.$$

Therefore, in the absence of debt the demand curve is horizontal at a level that equals the discounted mean of the productivity shock, and whenever the condition on $\theta_c(\cdot)$ is satisfied, the demand price approaches this value asymptotically as the investment level goes to infinity.

Figure 3 describes a situation with a unique equilibrium, determined by the intersection of the demand and supply curves at point 1. These curves were generated from explicit functions and a debt level $D = 0.25$.[2]

---

[2] In this example the following parameters and functions are used: $R = 1$, $t = 0.5$, θ is uniformly distributed on $[0,1]$, and $E(I) \equiv 1 - 10\log 0.27 + 10\log(0.27 + 0.1I)$.

Figure 4 describes curves that were generated from the same functions
with a debt level $D = 0.50$. They intersect twice, and the demand curve
is below the supply curve at low investment levels. Consequently, there
are three equilibria: at points 1, 2, and a third one with zero investment.
The third equilibrium is supported by every equity price in the range
$[\bar{q}, \underline{q}]$. The first and third equilibria are stable under the usual adjustment process while the second is not. Inspection of Figures 3 and 4 and
the fact that the demand curve shifts up when debt declines imply:

Proposition 1   In the presence of free capital mobility debt reduction
stimulates investment at stable equilibria with positive investment.

First, observe that a unique equilibrium exists for sufficiently low debt
levels as long as the supply price at zero investment is below the expected
present value of $\bar{\theta}$, and that positive investment prevails in this equilibrium. Therefore, whenever there exists an equilibrium with zero investment, small debt reductions may not eliminate it but sufficiently

Figure 4

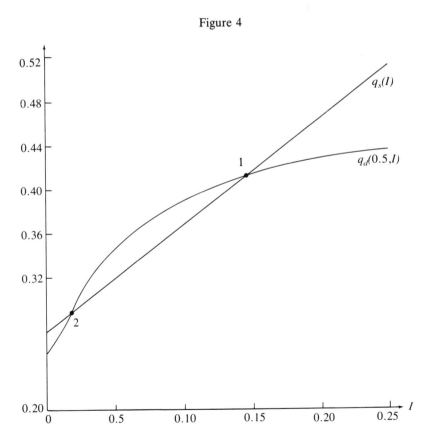

Figure 5

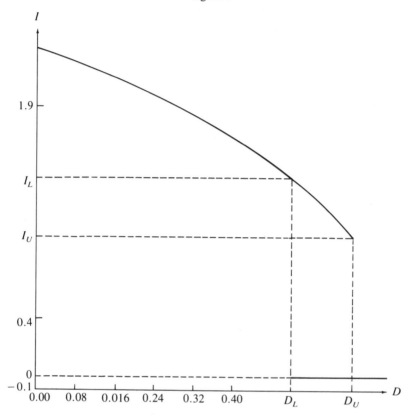

large debt reductions will. Second, in the presence of multiple equilibria the economy can be trapped in a low investment equilibrium, which hurts the creditors and the debtor (see the following section). Nevertheless, no competitive forces ensure a switch to a better equilibrium. When a single financial investor calculates the benefits of an additional unit of equity holding, he takes as given the tax structure and therefore the expected net return on equity. If he expects lower tax rates he is willing to pay a higher price for equity. Higher equity prices lead to higher investment. Higher investment, in turn, reduces tax rates in states of full repayment, thereby justifying the expected high return on equity. This mechanism is responsible for the multiplicity of equilibria.[3]

Figure 5 describes the relationship between debt and equilibrium in-

[3] Multiple equilibria appear also in other models of debt; see, for example, Eaton (1987) and Calvo (1988).

vestment in the example given in footnote 2 (it is also easy to see the following results by direct inspection of Figures 3 and 4). For debt levels below D_L or above D_U a unique equilibrium exists, which features positive investment in the former interval and zero investment in the latter. For debt levels in the interval $[D_L, D_U]$, however, there exist two equilibria; one with positive investment and one with none. This feature can bring about sharp investment responses to small changes in debt. In order to appreciate the importance of this point consider the following experiments. First, suppose debt is close to D_U but below it, and the economy is at the positive investment equilibrium. A small increase in debt that brings the debt level above D_L shifts the economy to the single no-investment equilibrium. Hence, a small debt increase brings about a decline of investment from above I_U to zero. Next, suppose debt is close to D_L but above it and the economy is trapped at the no-investment equilibrium. Now a small debt reduction that brings the debt level below D_L shifts the economy to the single positive investment equilibrium. Hence, a small debt reduction raises investment from zero to a level that exceeds I_L.

Proposition 2   In the presence of free capital mobility a debt increase may bring about a discontinuous drop in investment, and a debt reduction may bring about a discontinuous rise in investment.

As in many other models with multiple equilibria, it is hard to predict which equilibrium the economy will choose. It is, however, clear that for debt levels in the interval $[D_L, D_U]$ the economy settles on the positive investment equilibrium when portfolio holders expect low future tax rates and on the no-investment equilibrium when portfolio holders expect high future tax rates. Hence, expectations of future tax rates determine the quilibrium outcome, and both low and high tax rate expectation are self fulfilling.

No Capital Mobility

Next consider the case with no international capital mobility in the debtor country (the following results apply also to cases of binding quantative restrictions on capital movements). In this case investment equals saving and we need to specify saving behavior in order to analyze investment levels. I employ a simple two-period model.[4] The second period was described in the previous sections. In the first period residents of the debtor country consume c_0 and acquire e real equities. Firms

---

[4] This subsection follows closely Helpman (1988, Section IX).

invest I. Let y be output in this period. Then the representative resident faces the budget constraint

$$c_0 + qe \leq y + qE(I) - I, \tag{13}$$

where the last two terms on the right-hand side represent the net value of initial share holdings.[5] Individuals evaluate first period consumption and portfolio holding by means of their discounted expected utility

$$U(c_0, e; D, I) \equiv v(c_0) + \delta \int_0^\infty u[\eta(\theta; D, I)e]dG(\theta), \tag{14}$$

where $v(\cdot)$ and $u(\cdot)$ are concave functions, δ denotes the subjective discount factor, and $\eta(\theta; D, I)e$—which represents the return on portfolio holding—represents second period consumption. Maximization of $U(\cdot)$ subject to (13) yields the first order condition

$$q = s(c_0, e; D, I), \tag{15}$$

where $s(\cdot) \equiv U_e(\cdot)/U_{c_0}(\cdot)$ denotes the marginal rate of substitution between real equity and first period consumption, defined by

$$s(c_0, e; D, I) \equiv \delta \int_0^\infty u'[\eta(\theta; D, I)e]\eta(\theta; D, I)dG(\theta)/v'(c_0). \tag{16}$$

This function is increasing in c_0 as long as $v(\cdot)$ is strictly concave and declining in e as long as $u(\cdot)$ is strictly concave. The latter applies whenever residents of the debtor country are risk averse. The separate functional forms for first and second period utility are designed to separate considerations of second period risk aversion from intertemporal substitution.

Equations (15) and (16) apply to every distribution of returns on real equity and can be combined to yield a demand price for equities. In our case (2) and (11) can be used to derive the rate of return function. They imply that in states of full repayment the rate of return is declining in debt and increasing in investment, and the rate of return is constant in states of partial repayment. Hence, if the Arrow-Pratt measure of relative risk aversion $\rho(c) \equiv -u''(c)c/u'(c)$ is larger than 1, the product $u'[\eta(\theta; D, I)]\eta(\theta; D, I)$ increases in debt and declines in investment. If the measure of relative risk aversion is smaller than 1, this product declines in debt and increases in investment. Therefore we have

---

[5] It is easy to add a domestic bond market to the model. In the absence of capital movements, however, this market has to clear at zero indebtedness. Consequently, the following analysis would not be affected by this modification. In fact, one can calculate from what follows the equilibrium interest rate on this bond market.

Lemma If the relative degree of risk aversion is larger than 1 $s (c_0, e; D, I)$ increases in debt and declines in investment, and if the relative degree of risk aversion is smaller than 1 $s (c_0, e; D, I)$ declines in debt and increases in investment.

The intuition behind this result can be explained as follows. An increase in debt reduces the return to equity in every state with full repayment. This generates an income effect and a rate of return effect. The income effect stems from the fact that given equity holdings future income falls in some states but does not rise in others. Consequently, the value of assets that transfer income from the present to the future increases, including the value of equity. On the other hand, a decline in the rate of return on equity reduces its value as an asset. Therefore the net effect on $s (\cdot)$ depends on whether the income effect dominates the rate of return effect or vise versa. The income effect dominates under high risk aversion (i.e., $\rho(c) > 1$) while the rate of return effect dominates under low risk aversion.[6]

Next observe that, in the absence of capital mobility, debtor country residents hold all domestic equity; that is, $e = E (I)$. Together with (13) this condition implies $c_0 = y - I$. Namely, first period consumption equals output minus investment. Substituting these results into (15) yields the derived demand price function

$$q_d (D, I) \equiv s [y - I, E (I); D, I]. \tag{17}$$

Investment affects the demand price through three channels: first period consumption, the stock of real equities, and the rate of return on equity. Higher investment reduces the demand price via the first two channels and reduces it via the third channel if and only if the degree of relative risk aversion is larger than 1 (see Lemma). The last condition also ensures that the demand price increases in debt. Hence, the demand curve slopes downward when risk aversion is high, as in Figure 6, and debt reduction shifts the demand curve downwards, thereby depressing investment.

Proposition 3 If there is no international capital mobility and the degree of relative risk aversion is larger than 1, then:

- A unique level of investment is associated with every debt level.
- Debt reduction depresses investment.

When the degree of relative risk aversion is smaller than 1, the effect of investment on first period consumption and the stock of real equities

---

[6] A diagrammatic exposition of the income effect is available in Helpman (1988). See also Corden, below, in this volume.

Figure 6

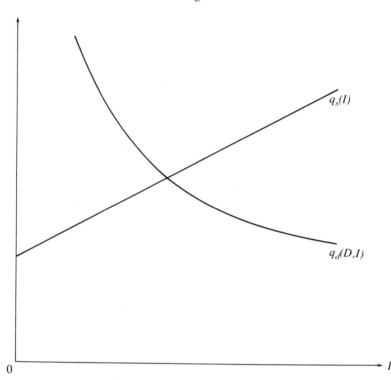

may still cause the demand curve to slope downward. In this case, however, debt reduction shifts it upwards (see Lemma), thereby stimulating investment. It is also clear that even if—as a consequence of low risk aversion—the demand curve slopes upwards, debt reduction stimulates investment at every stable equilibrium point (i.e., points at which the demand curve is flatter than the supply curve), because it brings about an upward shift of the demand curve.

Proposition 4 If there is no international capital mobility and the degree of relative risk aversion is smaller than 1, debt reduction increases investment at every stable equilibrium with positive investment.

Propositions 1–4 summarize the effect of debt reduction on investment; it can be positive or negative, depending on the degree of capital mobility and attitudes toward risk.[7]

---

[7] Estimates of relative risk aversion are typically larger than 1. In linear regressions of the investment/GDP ratio on the debt/GDP ratio for the 15 most heavily indebted countries, I found only in 8 of them a negative coefficient that is significantly different from zero (the sample period is 1973 to 1986 or 1987).

More insight can be gained by identifying links among these results. Free capital mobility leads to a linear evaluation of equities. Therefore, in the presence of restrictions on capital mobility, one expects low risk aversion to generate results that are closer to the case of perfect capital mobility than high risk aversion, which indeed happens. In particular, risk neutrality implies (see (16) and (17))

$$q_d(D, I) = \delta u'(0) \int_0^\infty \eta(\theta; D, I) \, dG \, (\theta)/v'(y - I). \tag{17'}$$

In this case the income effect vanishes and debt reduction increases the demand price via the rate of return effect, just as in the case of free capital mobility. The price is also proportional to the mean return, except that the factor of proportionality depends on investment. The latter dependence disappears altogether when the elasticity of substitution between present and future consumption goes to infinity. Under these circumstances the effects of debt forgiveness on investment are the same as under free capital mobility. For this reason we have:

Proposition 5   If there is no international capital mobility, the degree of relative risk aversion is smaller than 1, and the elasticity of intertemporal substitution is sufficiently high, the relationship between debt and investment is the same as in the case of free capital mobility.

I should like to emphasize that the similarity in results that is pointed out in this proposition applies not only to the response of investment to debt but also to the possibility of multiple equilibria.

V. Welfare

The typical analysis of the effect of debt on investment does not draw a clear distinction between equilibrium and welfare-maximizing investment levels (see, for example, Sachs (1988)).[8] This difference is, however, important. For example, models with optimal investment preclude the possibility of multiple equilibria of the type described in the previous section. I assume that investment is governed by market forces. The following analysis is concerned with the welfare implications of debt reduction for the debtor and the creditors, taking into account investment responses. I emphasize the role of the degree of capital mobility and attitudes toward risk.

As far as the debtor is concerned, its welfare is measured by the utility level that is attained when (14) is maximized subject to (13). Let the implied indirect utility function be $U^{IN}[q, y + qE(I) - I; D, I]$; it depends

---

[8] See also Krugman (below) and Corden (1988) for reviews.

on the price of equity, net wealth, and directly on debt and investment, which determine the rate of return on equity via the tax rates. It has the usual properties of indirect utility functions. Hence,[9]

$$dU^{IN}/v\,'(c_0) = [E(I) - e]\,dq + [qE\,'(I) - 1]\,dI$$
$$+ \delta e \int_{\theta_c(D,I)}^{\infty} u\,'[\eta(\theta;D,I)\,e][\eta_D(\theta;D,I)\,dD$$
$$+ \eta_I(\theta;D,I)\,dI]\,edG(\theta)/v\,'(c_0). \qquad (18)$$

The first term on the right-hand side represents the assets terms of trade effect. If there are restrictions on capital mobility and $e = E(I)$, it is zero. In the presence of free capital mobility I make the reasonable assumption that domestic residents hold only part of their equity; that is, $E(I) > e$. In this case debt reduction raises investment and the price of equity at stable equilibria (unless the economy jumps to a different equilibrium) and the debtor gains on account of better asset terms of trade (see Proposition 1).[10] The second term is always zero, because firms maximize net value (see (9)). The third term describes the direct effect of debt and investment on welfare through the rate of return, or equivalently, through the tax rates. Debt reduction raises investment at a stable equilibrium when capital moves freely. In this case tax rates decline in states of full repayment both as a result of lower debt service payments and higher investment. Consequently, the rate of return rises in these states and the debtor gains.

In the absence of capital mobility only changes in the rate of return affect the debtor's welfare, and I have shown in the previous section that under these circumstances debt reduction increases investment at stable equilibria if and only if the degree of relative risk aversion is smaller than 1 (see Propositions 3 and 4). Hence, when the degree of relative risk aversion falls short of 1, debt reduction increases the rate of return on equity in states of full repayment, both through the direct effect of lower debt and the indirect investment effect on tax rates. Consequently, the country gains. In the absence of capital mobility and a larger-than-1 degree of relative risk aversion, debt forgiveness reduces investment. In this case the rate of return rises as a result of the direct effect of lower debt and falls as a result of the indirect investment effect on tax rates.

---

[9] Changes in debt and investment change the critical state θ_c. Changes in the critical state, however, have second order effects (because the rate of return function is continuous despite the fact that its derivatives are not) and are therefore disregarded in this formula.

[10] In the presence of free capital mobility the country may be trading additional assets. My results do not change as long as the price of these assets is not influenced by either debt or investment.

The former effect dominates, however, and rates of return increase in states of full repayment.[11] This establishes

Proposition 6   The debtor gains from debt reduction when the economy is at a stable equilibrium and does not jump to another equilibrium.

Note that in the absence of capital mobility the response of investment to debt reduction hurts the debtor whenever the degree of relative risk aversion exceeds 1 (it is welfare increasing in the other case). We have established, however, that this negative feedback does not suffice to make the debtor worse off.

Next I considered the welfare ranking of multiple equilibia. As before, in the absence of capital mobility $e = E(I)$ and in the presence of capital mobility $e \le E(I)$. Under these conditions we have the following result:

Proposition 7   Given the degree of capital mobility and the level of debt the debtor prefers an equilibrium with higher investment.

Proof   First consider the case of no capital mobility. (Naturally, in this case multiplicity of equilibria can arise only when the degree of relative risk aversion is smaller than 1 and there is sufficient intertemporal substitution in consumption (see Proposition 5).) Figure 7 presents two equilibrium points, 1 and 2. The curve TT describes the trade-off between first period net resources $y - I$ and real equity $E(I)$. In the absence of capital mobility, first period consumption and equity holdings have to be on this curve. An equilibrium is characterized by the tangency of an indifference curve to TT, where the indifference curve is defined by combinations of (c_0, e) that maintain a constant level of $U(c_0, e; D, I)$ (defined in (14)) and I is the investment level at the tangency point. Points 1 and 2 satisfy this requirement. Since these indifference curves have the usual shape, they have to intersect. In the figure they intersect at point 3. Now, since higher investment implies lower tax rates, $U(c_0, e; D, I_2) > U(c_0, e; D, I_1)$ for all (c_0, e), and in particular for the pair at point 3. This establishes $U_2 > U_1$.

In the presence of capital mobility, the production point is on TT, but the consumption point can be anywhere on the implied budget line. The production point is determined by the tangency of a line with slope

---

[11] *Proof*   From Proposition 3 we know that under these circumstances debt forgiveness depresses investment. On the other hand,

$$q_d(D, I) \equiv s[y - I, E(I); D, I] = q_s(I).$$

Lower investment implies a lower value of $q_s(\cdot)$ and a higher value of $s(\cdot)$ for constant rates of return. Therefore, given that the relative degree of risk aversion is larger than 1, rates of return in states of full repayment have to be higher for the demand price for equity to equal the supply price (see Lemma); namely,

$$\eta_D(\theta; D, I) + \eta_I(\theta; D, I)dI/dD > 0 \qquad \text{for} \qquad \theta > \theta_c(D, I).$$

Figure 7

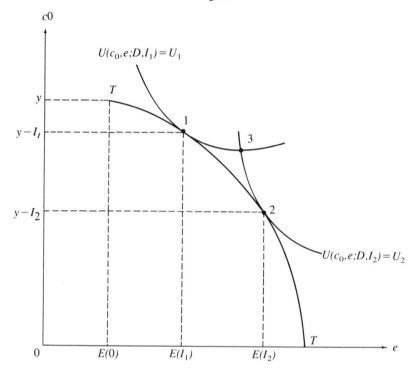

$q_d(D, I)$ (defined in (12)) to TT, where I is the investment level at this point. The resulting line is the budget line on which consumption is chosen. Point 1 in Figure 8 describes a production equilibrium. The corresponding consumption point is $1'$, at which an indifference curve for the investment level I_1 is tangent to the budget line. Since $1'$ is to the left of 1, $e < E(I_1)$. Now suppose that 2 is also a production equilibrium with higher investment. Then the budget line that is tangent to TT at 2 (not drawn) intersects the indifference curve. It implies that with preferences $U(c_0, e; D, I_1)$ it is now possible to reach a higher welfare level. Since $U(c_0, e; D, I_2) > U(c_0, e; D, I_1)$, it is certainly possible to reach a higher welfare level with $U(c_0, e; D, I_2)$. Hence, the equilibrium with higher investment is preferable.

I have shown that the debtor prefers equilibria with higher investment. But so do the creditors. Their welfare is measured by the market value of debt $V(D, I)$ (see (5)). Since this function increases in investment,

Proposition 8   Given the level of debt, creditors prefer an equilibrium with higher investment.

Figure 8

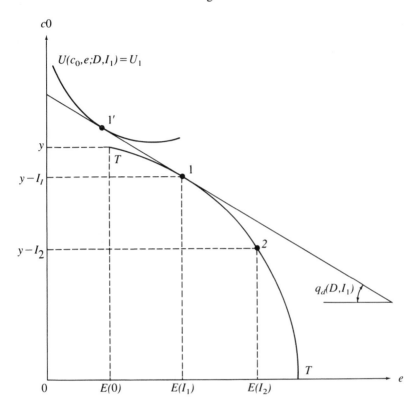

Creditors prefer equilibria with higher investment, because the higher the investment level the larger the set of states with full repayment and the larger repayment per unit debt in states of partial repayment. Since the debtor also prefers equilibria with higher investment, no conflict arises between the debtor and the creditors in the ordering of these equilibria. Nevertheless, when the economy settles on a low investment equilibrium they cannot switch to a better one without explicit coordination.

Now consider the incentive of creditors to write down debt. In this section they are treated as a single entity; the incentives of individual creditors are discussed in the following section. First, observe that a debt write-down has a direct adverse effect on the creditors' welfare, because $V(D, I)$ increases in D. Therefore, creditors benefit from debt relief only when it stimulates investment to a sufficiently large degree to outweigh the negative direct effect. Consequently, voluntary debt reduction will not be observed when it depresses investment. In view of Proposition 3 this implies

Proposition 9   If there is no international capital mobility and the degree of relative risk aversion is larger than 1, creditors do not benefit from debt reduction.

In other cases creditors may or may not benefit from debt reduction. Take, for example, the case in which a unique equilibrium exists for every debt level. Let $I(D)$ be investment as a function of debt, assumed to be differentiable. Then from (5) we obtain

$$\frac{d}{dD} V[D, I(D)] = 1 - G\{\theta_c[D, I(D)]\}$$
$$+ \int_0^{\theta_c(D,I)} \theta\{tE'[I(D)]/R\} dG(\theta) I'(D).$$

For $D = 0$ this expression is equal to 1, implying that the market value of debt rises with its face value for small debt levels even when one takes account of changes in investment. It is also clear that for sufficiently large values of debt $1 - G\{\cdot\}$ is close to zero. Therefore, if $I'(D) < 0$ the right-hand side may be negative for large debt levels, which would imply a market value that declines with debt. Figure 9 depicts two simulated market value curves from the same functional forms, each panel representing a different value of a parameter a in the function $E(I)$.[12] In the upper panel the market value rises with debt for all debt levels. In the lower panel the market value rises for low debt levels and declines thereafter. In the first case creditors have no incentive to reduce debt. In the second case creditors benefit from debt reduction when $D > D_0$ (see also Sachs (1988), Krugman (below), and Froot (1988)). Whenever debt exceeds D_0 creditors jointly benefit from its reduction to D_0. In addition, the debt's market value may drop discontinuously in response to an increase in its face value when multiple equilibria exist, as I explain in what follows. Therefore,

Proposition 10   If there is free capital mobility or there is no capital mobility but the relative degree of risk aversion is smaller than 1, there may exist sufficiently large debt levels at which the creditors benefit from debt reduction.

Observe that a negative effect of higher debt on investment does not guarantee voluntary debt reduction. The point is that even under these

---

[12] The curves in Figure 9 were simulated from the following data: $R = 1$, $t = \frac{1}{2}$, $G(\theta) = 1 - \exp(-\theta)$, and $E(I) = a + \log 2 + \log(0.5 + I)$. In the upper panel $a = 1$; in the lower panel $a = 0.4$.

Figure 9

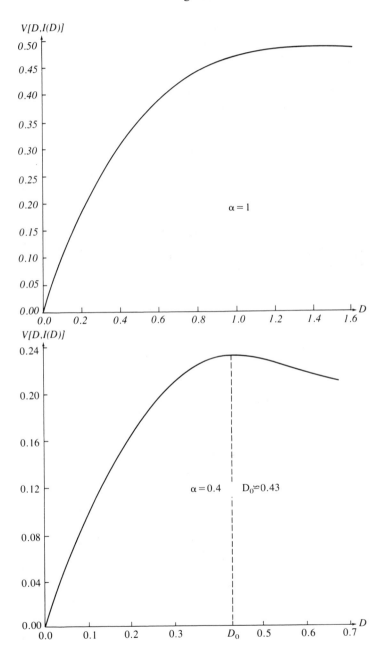

circumstances the market value of debt may be rising with its face value, and even when it does not always rise with the debt's face value, voluntary debt reduction requires the initial debt to be sufficiently large.

Particularly interesting features of the debt relief problem arise when there are multiple equilibria. Consider the situation described in Figure 5, where two equilibria exist for every debt level in the range $[D_L, D_U]$. This may arise in the presence of unrestricted capital mobility, or in the absence of capital mobility but a smaller-than-1 degree of relative risk aversion and a high elasticity of intertemporal substitution (see Proposition 5). Suppose that debt slightly exceeds D_L and the economy is trapped in the low investment equilibrium. Then both parties prefer to switch to the high investment equilibrium (see Propositions 7 and 8). The problem is, however, that there do not exist market forces that automatically bring about a switch. On the other hand, the creditors can orchestrate a switch by a small amount of debt forgiveness, because once debt is below D_L the economy moves to the high investment equilibrium. Given I, a small amount of debt forgiveness reduces $V(D, I)$ by a small amount. On the other hand, a discrete increase in investment brings about a discrete increase in $V(D, I)$. Therefore in this case debt relief benefits the creditors as well as the debtor (although the creditors prefer a switch to the high investment equilibrium without debt reduction). In this situation debt reduction can perform the important function of a trigger that shifts the economy to a better equilibrium.

Figure 10 describes the market value of debt as a function of its face value for the example presented in footnote 2. In the range $[D_L, D_U]$, in which there are two equilibria, the upper curve plots values for the high investment equilibrium, while the lower horizontal line plots values for the low investment equilibrium. In this example the low investment equilibrium has always zero investment and the market value of debt does not change with its face value in the low investment equilibrium. Clearly, in the zero investment equilibrium creditors lose nothing by collectively reducing debt to D_L, and they stand to gain a lot by a slight further reduction. Hence,

Proposition 11   In the presence of multiple equilibria, debt reduction benefits the creditors whenever the economy would otherwise be in the zero investment equilibrium.

The fact that the creditors have a collective incentive to provide debt relief does not imply that individual creditors have the same incentive. This is known as the free-rider problem. The following section discusses possible outcomes, taking into account the incentives facing individual creditors.

Figure 10

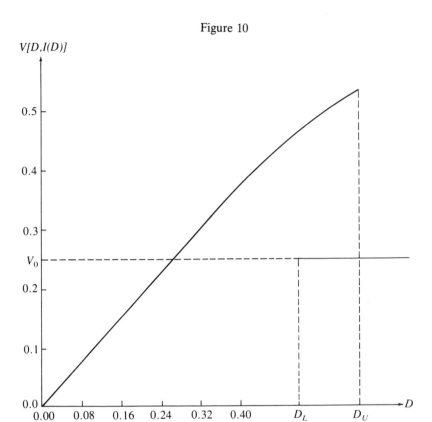

VI. Equilibrium Debt Reduction

We have seen that there exist circumstances in which the market value of debt $V[D, I(D)]$ rises with its face value; other circumstances in which it rises for low face values and declines for high face values; and that it can in fact drop discontinuously. Whenever market value rises with face value, creditors lose from debt reduction, unless there is more than one investment equilibrium and debt reduction switches the economy from a low to a high investment equilibrium. In the latter case—as well as in the case in which the face value of debt falls into a range in which market value declines with face value—creditors are interested to provide debt relief. This, however, is a collective interest. A frequent argument states that even when debt reduction serves the collective interest of creditors, a single creditor stands to gain more by not participating in a relief program. Because once debt is forgiven by others, he fully enjoys higher repayments per unit debt without diluting the face value of his holdings. I show that in the single equilibrium case this argument has no justification; a single creditor can benefit from a voluntary reduction of his claims. It may, however, apply in the presence of multiple equilibria.

In order to examine this issue I formulate the relief decision as a non-cooperative game among creditors. For simplicity I only discuss symmetric games and their corresponding symmetric equilibria (i.e., games in which every creditor owns the same face value of debt). First, consider the case in which a single investment equilibrium exists for every level of debt (i.e., $I(D)$ is a function), and the lower panel of Figure 9 describes the market value of debt curve. Equation (6) gives the price of a unit of debt. Taking account of the response of investment to changes in debt, the price can also be expressed as

$$P(D) \equiv p[D, I(D)]. \tag{19}$$

This function declines in D.

The game is formulated as follows. A single creditor owns D/n units of debt, where n denotes the number of creditors. He can choose to reduce his holding to $d \leq D/n$. He wishes to maximize the market value of d. Therefore, if the other creditors' holdings after their forgiveness decision is denoted by D^-, he solves the following problem:

$$\max_{d} [P(D^- + d) d \,|\, s.t. \ d \leq D/n]. \tag{20}$$

This game resembles a Cournot oligopoly in which firms maximize revenue and sales are limited by a capacity ceiling. Assuming that the marginal revenue curve $MR(D) \equiv P(D) + P'(D) D$ slopes downward, the symmetric solution satisfies:

For $MR(D) \geq 0$; $d = D/n$ and no debt reduction takes place;

For $MR(D) \leq 0$; d is implicitly defined by $m(nd) = 0$ and voluntary debt reduction takes place;

where

$$m(D) \equiv \frac{1}{n} MR(D) + \left[1 - \frac{1}{n}\right] P(D)$$

(see Helpman and Krugman (1989, Chap. 4)).[13] Figure 11 describes this

---

[13] The individual creditor's marginal revenue is $P(D^- + d) + P'(D^- + d)d$. His objective function is maximized when this is equal to zero. When this is achieved at $d \leq D/n$, this is also the solution to (20). If, however, this is achieved at $d > D/n$, his ceiling constraint is binding and he chooses $d = D/n$. In a symmetrical equilibrium we examine marginal revenue $P(nd) + P'(nd)d$, which is given by $m(nd)$.

Figure 11

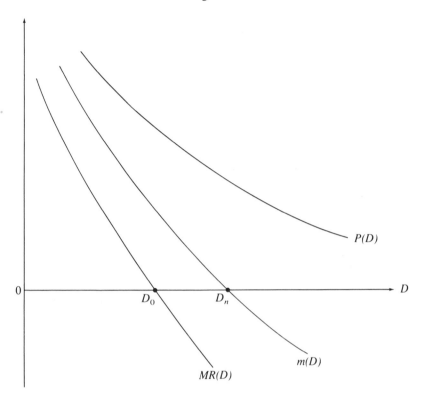

solution. Curve $m(D)$ is located between the demand and the marginal revenue curves; it coincides with the marginal revenue curve when $n = 1$ and with the demand curve when there are infinitely many creditors. A single monopoly creditor provides voluntary debt reduction whenever debt exceeds D_0, where D_0 in Figure 11 corresponds to D_0 in Figure 9.[14] Hence, a single creditor provides relief that maximizes the market value of debt, just like a monopolist who chooses output to maximize total revenue in the absence of costs. Several non-cooperating creditors provide debt reduction to D_n whenever $D > D_n$. Their joint forgiveness is not as large as the single creditor's, but they do forgive nevertheless. For every finite number of creditors the non-cooperative solution implies debt reduction for sufficiently high debt levels. These results are summarized in the following proposition:

[14] From the definition of $MR(D)$ it is clear that $V[D, I(D)] \equiv P(D)D$ reaches a maximum at $MR(D) = 0$.

Proposition 12 If (a) there exists free capital mobility or there is no capital mobility but the degree of relative risk aversion is smaller than 1; (b) a single investment level corresponds to every debt level; (c) the market valve curve declines with debt for inefficiently high debt levels, then:

- For every finite number of creditors there exists a minimal debt level at which creditors provide voluntary debt reduction.
- The minimal debt level increases with the number of creditors, and the post-relief face value of debt exceeds the market value maximizing level (unless $n = 1$).

Multiple equilibria introduce new possibilities. In order to clarify

Figure 12

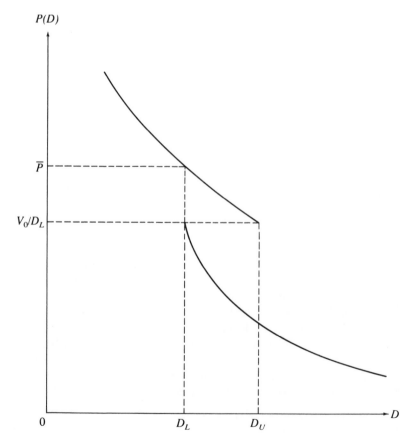

them, consider the example developed in Figures 3, 4, 5, and 10. The demand curve $P(D)$ has two separate portions, as depicted in Figure 12; the upper portion corresponds to equilibria with positive investment, while the lower corresponds to equilibria with zero investment. The lower portion is defined by $PD \equiv V_0$, implying a marginal revenue of zero. Therefore, as long as creditors perceive changes along this curve (namely, they believe that their contribution to debt reduction will not bring about a shift to the positive investment equilibrium), they have no incentive to reduce debt. In these circumstances there exists a non-cooperative equilibrium with debt forgiveness only when every creditor is willing to provide the marginal debt reduction that reduces the debt's face value just below D_L. A direct calculation shows that

$$\frac{V_0}{\bar{P}D_L} < \frac{1}{n} + \left[1 - \frac{1}{n}\right]\frac{D_L}{D}, \tag{21}$$

is necessary and sufficient for the existence of an equilibrium with debt reduction, where $\bar{P}$ is the price of debt at D_L in the high investment equilibrium. The left-hand side is smaller than 1 (see Figure 12).[15] Condition (21) is satisfied when $n = 1$; a single creditor provides relief. For every other $n > 1$ there exists D close enough to D_L that fulfills (21).

On the other hand, the satisfaction of (21) does not exclude an equilibrium with no debt reduction. The following provides a necessary and sufficient condition for the existence of an equilibrium without debt relief:[16]

$$\frac{V_0}{\bar{P}D_L} > n - (n - 1)\frac{D}{D_L}. \tag{22}$$

Conditions (21) and (22) can be satisfied simultaneously. For example, they are satisfied when $n = 2$ and $D/D_L = 3/2$. Hence,

Proposition 13 If there exist multiple investment equilibria for a given debt level, then an equilibrium with debt reduction may coexist with an equilibrium without debt reduction.

---

[15] In a symmetrical equilibrium D_L is reached when every creditor forgives $(D - D_L)/n$, $D \geq D_L$. When $n - 1$ creditors forgive their share, the remaining face value of debt is $D_L + (D - D_L)/n$ and its price in the secondary market is $V_0/[D_L + (D - D_L)/n]$. If the remaining creditor does not forgive, the market value of his claims is $(D/n)V_0/[D_L + (D - D_L)/n]$. If he forgives his share, the market value of his claims is $(D_L/n)\bar{P}$. The latter exceeds the former if and only if (21) holds.

[16] When $n - 1$ creditors do not provide debt relief, the nth creditor's debt is worth V_0/n if he does not provide relief and it is worth $\bar{P}[D/n - (D - D_L)]$ if he provides relief $(D - D_L)$ so as to induce a jump to the high investment equilibrium. The former exceeds the latter if and only if (22) is satisfied.

This result shows that debt reduction is not guaranteed even when it is an equilibrium phenomenon, because it may coexist with an equilibrium in which there is no debt reduction. Which one emerges depends on expectations. If creditors believe that others will forgive debt, they also choose to forgive, and debt reduction obtains. If, on the other hand, creditors believe that others will not forgive, they also choose not to forgive, and no debt reduction takes place. This happens only when the economy is trapped in a low investment equilibrium. It represents a clear instance in which cooperation has a high return.

VII. Conclusions

My results show that the desirability and likelihood of voluntary debt reduction depend on circumstances. Creditors benefit from a write-down of debt in some circumstances and lose in others. Theory helps to identify important features of those circumstances. But once those features are known, there is no substitute for a careful examination of their applicability to concrete countries. In particular, estimates of the function $V[D, I(D)]$ are needed in order to form a judgment on whether debt reduction helps the banks. This function can, in principle, be recovered from data on secondary market prices. Unfortunately, these data exist only since 1986, which precludes accurate estimation. Recently Claessens (1988) used a cross-section procedure to estimate this curve. His results are preliminary, however, and need to be refined.

Thirteen propositions describe the main findings of this paper and I shall not repeat them in this section. I consider instead some policy implications. The following discussion is only tentative; reliable policy conclusions require further analysis.

One thing to note is that my results identify circumstances in which creditors provide voluntary debt reduction without complete coordination. Recent reschedulings in which suitable risk premia have not been built into contractual interest rates represent a form of voluntary forgiveness (see also Corden (1988) on this point). We have seen, however, that even when non-cooperative debt reduction emerges in equilibrium, its extent falls typically short of the level desired by the debtor and creditors alike. In this case an explicit policy can help. For example, the debtor can remedy the shortfall by means of a unilateral partial moratorium on debt that reduces its face value to the market value maximizing level. This policy helps the debtor and the creditors. In those circumstances one expects creditors to abstain from using sanctions against the debtor who helps them out. But will they?

Another example concerns the low investment trap. I have shown that when the debtor country is trapped in a low investment equilibrium the debtor and creditors desire to switch to a high investment equilibrium. Nevertheless, market forces may not bring about a switch. In this case voluntary debt reduction can play a useful role in inducing the desired switch. However, debt reduction fails to fulfill this role if expectations are pessimistic. In this case the debtor country government can improve on the free market outcome.

Suppose, for example, that lump-sum taxes are available in the debtor country in the first period. Then the government can use them in order to raise revenue and subsidize investment. An investment subsidy shifts down the $q_s(\cdot)$ curve (see Figure 4) and thereby raises investment at every stable equilibrium. In addition, sufficiently high subsidies eliminate the zero investment equilibrium, thereby benefiting the debtor and the banks. But lump-sum taxes are seldom available. Therefore an optimal policy from the debtor's point of view needs to take into account the dead-weight loss associated with the use of distortionary taxes. This dead-weight loss tilts the cost-benefit analysis against investment subsidies.

I have described several examples of policy applications. Many other policies can be considered, such as alternative forms of taxation, changes in public spending, and control of international capital flows. The desirability of debt reduction depends on these policies.

REFERENCES

Calvo, Guillermo A., "Servicing the Public Debt: The Role of Expectations," *American Economic Review* (Nashville, Tennessee), 1988, forthcoming.

Claessens, Stijn, "The Debt-Laffer Curve: Some Estimates" (unpublished; Washington: World Bank, July 1988).

Cline, William R., *Mobilizing Bank Lending to Debtor Countries,* Policy Analyses in International Economics, No. 18 (Washington: Institute for International Economics, June 1987).

Corden, Max W., "Is Debt Relief in the Interest of the Creditors?" IMF Working Paper WP/88/72 (unpublished; Washington: International Monetary Fund, August 1988).

Diamond, Peter A., "The Role of a Stock Market in a General Equilibrium Model with Technological Uncertainty," *American Economic Review* (Nashville, Tennessee), Vol. 57 (1967), pp. 759–76.

Eaton, Jonathan, "Public Debt Guarantees and Private Capital Flight," *World Bank Economic Review* (Washington), Vol. 1 (1987), pp. 377–96.

Froot, Kenneth A., "Buy-Backs, Exit Bonds, and the Optimality of Debt and

Liquidity Relief" (unpublished; Cambridge, Massachusetts: Massachusetts Institute of Technology, 1988).

Helpman, Elhanan, "The Simple Analytics of Debt-Equity Swaps and Debt Forgiveness," IMF Working Paper WP/88/30 (unpublished; Washington: International Monetary Fund, March 1988).

———, and Paul R. Krugman, *Trade Policy and Market Structure* (Cambridge, Massachusetts: MIT Press, 1989 forthcoming).

———, and Assaf Razin, *A Theory of International Trade under Uncertainty* (New York: Academic Press, 1978).

Kenen, Peter B., *New York Times,* March 6, 1983.

Sachs, Jeffrey, "The Debt Overhang of Developing Countries," in *Debt, Growth, and Stabilization: Essays in Memory of Carlos Diaz Alejandro,* ed. by Ronald Findlay (Oxford: Blackwell, 1988).

Debt-Equity Swaps

MICHAEL BLACKWELL and SIMON NOCERA*

This paper describes the development of debt-equity swaps in the years following the emergence of the international debt crisis. It discusses some of the possible advantages and disadvantages offered by such swaps to commercial banks, investing companies, and the indebted countries. It also provides an analysis of how these swaps are treated in the balance of payments accounts of an indebted country and discusses their possible effects on that country's money supply, foreign exchange rate, and economic growth. The paper concludes that debt-equity swaps can help to make a country's debt burden more manageable and can contribute to economic growth, but only to a limited extent.

CONVERSION OF DEBT into equity has figured prominently in "menus" of financial options for dealing with debt problems and is the subject of a growing body of literature. This paper provides a general overview of the development of debt-equity swaps and the manner in which such swaps affect commercial banks, investing companies, and debtor countries.

The regulations governing how countries permit the swap of their commercial bank debt for equity in particular economic sectors differ from country to country; even within individual countries, conditions applied to such transactions can vary according to why the swap is undertaken, monetary policy considerations, and other factors. Most debt-equity swaps conform, however, to the following basic pattern. First, a bank sells at a discount an outstanding loan made to a public sector agency—or sometimes to a private sector enterprise—in an indebted country that is experiencing difficulty in adhering to an agreed

* Mr. Blackwell is an economist in the Treasurer's Department of the International Monetary Fund and is a graduate of the University of East Anglia.

Mr. Nocera is a graduate of the University of Milan and is an economist in the Treasurer's Department of the International Monetary Fund.

repayment schedule. Second, an investor, most often a multinational manufacturing company, buys the loan paper at a discount and presents it to the central bank of the indebted country, which redeems all or most of the face value of the loan in domestic currency at the prevailing market exchange rate. Third, the investor acquires equity using this domestic currency, which it has in effect purchased on terms more favorable than can be obtained through regular foreign exchange market transactions. This paper focuses primarily on this type of debt-equity swap.

The growth in the volume of debt-equity swaps in recent years derives not only from increasing recognition in debtor countries that foreign investment can contribute to economic growth, but also from the development of a flourishing secondary market in country debt obligations among the international banks and from the current global trend toward the securitization of debt. Moreover, the growth in debt-equity swaps can also be attributed to benefits that such transactions offer the participating parties. The international bank that sells an outstanding loan at a loss, reflecting the difference between its face value and its value in the secondary debt market, can realize the cash value of a problematic asset, liquidate any reserves set aside to cover possible losses on the loan, and employ these resources more profitably in other investments. The indebted country is able to reduce its interest payments and shift the risk of servicing the claim to the foreign investor; moreover, depending on the buyer of the debt, the conversion of debt to equity may provide a mechanism for the repatriation of flight capital and encourage domestic investment. Finally, the investing company is able to acquire investment capital on more favorable terms than those available through direct exchange market purchases of domestic currency.

Although advantages may be realized by participants in the debt-equity swap, potential difficulties and costs may obtain. For example, for banks the sale of outstanding loans at a discount may require provisioning and ultimately the writing down in value of other assets, which in turn may give rise to a number of regulatory and accounting problems. For investing companies, debt-equity swaps can be subject to more onerous conditions governing capital repatriation and profit remittances than is regular direct investment. For the debtor countries, debt-equity swaps can have adverse budgetary and monetary consequences and may be regarded as infringments on national economic sovereignty.

These advantages and disadvantages of debt-equity swaps are addressed in more detail in the body of the paper. The first section identifies the countries that have participated in debt-equity swaps and describes the main features of their policies; it then gives some indication of the present volume of such swaps and discusses possible trends. Section II identifies the types of banks that are most involved in debt-equity swaps and describes the workings of the secondary market in debt. Section III analyzes the possible advantages and disadvantages for international companies using debt-equity swaps. Section IV analyzes how debt-equity swaps are treated in the balance of payments accounts of indebted countries and discusses possible effects in these countries on the money supply, the foreign exchange rate, and economic growth. Section V provides some concluding remarks.

I. Overview

The present debt-equity swaps market emerged with the onset of the debt crisis in the summer of 1982, although several isolated instances of such swaps had been recorded earlier. For example, in Brazil since 1962, certain nonresidents had been allowed to convert external debt into equity investments at face value and at the official exchange rate. In Turkey, in 1980 the authorities enacted legislation dealing with the settlement of some $1.4 billion of foreign arrears claims and providing for creditors to be paid either in foreign exchange over ten years or in local currency on demand. The local currency could be used for a wide variety of purposes, including the purchase of equity. Soon after the enactment of this legislation a certain amount of trading in Turkish debt began, with debt paper being sold at a discount from its face value.[1]

The first debt-equity swaps after the emergence of the debt crisis took place in Brazil in 1983. As part of a major rescheduling package agreed that year, private sector borrowers were required to deposit with the Central Bank of Brazil the cruzeiro equivalent of their foreign currency borrowings when those borrowings became due for repayment. Some creditors decided to relend this money in Brazil and some decided to use it for the purchase of equity. Several creditors, however, decided to sell their loans, and thus the right to use the corresponding cruzeiro deposits, to a multinational corporation or similar institution planning to invest in Brazil. In this manner the first of the post-debt crisis debt-equity swaps was introduced.

The Central Bank of Brazil imposed conditions on debt-equity transactions designed to prevent repatriation of capital before the scheduled date for the repayment of the loan and to ensure, in the interim, there would be no repatriation of profits from the venture that would exceed

---

[1] UNCTAD (1984), p. 13. See also Dillon (1985).

interest payments on the original loan.[2] In the summer of 1984, the Brazilian authorities became concerned that the scheme might discourage the inflow of new money from direct investors and so restricted authorizations for debt-equity swaps to the original creditors. From 1983 to mid-1987, almost $2 billion worth of Brazil's external debt was converted into equity. In February 1988, the authorities introduced a new debt-equity swap scheme intended to increase the volume of transactions. During the first three months of its operation, external debt was reduced by over $500 million.

Toward the end of 1984, Argentina also began debt-equity swaps. The Argentine scheme was related to a rescheduling package, but took a different form. The Argentine authorities issued promissory notes (BONODS) for debt covered by the package and then permitted the conversion of these notes to equity on a case-by-case basis. This scheme provided the only mechanism by which creditors provided with an exchange rate guarantee could realize immediately the capital gain that was associated with this guarantee. This particular debt-equity swap arrangement was discontinued before the end of 1985 after about $500 million worth of debt had been converted. According to banking sources, the scheme was terminated because of concern, as in Brazil, that the investment associated with debt-equity swaps would substitute for inflows that would have taken place in any event, and that such swaps would lead to increased credit expansion. In June 1987, the Argentine authorities introduced a new scheme that allowed debt-equity swaps as long as the face value of the swapped debt was matched by the investment of an identical amount of "new" money. The limited demand for debt-equity swaps in Argentina during the ensuing months seemed to provide evidence that this provision was reducing the scheme's attractiveness. Several changes in the debt-equity scheme were made in the series of economic reforms announced in October 1987, including an increase in the 50/50 ratio of debt to new money to a 70/30 ratio, and a modification to permit the new money requirement to be met by local as well as foreign currency. Following these reforms some debt-equity swaps were agreed and by October 1988 some $325 million of debt had been converted at an average discount of 50.6 percent.

In May 1985, Chile introduced a more comprehensive scheme than those then operated by Brazil and Argentina.[3] The scheme provided for

---

[2] These conditions applied only to debt-equity conversions tied to the rescheduling agreement with banks. For other conversions, the same rules on repatriation applied as to foreign investment.

[3] Chile had a type of debt-equity conversion scheme in place as early as 1977, under which the original creditor could directly convert its claims into equity of the original debtor.

debt-equity conversion through the use of mechanisms designed to avoid any expansion of the monetary base. The provisions were set out in Chapters 18 and 19 of the *Compendium of Rules on International Exchange* issued by the Chilean Central Bank. Under the provisions of Chapter 18, the Central Bank holds a monthly auction at which local banks bid for the right to engage in transactions to convert a specific limited amount of foreign debt into domestic currency. The banks act as agents by assisting the holders of the foreign debt to convert it, with the consent of the local debtor, into cash or a peso-denominated asset, which can be resold. These provisions were the first to permit a country's own residents to exchange foreign debt obligations purchased at a discount for domestic currency or instruments denominated in domestic currency. The proceeds of the conversion may be used to repay debts to local financial institutions, acquire assets of those institutions, or be held as an investment. Under certain conditions, the proceeds may be used to acquire equity in local firms without going through the auction process. Thus, these regulations effectively permit the repatriation of capital sent out of the country as part of the capital flight of earlier years. On the one hand, Chapter 18 does not require that the domestic currency obtained be used for specific types of investment; on the other, it does not provide for transfer abroad of capital or dividends.

The provisions of Chapter 19 allow nonresidents to convert into equity certain external debt claims, which can be purchased on the secondary market without going through the auction mechanism. The domestic currency obtained must be used for approved investments, however, and repatriation of capital or dividends is subject to a number of conditions. The Central Bank considers each application on a case-by-case basis and during 1988 began to insist that each conversion be accompanied by at least a small amount of new money.

In September 1987, Chile's Central Bank announced an extension of the country's debt-for-equity scheme to allow the formation of foreign investment societies, whose funds—obtained through the purchase of discounted debt—could be invested in a range of Chilean shares and financial instruments. The investment societies will be required to maintain 60 percent of their portfolios in shares, while the remainder can be invested in local bonds and other financial instruments. No society will be allowed to take a majority holding in any company.

In 1986, Mexico, the Philippines, and Ecuador introduced arrangements for making debt-equity swaps. Under the Mexican arrangement, until its suspension in November 1987, the Bank of Mexico was empowered to redeem foreign currency public-sector debt at a discount related to the perceived utility to the economy of the proposed investment of the proceeds of the swap. The Bank of Mexico would offer to purchase Mexican debt paper at face value when the domestic currency was to be used to acquire state-owned firms; at 95 percent of face value when it was to be used for investment that would create new employment and introduce new technology in a firm that exported 80 percent or more of its production; and at other fractions of the face value down to 75 percent. The scheme was suspended in November 1987, as the authorities became concerned at the possible inflationary consequences of debt-equity swaps and at the possibility that such swaps were effectively subsidizing investments that would have been made without this added incentive.

In the Philippines, the authorities introduced in August 1986 a program for debt-equity swaps intended to provide incentives for investment in designated priority sectors, to reverse capital flight, and to reduce the burden of external debt. As amended in October 1987, the program provides for the exchange of specified types of debt paper for domestic currency at face value with a conversion fee amounting to 0.0 percent to 20.0 percent for investment in certain preferred sectors and to 0.0 percent to 24.0 percent for investment in less preferred sectors. The amount of the fee is determined by the amount of "fresh money" accompanying the investment. For example, in the preferred sectors an investment financed entirely by debt-equity conversion would incur a conversion fee equivalent to 20 percent of the face value of the debt, whereas no conversion fee would be charged where the amount of debt to be converted is matched by the same amount of "fresh money." (There are four intermediate points between these two extremes.) Investors are free to choose their own combination of conversion fee and fresh money, with their choice influenced by the magnitude of the discount in the secondary market. Since fees cannot be funded from the peso proceeds of the converted debt, every conversion will involve some fresh money unless the investor can borrow from the Philippine banking system or has access to other peso funds. The conversion fee and fresh money requirement ensure that the Philippine authorities obtain some benefit from the secondary market discount on the country's external bank debt. Gradual capital repatriation is allowed after three years for investments in the most preferred sectors and after five years for those in the less preferred sectors. Dividend payments abroad can be made out of profits realized from the outset in the most preferred sectors and after four years in the less preferred.

In determining whether to approve proposals, the authorities wish to ensure that the swap will increase foreign resources available to the economy rather than merely providing a means for converting at a more beneficial rate to the investor those funds already intended for investment in the Philippines. In general, therefore, approval is not given for the purchase of claims of current stockholders on existing assets, or for increasing working capital or paying off the obligations of existing firms. However, an exception to this rule is made for the purchase of non-performing assets of government financial institutions, which are being disposed of by the Asset Privatization Trust. Attention is also paid to the monetary impact of the debt-equity swap, particularly with regard to the conversion of Central Bank debt instruments.

In February 1988, the authorities introduced a number of further changes to the debt-equity conversion program. An indicative limit for the conversion of Central Bank paper was set to contain the expansionary monetary impact of debt-equity swaps. No limitation was placed on the conversion of private corporate debt since the redemption of this debt does not involve additional credit creation. Fees for the conversion of private debt were also waived since, in practice, the purpose of the fees—capturing part of the discount on the debt—could be achieved by the debtor in negotiations over the terms of the swap agreement. The authorities also announced that they would be guided, in their decision to approve debt-equity swaps, by the extent to which the investments that would be financed met the following criteria: (i) at least 80 percent of production is for exports; (ii) a new export product is involved; (iii) the export product is not subject to foreign quotas; (iv) employment is generated; (v) the productive process involved is labor intensive; and (vi) location is in the regions that are not heavily industrialized.

In Ecuador, the authorities announced their intention to introduce debt-equity swaps in November 1986 and issued regulations in February 1987, which essentially specified that all applications under the scheme would be handled on a case-by-case basis. By August 1987, however, the scheme had been suspended because a significant proportion of the operations originated from domestic residents which, in the authorities' view, tended to put excessive pressure on the exchange rate. In practice, debt-equity swaps continued to be made at the discretion of the authorities until August 1988.

In April 1987, the Venezuelan authorities issued a number of rules covering the conversion of public external debt into foreign direct investment. Essentially, conversion can be authorized if the proceeds are invested in import-substituting or export-oriented industries or in industries in one of 11 designated priority sectors. The proceeds can also be used to invest in enterprises in danger of being closed down. The rules limit profit remittances to a maximum of 10 percent of the converted debt during the first three years and to 20 percent plus LIBOR thereafter. No capital repatriation from converted equity is allowed during the

Table 1.   *Selected Indicators for Countries Engaged in Debt-Equity Swaps*
(In billions of U.S. dollars and in percent[1])

Country	Debt Conversion (1983–1987[2])	Market Capitalization (1985[3])	Direct and Portfolio Investment Inflows (1980–85)[4]	Total Debt Outstanding to Commercial Banks[5]
Chile	3.3 (23.5)	2.0 (12.5)	1.3 (8.1)	13.9 (86.7)
Brazil	2.2 (1.1)	42.9 (21.6)	40.7 (20.5)	78.8 (39.8)
Mexico	1.8 (1.1)	4.2 (2.6)	7.6 (4.8)	73.7 (46.3)
Argentina	0.5 (0.88)	1.4 (2.8)	7.6 (12.9)	31.3 (53.0)
Philippines	0.2 (0.77)	0.7 (2.4)	n.a.	14.1 (48.0)

[1] Percentage value in relation to 1985 GNP in U.S. dollars.
[2] Estimates from various sources.
[3] Source: International Finance Corporation.
[4] Source: International Monetary Fund, *Balance of Payments Statistics,* Volume 37, Yearbook, Part 1, 1986.
[5] Estimates from U.S. Federal Financial Institution Council and Bank for International Settlements, quoted by Cline (1987).

first five years; afterwards, repatriation can be made in eight equal yearly installments.

Colombia, Costa Rica, Dominican Republic, Jamaica, Morocco, Nigeria, Peru, and Uruguay are also introducing or are contemplating the introduction of debt-equity swap schemes.[4]

Although details differ from country to country, the arrangements for debt-equity swaps in these countries have a number of common features. Most arrangements provide some opportunity for the debtor country to share part of the discount on the debt, either through auction proceeds or through redemption charges; most give some direction with regard to the sectors of the economy from which equity can be purchased; and most place some restrictions on the volume and frequency of payments that can be made abroad in the form of dividends or repatriated capital.

Can a country's propensity to engage in debt-equity swaps be correlated with its market capitalization, its volume of direct and portfolio investments, and its outstanding debt? Excluding Chile from Table 1 and looking at absolute values, it would appear that there might be a positive correlation between the amount of debt converted and each of these indicators. In normalizing these figures in terms of GNP these correlations disappear, however. This would tend to confirm the view of the

[4] See, for example, Houghton (March 1987), pp. 151–57, Bruce (May 1987), p. 117, and Debs (1987), p. 22.

banking community in the industrial countries that a commitment to debt-equity swaps depends not so much on economic and financial considerations as on the political climate in the country concerned.

Market Volume

Table 2 lists some of the countries that have been engaged in debt-equity swaps over the past few years and gives some indication of the volume of debt being converted into equity in comparison with total debt outstanding.

While the volume of conversion of debt into equity has made only a modest contribution to the reduction of debt and therefore of contractual interest repayments of developing countries as a whole, it has not been insignificant for particular countries. In Chile, for example, it has been estimated that almost $1 billion worth of debt was converted into equity in 1986, thus reducing Chile's external debt by about 5 percent.

The consensus among banking sources seems to be that the volume of debt-equity swap transactions could well expand from present levels but is unlikely to advance much beyond $3–5 billion a year. Even the strongest proponents of debt-equity swaps doubt that more than 10 percent of developing country debt will ever be swapped for equity. As is explained in detail below, there are limits on the volume of such transactions that reflect debtor countries' need to contain the potentially adverse financial consequences of converting foreign debt into domestic currency and their concern over the consequences of increasing the foreign ownership

Table 2. *Debt Conversion and Total External Debt Outstanding*

(In billions of U.S. dollars)

Country	Total Debt Outstanding to Industrial Country Banks[1]	Debt Conversion (1983–87[2])
Argentina	31.3	0.50
Brazil	78.8	2.20
Chile	13.9	3.30
Ecuador	5.3	0.13
Mexico	73.7	1.80
Philippines	14.1	0.20
Venezuela	26.4	0.00
Total	243.5	8.13

[1] Estimates from U.S. Federal Financial Institution Council and Bank for International Settlements, quoted by Cline (1987).

[2] Estimates from various sources.

of profitable domestic industries. The commercial banks may also limit the volume of their transactions for accounting and balance sheet considerations and, possibly, because of the limited opportunities for substantial profitable investment in the most heavily indebted countries.

Possible Future Developments

The difficulty in identifying suitable investment opportunities for which debt can be swapped—either because there are none available or because the authorities withhold permission—could well lead to the swapping of debt for other assets. According to banking sources, a few countries are contemplating the introduction of debt-for-products and debt-for-commodities schemes. Peru pioneered this type of transaction and in the late summer of 1987 announced deals in which the Midland Bank and First Interstate Trading Company would arrange for the sale of Peruvian export goods and retain about one third of the receipts to repay outstanding debt.[5]

Perhaps of greater potential significance is the development of trust funds that can at least in part be financed by the proceeds of debt-to-equity conversion. In late 1987, the International Finance Corporation (IFC) was in the process of establishing trust funds in which some of its own resources would be added to loan claims from a number of banks for the purchase of investments or shares in private companies in debtor countries. These funds, which will be managed professionally, will work in the same way as established country-specific mutual funds.

A different type of scheme mooted by the U.S. investment firm of Drexel Burnham Lambert in the late summer of 1987 involved packaging Latin American loans purchased on the secondary market and selling them to investors as high-risk yet potentially high-yield investments—along lines similar to the domestic "junk" bonds this firm had been active in promoting. The attraction of such schemes to investors would be that if they could buy debt at 50 cents on the dollar, the interest rate they would receive—assuming the debtor country was current on its debt obligations—would be doubled, as would the amount of their investment should the debt paper ever be redeemed at par. The chances of such schemes succeeding would appear doubtful, however, as debtor countries would probably object to their loans being transferred to private

[5] Reuters reported (September 16, 1987) that the Midland Bank agreed to arrange for the sale of $23 million worth of Peruvian goods in international markets, to retain $8.8 million of the proceeds to cancel part of Peru's outstanding debt, and to return the remaining cash to the Peruvian authorities.

investors who have no interest in providing additional investment to the country; moreover, investors would probably not be greatly attracted by claims on which the terms could change and which might never be repaid.

Another approach to debt conversion involves the swapping of debt paper for equity, which is then sold to a syndicate of buyers, with the returns on the investment determined by the profits realized by the equity involved. Investments in the hotel and tourist industries have been particularly attractive in this context. The success of any of these schemes for mutual funds depends above all on the willingness of the creditor banks to sell significant amounts of debt paper at a substantial discount, an action that most major banks still seem reluctant to take.

Opinions are divided with regard to the length of time the debt-equity swap market will be active. Martin Schubert, chairman of one of the most active finance corporations in this field, concluded at a recent conference on debt-equity swaps:

> At best, the debt equity conversion may have a useful life of two to three more years. During that time, what major investment opportunities have not already been taken up, will have been grabbed by shrewd venturesome entrepreneurs, both locally and externally. Valuable government properties which have been set out for privatization will have been privatized. Important undervalued properties will have been taken up or their market values driven up by anticipation, or by government discount practices, to where they no longer have the same attraction. One should not expect that governments will massively give over their resources in exchange for debt which they more and more are coming to the conclusion that they cannot, and will never be able to repay.[6]

These remarks were probably designed to encourage listeners from the multinational corporations to reach more rapid decisions about their investment plans, but they nevertheless contain several valid points. One further point that could be made is that debt-equity swaps will no doubt be discontinued in countries which regain liberal access to the capital markets, since presumably at that time the discounts on those countries' existing debts in the secondary market would have disappeared.

II. Banks

Since the onset of the debt crisis in 1982, commercial banks with large exposures to financially troubled countries have engaged in sales or swaps of loan claims with the principal objective of reducing or di-

---

[6] Schubert (1987).

versifying their credit exposures. Several commercial and investment banks set up special departments to serve as intermediaries in such deals; eight of these banks account for about 85 percent of the volume of all transactions.[7] According to market sources, about $15 billion worth of loans will be traded at least once in 1988, more than three times the 1985 level.[8] In 1987 it was established that probably 60 percent or more of the transactions were part of a chain leading ultimately to the actual conversion of debt held by commercial banks into equity.[9]

Banks often seek to reduce their credit exposure in order to avoid or reduce the need to increase it later during a country debt rescheduling arrangement. In many rescheduling programs, a creditor bank is expected not only to accept postponement of overdue principal repayments but also to join other creditor banks in committing new loans in order to cover the debtor country's financing needs during an agreed adjustment period. A failure to comply with the rescheduling agreement could result in a creditor bank's original loan being placed in a non-accrual or non-performing status, with adverse implications for the bank's earning statement.

Moreover, even if a bank is prepared to increase the amount it is willing to loan to a particular country, the combined impact of rescheduling existing loans and making a new loan might cause it to contravene the limits on lending or on country exposure set by internal or regulatory capital requirement policies. Another reason for engaging in a loan sale is that a bank may from time to time experience liquidity constraints that will force it to scale down its asset base. Finally, a bank's management may find it to be more profitable to sell debt paper at a discount and reinvest the proceeds than to hold onto the debt with uncertain prospects for repayment of interest and capital. By selling such a loan, the bank could improve its capital assets ratio as the amount of loan loss reserves set aside previously grows in relation to the stock of outstanding problematic assets.

Parallel to the outright sale of loans, banks have also actively engaged in asset trading. In this type of transaction, two or more parties agree to assign to each other debt obligations of different borrowers, with a possible cash settlement reflecting the different market values of the loans exchanged. Banks willing to maintain their current level of outstanding credit but wishing to diversify their loan portfolio or to concen-

---

[7] Schubert (1987), p. 4.
[8] *Economist* (March 7, 1987), pp. 87–90.
[9] Ibid.

trate it in more familiar markets have found asset swaps to be extremely advantageous. Some banks pursuing portfolio readjustment programs may find specific loans more appealing than others; they may, for example, be able to take advantage of the inefficiency of the secondary market in pricing loans arising from differences in perception of country risk and expectations of the collectability of the loan. There are various reasons why one bank may find a particular loan asset more appealing than its current owner; for example, banks can have different views about the prospects for a particular debtor country making an orderly return to debt service. In addition, some banks might feel that the special relationship they enjoy with the government of a country might increase their chances of exercising their credit rights. Also, where banks are required by regulators to write down the loans of a particular country, they may find it useful to swap all or part of their loans to that country for loans to another country that do not require a mandatory reserve increase, even if this entails a cash settlement to close the transaction. Finally, a bank wishing to obtain equity in a particular country may swap loans against debt paper suitable for a debt-equity conversion in that country. For these reasons, banks have shown an increasing interest in swapping assets as a means of fine-tuning their asset management practices in order to achieve their desired credit exposure.

Following the success of many debt-equity conversions, the swapping of debts has become much more frequently an early and preparatory step in the debt-equity conversion process. Banks prepared to participate in the sale of a loan at a discount generally try to avoid publicity; they do not want the news that they are selling off a customer's paper to convey disturbing signals to the market, as this could lower the perceived value of similar assets in their portfolios and could, in addition, undermine their relation with the borrower. By swapping loans in the interbank market instead, banks can reach a desired level of confidentiality and reduce the risk of sending disturbing signals. It is generally acknowledged in the market that behind each series of asset swap transactions, there is probably an outright buyer of a loan.

As participants have gained experience in the secondary debt market, they have gone beyond the straightforward debt-debt and debt-equity transactions and have used the market for increasingly more sophisticated deals. Some banks, for example, have traded developing country debt paper for U.S. domestic debt paper, junk bonds, or zero coupon Treasury bonds; some have swapped debt paper, with a cash adjustment, for debt paper of a perceived different quality of the same country; and some have donated debt paper to charities for tax deductions based on the local currency received at the swap. A similar related action has been donations of debt paper for rain forest preservation, as in the Bolivian "nature swap."[10]

Accounting and Regulatory Constraints

While debt-equity swaps have certain advantages for banks, as described above, they do not provide a comprehensive solution for lowering or diversifying a bank's credit exposure. When it first began, activity on the secondary market for the debt obligations of financially troubled countries was relatively unimpeded, but it soon became constrained by a number of legal, accounting, and regulatory factors, particularly in the United States.

First, it became evident that an original lender might not be absolved from the obligations attached to a loan that it had swapped or sold. As noted above, a creditor bank participating in a rescheduling program may be required to commit new funds in an amount equal to the percentage of its total credit exposure in the rescheduling country. This percentage is calculated on the basis of the outstanding credit at a particular base date, which is normally, but not always, the day on which the debtor country announces a moratorium on its debts. Consequently, some banks engaged in loan sales or swaps may later find out that they have not been released from these obligations to provide new funds, as they had engaged in such transactions prior to the base date. Some banks have tried to overcome this problem by entering into agreements whereby the purchaser relieves the original lender of any future obligation to contribute new funds to the rescheduling country. The legal validity of such agreements in some regulatory environments has not been established, and therefore the incentive to sell or swap loans as a way of avoiding both increases in credit exposure and the burden of participating in rescheduling programs has been somewhat reduced. According to some banking sources, however, a consensus is growing that debt converted under official debt-equity conversion schemes will be excluded from future new money packages—at least on a case-by-case basis.

The single most important factor constraining U.S. banks from actively participating in loan sales and swap transactions was the release in May 1985 by the American Institute of Certified Public Accountants (AICPA) of a "Note to Practitioners Regarding Accounting for Loan Swaps."[11] The premise of the AICPA note is that an asset swap repre-

---

[10] Schubert (1987), p. 16.

[11] Although the AICPA has jurisdiction only over U.S. accounting practice, its positions are often influential in the shaping of policies in other accounting environments.

sents a market transaction that should be accounted for by banks at current fair value. If the value of the proceeds from a swap is less than the recorded original investment, the bank should record a loss equal to the difference between the amount of the acquired loan, plus any cash paid, and the current fair value of the original loan, plus any cash received. The determination of the current fair value is, however, difficult and subjective. The AICPA itself has recognized in its document that the determination of this value is difficult to make because of the highly judgmental nature of the valuation process in the swap transaction. In fact, the various parties involved may very well reach different conclusions on the value of the asset they are exchanging. Even if the loan is swapped at a particular agreed price, it could be legally recorded at different prices in the books of the two banks involved in the transaction. Moreover, under normal accounting rules, a bank may be perfectly correct in recording the face value of the loan it acquired at a discount, if the bank's management intends to, and is considered able to, hold the loan to maturity.

In its "Note" the AICPA also suggested that when the swap involves loans to countries experiencing financial difficulties, the estimated fair value of the asset acquired will generally be less than its original face value, resulting therefore in a loss for the banks participating in the swap. The recognition of a loss, however, has raised the question of whether the exchange of loans at a discount should trigger a reassessment of the value of assets similar to those swapped, but that are still retained in the bank's portfolio, on the grounds that if a bank is selling a loan at discount because of its management's concern about the loan's ultimate collectibility, it seems plausible that other assets with similar credit characteristics should be written down or provided for in order to reflect their current market value. As a result, many banks have interpreted the AICPA rules as implying that if they record a loss on one specific loan that has been swapped, they should provide for possible losses on the value of similar assets held on their balance sheets.

Shortly after the publication of the AICPA document, the Office of the U.S. Comptroller of the Currency (OCC) published a banking circular on the same subject[12] which took an even more explicit position on the appropriateness of recording discounted loans acquired through swaps at face value. This circular made clear the presumption of the OCC that swapping debts of financially troubled countries at market value could result in a loss for the creditor and in that case banks under

---

[12] Office of the Comptroller of the Currency, "Accounting for Loan Swaps," Bank Circular-200, May 22, 1985.

its jurisdiction should reconsider the level of their provisions[13] against loan losses with respect to other similar assets retained in their portfolio.

As a result of the potential need to recognize losses in conformity with the publications of the AICPA and the OCC, sales or swaps of loans by commercial banks were sharply reduced in the United States and, because of the influence of these two institutions in other regulatory environments, in other creditor countries as well. Major U.S. banks in particular were concerned that if they sold a specific loan at a discount from their own portfolio and consequently recorded a loss, they might ultimately have to adjust (mark-to-market) the value of similar assets remaining in their portfolios. This would have had a direct and substantial impact on banks with large credit exposures and, therefore, a large potential need to increase capital in order to comply with minimum reserve requirements. In other words, the financial benefit of selling or swapping a loan could have been more than offset by the potential loss.

Citibank's decision in May 1987 to increase its loan loss reserves by an unprecedented $3 billion, which was followed by similar moves in other banks, indicated a change in the attitude of major banks toward their credit exposure in financially troubled countries and removed some of the constraints imposed by accounting regulations. Specifically, they are in a better position to absorb losses that may be occasioned by any requirement to mark-to-market their portfolio. Setting aside large voluntary provisions has therefore opened up to the banks the possibility of swapping their own debt paper for equity or of selling it outright at a discount.

Another constraint on U.S. banks contemplating debt-equity swaps relates to the operation of Regulation K of the Federal Reserve Board. Until August 1987, this regulation prohibited U.S. banks from owning more than 19.9 percent of any foreign nonfinancial company. In August, the regulation was liberalized to permit a U.S. banking organization to acquire as much as 100 percent of the shares of a foreign nonfinancial company as long as that company is in the process of being transferred from public to private ownership and is located in a heavily indebted developing country. It also required shares in the company to be acquired through a debt-equity swap and to be held by the bank holding company or its subsidiaries, and, finally, that the ownership interest would be divested within five years unless the Federal Reserve Board extended the period for good cause, but, in any event, within ten years. Although the banks welcomed this liberalization, most found that it did

---

[13] The term "provisions," as it is used throughout this paper, refers only to the amount of capital set aside as a reserve against loan losses.

not go far enough and have made representations to the Federal Reserve Board asking for the regulation to be liberalized further.

Finally, uncertainty about tax considerations has also constrained debt sales by U.S. banks. The Internal Revenue Service has not yet made any ruling on the tax treatment of debt-equity swaps. There is some concern in banking circles, however, that in determining whether the sale of a debt obligation at a discount qualifies for a tax deduction, the Service may well wish to consider the face value of the foreign exchange received in exchange for that debt obligation.

As a general rule, commercial banks outside the United States have been rather less constrained in the sale of their debt paper. In the United Kingdom, the sale of one or more debt obligations from one country is not considered a cause for marking-to-market other loans to the same country still held in the portfolio of the bank concerned. In addition, the difference between the face value of the debt paper and the sale price in the secondary market is considered by the tax authorities as a realized loss that can be offset against profits. With regard to provisioning, the Bank of England has encouraged banks to increase their provisions against their developing country debts. The Bank of England suggested that the level of provisions should be set on the basis of 15 factors grouped into three areas: present repayment record, past repayment record, and the economic prospects for the country concerned. In the United Kingdom, according to banking sources, the major banks have provisioned against about 30 percent of the value of their developing country debt portfolios. On the European continent, provisions are generally much higher, in some countries exceeding 60 percent.

Market Players

At present, banks account for almost all transactions in the secondary debt market, with European and small U.S. regional banks being virtually the only net sellers of loans at a discount. Because of the decline in prices for debt paper, some banks have suffered losses in this market and are now not prepared to take positions. The need to recognize losses has made the large U.S. commercial banks and banks with substantial exposure in financially troubled countries reluctant to sell or swap loans out of their own portfolios. As discussed above, engaging in swap transactions at a market-determined discount could trigger a reassessment of the remaining assets with similar credit characteristics still held at face value in a bank's balance sheet. Obviously, the consequent losses resulting from the strict application of this accounting rule would be proportional to the level of outstanding credit, that is, the larger the exposure, the larger the losses. The substantial negative impact on the balance sheet of banks with large exposure would therefore largely offset any potential advantage of selling part of a portfolio of problematic loans at a discount. Only banks with a limited exposure in debtor countries can afford to absorb such losses. According to commercial banking sources, many small regional U.S. banks that began lending to developing countries shortly before the emergence of the debt crisis have by now sold or written off a substantial portion of their portfolios. Because of their small exposure, and the consequent small losses entailed in a complete write-down of their portfolio, they have been able to clear their balance sheet of problematic assets.

The reserve policies exercised in the various regulatory environments have also played a role in shaping the supply side of the market. Because of their high level of provisioning (both mandatory and voluntary), European banks have been able to absorb larger losses resulting from the sale of a loan at a discount. In fact, banks in some European countries have accumulated such a high level of reserves against nonperforming loans that the sale or swap of a loan at the prevailing market discount rates could result in a profit. For example, should a bank having provisioned for a 40 percent loss against a particular loan sell that loan at a discount of only 20 percent (assuming that such a sale would be possible under the existing accounting regulations), the net effect would be a profit of 20 percent.

U.S. financial institutions have not left the market entirely. Large commercial banks and investment banks alike have in fact come to see debt-equity conversions as a sizable source of income. Partly reflecting the accounting constraints described above, the larger banks have been active in the market as intermediaries. They have specialized in arranging a complex series of transactions ranging from the acquisition of debt paper on the secondary market to the negiotiation of the conversion terms with the authorities of the debtor country without utilizing any loans or assets recorded in their own books. Banking analysts have estimated that in early 1987 90 percent of the activity of major U.S. financial institutions in debt-equity swapping was that of a broker rather than of a principal. Fees for arranging typical transactions were reportedly running as high as $1 million for every $100 million of debts converted.

Factors Affecting the Discount on Bank Loans

The discount applied to the sale of bank loans is largely linked to the market's perception of the creditworthiness of the debtor country.

Dooley has argued[14] that the market value of a debt will tend to equal the market's expectation of the future cash flow to the holder of the debt. This factor, however, is only a benchmark. There are other factors which enter into play. For example, the discount will tend to vary according to the different provisioning policies implemented by bank regulators. If these policies are adjusted to require a greater amount of capital reserves to be set aside against doubtful loans, the discount on the secondary market may deepen, as the banks will be less constrained by potential losses in selling their debt paper. Even within the same regulatory environment, different risk assessments or repayment expectations by bank officials could result in different prices on similar debt instruments in the same market. The level of the discount will also respond to supply and demand forces; for example, the easier it is to convert debts into equity, the higher will be the demand for the discounted debt in the secondary market and the lower the discount will become.

In light of the above considerations, it is difficult to identify a single market price for loans to a particular country. Only a relatively small number of financial institutions actively engage in this market, and the volume of transactions is still quite small. Even though a few banks regularly post quotes for the sale of debt paper, most transactions, especially outright sales, result from individual case-by-case negotiations. Spreads and discounts can be highly misleading as the market remains volatile and relatively illiquid. Some bankers have in fact said that the outright purchase of as little as $50 million worth of paper of a particular country could radically move the market. Finally, a debt-equity swap incorporates a number of financial goals and strategies chosen by different players. The complexity of each individual transaction, the lack of information on similar potential deals, and the lack of standardized procedures can understandably lead to wide variation in the pricing of debt obligations.

Table 3 shows some prices quoted over the past two years by a New York investment bank (Shearson Lehman Brothers) for debt obligations of major debtor countries. These quotes are purely indicative, and the generally declining trend shown in the table does not necessarily reflect fundamental changes in the market. It is generally believed, however, that the sharp decline since May 1987 reflects the decision taken by several U.S. banks during that month to set aside reserves against potential loan losses, a decision that was interpreted as a tacit recognition by these banks that their developing country loans were unlikely to be repaid in full.

---

[14] See Michael P. Dooley, "Buy-Backs, Debt-Equity Swaps, Asset Exchanges, and Market Prices of External Debt" in this volume.

Table 3. *Price of Debt Obligations on the Secondary Market, 1986–87*
(In percent of face value)

	January 1986	December 1986	June 1987	December 1987	November 1988
Argentina	62–66	62–66	58–60	35–38	20–21
Brazil	75–81	74–77	62–65	45–47.5	42–43
Chile	65–69	65–68	67–70	60–63	57–59
Colombia	82–84	n.a.	85–88	67–72	60–61
Ecuador	68–71	63–65	52–55	34–38	14–16
Mexico	69–73	54–57	57–60	51–54	45–46
Peru	25–30	16–19	14–18	2–7	5–8
Philippines	n.a.	72–76	70–72.5	49–52	51–53
Poland	50–53	41–43.5	43–45.5	41–43	37–38
Romania	91–94	86–89	86–89	81–83	96–100
Venezuela	80–82	72–74	72–74	49–52	44–45
Yugoslavia	78–81	77–81	77–80	—	47–48

Source: Shearson Lehman Brothers.

III. The Investing Companies

A company wishing to invest in an indebted country stands to derive considerable benefits from a debt-equity swap scheme, the most obvious being the possibility of obtaining local currency for investment on terms more favorable than can be obtained through regular foreign exchange market transactions. There are, however, some possible disadvantages that companies following this investment path need to take into consideration.

Probably the most serious potential disadvantage is that the recipient indebted country may impose stricter conditions regarding capital repatriation and profit remittances on investment financed by debt conversion than on regular foreign direct investment. Some countries have, for example, specified that foreign capital repatriated must not exceed the amount that would have been repatriated in repayment of the original debt before it was swapped for equity. Another possible disadvantage is that the debtor country might place restrictions on the type of equity it is prepared to sell in exchange for debt paper that it would not place on sales of equity for "new" foreign investment. In Mexico, for example, the rate at which the authorities bought back their country's debt was related directly to their assessment of the degree to which the intended investment would meet government priorities and objectives. Moreover, the paperwork and other formalities connected with the completion of debt-equity swaps may be more burdensome and time consuming than regular direct investment transactions. Finally, there are a number of unresolved tax issues; it is possible, for example, that the difference between the purchase price and the redemption price of the debt paper, measured in terms of the currency of the country in which the company is headquartered, might be considered as a profit subject to tax.

The benefits to an investing company are illustrated by what has become the classic case study of a debt-equity swap—the Nissan/Citicorp/Mexico deal. In this transaction Nissan, through the offices of Citicorp, was able to obtain $54 million worth of pesos for $40 million, that is, at a discount of some 26 percent from the free market exchange rate at the time of the transaction. It would therefore appear that Nissan's action was more advantageous than the two other basic options available: borrowing pesos in the domestic market at the very high nominal rates of interest then prevailing in Mexico (and that prevail in most indebted countries) or buying pesos at the current market exchange rate with "new" money.

The most often quoted case of a bank swapping its own debt holdings into equity is the transaction in which Bankers Trust swapped about $44 million worth of debt for a controlling share in the Provida Pension Fund and an affiliated insurance company in Chile. U.S. banks swapping their own debt for equity are likely to concentrate their attention on financial institutions such as these, not only because this is the sector in which they have expertise but also because, notwithstanding the liberalization of Regulation K, banking regulations still limit the range of companies in which banks can hold more than 19.9 percent of the equity and act as anything more than passive investors.

The major question of concern for a company investing in an indebted country through means of debt-equity swaps is whether the regulations concerning the repatriation of profits earned by the new investment or concerning the investment capital itself will be tighter than had the investment been made with "new" money. In many cases regulations governing repatriation have been more restrictive; for example, in Brazil the authorities specified that for debt-equity swaps tied to rescheduling agreements with banks, the repatriation of profits and capital could not exceed the scheduled payment of interest and capital on the particular debt that was swapped. In Mexico, the authorities did not allow debt-equity swaps to be made for investments that benefit from guaranteed dividends payable irrespective of earnings and profits, but otherwise they tried to apply the scheme without restrictions. In some countries conditions of repatriation are worked out on a case-by-case basis.

In general terms, the more an investment is perceived by the host country to stimulate economic growth, the more favorable the conditions of the debt-equity conversion are likely to be for the investor. In the final analysis, however, the decision on whether or not to invest can only be taken on a case-by-case basis with the overall costs and likely returns on each scheme carefully assessed by the management of the investing company.

IV. The Effects on the Indebted Country

The following analysis of the impact of debt-equity swaps on the balance of payments is based on an example of a country that borrows $100 million abroad in order to finance its public sector deficit. The manner in which the debt-to-equity conversion is recorded in the balance of payments depends on the value at which the country redeems the paper presented by the foreign investor (i.e., the redemption value of the loan). It is useful to consider the three cases indicated below, which are illustrative examples of transactions denominated in U.S. dollars.

Case	Loan Face Value	Discounted Value[1]	Redemption Value[2]
	(In millions of dollars)		
1	100	70	100
2	100	70	90
3	100	70	70

[1] The discounted value is the market price that the foreign investor pays to acquire the debt on the secondary market—a transaction that does not involve the indebted country directly.
[2] The redemption price is the price that the government agrees to pay in order to redeem its external liability.

In recording the transaction in the balance of payments, it is necessary to decide which redemption value is to be used. On this point, the IMF *Balance of Payments Manual* is clear. Paragraph 75 states that the market price is the only value at which transactions should be recorded. This criterion excludes the possibility of recording the face value of the loan, leaving a choice between the discounted value and the redemption value of the loan. Although one of the partners to the swap is a government agent, it seems reasonable to regard this transaction as market determined in that it takes place between an independent and voluntary buyer and an independent and voluntary seller, both of whom are motivated by commercial and financial considerations.[15] As the redemption price is what is paid by the government, it should therefore be considered to be the value at which the debt-to-equity conversion is recorded.

To simplify the analysis, it is assumed that both the original loan and the subsequent debt-equity conversion are carried out in the same period covered by the balance of payments statistics so that the net result of the transactions can be considered as the flow affecting the stock of the country's external liabilities[16] in that period. When the initial loan transaction is executed, it would be recorded in the capital account (including reserves) in the following way:

Debit: foreign exchange assets $100 million
Credit: external liabilities $100 million

At the next stage when the conversion of the debt into equity takes place, no cash payment in foreign currency is required by the debtor for the redemption of the debt. It is, therefore, simpler to view the two transactions taken together in terms of balance of payments statistics as an exchange of two financial claims, that is, an external debt and a direct investment. For the first case, the balance of payments transactions would appear as follows:

Debit: external liabilities $100 million
Credit: direct investment $100 million

Consolidating this with the loan record gives the following:

Credit: external liabilities   0.0
Debit: foreign exchange assets $100 million
Credit: direct investment $100 million

The net results for the debtor country are a reduction in its external liabilities, an equivalent increase of foreign direct investment, and an unchanged amount of foreign exchange assets. It would appear that the evaluation of the impact of a debt-to-equity conversion is simply a comparative analysis of two forms of external obligations: debt vs. equity. However, the net effect on the economy will also depend on how the debtor country finances the domestic currency counterpart of the conversion of the debt into equity. This topic is analyzed below.

---

[15] These are the considerations that are in paragraph 76 of the *Balance of Payments Manual* which are used to identify the "market price."

[16] The term "external liabilities" is not consistent with the terminology adopted in the *Balance of Payments Manual,* but has been used here in the interests of simplicity.

In the second case, the results will be slightly different. When the debt-equity swap takes place, the record on the balance of payments will be as follows:

Debit: external liabilities $90 million
Credit: direct investment $90 million

Consolidating this entry with the loan record gives the following:

Credit: external liabilities $10 million
Debit: foreign exchange assets $100 million
Credit: direct investment $90 million

The residual in the external liabilities account needs some explanation. According to the *Balance of Payments Manual,* [17] changes in the market value of financial instruments are recorded in the balance of payments only when their ownership is transferred, in which case there will be a realized gain or loss. In the above example, not only is the ownership of the external liability temporarily transferred but also the debt is reclassified under a different heading, that is, direct investment. It is, therefore, more appropriate to credit the $10 million to a contra account called "realized capital gain" after having debited the full face value of the loan to the external liabilities account. The consolidation will now be as follows:

Credit: external liabilities   0.0
Credit: realized capital gain $10 million
Debit: foreign exchange assets $100 million
Credit: direct investment $90 million

The net result will be an unchanged amount of foreign exchange, a realized gain of $10 million, and a simultaneous change, that is, a swap, of external debt for direct investment and reduction in liabilities to the rest of the world.

Thus far the analysis has referred to balance of payments figures recorded in terms of U.S. dollars. However, a country will usually compile its balance of payments in national currency. In such a case, assuming a foreign exchange rate of two units of domestic currency (*dc*) for every U.S. dollar, when the loan takes place the following will be recorded in the balance of payments:

Debit: foreign exchange assets (at 2 *dc* per dollar)   200 million
Credit: external liabilities (at 2 *dc* per dollar)   200 million

---

[17] Par. 373i, *Balance of Payments Manual.*

When the debt-to-equity conversion is carried out, the price paid by the country in foreign currency terms will still be the market price, but in this case the redemption value of the loan will reflect an implicit foreign exchange rate that is different from the official rate. The records will be as follows:

Debit:	external liabilities (at 2.22 *dc* per dollar)[18]	200 million
Credit:	direct investment (at 2.22 *dc* per dollar)	200 million

The net consolidation will now be:

Credit:	external liabilities	0.0
Debit:	foreign exchange assets	200 million
Credit:	direct investment	200 million

The result will be a "swap" of external liabilities for direct investment with exactly the same entries as in the first case but evaluated in domestic currency. The explanation of these results can be found in the *Balance of Payments Manual.* [19] If there are two or more exchange rates for the same currency but for different classes of transactions, the net effect of the difference between rates can be seen as equivalent to a tax on, or subsidy to, a domestic economic agent. This amount will be equal to the difference between the exchange rate at which the transaction is valued and the official exchange rate prevailing in the market. The profit or loss realized by the country following the application by the government of a multiple exchange rate system will have, essentially, a domestic origin; for this reason, it will not be included in the balance of payments.

The third case, while unlikely to be realized, raises a few interesting points. Recording the transactions gives:

Debit:	external liabilities	$70 million
Credit:	direct investment	$70 million

The net consolidation will provide the following results:

Credit:	external liabilities	0.0
Debit:	unrealized capital gain	$30 million

---

[18] $\dfrac{200 \text{ million of } dc}{90 \text{ million of dollars}} = 2.22.$

However, it should be noted that this is not the relevant implicit exchange rate for the foreign investor. This rate is equal to

$$\frac{\text{redemption value} \times \text{official exchange rate}}{\text{discounted value}}$$

i.e., ($90 × 2)/($70) = 2.57.

[19] Pars. 129–130, *Balance of Payments Manual.*

Credit: foreign exchange assets $100 million
Debit: direct investment $70 million

There is no obvious advantage for the foreign investor to enter into a debt-to-equity conversion agreement on these terms compared with investing $70 million of new money in the debtor country. Thus the foreign investor would be unlikely to engage in a swap of this kind. For the debtor country the unrealized capital gain would be quite substantial. By explicitly admitting a diminished value of its own external liabilities, however, the debtor country could jeopardize its relationship with major creditors, and its credit rating in the international capital market, which could increase the cost of future external finance and offset the initial capital gain.

The accounting analysis described above has shown that a swap of equity for debt has little or no effect on a country's net liability position. In most cases, the claims of the rest of the world on the country are merely reclassified, that is, there is no net capital inflow. Through a debt-equity swap a country simply exchanges one form of external liability for another—a debt with fixed service and continuing repayment obligations for direct investment.

The conversion of debt into equity may have an impact, however, on the balance of payments through the overall cumulative effect on net factor payments. If no restrictions are applied to the direct investment— for example, with regard to repatriation of capital or remittance of dividends—the balance of payments could be adversely affected to the extent that the payments abroad associated with the equity investment exceed the interest payments on the redeemed external debt. However, instead of having to service its debts at a rate of interest determined largely by factors beyond its control, the dividends and profits remitted by the debtor country would be influenced by the profitability of the investment, and this would be more directly linked to its capacity to service its obligations to the rest of the world. In this way, a swap could alleviate the debt service burden of an indebted country.

Impact on Money Supply

A useful first step in evaluating the financial implications of a debt-to-equity swap is to consider the highly simplified balance sheet of the consolidated banking system (central bank plus commercial banks) that is set out below. This type of presentation has the advantage of focusing on the banking system's acquisition of net foreign assets and permits a closer tracking of possible "swaps" between domestic and external sources of finance in the debtor country's economy.

Assets	Liabilities
Net foreign assets (NFA^b)	
Net domestic assets (NDA^b)	Monetary aggregate (M)

From this we have the following accounting identity:

$$M \equiv NDA^b + NFA^b. \tag{1}$$

Net domestic assets can be further disaggregated into claims on the government (DC^g) and claims on the nonbanking sector (DCn^b):

$$NDA^b \equiv DC^g + DC^{nb}. \tag{2}$$

Substituting the right-hand side of this equation into (1) gives:

$$M \equiv DC^g + DCn^b + NFA^b. \tag{1a}$$

This equation shows that the monetary aggregate depends on the claims of the consolidated banking system on domestic and foreign residents.

On the assumption that the government is running a deficit, two possible sources of finance—domestic and foreign—can be identified. These two sources appear in the government's budget constraint:

$$G - T \equiv \Delta DC^g - \Delta NFA^g, \tag{3}$$

where G is public spending, T is total government revenue, and NFA^g denotes net foreign assets of the government. Note that when there is net foreign borrowing by the public sector, there will be a decline in NFA^g. Rewriting (3) in terms of DC^g gives:

$$\Delta DC^g \equiv G - T + \Delta NFA^g. \tag{3a}$$

Equations 1a and 3a can be used to derive a particularly useful relationship between the financing of the government deficit and the change in the monetary aggregate:

$$\Delta M \equiv G - T + \Delta NFA^g + \Delta DC^{nb} + \Delta NFA^b. \tag{4}$$

This accounting identity can be used to analyze the effects on the money supply of first borrowing abroad by the government to finance a deficit, and then the conversion of the foreign debt of the government into domestic equity. For simplicity, the assumption will be made that the exchange rate is set at two units of domestic currency per dollar, that it does not vary from the time the loan is contracted, and that the government redeems the full face value of the government debt. When the government borrows on the external credit market, so that there is a decline in NFA^g, and transfers the proceeds of the borrowing to the banking system, then the net effect will be an increase in NFA^b of dc

200 million ($100 million at $2dc$ per dollar) and an equivalent increase in M associated with the foreign financing of the government deficit:

$$\Delta M \equiv (G - T) + \Delta NFA^g + \Delta DC^{nb} + \Delta NFA^b, \text{ or}$$

$$200 \equiv 200 - 200 + 0 + 200.$$

At the second stage when the debt-to-equity conversion is carried out, the government's external liabilities will decrease by dc 200 million ($100 million face value of the loan at $2dc$ per dollar), that is, NFA^g will be equal to $+200$ million. This is matched, as shown above, by a 200 million increase in equity claims. The effect on M will depend on whether or not the government finances the domestic transaction, that is, the domestic currency counterpart of the equity investment, through the consolidated banking system. If it chooses to do so, the domestic claims on the government (DC^g) will increase by an equivalent amount, that is, $+200$ million, and there will be a direct effect on the monetary aggregate. This can be seen directly in equation (1a), where a change in DC^g is matched by an equivalent change in M. If instead the government finances the transaction through the nonbanking system by selling securities to the public, then none of the variables included in (1a) will be affected, and consequently, there will be no effect on the domestic money supply.

Debt-equity swaps can therefore have a significant impact on the monetary and fiscal policies of the country redeeming the debt, particularly if a substantial volume of swaps take place. If the swap involves the conversion of private sector debt into private sector equity, however, there will be no monetary impact. The net result will be a transfer of existing liquidity from the private debtor to the equity holder without the intermediation of the banking system and without domestic credit creation or pressure on the domestic capital market.

Nonetheless, as most debt-equity swaps involve central bank or government liabilities, there will typically be some monetary or fiscal policy action. In such cases, the monetary impact will depend on how the domestic side of the transaction is financed. On the one hand, if the government issues a bond and floats it in the private sector, there will be no net monetary impact. However, the additional demand on the domestic capital market could well lead to upward pressures on interest rates. On the other hand, if the government finances the transaction through the consolidated banking system, there will be an equivalent increase in the monetary aggregate and possible inflationary pressures. In both cases, therefore, there are domestic financial effects of debt-equity swaps that may place constraints on the amounts that can be accommodated by the indebted country.

Table 4. *Potential Monetary Impact of Converting Debt to Equity Through the Creation of Money*

Country	Total Debts[1] Outstanding to Commercial Banks (In billions of dollars) (1)	Money Supply (M)[2] (In billions of dollars) (2)	Potential Effect on M of 5 Percent Conversion[3] (In percent) (3)
Argentina	31.3	4.5	35.8
Brazil	78.8	12.08	32.62
Mexico	73.7	6.3	58.5
Philippines	14.1	2.1	33.6

[1] Estimates from U.S. Federal Financial Institution Council and Bank for International Settlements, quoted by Cline (1987).

[2] With the exception of Brazil, figures are estimates for end-1986 quoted in dollars. The money stock is considered as the sum of currency outside banks plus demand deposits held with the monetary system by the rest of the domestic economy, other than the central government. For Brazil, figures are for September 1987.

[3] $[(1) \times 0.05 \times 100]/(2) = (3)$.

In many countries, resorting to domestic credit creation for the conversion of even a small proportion of external debt into equity could result in a significant increase in the money supply. Cline illustrated this point by relating the amount of external debt to existing money supply levels.[20] Following this approach, Table 4 shows the impact on the domestic money supply of a group of selected indebted countries that could be associated with the conversion of 5 percent of their outstanding debt to commercial banks.

The figures in column 3 indicate the dimension of the problem faced by the domestic monetary authorities. The most significant example is Mexico, where the conversion of 5 percent of outstanding external debt to commercial banks could result, other things remaining equal, in an increase of almost 60 percent in the money supply.

Nevertheless, even if the authorities of the debtor country take a different approach and decide to finance the swaps directly by selling public bonds to the private sector, they will not necessarily avoid difficult financial problems. Financing debt-equity conversion by drawing on domestic capital markets could well result in substantial crowding-out effects by placing upward pressures on interest rates and thereby squeezing out domestic economic agents. The limited size of the domestic

[20] Cline (1987).

capital markets existing in most major debtor countries would appear to offer little scope for the absorption of public debt that would be required for substantial debt-equity conversions. Domestic monetary authorities would, therefore, appear to face limitations with regard to the volume of debt-equity conversions that they can reasonably accommodate.

On the fiscal side, the substitution of foreign liabilities with domestic obligations—whether to the consolidated banking system or the private sector—may result in an increase in the domestic-currency debt service obligation of the government to the extent that the domestic real interest rate is higher than the rate applied to the external debt. This cost, as well as the financial implications of the early repayment of external debts, must be taken into account in the government's financial program.

Impact on Foreign Exchange Rate and Reserves

It is difficult to make a general statement regarding the impact of debt-equity conversions on the foreign exchange value of the domestic currency concerned. In most cases, as the debt-equity swap is not settled in or through the foreign exchange market, there is unlikely to be any direct linkage with the foreign exchange rate of the debtor country involved. If net factor payments decrease as a result of the conversion, however, the consequent reduction of foreign currency disbursements, even if marginal, could ease possible pressures on official reserves. This short-term improvement in the reserve position could prove to be beneficial in helping to restore the international creditworthiness of the country, particularly in present circumstances when many debtor countries do not have access to new bank lending. This beneficial effect on reserves could, however, be offset to some extent by the fact that when investment is made through debt-equity conversion instead of through direct purchases of domestic currency in the foreign exchange market, potential additions to foreign currency reserves will have to be forgone.

The longer-term impact of debt-equity swaps on the foreign exchange rate will depend on a combination of factors, such as the overall volume of debt converted into equities, the impact on the monetary aggregates and the domestic capital market, and ultimately on the profitability of the investments. As described above, either the money supply could increase or domestic interest rates could rise, both of which developments could exert substantial, although divergent, pressures on the exchange rate.

Impact on Economic Growth

All debt-equity swaps, whether they involve the conversion of public or private debt, are significantly influenced by the policies of the government of the indebted country concerned. The government can screen potential investors and decide which ones it will allow to engage in debt-equity swaps. It can decide to redeem the debt paper at less than face value and thus reduce the incentive to the foreign investor to engage in particular transactions. More important, when a government specifies the sectors into which the local currency proceeds of a debt conversion can be channeled, it is in effect pursuing an investment program that is not guided by purely market signals. The investment activities associated with such a program may not reflect an efficient allocation of resources and could, therefore, lead to distortions.

However, it should also be noted that the direct investment may confer certain advantages to the economy. Direct investment is often concentrated in import-substituting or export-oriented industries where it can contribute to improvements in the trade performance of the recipient country. Successful investment of this nature can create employment either directly or indirectly through increasing demand for domestically produced inputs and can, in consequence, expand the country's tax revenue base. Moreover, direct investment often includes new technology and management expertise, which can bring significant increases in productivity. For this reason, the financial value of direct investment may understate its overall benefits to the recipient country.

In assessing the benefits of debt-equity swap programs, the debtor countries have focused much attention on whether or not such swaps substitute for the flow of new money for direct investment, that is, whether or not they create additional direct investment. According to banking sources, concern that there would be such a deterrent effect was the reason why Brazil restricted its program in 1984 and why Argentina formulated a program in which the debt swapped for equity would have to be accompanied by new money. This concern has some backing in the academic community; for example, Rudiger Dornbusch of the Massachusetts Institute of Technology has claimed that some investments financed by swaps would have happened anyway and that for the others only the subsidy makes them artificially viable.[21]

Not all countries accept these arguments. For example, after the March 1987 announcement that American Express Bank would convert

---

[21] *Economist*, March 7, 1987, pp. 87–90.

$100 million of its debt for an equity share in new Mexican hotels, Mexican officials claimed that the project would create 15,000 jobs, would attract 240,000 extra tourists each year, and would lead to annual foreign exchange earnings of $80 million. Some investment bankers believe that many companies are not prepared to invest in the debtor countries at prevailing market exchange rates but that they might well do so if the price is right, that is, if the discount on the debt is great enough to provide what would in effect be a subsidized exchange rate.

One reason why the authorities of some countries are reticent in promoting debt-equity swap programs comes from their anxiety not to cede any sovereignty in the control of their domestic economies. It was partly this concern that made foreign bank lending more attractive than equity investment during the 1970s. The authorities of those countries who believe that the domestic resources must remain in national hands are less likely to encourage debt-equity swaps.

V. Concluding Remarks

This paper has attempted to identify some of the potential advantages and disadvantages of debt-equity swap programs for commercial banks, foreign direct investors, and the indebted countries. In doing so, the paper draws some conclusions with regard to the limited role such swaps might play in the resolution of the debt crisis.

For the banks participating in debt-equity swaps, probably the most important advantage is the opportunity of clearing their books of problematic loans that might still confer upon them an obligation to commit new funds to the same debtor country in any rescheduling agreement. At first, European and small U.S. regional banks were virtually alone in being net sellers of loans in the interbank market. The major U.S. banks largely refrained from making such sales because of accounting and regulatory policies they believed could ultimately oblige them, after the sale of a loan at a discount, to mark down the value of all their remaining loans to the relevant country to the same extent. In the early summer of 1987, however, a number of these banks decided to set aside additional and relatively substantial reserves in recognition of the problematic nature of loans to certain developing countries. This action would tend to suggest that the accounting and regulatory constraints are losing some of their significance; if this is the case, it is quite possible that in the near future some of the major U.S. banks might become net sellers in the secondary debt market.

Those countries permitting the swap of their external debt obligations for domestic equity have done so because they perceive a number of advantages. These include the replacement of fixed external payment obligations with a repayment stream that depends on the profitability of the equity investment; the stimulation of growth in export-oriented or import-substituting industries and the concomitant improvements in the country's trade performance, its balance of payments, and ultimately its overall external position; and the possible stimulus to the development of local equity markets, which subsequently can provide attractive uses for domestic savings and reduce the motivation for, if not reverse altogether, capital flight.

Nevertheless, in appraising the possible advantages that may be associated with debt-equity swaps for indebted countries, a number of considerations must be borne in mind. First, as discussed in Section IV, the conversion of foreign debt into equity does not in and of itself provide additional foreign resources to the country; only the form of foreign claims on the resources of the indebted country changes. This change in form may confer certain benefits in that the fixed repayment obligations of interest and principal to banks are replaced by the remittance of profits and dividends and the repatriation of capital that depends on the profitability of the investment itself and, in addition, on regulations affecting such remittances and capital repatriation that the host country chooses to implement. Thus the risk of not meeting an international repayment obligation is shifted somewhat from the borrower to the foreign investor. To the extent that the terms on which the borrowing country can service its foreign obligations become more favorable, as measured by the change in the present discounted value of net factor payments abroad associated with the shift from bank loans to equity investment, a debt-equity swap may appear to be advantageous to the indebted country.

However, it is also necessary to consider the transaction from the point of view of the equity investor, who presumably engages in the transaction expecting to make a profit on the investment in the host country and at some point to be able to remit that profit as well as the original investment. Numerous factors influence the investor's decision, among the most important of which are the discount at which the debt is purchased and the redemption price at which this principal can be converted into local currency. The more attractive the redemption price and the larger the discount, the greater the incentive to engage in the transaction. The difference in costs between a debt-equity swap transaction and a regular foreign direct investment transaction, that is, the effective subsidy, may have to be quite high to compensate the investor for the economic risks associated with the particular investment as well as those arising from possible changes in government policies affecting the profitability of the local investment or the repatriation of profits and capital.

The effective subsidy may involve a cost to the country to the extent that the swap of debt for equity substitutes for investment that would have been made in any event without the incentive provided by the swap. Such investment would add to the foreign exchange resources of the country; to the extent that these investment flows qualify for access to domestic currency by means of the swap arrangement, there would be a decline in the foreign exchange that would be converted into domestic currency. A debt-equity swap may therefore involve a cost to the country in the form of reduced demand for its currency in the foreign exchange market.

Another issue associated with the effective subsidy to foreign investment provided by the swap is the reallocation of investment that may be involved. Debt-equity swap arrangements lower the cost of capital to particular qualifying sectors of the economy and it can be seen as part of an "industrial policy" on the part of the countries involved. Viewed against the standard of a well-functioning capital market that allocates funds efficiently to their most productive uses, the incentives for investment that are the essential feature of swap arrangements should be regarded with some caution. However, where considerable distortions in domestic capital markets already exist, it is difficult to judge whether an additional distortion will result in a substantial misallocation of resources. In any case, in appraising the usefulness of debt-equity swaps, it is important to view them as providing subsidies to particular sectors of the economy in the sense that investors in these sectors can acquire funds more cheaply than otherwise, and therefore it is necessary to consider whether there are not more efficient ways of achieving the same objectives.

In addition to the microeconomic aspects of debt-equity swaps, there are important macroeconomic implications. The analysis in Section IV pointed out the need to take account of the monetary and financial effects associated with the domestic financing of the swaps. As the conversion of debt into equity does not necessarily provide any additional foreign capital (indeed, the swap may substitute for additional foreign funds), some portion of the resources for any increase in gross investment will need to come from the domestic economy. To the extent that these are unemployed resources, the additional expenditure generated by the swaps can perhaps be accommodated with little increase in the price level or domestic interest rates. If the economy is operating close to capacity, however, any increase in investment spending must either crowd out other domestic expenditure as a result of higher prices or higher interest rates, or result in an increase in imports. An increase in the share of output (or expenditure) devoted to investment is no doubt desirable, but the consequences for the rest of the economy must be taken into account.

Overall, debt-equity swaps can to some extent alleviate the debt burden by making more manageable the servicing of obligations to foreigners. They can also make a contribution to economic growth to the extent that aggregate investment in efficient sectors of the economy is increased as a share of domestic output or spending. Nevertheless, the magnitude of this contribution of swaps in these two areas would appear to be rather limited.

REFERENCES

Andersen, M., "Buenos Aires Officials Elated . . . ," *Washington Post,* April 15, 1987, pp. E1, 3.

Bruce, Rupert, "Who are Debt/Equity Swappers?" *Euromoney* (May 1987). p. 117.

Cline, William R., *Mobilizing Bank Lending to Debtor Countries,* Policy analyses in International Economics, No. 18 (Washington: Institute for International Economics, June 1987).

Debs, Richard A., David L. Roberts, and Eli M. Remolona, *Finance for Developing Countries* (New York: Group of Thirty, 1987).

Dillion, K. Burke, and others, *Recent Developments in External Debt Restructuring,* International Monetary Fund Occasional Paper 45 (Washington: International Monetary Fund, 1985).

Houghton, Lyal, "Getting to Grips With Debt Equity Swaps," *Euromoney,* March 1987, pp. 105–6.

International Monetary Fund, *Balance of Payments Manual,* Fourth Edition (Washington: International Monetary Fund, 1977).

Officia of the Comptroller of the Currency, "Accounting for Loan Swaps," Bank Circular 200 (Washington, May 22, 1985).

Schubert, Martin W., Address delivered at the debt-equity swap market conference organized by the Institute for International Research (unpublished; New York, October 19, 1987).

UNCTAD (United Nations Conference on Trade and Development), "The Role of Foreign Direct Investment in Development Finance: Current Issues," TD/B/C.3/196, December 14, 1984.

The Strategy of Debt Buy-Backs: A Theoretical Analysis of the Competitive Case

CARLOS ALFREDO RODRIGUEZ*

This paper is concerned with analyzing the strategy of a debtor country repurchasing its debt at market prices. The main result, for the case in which unpaid interest is rolled over, is that a strategy of announced debt repurchases at market prices, under competitive conditions and rational expectations, will only allow the country to recover debt at par value whenever the market expects the remaining debt to be fully served at some time in the future. When debt holders are myopic with respect to future debt repurchases, a strategy can be devised by which all the "excess" debt is repurchased at a price equal, in present value, to that prevailing before the policy was announced.

T HE DEBTS of several developing countries are traded well below par in financial markets. To a great extent this is a reflection of the fact that service payments by debtor countries fall short of contractual interest. Unpaid interest on syndicated loans with commercial banks is rolled over, and the total contractual debt keeps rising over time. This continuous increase in contractual debt, with no improvement in service payments, is bound over time to lower the price at which this debt is traded.

*Mr. Rodriguez is a staff member of the Argentine Center for the Study of Macroeconomics (CEMA) in Buenos Aires. He wrote this paper when he was consultant in the Research Department of the IMF. He is indebted to Paul Lizondo, Michael Dooley, and others in the Research Department for their comments.

We define excess debt as the difference between total outstanding debt and that amount of debt that can be fully served. It may be to the advantage of debtor countries to obtain additional funding, other than that devoted to servicing interest, in order to repurchase their outstanding debt at prices well below par. Ideally, the purchases should retire enough debt that service payments can service fully the remaining amount. At this point the debt problem disappears, as the remaining debt can be fully serviced and can therefore be traded at par. The country has recovered access to the international financial markets.

In evaluating buy-backs, several questions come to mind. First, is it possible for the debtor country to retire all the excess debt at prices below par? Second, to the extent that in the absence of buy-backs the price of the outstanding debt converges asymptotically to zero, would it be possible to retire all excess debt with just a minimal amount of cash devoted to buy-backs per unit of time?

The answers to these questions depend fundamentally on the strategies the participants in this game are assumed to play. This paper is concerned with only one strategy, denoted as the "competitive" strategy. Basically this strategy assumes that the debtor country has a fixed trade surplus (T) devoted fully to the service of the outstanding debt. The country also has an amount of additional cash probably coming from a donation or from sales of domestic assets that is devoted to repurchase outstanding debt at the going market price (i.e., the country bids competitively for its outstanding debt). The creditors are fully competitive, have full information about the debtor country strategy, and are also willing to sell debt at the going market price. Since the market price at which transactions are carried depends on actual and expected future developments, it is assumed that those expectations are formed rationally.

Since we will not be considering uncertainty, the dynamic equilibrium to be derived will be represented by that perfect foresight path that converges to the steady state (a concept that will have to be defined later, particularly for the case in which the price of debt falls continuously).

We will analyze two distinct cases depending on what is done with the unpaid fraction of contractual interest. As presently happens, the unpaid interest is rolled over and therefore increases the outstanding stock of debt. This point is particularly relevant if the cash buy-back strategy aims at repurchasing all the outstanding excess debt. In this context it will be shown that such a cash buy-back strategy, under rational expectations, requires in every period an amount of cash investment in buy-backs larger than the amount of unpaid interest. In this case all cash buy-backs will have to be made at par. In summary, if the cash buy-back strategy is expected eventually to recover all the excess debt, the country must repurchase all its excess debt at par whenever the unpaid interest is rolled over. These, of course, are the only results consistent with a rational expectations equilibrium. Other assumptions regarding expectations will yield different results.

If debt holders view future debt repurchases myopically and consider each repurchase as the last, a strategy of continuous debt repurchase at a minimum feasible rate amounts, in present value, to repurchasing all the excess debt at the market price prevailing the instant before the repurchases are announced.

The alternative to the rollover of interest is forgiveness of unpaid interest, provided the stipulated amount T per period is devoted to servicing the debt. It is assumed that T is the maximum amount the country can commit to the service of interest.

It is obvious that if the debtor can service indefinitely, and with certainty, only a fraction of the contractual interest, the debtor must eventually become insolvent. If the debtor becomes insolvent, bankruptcy laws in most countries freeze interest charges with consequences similar to forgiving the unpaid fraction of contractual interest. In this case, any amount in excess of T that can be devoted to cash buy-backs at market prices will eventually be successful in repurchasing the total amount of excess debt. Furthermore, the debt will be repurchased at a price below par and along the rational expectations path. A lower rate of cash purchases per unit of time will result in a lower purchase price for the debt although a longer time will be required to retire the entire amount of excess debt. It can be shown, however, that the present value of all cash payments will also fall. The debtor country therefore faces a negative trade-off between the present value of the cost of retiring its excess debt and the length of time required to do so. This case is interesting to analyze because the present value of all cash payments for debt repurchase could be taken as a measure of the amount that debtors would accept as a once-and-for-all exchange of cash for excess debt.

I. Cash Buy-Back With Rollover of Unpaid Interest

In order to simplify the analysis we make only those assumptions that are absolutely essential to describe the dynamic consequences of debt buy-backs. We therefore assume that the debt of the country is structured as a perpetuity, paying a contractual interest equal to the competitive rate, that we denote by i. The total face value of outstanding debt is denoted by B. Per unit of time, the debtor has available for interest service only the fixed sum T, that is less than contractual interest service due ($i.B$). The amount T is distributed proportionally among all existing titles. Each title, therefore, is paid an amount equal to T/B. In addition, the unpaid interest is documented as a new issue of debt in an amount of ($i - T/B$) per existing title of \$1.

The model we will analyze is determined by two equations. The first describes the trajectory of the equilibrium market price for the outstanding debt, while the second describes the trajectory of the outstanding debt as a function of unpaid interest and the rate of debt repurchases.

At any moment, the holder of one title of debt promising to pay an interest rate of i in perpetuity faces the following alternatives. First, he can sell his title at a market price of p dollars per dollar of face value of the debt and reinvest the proceeds at the rate i. The return is $i.p$. Second, he can keep the title and collect (T/B) in cash and an additional amount of debt titles equal to ($i - T/B$) on account of unpaid interest. This last payment amounts to the rollover of the unpaid interest and has a market value of $p.(i - T/B)$. In addition, by keeping his debt title, the holder is entitled to the expected rate of capital gain Dpe. The total return of keeping the debt title is therefore $(T/B) + p.(i - T/B) + Dpe$. Since we are assuming rational expectations with perfect foresight, the expected change in the price is equal to the actual change, $Dpe = Dp$. Throughout the paper we will use the notation $Dx = dx/dt$.

Market equilibrium requires that the time path of p be such that the debt holder be indifferent between keeping the debt title or selling it. This implies that the return be identical under both alternatives:

$$i.p = (T/B) + p.(i - T/B) + Dp. \tag{1}$$

Equation (1) is fully equivalent to the following expression showing the actual market price as the present discounted value of all future expected returns on the asset:

$$p(t) = \int_t^\infty \frac{\{T + p(s).[i.B(s) - T]\}}{B(s)} \cdot \exp[-i.(s - t)].ds. \tag{2}$$

From equation (1) we obtain the following differential equation describing the equilibrium trajectory of the market price, p:

$$Dp = (T/B).(p - 1). \tag{3}$$

The differential equation (3) describes the path of p, given the initial value (still to be determined) and the trajectory of B.

The outstanding stock of debt increases over time on account of the interest unpaid and falls on account of current cash buy-backs (A/p).

$$DB = i.B - T - A/p. \tag{4}$$

Cash buy-backs are supposed to continue, i.e., $A > 0$, until all excess debt is repurchased. We define the sustainable level of debt as that level that can be fully served with the current trade surplus,

$$B^* = T/i. \tag{5}$$

Using the concept of sustainable debt, we define excess debt as $B - B^*$. If $B = B^*$, it is assumed that $A = 0$ and by (4), B will remain unchanged at the level B^*. Given the values of A, T, i, $p(0)$ and $B(0)$, equations (3) and (4) describe the time path of the stock of outstanding debt and its equilibrium market price.

The initial level $p(0)$ under rational expectations is determined by the condition that the system converge to its stationary state. Whenever this stationary state exists, we show that the initial value $p(0)$ is unique. Occasionally, however, a stationary state for p and B is not feasible. In those cases, however, there exists a balanced growth path along which the market value of the outstanding debt, $Z = p.B$, remains constant. We assume that rational traders will choose this balanced growth path as the alternative to the nonexistent stationary state; also in this case we show that the initial value of $p(0)$ is uniquely determined.

Steady State With $A = 0$

Let us first analyze the case in which there are no debt repurchases, that is, when $A = 0$ at all times.

The behavior of p and B is described in this case by equations (3) and (6):

$$Dp = (T/B).(p - 1), \tag{3}$$

$$DB = i.B - T, \ B > T/i = B^*. \tag{6}$$

The only steady state is for $p = 1$ and $B = B^*$. However, this steady state is not attainable since by assumption the initial stock of outstanding debt is $B > B^*$ and therefore, by (6), B will grow without bounds. We will show, however, that there is an initial value of $p(0)$ consistent with a constant market value of outstanding debt equal to the present value of cash payments being made by the debtor country, that is, $Z^* = T/i = p(t).B(t)$ for all t. To show this, we use (3) and (6) to obtain the differential equation describing the behavior of $Z(t)$:

$$\begin{aligned} DZ/Z &= Dp/p + DB/B \\ &= (T/Z).(p - 1) + i - p.T/Z \\ DZ/Z &= i - T/Z. \end{aligned} \tag{7}$$

Equation (7) has a stationary state at $Z^* = T/i$ and is dynamically unstable. Under rational expectations this means that only the value $Z(t) = Z^*$ for all t is consistent with market equilibrium. This means that at all times it will be $p(t) = Z^*/Bt$. In particular, at $t = 0$, the initial value of $p(0)$ is determined by $p(0) = Z^*/B(0) = T/i.B(0)$.

Over time B grows at the rate $DB/B = i.T/B$ and p grows at the rate $Dp/p = (T/B).(p - 1)$. Since at all times $p.B = T/i$, it is easy to see that the sum of both growth rates is equal to zero at all times. The stationary state solution $Z = Z^*$ is therefore feasible and consistent with the equations describing the behavior of p and B.

We conclude that in the absence of debt repurchases, the equilibrium market price of outstanding debt is determined by the condition that the market value of the outstanding debt be equal to the present value of all future cash payments by the debtor country. If those payments are not enough to pay the full contractual interest, the outstanding stock of debt will be growing over time, and p will be falling at exactly the negative of the growth rate in B.

Figure 1 describes the equilibrium when $A = 0$. The locus $DB = 0$ is represented by the vertical line at $B = B^* = T/i$ and the locus $Dp = 0$ is the horizontal line at $p = 1$. The arrows indicate the direction of the motion of p and B that follows from the differential equations (3) and (6). The rectangular hyperbola $p = T/i.B$ represents the unique balanced growth path consistent with the rational expectations trajectory for p and B.

Figure 1. *Market Equilibrium without Buy-Backs*

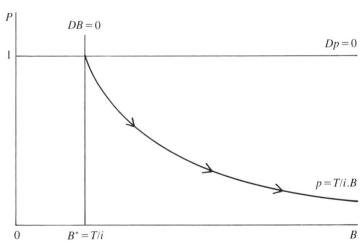

Assume now the debtor country is granted a gift of $A > 0$ per unit of time to be applied exclusively for debt repurchases at market prices. The gift is supposed to remain in effect as long as $B > B^*$. The dynamic behavior of p and B is now described by equations (3) and (4).

$$Dp = (T/B).(p - 1), \tag{3}$$

$$DB = i.B - T - A/p. \tag{4}$$

To the extent that $A > 0$ there is a stationary state at the values $p = 1$ and $Ba = (T + A)/i > B^*$. Figure 2 shows the face diagram for the case $A > 0$. It is easy to see that the stationary state at $(1, Ba)$ is unstable, meaning that no initial pair of $p(0)$ and $B(0)$ will converge to it other than the pair $(1, Ba)$. Such a stationary state is consistent with rational expectations only if by chance $B(0) - Ba$.

Notice that $B(0) = Ba$ implies $i.B(0) - T = A$ and therefore a stationary state at $(1, Ba)$ will only be feasible if the amount of cash devoted to buy-backs is exactly identical to the initial amount of unpaid interest.

If $B^* < B(0) < Ba$, there is a unique rational expectations solution for which $p(t) = 1$ for all t. For $B(0)$, as drawn in Figure 2, any $p(0)$ different from unity will lead to p rising or falling without bound or, alternatively, to the stock of debt reaching B^* at a time when p differs from unity. These trajectories are ruled out under rational expectations because as B reaches B^* it is required that $p = 1$. If at that moment p differs from 1, it would have to jump up to that level, and this is ruled out under the

Figure 2. *Market Equilibrium with Buy-Backs*

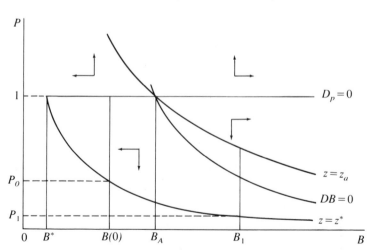

assumption of rational expectations since it would imply an anticipated infinite rate of return for that instant.

The equilibrium trajectory, therefore, requires $p = 1$ and B gradually falling along the $DP = 0$ line. As B reaches B^*, A becomes zero and the $DB = 0$ schedule reverses to the vertical line at $B = B^*$. The steady state for the new system is at $(1, B^*)$, which is exactly where both p and B happen to be at that time. As required for a rational expectations path, there are no jumps in the price of debt at the time that the cash buy-backs end.

Assume now that A is less than the amount of unpaid interest at time 0. In that case initial debt must be greater than Ba. Such a level is indicated as $B1$ in Figure 2. In the absence of buy-backs, the market price of $B1$ would have been $p1 = T/i.B1$, along the $Z = Z^*$ rectangular hyperbola. It can be seen that there is no initial value of $p(0)$ such that it will converge to unity in the exact time that $B1$ converges to B^*. This means that for the actual levels of A and $B1$, the debt repurchase strategy is not feasible, in the sense that debt cannot be reduced to the self-sustainable level B^* along a rational expectations path. If, however, A is to remain at its present level forever (of course one would wonder why it should), the rational expectations equilibrium would imply that p and B move along the rectangular hyperbola described by the locus $Z = Za = (T + A)/i$. This means that p will jump from the level $Z^*/B1$ to the higher level $Za/B1$. The absolute increase in p as a consequence of the announcement of the $A > 0$ policy is then $A/i.B1$; that is, p rises by the capitalized amount of the new money available for buy-backs. After the initial rise, p starts falling as B rises, both moving along the $Z = Za$ locus. Eventually p will again reach the level it had before the announcement of the buy-back policy.

We conclude that the only buy-back policy able to bring debt to the sustainable level, under rational expectations, is one in which the amount of money devoted every period for debt repurchase is larger than the amount of interest being rolled over. It is also the case that under this policy all debt repurchases will have to be made at par. If the unpaid interest is rolled over, there is no debt forgiveness whatsoever although countries are allowed to repurchase their excess debt at market prices. If debt is finally reduced to the sustainable level, the excess debt would have been bought at par. If the amount of cash buy-backs is not sufficient to bring debt back to the sustainable level, the market price of debt will rise in response to the capitalized value of the cash devoted to the buy-back, but it will eventually fall below the pre-buy-back level as debt keeps accumulating.

Our conclusion that cash buy-backs of outstanding debt may not represent any long-run advantage to the debtor country reflects the model in which it was derived. Not only have we assumed perfect foresight and rational expectations, but we also assumed that the buy-back policy is openly announced. This implies that title owners can discount the fact that all of their titles, actual and forthcoming, will be quoted at par eventually, if the policy is to be successful in bringing debt back to the sustainable level. This leads to the only feasible alternative under rational expectations, implying that all debt titles start being quoted at par from the very moment the buy-back policy is announced.

Myopic Expectations With Respect to Buy-Backs

An alternative view is that all buy-backs are considered to be the last one by titleholders. At the limit, if the market is totally myopic with respect to the buy-back policy, titleholders will not consider that $A > 0$ will remain in the future and in consequence will sell their assets along the $Z = Z^*$ curve in Figure 2. The market price of outstanding debt will only rise gradually as the stock of debt is reduced by the continued purchases. In this limiting case, the total amount of cash payments necessary to recover the excess debt will be the area under the $Z = Z^*$ curve between B^* and $B(0)$ plus the value of the accumulated amount of rolled-over interest during the period. The length of the period required to repurchase the debt in turn depends on the rate of cash buy-backs and the initial stock of excess debt.

The length of the period required to repurchase the excess debt under the myopic assumption can be calculated in the following manner.

First solve for $B(t)$ from (4) after substituting $p(t) = T/i.B(t)$. Defining $x = (A/T) - 1$, the solution for $B(t)$ is

$$B(t) = - (B^*/x) + [B(0) + B^*/x].\exp(-ixt). \tag{8}$$

Equating $B(t)$ in (8) to B^* we can compute the length of time required to complete the purchase of the excess debt, t^*.

$$t^* = (1/ix).Ln.[(1 + x)/(1 + x.B(0)/B^*)]. \tag{9}$$

There will be a positive solution for t^* only if $1 + x.B(0)/B^* > 0$, a condition that implies that debt repurchases are larger than unpaid interest.

The present value of cash expenditures is therefore:

$$PV = (A/i).[1 - \exp(-it^*)] = (1 + x).B^*.[1 - \exp(-it^*)]. \tag{10}$$

Consider now the limiting case where $x = - B^*/B(0)$ for which t^* tends to infinity. This is the case where the debt that can be bought by A, at the going market price of $p = T/i.B(0)$, is exactly equal to the amount of interest being rolled over. With fully rational expectations, p will jump to 1, and the debt will remain forever at $B(0)$. With myopic expectations regarding the $A > 0$ policy, as A tends to this level, the stock of debt also tends to B^* as t^* tends to infinity and the present value of cash payments tends to

$$PV \rightarrow PV^* = (1 - B^*/B(0)).B^* = [B(0) - B^*].[B^*/B(0)]. \qquad (11)$$

The present value of cash payments per unit of debt bought, $PV^*(p)$, is therefore the ratio of PV^* to $[B(0) - B^*]$:

$$PV^*(p) = B^*/B(0),$$

which is identical to the initial price prevailing just before the debt repurchase plan was to be announced.

The above means that with myopic expectations regarding future cash buy-backs, a policy of the minimum feasible cash buy-back will in fact repurchase all the excess debt (in infinite time) at an actual net present value identical to the market value of the existing excess debt prevailing the instant before the buy-back policy is announced. It would be fully equivalent (in present value terms) to an agreement to purchase all the excess debt at the current market price (equal to $B^*/B(0)$).

The former transaction, however, could never be duplicated in practice with a single repurchase offer for the total stock of excess debt at the current price since the price will immediately jump to unity. Such an offer would imply that the debtor loses the informational advantage he had thanks to the myopic expectations assumed on the part of the holders of debt.

II. Cash Buy-Backs Without Rollover of Unpaid Interest

In what follows we will assume that unpaid interest is simply forgiven instead of being rolled over. This would be a natural outcome under bankruptcy laws of most countries if the debtor is in fact bankrupt. It may also come about as a consequence of an agreement with the country's creditors in which they accept a settlement freezing the level of the debt in exchange for a fixed payment per period. To make the analysis relevant we assume that the fixed payment per period (T) is not enough to serve the existing stock of debt (Bo) at competitive interest (i).

It is assumed that the country, in addition to the fixed payment of T dollars per unit of time, can also devote A dollars per unit of time to debt repurchase at market prices. As before we will assume that $A > 0$ whenever $i.B > T$ (and $A = 0$ otherwise).

The following equations describe the dynamic behavior of the market price and the outstanding stock of debt.

$$Dp = i.p - (T/B),\tag{12}$$

(derived from (1) setting the second term in the RHS equal to 0, since there is no rollover of interest)

$$DB = -(A/p).\tag{13}$$

If cash buy-backs are zero, equation (13) is substituted for $DB = 0$. With $A = 0$, the stock of debt remains at $B(t) = B(0)$ and the rational expectations solution for p is $p(t) = T/i.B(0)$ at all times.

Figure 3 shows the dynamic configuration described by equations (12) and (13) for $A > 0$. There is only one steady state at $B = B^* = T/i$ and $p = 1$. The system has saddle path stability and the rational expectation solution lies along the saddle path, denoted by the dotted curve SS in Figure 3.

Before the announcement of the buy-back policy, the initial equilibrium was at the intersection of the $Dp = 0$ line and the initial stock of debt $B(0)$. Also, DB was equal to zero at all times.

With the announcement of the $A > 0$ policy, DB becomes negative and the unique solution under rational expectations requires a jump in

Figure 3. *Market Equilibrium without Rollover of Unpaid Interest*

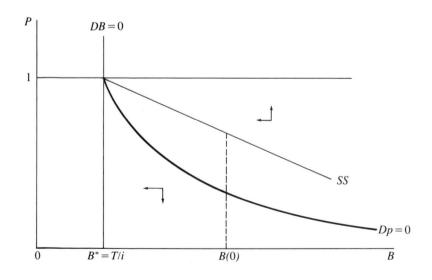

p to the corresponding level along the saddle path. After the initial jump in p, both p and B move along the saddle path toward the long-run equilibrium at $(1, B^*)$.

The lower the rate of debt repurchase, A, the closer will the saddle path be to the $Dp = 0$ line, and therefore the smaller will be the initial jump in p at the moment the policy is announced. Nevertheless, for any $A > 0$, both p and B eventually converge to the long-run equilibrium $(1, B^*)$.

In the limit, as A grows smaller, the saddle path approaches the $Dp = 0$ line and all purchases are made at the price indicated by this line (or infinitely close to it). The undiscounted sum of cash disbursements will approach the area under the $Dp = 0$ curve; this area can be calculated as follows.

Denote the area under the $Dp = 0$ curve between B^* and $B(0)$ by Cmin. We can see by integration of $p = T/iB = B^*/B$ that:

$$Cmin. = B^*.Ln.(B(0)/B^*).$$

Consider a situation in which $B(0) = 2B^*$ so that initially p was equal to .50. In this case the Cmin. equals $0.693 \cdot (B(0) - B^*)$. This means that as the rate of cash buy-backs tends to zero, the excess debt can be retired for a total cash expenditure that tends to 69.3 percent of its face value. The actual present value of disbursements, however, will also depend on how long it actually does take to do the operation. As A grows smaller, not only does the undiscounted sum of required cash disbursements fall, but also the required time over which that sum is uniformly spent rises. On both counts, the net present value of the cash disbursements tends to fall.

It can be formally shown that as A tends to zero, the net present value of the disbursement also tends to zero. This means that in the limit, all of the excess debt could be retired for a zero investment in terms of its net present value. Intuitively, this result can be illustrated as follows:

The present value (PV) of a constant rate of purchases A during a period of time t, is:

$$PV = (A/i).[1 - \exp(-it)].$$

Multiplying and dividing the RHS by t, and defining $C = A.t$ as the undiscounted sum of disbursements, PV becomes

$$PV = (C/i).[1 - \exp(-it)]/t.$$

We know that as A becomes smaller, C falls towards Cmin. and t tends to infinity. It is easy to see, therefore, that as A goes to zero, so also does PV.[1]

The country, therefore, faces a trade-off between the present value of the cost of retiring its excess debt and the time required to do it.

III. Conclusions

The main result of this paper, in the case in which unpaid interest is rolled over, is that a strategy of announced debt repurchases at market prices, under competitive conditions and rational expectations, is not bound to help debtor countries to recover all their excess debt at prices below par value. Only when debt holders are myopic with respect to future debt repurchases can a strategy be devised by which all the excess debt is repurchased at a price equal, in present value, to that one prevailing before the policy was announced.

If unpaid interest is forgiven, a case that may happen if an agreement is reached by which debtor countries pay only a stipulated fixed amount per unit of time (e.g., a fraction of the trade surplus or exports), any constant rate of debt repurchases will succeed in bringing debt down to that sustainable level where the fixed payment equals the service at competitive interest. However, the present value of those purchases falls as the rate of purchase decreases. There is therefore a trade-off between the present value of the cost of repurchasing the excess debt and the time required for the debt to be quoted at par.

We have only analyzed the competitive case, in which creditors are not faced with noncompetitive offers of the "take it or leave it" type. All bids for debt repurchase are assumed to be competitively made and openly announced.

Many strategies of debt repurchase other than those presented here can surely be found. This paper offers what can be considered to be the competitive frame of reference, within which the other alternatives can be compared and evaluated.

---

[1] From the integration of (12) and (13) and the condition that at the time t^* when $B(t^*) = B^*$ it must be $p(t^*) = 1$, we can derive the saddle path, as well as the value of t^* and of PV. In particular, the present value of any rate of purchases A over the amount of time required to retire all the excess debt is given by:

$$PV = B^*.q.\{1 - (1 + q).[q + (B(0)/B^*)^{\wedge}((1 + q)/q)]^{(-1)}\},$$

where $q = (A/T)$. It can be seen that as q (and A) tends to zero, PV also tends to zero. Similarly, as q tends to infinity, implying that all the excess debt is rescued instantaneously, PV tends to the value $B(0) - B^*$, meaning that all the debt is retired at par value.

Mexican Debt Exchange: Lessons and Issues

DAVID FOLKERTS-LANDAU and CARLOS ALFREDO RODRIGUEZ*

Mexico undertook its first debt-exchange program—an exchange of discounted restructured loan debt for new bonds with improved debt-service characteristics—in early 1988. The rate at which old restructured debt was exchanged for the new bonds was determined in an auction; this note analyzes the outcome of the auction and the valuation of the new bonds with a simple asset pricing model and data from the secondary market for restructured loans.

D EBTOR COUNTRIES that experience unexpected changes in current or anticipated cash flows[1] may find it beneficial to modify the stream of debt service payments mandated under existing contractual debt obligations by exchanging outstanding debt for new debt with different debt service characteristics. Such a voluntary debt exchange, frequently employed in U.S. capital markets, offers the debtor the opportunity to match the contractual stream of debt service payments more closely with current and anticipated cash flows. In addition, the debtor can affect a buy-back of outstanding debt at market prices, by issuing credit-enhanced, that is, collateralized, debt in return for outstanding debt.

These considerations led Mexico to undertake its first debt-exchange program in early 1988. Under this program, Mexico was prepared to

* Mr. Folkerts-Landau is the Assistant Division Chief of the Financial Studies Division of the Research Department. He is a graduate of Harvard University and holds a doctorate from Princeton University. He was an Assistant Professor of Economics and Finance in the Graduate School of Business, University of Chicago, before joining the International Monetary Fund.

Mr. Rodriguez is a staff member of the Argentine Center for the Study of Macroeconomics (CEMA) in Buenos Aires.

[1] Such cash-flow variations may arise with changes in the country's trade balance or external financial flows.

issue up to $10 billion of a new negotiable bond debt in exchange for rescheduled bank debt. The bond obligations were to have a higher coupon than recently rescheduled bank debt, and the bond principal was to be fully collateralized. The rate at which old restructured debt was exchanged for the new bond obligations was determined in an auction in which banks tendered restructured loans for new bonds at specified ratios and amounts. In the event, Mexico issued $2.6 billion of the new bonds in exchange for $3.7 billion of restructured bank debt.

This note analyzes the outcome of the auction with a simple asset pricing model which relies on data from the secondary market for restructured bank loans to obtain a valuation of the new bond obligations. By comparing the predicted prices for the new bond obligations with actual prices prevailing in the secondary market for the new bonds since the auction, it is possible to obtain an indication of the validity of the model and of the efficiency of the secondary market for bank debt of indebted developing countries. We then compare the debt exchange to cash buy-backs and raise some general issues associated with the securitization of external debt.

I. Debt Exchange Program

Mexico was prepared to issue up to $10 billion of 20-year marketable international bonds to its bank creditors at a spread of 1⅝ percent above the 6-month London Interbank Offered Rate (LIBOR—double the spread on rescheduled Mexican bank debt), payable semiannually. The new bond will be amortized in a single payment at the end of 20 years (corresponding to the maturity of eligible rescheduled bank debt), but will have call provisions permitting earlier amortization at the discretion of the Mexican authorities. The new bond obligations are listed on the Luxembourg Stock Exchange and are traded and cleared through the Eurobond market system. They are fully marketable on issuance subject to normal Euromarket practices. Any tranche of the new bond obligations issued within the United States will be on a private placement basis and may be traded in the private placement market in the United States, but the issue will not be registered with the Securities and Exchange Commission (SEC) under the U.S. Securities Act and thus cannot be publicly offered or traded in the United States.

In addition to a higher interest spread, the principal of the new bond is collateralized with a nonmarketable foreign series zero-coupon U.S. Treasury security maturing in 20 years. The zero-coupon collateral is held in escrow by the Federal Reserve Bank of New York in the form of a book entry. The actual face value of the zero-coupon U.S. Treasury security was determined once the volume and price of bank claims to be exchanged became known, while the amount of Mexican foreign exchange reserves required to purchase the zero coupon bonds depended on the prevailing market interest rates.

Bank debt eligible to be included in the program consisted of claims under the 1985 debt restructuring agreement and the 1983 and 1984 credit agreements, but the 1986/87 new money package, short-term credits, and private sector debt are excluded. The total eligible volume was estimated at about $53 billion.

Before the exchange could take place, the sharing procedures relating to prepayment of loans, the pari passu clauses relating to the priority ranking of payments, and the negative pledge clauses under existing agreements all had to be waived. Since the restructuring agreements covering the eligible debt permitted such waivers to be based on the simple majority of the eligible bank exposure to Mexico, only 50 banks, compared with about 500 banks that originally signed these documents, were needed to amend some 92 loan agreements. Negative pledge clauses contained in the agreement with the World Bank and the Inter-American Development Bank also were waived. To avoid negative pledge problems with other holders of existing Mexican bonds, these international bonds would have had to have their creditworthiness similarly enhanced.[2] The new bonds carry a pari passu clause that requires them to be treated on similar terms as all other external debt including obligations to international organizations, such as the Fund.

II. Pricing New Bond Obligations

The basic assumption of the valuation model is that the banks holding Mexican obligations are risk neutral. This assumption implies that the market value of Mexican debt will equal the expected present value of principal and interest payments. We assume there exist two states of the world.[3] In the first state, the debt service payments are made in full; in the second state no debt service payments are made. If the probabilities that interest and principal are paid in full are denoted by π_1 and π_2, respectively, then the market value of Mexican debt of N period maturity,

---

[2] The credit enhancement of Mexico's outstanding international bonds is estimated to have cost about $100 million.

[3] Since bank creditors are assumed to be risk neutral, the specifications of the probability model for debt service payments affect the valuation only through expected values. Hence, we can simplify the exposition without loss of generality by assuming that only two states can occur.

face value of FV, and an interest spread of s percent above r_i, the LIBOR expected to prevail in period i, will be given by:

$$MV = \pi_1 \sum_{i=1}^{N} \frac{(r_i + s)}{R_i} + \pi_2 \frac{FV}{R_N} , \tag{1}$$

where $R_i = \prod_{j=1}^{i} (1 + r_j)$.

Since LIBOR is the banks' cost of funds, it is used as a discount rate for the expected debt service payments. The bonds that are being priced are floating-rate obligations, that is, the coupon is reset at regular intervals by adding a spread to the then prevailing LIBOR. The forward LIBOR rates r_i, used for discounting, are obtained by adding a constant spread to the forward interest rates extracted from the zero-coupon U.S. Treasury obligations, with the spread equal to the anticipated difference between the U.S. Treasury obligations and LIBOR.[4] Since payments can be designated arbitrarily as payments for interest or principal, by the debtor as well as creditor, when such payments fall short of full contractual requirement payments, we can assume that $\pi_1 = \pi_2 = \pi$.

We can solve for $\pi(=\pi_1 = \pi_2)$ in equation (1)

$$\pi = \frac{MV}{\sum_{i=1}^{N} \frac{(r_i + s)}{R_i} + \frac{FV}{R_N}} , \tag{2}$$

where $R_i = \prod_{j=1}^{i} (1 + r_j)$.

Since principal payments of the new bonds are guaranteed, we set $\pi_2 = 1$, while $\pi_1 = \pi$. Thus, given the spread above LIBOR on the new bond as $2s$, the market value of the new bonds will equal:

$$MV^* = \pi \sum_{i=1}^{N} \frac{(r_i + 2s)}{R_i} + \frac{FV}{R_N} , \tag{3}$$

where $R_i = \prod_{j=1}^{i} (1 + r_j)$.

An alternative, but equivalent, method of pricing the new bond is to assume that the discount rate applied to the uncertain interest and principal payments is equal to the internal rate of return (IRR) that equates the contractual debt service payments with the observed market value, that is,

$$MV = \sum_{i=1}^{N} \frac{(r_i + s)}{(1 + \rho)^i} + \frac{FV}{(1 + \rho)^i} . \tag{4}$$

[4] This is the so-called TED (U.S. Treasury Eurodollar) spread.

Since the principal payments of the new bonds are certain, the bonds will be valued in this model at:

$$MV^{**} = \sum_{i=1}^{N} \frac{(r_i + 2s)}{(1 + \rho)^i} + \frac{FV}{(1 + r_\rho)^N},$$ (5)

where $\rho(\text{IRR})$ is the discount rate for interest and principal payments.

The valuation model developed above relies on four assumptions. *First, Mexico's ability to service external debt has increased* by the amount necessary to pay for the collateralization of principal. In the case at hand, the increase in Mexico's foreign exchange reserves prior to the debt exchange is thought to justify this assumption. If instead Mexico's ability to service external debt had remained unchanged, the increase in expected payment of principal would merely have reduced the expected payment of interest, and collateralization would be ineffective.

Second, investors' assessment of the probability of debt service payments being made in full has not changed as a result of the assumed increase in its ability to make such payments.[5] This assumption is clearly valid only as long as the share of debt service payments that is collateralized does not become large relative to total debt service payments.

Third, investors perceive the likelihood of interest payments being made on the new secured debt to be the same as the likelihood of interest payments being made on outstanding rescheduled bank loans (that is, the new bond obligations are not perceived to be senior claims).

Fourth, arbitrage will ensure that yields on unsecured restructured bank loans and unsecured bonds of equal structure (coupon, maturity) will be equalized in the secondary markets (in particular, once the stock of secured bonds outstanding reaches a significant proportion of the stock of syndicated loans outstanding).[6]

---

[5] For an analysis of how debt conversions might affect the probability of debt service payments see Michael P. Dooley, "Buy-Backs, Debt-Equity Swaps, Asset Exchanges, and Market Prices of External Debt," above.

[6] Negotiability of the bond debt instrument by itself would tend to reduce its yield because of larger institutional demand and increased liquidity, but negotiability may also reduce the ability of the creditors to enforce the bond contract, and this would tend to raise yields. In the case at hand, the enforceability of negotiable bond contracts may well be significantly worse than that of the existing syndicated loan contract. The bank syndicates, with the backing of financial authorities concerned about systemic financial problems arising from the erosion of bank capital, generally have a greater ability to increase the likelihood of debt service than bondholder councils. We assume that the combined effects on yield of negotiability and enforceability will offset each other. Finally, the possibilities of exiting from credible new money obligations by exchanging syndicated bank debt for negotiable collateralized bonds might act to increase the attractiveness of the new bonds to some banks, thus permitting a lower yield to be offered initially.

III. Auction Outcome

In January 1988, 20-year floating-rate Mexican restructured debt had a coupon of about 8.75 percent (LIBOR was 7.94 percent), a spread of $^{13}/_{16}$ percent, and traded at a discount of about 50 percent (yield-to-maturity of 18.2 percent). A 50 percent discount suggested that the expected present value of total debt service payments on a bank loan of $100 face value was $50 (equal to its market value). The prevailing LIBOR of 7.94 percent implied that the present value (PV) of full principal repayment and full interest payment was $21.70 and $86.31, respectively.[7] The credit market's view about the probability of full payment being made on the outstanding bank loans is equal to the ratio of the market value of the old restructured bank loans and can be obtained from equation (2), that is, as the ratio of the market value of the restructured loans to the present value of its total contractual payments (0.463). The expected PV of principal and interest payments were then $10.05 and $39.95, respectively, totaling to a market value of $50.

The new bond was to have a coupon of LIBOR + 1.625 percent (about 9.56 percent in February 1988), and principal repayment was secured with a zero-coupon bond of equal face value. The present value of principal repayment was $21.70, and the present value of interest payments was $94.32 on $100 face value of the new bond. Collateralization of principal implied that the expected present value of principal payment was equal to the PV of full principal payment, $21.70. Hence, the expected value of the interest payments on the new bonds was $43.65, and the predicted market value of the new bond, that is, the sum of the expected value of principal and interest payments, was $65.35; or equivalently, the predicted market discount on the new bond was 34.65 percent. The relatively higher market value and yield of the new bond obligations compared with restructured bank loans are the result of the higher coupon and the collateralization of principal repayment.

The amount of outstanding bank debt that could be expected to be offered in exchange for a given amount of new secured debt can be calculated from the predicted market discounts on these two types of debt. In particular, the market discount of 50 percent on restructured bank loans and the predicted discount of 34.65 percent on the new collateralized bond suggested that an average of $1.31 of face value of the old syndicated loans would be offered for $1 of face value of the new

---

[7] The present value is computed using the currently prevailing LIBOR as discount rate, instead of using the rates implied in the term-structure as indicated in equation (1).

secured debt. If the entire proposed $10 billion of new bond obligations were issued, the reduction in total indebtedness would have been $3.1 billion. The higher the market discount on old bank loans, the larger the amount of syndicated loans that was offered in exchange for a given amount of secured debt and greater the reduction in total indebtedness for various assumptions about the magnitude of the market discount of syndicated loans.

The reduction in market discounts and in total indebtedness made possible with the collateralization of principal was limited by the fact that at the prevailing nominal U.S. dollar interest rate levels, the PV of interest payments on debt of 20-year maturity was about 80 percent of the PV of all payments, while the PV of principal was only about 20 percent of all payments.

The Mexican auction was completed on February 26, 1988, with 139 banks making bids covering $6.7 billion in restructured debt. Mexico accepted bids from 95 banks for $3.7 billion in claims. Among successful tenders, Japanese banks offered the largest amount followed by U.S. and Canadian banks. Only two or three money-center banks participated out of about 30 U.S. banks that tended bids. These claims were exchanged for $2.6 billion in new bonds, at an average exchange rate of $1.42 of restructured debt for $1 of new bond obligations. Mexico's debt will be reduced immediately by $1.1 billion and contractual interest savings amount to about $65 million a year.

Mexico ranked accepted bids in descending order of bid ratio (amount of eligible debt tended in exchange for new bonds) to maximize the amount of eligible debt retired, and the accepted bid was at the bank's bid ratio. The Mexican Government thus determined the amount and price at which such offers were accepted. The dispersion of bids was such that the highest bid was $2.08 and the lowest was $1.12 with about three quarters of bids concentrated in the range of $1.33 to $1.67. Within this band, most exchange offers lay between $1.44 and $1.54 of old bank debt per dollar of face value of the new bank debt. This dispersion in bid prices was the result of differing beliefs about the seniority of the new bonds and about the ability of the secondary market for restructured bank debt to absorb large amounts of debt.

The auction procedure adopted by Mexico thus made it possible for Mexico to accept bids in descending order of price down to its reservation price of $1.33 of old bank loans per dollar of new bonds and to achieve an average exchange rate of $1.42. According to the model developed above, Mexico's reservation or limit price of $1.33 of old bank debt per dollar of new bank loans corresponded closely to the discount of 50 percent then prevailing in the secondary market for restructured bank debt.[8] This type of auction thus made it possible for Mexico to accept only bids above the current market price and to exchange a modest amount of new collateralized bond debt at "better-than-market" terms for restructured bank debt.

IV. Market Valuation of New Bonds

Trading in the new bonds began shortly after the auction results were announced. Initially in April, the bid-ask spread for the price of the new bond with a face value of $100 ranged from $64 to $70. By July-August the bid-ask spread had narrowed, and transactions fell in the range of $62–68. The price of the new bond predicted by the model in March was about $65, while a higher LIBOR and lower price for restructured debt resulted in a lower predicted price of about $62 during the June-August 1988 period. Thus, the predicted value of the new bonds falls within the actual bid-ask range for the new bond (see Table 1).

The results in Table 1 appear to indicate that the simplified valuation model with risk-neutral investors and unchanging probabilities of debt service payments predicts the market value of the new bond reasonably well. The results also indicate that the secondary market for restructured bank loans and the market for the negotiable new bond obligations are being well arbitraged according to the valuation model employed above. Thus, the fact that the new bond is fully negotiable and not encumbered by the same kind of regulatory and fiscal constraints as are bank loans has not influenced the pricing very much. In other words, there appear to be no special features present in the market for bank loans that should lead us to doubt the usefulness of the prices observed in this market as indicators of country risk.

V. Comparison of Debt Exchanges With Cash Buy-Backs

As was shown above, a market discount of 50 percent on restructured loans (LIBOR of 7.9 percent) would on average result in $1.30 of restructured debt being exchanged for $1.00 of new bond obligations. If Mexico had bought about $2 billion of U.S. Treasury zero-coupon bonds as collateral for $10 billion of new bonds, then these new bonds could be exchanged for $13 billion of restructured loans. Since the new bonds would trade at a discount of about 35 percent, Mexico can buy back the

---

[8] The reservation price predicted was $1.31 of old bank debt per $1.00 of new bank debt.

Table 1. *Valuation of Restructured Bank Loans and Collateralized Bond Debt*

	Market Price of Restructured Bank Loans (In dollars per $100 of face value)	Market Price of New Bond Debt (In dollars per $100 of face value)	Predicted Price of New Bond Debt (In dollars per $100 of face value)	LIBOR (In percent)	Loan Coupon	Bond Coupon
March 1988	49–51	64–70	65	7.9	8.7	9.6
June 1988	48–50	63–68	63.8	8.5	9.3	10.1
August 1988	47–48	62–66	61	9	9.8	10.6

Source: *International Financing Review*, various issues.

new bonds with $6.5 billion of reserves. Thus Mexico would have retired $13 billion of restructured bank loans with a cost outlay of $8.5 billion, of which $2 billion are invested in the zero-coupon bonds. After selling the zero-coupon bond Mexico's net expenditure is $6.5 billion, that is, the same result as could have been achieved through a direct cash buy-back of restructured bank debt. Hence debt exchanges and cash buy-backs are equivalent in their economic outcome.

In actual fact, the collateralization of principal cost Mexico about $500 million in foreign exchange reserves, and Mexico recovered about $1.1 billion in par value of rescheduled bank debt. In addition, Mexico does not have to fulfill the obligation to pay $3.7 billion of old bank loans in 20 years since this payment is covered by the maturing U.S. Treasury zero-coupon bond. If the discount on old Mexican debt is 50 percent, then the market's expected present value of Mexico's promise to pay $3.7 billion of bank loan principal in 20 years is about $300 million. Thus, the net present cost to Mexico of reducing its nominal debt by $1.1 billion was about $200 million. A direct cash buy-back of $1.1 billion of old bank debt would have required $550 million of foreign reserves at the currently prevailing discount on bank loans of 50 percent. Thus, by accepting only bids offering more than $1.33 of old bank debt for $1 of new bond obligations, Mexico has been able to keep the average exchange ratio above the exchange ratio implied by the market discount of 50 percent of old bank debt, and hence was able to outperform a direct cash buy-back. If, however, Mexico had accepted a volume of bids sufficiently large that the average exchange ratio of old bank debt for new bonds coincided with the ratio implied by the prevailing market discount, the debt exchange would have been equivalent to a direct cash buy-back.

VI. Systemic Implications of the Mexican Debt Exchange

The systemic implications of the Mexican proposal derive almost entirely from the creation of a *liquid secondary market in the new bonds* with price quotations published daily in the financial press. For the first time since the 1920s, there exists a market for external obligations of a major developing country, which can provide continuous data on the market's assessment of Mexico's willingness to repay such obligations. Currently, Mexico's outstanding syndicated loans are being exchanged among banks (and some nonbank investors) attempting to modify their exposure, and the prices at which such exchanges take place are frequently thought to be distorted by the peculiarities of the participants, for example, tax considerations, absence of a significant number of nonbank participants, new money obligations, high transactions costs, and thin markets. Thus, while these prices undoubtedly reflect the banks' assessment of Mexico's creditworthiness, they have not attained the credibility and information content that are normally associated with Eurobond prices of major issuers.

Credible daily price quotations in the external obligations of a major debtor have three implications for the overall debtor-creditor relationship. First, the pricing of new money, in whatever form, will have to respect the price information available from secondary markets. It would, for example, expose the directors of U.S. banks to liability arising from shareholder suits if a bank participates in new money packages at interest rates significantly below those observable in the market for the new bonds (adjusted for the collateral).[9] If the new Mexican bond continues to trade at yields of about 18 percent, any new financing for Mexico will have to be at a cost of about 18 percent. Similarly, new money for other developing country debtors would have to be priced in relation to the yield on the Mexican bonds. The market pricing of the credit risk associated with developing country borrowers may in the long run lead to a more efficient allocation of credit.

Second, it is likely that the market prices of Mexico's external obligations will decline further from the level currently observed in the market for restructured loans. The yields currently obtainable in the U.S. high-yield corporate bond markets are generally in excess of 15 percent. The nonbank investors in the new Mexican bonds can be expected to ask for a yield in excess of U.S. corporate high-yield bonds because of the difficulty in claiming any residual assets. Therefore, to be competitive the new bond may well need to have a yield in excess of 20 percent in the absent of major policy adjustments. One reason why market prices of the external obligations of developing countries remained above those of high-yield corporate bonds is that the concentration of these obligations in the major banks gave these creditors greater influence over debtors than dispersed bondholders would have. However, the recent indication that bank holdings of developing country debt may be sold (e.g., Citicorp reserving) has already led to significant declines in market prices. For example, the price of Mexico's obligations fell from about 65 in April 1987 to 50 in January 1988.

---

[9] In particular, concern about shareholder suits forced Citicorp to postpone establishing reserves against its developing-country obligations until there was a clear deterioration of conditions (which was provided by Brazil's moratorium on interest payments).

Third, the implications for systemic stability of the banking system are largely positive. U.S. banks have nearly doubled their primary capital since 1982 and, with some exceptions, are able to cope with the implications of lower market prices of the external obligations of developing countries. The share prices of U.S. banks are thought to reflect the market value of banks' assets, rather than the book value of such assets. In any event, U.S. banks are being given an option to carry the new bonds at face value or to treat the bonds as a security and mark its value to market regularly. In the longer run, the ability to dispose of these assets, even at a substantial discount, may well serve to help the banking system to reduce its own cost of funds and thus improve its competitive position vis-à-vis the securities markets by reducing the amount of disintermediation that has taken place in recent years.

Thus the three systemic implications of the Mexican debt proposal are: (1) the cost of new financing for developing countries will be based on price information from bond markets; (2) further decline will occur in currently observable prices of syndicated loans; and (3) systemic stability in banking markets will improve. The Mexican proposal may therefore be regarded as the first step toward the system of development finance that existed before the 1930s, that is, development finance being provided through a broad-based bond market at risk-related yields, while collateralized trade finance is being provided by banks.

VII. Conclusion

According to the asset-pricing model employed in this paper, about $1.30 of restructured Mexican bank debt exchanges for $1.00 of the new Mexican bond. By accepting only bids of more than $1.30 of restructured bank loans for each $1.00 of the new bond, Mexico was able to exchange $2.6 billion of the new bond for $3.7 of restructured bank debt, that is, an average exchange rate of $1.40.

If Mexico had accepted a sufficient volume of bids so that the average exchange rate of restructured debt for the new bond had coincided with the equilibrium rate of $1.30, then the debt exchange would have been equivalent to a cash buy-back. That is, if the amount of foreign exchange needed to collateralize the new bond would have been used to buy back restructured debt at market prices, the reduction in external indebtedness would have been equivalent to the reduction achieved under the debt exchange.

The post-auction market valuation of the new Mexican bond obligation appears to be broadly in line with the observed prices for restructured bank debt according to the asset-pricing model with risk-neutral investors. Since the new bonds are fully negotiable Eurobonds, we conclude that prices observed in the secondary market for bank loans are not greatly distorted by special features of bank loans arising from their non-negotiability and regulatory or fiscal considerations.

Marked-to-Market Interest Rate Swaps: A Solution to the Interest Rate Risk Management Problem of Indebted Developing Countries

DAVID FOLKERTS-LANDAU*

Indebted developing countries have been prevented from hedging their exposure to volatility in short-term international interest rates by a lack of creditworthiness, a shortage of international reserves, and a lack of financial expertise. This paper uses the conventional interest rate swap contract—a contract between two parties to exchange a fixed payment stream for a floating payment stream without an exchange of principal—to construct an interest rate risk management tool that can overcome these difficulties. The proposed swap contract aims to reduce the credit risk borne by the counterparty in the swap transactions by shortening the performance period of the country through periodic resettlement of capital gains and losses on the existing swap contract combined with a recontracting at the prevailing market swap rate.

INDEBTED DEVELOPING COUNTRIES have been prevented from hedging their exposure to volatility in short-term international interest rates by a lack of creditworthiness, a shortage of international reserves, and a lack of financial expertise. This paper develops a risk management technique aimed at overcoming these difficulties.

The past ten years have seen a historically high volatility of financial yields. This development has led to increased emphasis on managing fi-

* Mr. Folkerts-Landau is the Assistant Division Chief of the Financial Studies Division of the Research Department. He is a graduate of Harvard University and holds a doctorate from Princeton University. He was an Assistant Professor of Economics and Finance in the Graduate School of Business, University of Chicago, before joining the International Monetary Fund.

nancial risk, that is, the risk of loss arising from open financial positions. Such open positions arise largely in the form of mismatched receipts and payments, as might occur in indebted developing countries, for example, when short-term financing is used for longer-term investment or when receipts and payments are denominated in different currencies. Financial risk assumes an added dimension when the country faces the possibility of illiquidity or default in the event of unfavorable movements in interest or exchange rates.

Active risk management has become an important element of financial management in most industrial countries. Efforts to deal with increased volatility of financial yields has led participants in the major financial markets to resort to the use of a large variety of hedging instruments and techniques. Most notable in this regard has been the increased use of financial contingent contracts, such as financial futures, forward, and options contracts, and such new contracts as interest rate and exchange rate swaps.[1] In some instances the underlying market value of trades in these contracts has come to exceed that of the underlying instruments.[2]

Indebted developing countries have been particularly adversely affected by the increased volatility of financial yields. First, the interest charges on external obligations of developing countries, which frequently constitute a large fraction of their external financing requirement, are indexed to short-term international interest rates, such as three- or six-month LIBOR or U.S. Treasury bill rates.[3] Since the timing and magnitude of variations in terms of trade or in receipts from investment projects have not generally coincided with variations in short-term index rates, the indebted developing countries have experienced a significant increase in financial risk.

Second, a lack of creditworthiness and of international reserves, as well as a lack of financial expertise, have severely limited the choice of risk-management instruments and techniques available to such countries. Indebted developing countries, particularly those with rescheduled debt, have generally been unable to refinance their floating-rate debt in the international fixed-rate debt markets.[4] The countries have, there-

---

[1] Financial hedging instruments (financial futures, forward, options and swap contracts) are contingent contracts entitling holders to payments that are conditional on the outcome of future interest rates.

[2] See M. Watson and others (1988).

[3] The LIBOR increase of about 3 percentage points over the past two years has resulted in increases in interest payments by indebted developing countries in excess of $5 billion annually.

[4] As has been noted elsewhere (e.g., Stiglitz and Weiss (1981)), some financial markets, in particular the market for bank loans and interbank funds, exclude

fore, been limited to hedging their interest rate exposure in the derivative markets.[5] Considerations of creditworthiness have denied indebted developing countries the use of forward interest rate contracts, such as forward rate agreements and interest rate swaps. Such contingent contracts generally require the indebted developing country to make unsecured payments on future dates and hence contain an element of credit risk. Furthermore, the lack of foreign exchange has limited the use of options contracts, such as interest rate caps, the purchase of which requires payment of an up-front premium. Such options entitle the country to receive payments should interest rates rise above a predetermined level. Finally, although the use of exchange-traded financial futures, such as the LIBOR futures contract, has not been much hampered by consideration of creditworthiness, which has been minimized through certain institutional arrangements, nor by lack of foreign exchange resources, it has nevertheless been severely restrained by the unavailability of liquid futures contracts with delivery dates extending into the medium term, that is, from 18 to 60 months. The absence of a sufficiently liquid market for medium-term futures contracts makes it necessary to sell and buy actively short-term futures to approximate the results of a medium-term hedge[6] through a stacking or sequencing of short-term contracts. The requisite financial expertise and the mechanisms to monitor delegated trading authority required for the management of the short-term futures positions designed for medium-term interest rate hedges are not yet readily available in most indebted developing countries. Furthermore, it is doubtful that the institutional framework necessary to support the acquisition and growth of such financial expertise can be created in the near future.

Thus, although most of the interest cost of the external obligations of indebted developing countries are tied to increasingly volatile short-term international interest rates, such countries have not been able to undertake active medium-term interest rate risk management, despite the benefits that greater interest rate certainty would have for the imple-

---

borrowers whose perceived credit risk exceeds a certain level, rather than demand a correspondingly higher risk premium. Such credit rationing behavior is readily apparent not only in international bank lending to developing countries but also in the markets for hedging instruments that expose bank intermediaries to credit risk (see Folkerts-Landau (1985)). The direct debt markets appear to be better able to price credit risk, as, for example, in the so-called noninvestment grade, that is, junk bond market.

[5] Indeed, such limitations have led to the inclusion of a short-term international interest rate index as contingent variable in the Fund's recently established compensatory and contingent financing facility.

[6] See *Managing Financial Risks in Indebted Developing Countries*, IMF Occasional Paper, 1989 (forthcoming).

mentation of medium-term adjustment programs or debt rescheduling agreements undertaken by indebted developing countries.[7]

This paper uses the conventional interest rate swap contract—a contract between two parties to exchange a fixed payment stream for a floating payment stream without an exchange of principal—to construct an interest rate risk management tool that can overcome a lack of creditworthiness and a lack of international reserves without making undue demands on the financial expertise of such countries. The proposed contract is designed to open up to indebted developing countries the possibility of achieving a period of desired length during which interest rates on external obligations remain fixed. It achieves this aim by reducing the credit risk borne by the counterparty in the swap transactions. This reduction is accomplished by shortening the performance period of the country through periodic resettlement of capital gains and losses on the existing swap contract combined with a recontracting at the prevailing market swap rate.[8] Furthermore, since interest rate swap contracts extend into the medium-term without requiring active management or an initial premium outlay, it is possible to avoid the problems associated with the lack of international reserves and of financial expertise. As is the case with futures contracts, however, the resettlement mechanism, while not demanding an increase in total cash outlays in present value terms, nevertheless requires cash-flow management over the period of the swap contract.

The great depth and liquidity of the interest rate swap market, estimated at $1.5 trillion of notional principal outstanding,[9] would comfortably permit a large-scale use of the proposed swap contract by indebted developing countries if the solutions to the various technical problem advanced in this paper are accepted by market participants.

Section I of this paper discusses the factors that prevent indebted developing countries from making more extensive use of the conventional interest hedging risk instruments (futures and forward contracts, conventional swap contracts, and options contracts). Section II discusses the proposed risk management instrument and its intended use. Section III addresses some additional problems and summarizes the paper.

[7] For a theoretical discussion of the general benefits of reduced risk for developing countries, see R. Brignoli and L. Seigel, "The Role of Noise in LDC Growth," presented at Roundtable Conference on Trends in International Capital Markets, Oxford, 1988.

[8] This recontracting and resettlement methodology has been successfully employed to eliminate the credit risk from short-dated futures contracts (see below).

[9] Estimate provided by the International Swap Dealers Association. Notional principal refers to the notional amount on which swap payments are based. The notional principal in an interest rate swap is never paid or received.

I. Impediments to Market-Based Interest Rate Risk Management by Indebted Developing Countries

Although it is generally recognized that active management of interest rate risk by indebted developing countries can reduce, inter alia, the threat to financial planning posed by higher volatility of short-term international interest rates, the use of market-based risk management has not become part of the financial policy of such countries.[10] This section points the way toward the design of an improved risk management tool for indebted developing countries by identifying the causes of their inability to make use of the existing instruments. Interest rate risk management tools that have been applied successfully and have stood the test of time can be classified into five broad categories: (1) choosing an *optimal period* during which interest payments remain fixed by refinancing floating-rate debt with fixed-rate debt in primary debt markets; (2) entering into *interest rate forward contracts*; (3) entering into *interest rate swap agreements*; (4) purchase of *interest rate options*; and (5) purchase or sale of *interest rate futures contracts*. The inability of indebted developing countries to make significant use of any of these five methods of reducing their exposure to short-term international interest rates has been attributable to lack of creditworthiness, lack of international reserves, and a lack of financial expertise.

Concern about the creditworthiness of indebted developing countries, particularly countries with rescheduled debt, has meant that such countries do not generally have access to the fixed-interest rate debt markets and thus are denied the possibility of lowering their exposure to volatile international interest rates through a lengthening of coupon periods.[11] Instead, 80 percent of the external obligations of developing countries carry a coupon period of six months or less. Their inability to alter the coupon period of existing debt directly forces indebted developing countries to do so indirectly through the use of derivative markets (forwards, futures, options, and swaps).

Considerations pertaining to the creditworthiness of indebted developing countries, many with rescheduled debt, have also made markets for interest rate forward contracts inaccessible to such countries. Interest rate forward contracts—contracts for the delivery of funds at a specified

---

[10] The one notable exception has been Chile, which in 1988 undertook a limited interest rate risk management operation involving the sale of Eurodollar futures contracts to hedge against increases in LIBOR before the next interest rate reset date.

[11] The coupon period is the period over which the interest payable on the liability remains fixed.

future date and interest rate—are pure credit instruments in that they expose counterparties to the risk of loss should the country renege on its payment obligations during the life of the contract.[12] For example, in order to offset a rise in the six-month LIBOR index rate at the next interest rate reset date of its external obligations, a debtor country could enter a forward rate agreement (FRA) for delivery of six-month funds at the reset date at a specified interest rate. If, under these circumstances, the six-month LIBOR at the delivery date is below the rate specified in the FRA, then the country owes interest payments to its counterparty in the FRA. Hence the counterparty is exposed to credit risk if rates fall. The longer the performance period, that is, the length of the forward contract, and the more volatile the interest rate of the underlying instrument, the greater the credit risk in forward contracts.[13] Such credit risk in forward interest rate contracts has meant that their use is largely confined to interbank markets.

The presence of counterparty risk has also resulted in the exclusion of indebted developing countries from the interest rate swap market. An interest rate swap is an agreement among two parties to exchange a stream of fixed interest payments for a stream of floating interest payments over a specified period without exchanging any principal payments. For example, the developing country would undertake to make fixed interest rate payments at a specified rate on a notional principal during a specified period, while the counterparty would make floating interest payments on the same notional principal. Since the country commits itself in the interest rate swap agreement to make unsecured future payments at regular settlement dates, up to a specified maturity date, the counterparty incurs credit risk. For example, a default on the fixed interest payments[14] by the country exposes the floating-rate payor to losses if fixed rates have declined since the beginning of the swap contract. Thus

---

[12] The predominant example of interest rate forward contracts is the forward rate agreement (FRA), a contract in which two counterparties agree on the interest rate to be paid on notional deposits of specified maturity at a specified future date. The market for FRAs has grown rapidly and is now estimated to exceed $100 billion outstanding in notional principal. Maturities of up to six months for delivery up to one year are most common.

[13] If, for example, the contracted interest rate on six-month funds is ρ and the spot rate at the delivery date is $r < \rho$, then the potential default loss for the counterparty is $(\rho - r)F/2$, where F is the nominal size of the contract. (The contract is usually cash settled, that is, by paying the interest differential without principal payments.) Hence, the longer the time to delivery and the more volatile the underlying interest rate the greater the likelihood that r differs from ρ.

[14] If one of the parties in an interest rate swap fails to fulfill its obligations under the swap contract, then the other party is released from making its payments.

Table 1. *Premia for Interest Rate Caps on Three-Month LIBOR*
in January 1989[1]

Maturity of Cap (In years)	Ceiling Interest Rate (In percent)	Premium (In basis points of face value)
Two	9	152
Two	10	74
Three	10	141
Three	11	79
Four	10	212
Four	11	125
Five	10	280
Five	11	180

[1] These premia are an average of premia quoted by major banks and securities houses in New York in January 1989. The three-month LIBOR averaged 9.5 percent during this period.

the swap participant's credit risk exposure depends on the potential movement of interest rates over the period of the swap and on the likelihood of a performance failure by the swap counterparty.

The lack of sufficient foreign exchange reserves has prevented indebted developing countries from purchasing interest rate caps. Such interest rate options have become an important and successful interest rate risk management tool, one whose use is not affected by the credit risk of the purchase of the cap. A floating-rate borrower, such as an indebted developing country, can obtain medium-term protection against an increase in the index rate by purchasing an interest rate cap. The market for caps is judged sufficiently deep and liquid to accommodate substantial participation by indebted countries.[15] Caps are sold by major commercial banks and securities houses. The main drawback of using interest rate caps to manage rate volatility is that the purchase of caps requires a fee, whose size is determined by the level at which the index rate is capped, the length of time over which the cap is in effect, and the expected volatility of the capped rate.[16] For example, the estimated cost of capping LIBOR 50 basis points above its current value for the next three years is about 141 basis points of the principal amount (see Table 1). Offsetting this price disadvantage is that, while caps limit

[15] It is estimated that in excess of $750 billion of LIBOR caps are outstanding. Available maturities run through ten years with most liquidity occurring for caps between one to five years of maturity.
[16] Conventional options pricing models can be used to determine the size of the premium.

upward movements, they do not deprive the country of the benefits of downward movements in rates. Indebted developing countries have, however, generally been unable or unwilling to use scarce foreign exchange resources for the interest rate caps. Since the indebted developing country does not incur obligations to make payments at future dates, the creditworthiness of such countries is not an impediment to the use of interest rate caps.

An important interest rate hedging instrument not affected by creditworthiness considerations or by lack of foreign exchange reserves is the exchange-traded interest rate futures contract. Such futures contracts are promises to deliver a particular financial asset at a predetermined price at a specified date in the future. The terms and the delivery dates of the contract are standardized as are the procedures for trading the contract. Furthermore, certain institutional arrangements, to be discussed below, serve to eliminate credit risk from the contract. The main shortcoming of using futures contracts to reduce the impact of interest rate volatility over the medium term is their relatively short time horizon, which limits its usefulness to indebted developing countries. The Eurodollar futures contract, which represents an obligation on the part of the holder of the contract to buy and represents an obligation on the part of the writer of the contract to sell at a predetermined price, on a specified future date, a Eurodollar time deposit of three- or six-month maturity, is the most successful of such contracts.[17] Sales of Eurodollar futures contracts can be used to lock in a forward LIBOR rate for some future date. Any increase in LIBOR will then be offset by profits on the country's short position in Eurodollar futures, while the benefits of a decline in LIBOR would be negated by corresponding losses on the contracts.

The market in the contracts for delivery of three-month Eurodollars up to one year is most liquid and is thought able to accommodate substantial participation by indebted developing countries. However, the markets for longer-dated contracts or for contracts for future delivery of six-month or one-year Eurodollars are not sufficiently liquid to accommodate substantial participation by indebted developing countries. Hence, the hedger has to employ a sequence (strip) or a stack of three-month contracts if he desires to lock in interest rates for periods in excess

---

[17] The Eurodollar futures market has grown rapidly to reach an open interest in excess of 250,000 contracts (contract size is $1 million) and a daily trading volume in excess of 80,000 contracts. The contract for the future delivery of U.S. Treasury bills is nearly as successful in terms of volume traded and open interest as the Eurodollar contract, but it does not allow a perfect hedge for the LIBOR index since the Treasury bill-LIBOR spread is not constant.

of one year.[18] Interest rate hedging with the liquid three-month Euro-dollar futures contract beyond 12 months is, therefore, not generally fully effective.

In addition, the hedging of interest rates risk beyond the immediate future with shorter term financial futures requires continuous adjust-ment in contract positions. Such activity requires skilled personnel capa-ble of dealing in wholesale hedging markets on a continuous basis. While these risk management services can to some extent be purchased from various financial institutions, even the evaluation of the quality and cost of these services requires considerable knowledge of market instruments and techniques. A further problem arises in designing and implementing an internal control mechanism that effectively limits the activities of risk managers to legitimate hedging operations. Recent experience in some prominent financial firms has shown that potentially large trading losses are possible if internal controls are inadequate. For this reason indebted developing countries have been slow to use this instrument for hedging interest rate risk over the medium term.

In contrast to the interest rate cap, futures contracts can be entered into by a country without a payment of an up-front premium. However, while in the former case the countries can still benefit from a decline in rates, a futures contract locks in a fixed interest rate. The greatest im-pediment to the use of the interest rate futures markets is, however, the limitation of the potential length of the hedge.

The discussion above thus shows that considerations of creditworthi-ness have closed access of indebted developing countries to fixed-rate debt markets, forward markets, and interest rate swap markets,[19] while the requirement of up-front premia deter the use of the interest rate options market. Finally, limitations on the feasible length of the hedge, and considerations pertaining to managing and monitoring futures po-

---

[18] A strip hedge covering one year consists of selling three-month Eurodollar contracts for delivery at the end of each of the four quarters. A stack hedge covering one year involves selling four times as many three-month futures con-tracts as the amount to be hedged. At the end of the first quarter, that is, the first LIBOR reset date, one quarter of the stack is closed out while the rest rolled over into the most nearby three-month contract. This procedure is repeated at each quarterly LIBOR reset date until the entire position is closed out at the end of the year. Prices for futures contracts traded at the end of each quarter are uncertain, however, and thus it is not possible to construct a precise hedge. In particular, the term structure of interest rates may twist, with short-term rates remaining relatively stable while medium- and longer-term rates rise. See Inter-national Monetary Fund (1989) for example of futures hedges.

[19] An important theoretical question remains unresolved concerning the pref-erence of lenders in such markets to ration access rather than to charge risk premia in accordance with their perception of the credit risk of countries.

sitions have limited the usefulness of interest rate futures as a medium-term risk management tool for indebted developing countries.

II. The Marked-to-Market Interest Rate Swap Contract

The discussion in the previous section underscores the fact that the special circumstances of indebted developing countries, particularly those with rescheduled debt, require an interest rate risk management tool that must satisfy a number of conditions before it can successfully be used to manage the interest rate risk facing such countries. First, the access of indebted developing countries to the risk-management tool should not be influenced by the markets' perception of the *creditworthiness* of the country. Second, the instrument should provide cover over the *medium term,* that is, from two to five years. In that case, it would add certainty to medium-term financial programs, as well as smooth cyclical movements in interest rates, enabling the indebted developing country to extend the coupon period on their external obligations from the conventional six months into the medium term. Third, the use of the risk management instrument should not require a large *up-front fee.* Instead, it is assumed that the indebted country is prepared to trade the benefits of downward flexibility of the rate to be hedged for limits on the upward movement of interest rates. Fourth, the risk management product must be easy to use and not require active *management of positions* or monitoring of delegated trading activity. Fifth, the market for the risk management product must be sufficiently deep to allow *large-scale participation* by indebted developing countries.

From the discussion of the previous section, it is apparent that none of the existing risk management products simultaneously satisfies these five requirements. Our strategy in the search for an interest rate hedge for use by indebted developing countries is to assume that it is not possible to design a *new* instrument that will gain sufficient market acceptance to provide the depth and liquidity necessary to allow indebted developing countries to hedge a significant part of their external floating-rate obligation. Furthermore, we also assume that it is not possible to improve the depth and liquidity of the longer-dated financial futures and forward contracts sufficiently to satisfy the medium-term hedging needs of indebted developing countries. Lastly, we rule out the possibility of external financial assistance for developing countries for the purchase of interest rate cap products.

By elimination, these assumptions point toward the interest rate swap contract as the only candidate for use in managing interest rate volatility.

The swap market possesses the necessary depth over the medium-term hedging horizon to accommodate substantial participation by indebted developing countries. Furthermore, entering into a medium-term swap contract does not require an up-front premium and can be done in a single transaction without a need for continuous monitoring. As was the case with forward rate markets, however, indebted developing countries do not enjoy access to the swap market because of the reluctance of market participants to expose themselves to the greater performance risks of such countries over a medium-term performance period. We conclude, therefore, that the only feasible solution to the interest rate risk management problem of the group of indebted developing countries is to modify the conventional swap contract to reduce or eliminate the risk of nonperformance from the conventional interest rate swap contract. In doing so, we shall take our cue from the futures markets in which certain institutional features have been employed to eliminate credit risk from the futures contract.

Conventional Interest Rate Swap

The conventional interest rate swap has become one of the most successful instruments for interest rate risk management.[20] In an interest rate swap the indebted developing country would pay a stream of fixed rate interest payments and receive a stream of floating rate payments over an agreed time period. The counterparty, usually a bank, would receive fixed and would pay floating. No actual principal would be exchanged either at the beginning or at the termination of the contract.[21] For example, at current swap rates, the country would have to pay a fixed 9.5 percent on a notional principal of, say, $100 million for five years and receive six-month LIBOR payments based on the same notional principal. A floating-rate borrower can thus achieve any desired medium-term lengthening of his interest rate period through the use of an interest rate swap. Although the market is an over-the-counter market, a significant amount of standardization in swap contracts and procedures has added greatly to liquidity in this market. Bid-ask spreads tend to be narrow, and maturities go out to 20 years, with most liquidity occurring within the three-to-ten year range. Money center banks have generally acted as counterparties in well over 80 percent of all interest rate swaps.

[20] See Watson and others (1988), Bank for International Settlements (1986).
[21] A wide variety of swap structures exists. We shall confine our discussion to the generic swap, in which fixed payments are exchanged for floating payments, on the same day, in the same currencies. See Kopprasch and others (1988).

Credit Risk in Swap Contracts

The credit risk of a swap contract with an indebted developing country at time t would be equal to the loss incurred by the counterparty when the country defaults on its fixed interest payments at time t. Assume c is the fixed interest coupon payable on a notional principal for a T period swap at the beginning of period 1. If the fixed rate for a T-1 period swap at the beginning of period 2 is also quoted as c, then either counterparty can replace the original swap agreed to at the beginning of period 1 with a new T-1 period swap at the beginning of period 2, without altering his payment stream. If, on the other hand, the quoted fixed rate had fallen to c' at the beginning of period 2, then the floating-rate payor (= fixed-rate receiver) would only be able to replace the original swap with one that paid lower fixed payments, that is, the counterparty of the country has suffered an unrealized loss. This loss would be realized if the country were to default on the swap agreement at the beginning of period 2.[22] Suppose, for example, an indebted developing country enters into an interest rate swap agreement with the bank under which the country pays 9.5 percent fixed interest on $100 million of notional principal for five years, while the bank pays LIBOR on the same notional $100 million for five years. Assume that at the beginning of year 2 the fixed interest rate swap rate on new four-year swaps has fallen to 8.5 percent. If the country defaults on its payment obligation, the bank will have to accept 8.5 percent fixed payments in return for LIBOR payments if it wants to replace the swap. Thus the bank will have lost 1 percent of $100 million for 4 years. If instead the fixed swap rate increases to 10.5 percent, a default by the country will not expose the bank to any losses. In this case, it can receive 10.5 percent fixed for its LIBOR payment. Potential losses are determined by the change in the fixed swap rate and not by its level, and no loss of principal is involved in a default on a swap contract. Thus, the credit risk on a medium-term swap contract is less than that of a loan contract of same principal. The potential losses over the period of the swap contract are a measure of the total *credit exposure* incurred by the counterparties. In order to determine the size of such exposure, it is necessary to determine the market value of swaps. The market value of the swap to the bank at the beginning of the second year is equal to the loss it sustains if the swap agreement became void through a default of the country. The replacement cost of a swap is equal to the market value

---

[22] We assume for the time being that the country makes the interest payment due at the beginning of period 1 and then announces its withdrawal from the swap agreement.

or zero, whichever is larger. The next section produces a method for valuing swaps.

Pricing Interest Rate Swaps

By market convention swap rates are quoted as the internal rate of return of the fixed payment stream of the swap against the floating index flat. For example, a ten-year interest rate swap might be quoted to a fixed-rate payor as "Treasury yield curve plus 70 basis points against six-month LIBOR."[23] If the current rate on ten-year U.S. Treasury bonds is 8.8 percent, then the fixed rate payor of such a swap with notional principal of $100 million makes fixed semiannual payments of $4.75 million for ten years. He receives in return six-month LIBOR flat for ten years, for example, $4.25 million in the first six-month of the contract if LIBOR is currently 8.5 percent.

Thus the swap market determines the swap rate for swaps of given maturities rather than swap prices.[24] Once the swap rate is known, that is, once the fixed payment stream is known, the market value of the swap can be computed.[25] The market value of the interest rate swap for the party receiving fixed payments is equal to the market value of the incoming fixed-payment stream less the market value of the outgoing floating-payment stream. It is convenient in this context to view a swap as an exchange of two hypothetical securities, that is, the fixed-rate payor sells a fixed-rate bond priced at par to the floating-rate payor who sells a floating-rate LIBOR note priced at par of equal maturity to the fixed-rate payor.[26] Since the notional principal amount of the swap is equal to the par amount of both hypothetical securities, there will be no net cash flows involving principal. The problem of determining the market value of a swap that has T fixed-rate payment periods left has then been transformed into one of finding the market value of these two hypothetical securities. The market value of the swap is the difference between the present value of the fixed rate payments and the present value of the floating rate payments.

---

[23] For example, in January 1989 quotations for U.S. dollar interest rate swaps were: two-year U.S. Treasury + (56-61); three-year U.S. Treasury + (57-62); five-year U.S. Treasury + (58-63); and ten-year U.S. Treasury + (64-70).

[24] Swap rates are determined by demand and supply in a screen-based market encompassing most larger banks and other financial institutions.

[25] In contrast, market makers for U.S. Government bonds quote the price of a given bond rather than its yields, which can be computed once the price is known.

[26] It is assumed that the payment dates of the fixed- and floating-rate payments coincide with the floating-rate reset dates.

A swap agreement entered into at the current swap rate[27] is called a *Par Swap*, in this case the present value of the fixed payments and the present value of floating payments are both equal to the par value of underlying notional fixed- and floating-rate securities and the market value of the swap is zero.

The market value of the outstanding swap with a remaining maturity of T payment periods changes with variations in the quoted swap rate for new swaps of T period maturity. For example, an increase in the five-year swap rate implies that the swap contracted earlier, with a remaining time to maturity of five years, attains a positive market value from the point of view of the fixed-rate payor and an equal negative value from the point of view of the floating-rate payor.

The present value of the fixed payment stream is given by[28]

$$P_{Fix} = \sum_{t=1}^{T} \frac{\frac{cF}{q}}{(1 + Z_t)^{K_t}} + \frac{\frac{F}{q}}{(1 + Z_T)^{K_T}}.$$ (1)

Where T = number of fixed-rate payment dates left;
q = number of fixed-rate payment dates per year;
F = notional amount of swap;
c = fixed-rate coupon for the swap in percent;
Z_t = annualized zero-coupon equivalent rate for fixed rate payment date t; and
K_t = number of days until the fixed rate payment date t divided by 360.

The hypothetical floating rate note is valued at par at the next payment date, hence its price is the sum of the present value of the next payment plus the par value, that is,

$$P_{Float} = \frac{rF \frac{n}{360}}{(1 + Z_1)^{K_1}} + \frac{F}{(1 + Z_1)^{K_1}}.$$ (2)

Where: n = number of days in the interest period of the floating note;
r = current floating rate index in percent.

The rates Z_t used to discount future payments are zero-coupon rates derived from the U.S. Treasury yield curve (Appendix I) rather than current swap rates, which are yields to maturity or internal rates of re-

---

[27] The quoted swap rate is equivalent to the yield to maturity or IRR of an underlying hypothetical fixed-rate security with the same coupon.
[28] The time convention in the interest rate calculations used here is 30/360.

turn on swaps entered now. The reason is that a swap with a fixed rate
different from the current market swap rate (off-market swap) has cash
flows different from the current par swap and hence has a different internal rate of return than the current par swap. The present value of the
off-market swap will thus depend on which internal rate of return (IRR)
is used. Zero-coupon rates on the other hand are independent of the
fixed rate of the swap and hence they are used to discount the fixed
payments of the off-market swap.[29]

The value to the fixed-rate receiver of a swap contract with T payment
periods until maturity is, therefore, equal to

$$P_{\text{Swap}} = P_{\text{Fix}} - P_{\text{Float}} \tag{3}$$

Any change in the U.S. Treasury yield curve will induce changes in
the zero coupon discount factors and hence the value of the swap will
change. For example, an upward shift in the Treasury yield curve would
increase the value of the swap to the fixed rate payor since P_{Fixed} decreases by more than P_{Float}.[30]

Since the country is not assumed to be free of default risk, the bank
counterparty in the swap contract will not use the risk-free zero-coupon
discount rates to determine the value of its swap, but instead will add a
risk premium to the discount rates. Hence, in order to enter into such
a swap, the country will have to pay a swap rate that reflects its default
risk. Once the bank has determined the discount rates it will use to discount the uncertain fixed-rate payment stream from the country it can
then determine the swap rate and a new swap rate can be found by
setting the initial market value of the swap equal to zero, that is,

$$0 = \sum_{t=1}^{T} \frac{\dfrac{\tilde{c}F}{q}}{(1 + Z_t + d_t)^{K_1}} + \frac{\dfrac{F}{q}}{(1 + Z_T + d_T)^{K_T}}$$

$$- \frac{rF \dfrac{n}{360}}{(1 + Z_1)^{K_1}} + \frac{F}{(1 + Z_1)^{K_1}}. \tag{4}$$

Where d_t are the risk premia added to t period risk-free zero coupon
           discount rates; and

        $\tilde{c}$ is the swap rate payable by the country with default risk.

[29] This valuation problem is thus strictly analogous to valuing a certain stream
of fixed payments made by risk-free payor to a risk-free borrower. In this case,
each payment would be discounted by the appropriate risk-free zero coupon rate
and the value of the stream would be equal to the sum of the terms.
[30] The longer maturity of the hypothetical fixed-rate security implies that its
present value changes by more with changes in interest rates than that of the
floating-rate security.

Marking-to-Market of Swap Contracts

In order to find a way to reduce credit risk in swap contracts, we first examine how the futures market has dealt with credit risk. The credit risk associated with the obligation to make future delivery under futures contracts has successfully been minimized through institutional features, such as daily resettlement, margin requirements, and futures clearing-houses. Any gains or losses that arise on the futures contract because of changes in the price of the contract are realized the next morning through cash settlements among the contracting parties, and the futures price is then marked-to-market.[31] Thus the performance period has been reduced to one day. In addition, market participants are required to post margins in the form of a performance bond, related to the estimated volatility of intraday futures prices, to cover any intraday losses. Thus the incentive to renege on the futures contract has been virtually elimi-nated. In addition, a clearinghouse interposes itself between transacting parties in all contracts, such that all contracts are with the clearinghouse as counterparty, which further reduces the risk of nonperformance. The homogenous nature of the futures contract and the bringing together of buyers and sellers in an organized futures exchange has resulted in a very liquid futures market.[32] Generally, the longer the performance period, the greater the probability that swap rates change in such a way as to pro-duce capital gains for the bank counterparty and the greater the credit risk. Hence, credit risk can be reduced by reducing the performance period.

The identification of the unrealized gains and losses occurring in swap contracts with changes in the swap rate makes it possible to design a similar mechanism of transferring the change in the swap's value from the losers to the gainers followed by a marking-to-market of the swap rate, as a way to reduce the credit risk of the swap contract. By making such transfers of the heretofore unrealized changes in the value of the swap contract at the beginning of each coupon period and by resetting

---

[31] For example, assume a country sells 1,000 contracts ($1 million per contract) for delivery of three-month Eurodollar deposits at a specified future date at 92 cents per dollar. If on the next day the futures interest rate on the three-month Eurodollar deposits has decreased by five basis points, that is, the price of the contract has risen by five basis points, then the country will have suffered a $125,000 loss on its short futures position. The resettlement procedure provided for the $125,000 to be paid to the holder of the contracts and for the interest rate at which the Eurodollar deposits will be supplied is to be adjusted upward by five basis points.

[32] The introduction of exchange-traded financial futures should be regarded as one of the most successful financial innovations of the past decade; see Miller (1986).

Table 2. *Marking-to-Market of Interest Rate Swaps*
(Five-year swap, semiannual, 9.8 percent fixed payment)

Date	Notional Principal (In millions)	Current Five-Year Swap Rate (In percent)	New MTM Swap Rate (In percent)	Fixed Interest Payment	Marked-to-Market Settlements[1] (In thousands)	Net Fixed Swap Flows
Jan. 1, 1989	$500	9.80	9.80			$(500,000)
July 1, 1989	500	10.40	10.40	$24,500	$(10,567)	13,933
Jan. 1, 1990	500	10.90	10.90	26,000	(7,934)	18,066
July 1, 1990	500	10.00	10.00	27,250	13,019	40,269
Jan. 1, 1991	500	9.40	9.40	25,000	7,687	32,687
July 1, 1991	500	8.80	8.80	23,500	6,603	30,103
Jan. 1, 1992	500	8.30	8.30	22,000	4,521	26,521
July 1, 1992	500	8.00	8.00	20,750	2,081	22,831
Jan. 1, 1993	500	9.00	9.00	20,000	(4,682)	15,318
July 1, 1993	500	9.40	9.40	22,500	(955)	21,545
Jan. 1, 1994	500			23,500		523,500

Total Flows: 244,773

Internal rate of return on net fixed payments (in percent):   9.80

[1] Amounts in brackets are resettlement payments to fixed-rate payor from floating-rate payor, while amounts without brackets are resettlement payments from fixed-rate payor to floating-rate payor.

the original swap rate to the prevailing market rate, we can reduce the size of losses to changes in the swap's market value occurring during a single coupon period.[33]

Consider for example (Table 2) a two-year swap of $500 million notional principal priced at 9.8 percent against six-month LIBOR flat with fixed-rate payment dates made to coincide with the floating-rate payment dates. At the end of the first half year, the fixed payor pays interest of $24.5 million[34] to the floating-rate payor. In addition, if the swap rate for a nine semester swap at the end of the first semester has moved from 9.8 to 10.4 percent then the fixed-rate payor has an unrealized capital gain of $(0.06) \times (500,000,000)$ for nine semesters, discounted at the new swap rate of 10.4 percent, that is, of $10,567,000.[35] Thus the country would receive this amount from its counterparty. The net fixed-rate payments would then amount to $13,933,000. If, instead, the swap rate for nine semester swaps at the beginning of the reset period were below the original coupon rate of 9.8 percent, then the fixed-rate payor would make a payment to the fixed-rate receiver. In either case, once such payments have been made the swap's fixed coupon rate is set equal to the new swap market rate, that is, to 10.4 percent in the example. The payment made at the time of the marking-to-market of the swap and the adjustment in the fixed coupon cancel out in present value terms, so that the effective fixed rate on the swap (the internal rate of return on all payments) is equal to the original coupon.

The shorter the performance period, the smaller the expected changes in swap rates during the period and the smaller the changes in market value from one settlement date to the next. For example, Table 2 is based on a semiannual settlement, while Table 3 is based on quarterly resettlement. It can be seen that the marked-to-market settlements are smaller when paid quarterly, that is, the credit risk is smaller, the smaller the performance period. It is theoretically possible to reduce the performance period to a single day, as is the case in the futures markets. The practical difficulty with shortening the performance period below three months is that then fixed-rate payments have to be made more than four times annually, and interest payment frequency higher than four times a year annum has been resisted by the market participants for administrative reasons.

---

[33] We assume that interest payment remains current up to the time the swap contract is declared nonperforming.

[34] $500,000,000 \times 0.098/2 = 24,500,000$.

[35] $\sum_{t=1}^{9} \dfrac{500,000,000 \times 0.06/2}{(1 + 0.104/2)^t} = 10,567,000$

Table 3. *Marking-to-Market of Interest Rate Swaps*
(Five-year swap, quarterly (30/360), 9.8 percent fixed payment)

Date	Notional Principal (In millions)	Current Five-Year Swap Rate (In percent)	New MTM Swap Rate (In percent)	Fixed Interest Payment	Marked-to-Market Settlements[1]	Net Fixed Swap Flows
					(In thousands)	
Jan. 1, 1989	$500	9.80	9.80			$(500,000)
April 1, 1989	500	10.00	10.00	$12,250	$(3,745)	8,505
July 1, 1989	500	10.40	10.40	12,500	(7,115)	5,385
Oct. 1, 1989	500	10.60	10.60	13,000	(3,386)	9,614
Jan. 1, 1990	500	10.90	10.90	13,250	(4,811)	8,439
April 1, 1990	500	10.50	10.50	13,625	6,134	19,759
July 1, 1990	500	10.00	10.00	13,125	7,307	20,432
Oct. 1, 1990	500	9.60	9.60	12,500	5,527	18,027
Jan. 1, 1991	500	9.40	9.40	12,000	2,588	14,588
April 1, 1991	500	9.20	9.20	11,750	2,405	14,155
July 1, 1991	500	8.80	8.80	11,500	4,445	15,945
Oct. 1, 1991	500	8.50	8.50	11,000	3,043	14,043
Jan. 1, 1992	500	8.30	8.30	10,625	1,825	12,450
April 1, 1992	500	8.20	8.20	10,375	807	11,182
July 1, 1992	500	8.00	8.00	10,250	1,400	11,650
Oct. 1, 1992	500	8.50	8.50	10,000	(2,935)	7,065
Jan. 1, 1993	500	9.00	9.00	10,625	(2,365)	8,260
April 1, 1993	500	9.20	9.20	11,250	(717)	10,533
July 1, 1993	500	9.40	9.40	11,500	(483)	11,017
Oct. 1, 1993	500	9.40	9.40	11,750	—	11,750
Jan. 1, 1994	500			11,750	—	511,750
Total Flows:						$244,549
Internal rate of return on net fixed payments (in percent):						9.80

[1] Amounts in brackets are resettlement payments to fixed-rate payor from floating-rate payor, while amounts without brackets are resettlement payments from fixed-rate payor to floating-rate payor.

Thus, in swaps with such mark-to-market provision only the risk of not receiving the net fixed interest payment due in the current coupon period remains. Such risk could be removed by a collateral deposit or performance bond similar to that required in the futures market. For example, for a five-year swap rate of 9 percent and LIBOR of 8 percent, the maximum interest payment lost could be 25 basis points of principal[36] plus, for example, another 10 basis points to account for intra-quarter volatility of swap rates. Thus, a performance bond of 50 basis points of principal would make such five-year swap contract almost riskless.[37]

III. Some Remaining Problems

The practice of periodic resettlement and marking-to-market of swap rates exposes the indebted developing country to potentially large variations in cash flows. However, such flows occur in the opposite direction of interest rate movements. As rates rise, the country receives payments, while a decline in rates leads to payments by the country. It is thus necessary to put in place an active system of management of cash-flows over the term of the hedge. The marked-to-market settlements in Tables 2 and 3 are subtracted from the fixed interest payments if the swap rate has risen (that is, the value of the swap to the fixed-rate payor had become positive) or added to fixed interest payments if the swap rate has declined (i.e., the value of the swap to the floating-rate payor has become positive). The resulting net fixed swap payments flow to be made by the country has, however, an interest rate of return equal to the initial swap rate (9.80 in the example in Tables 2 and 3). Thus, although the payments by the country to the swap counterparty, that is, the floating-rate payor, have become variable, the internal rate of return of the payments remains unchanged. It will generally not be possible for indebted developing countries to use the expected payments by the floating-rate payor as collateral for borrowing to finance the marked-to-market settlement payments. An early default by the country would result in a loss of floating-rate payments by the floating-rate payor since future payments from the floating rate payor are made only as long as the fixed-rate payor is not in default.

Since indebted developing countries have generally made interest payments on their external obligations there would appear to be scope for

---

[36] One percent over one year or 25 basis points per quarter.

[37] It is apparent from Table 2 and from equation (1) that changes in swap rates which occur early result in larger marked-to-market settlements than changes of the same magnitude occurring later into the contract.

multilateral lending agencies to facilitate such technical problems associated with the cash-flow requirement of converting floating rate payment into fixed-rate payment through an interest rate swap.

IV. Conclusions

In this paper we first showed that the interest rate swap is the most promising candidate among the currently available interest rate risk management tools that would satisfy the special requirements of indebted developing countries. Since collateralization of swaps is rejected because of lack of pledgeable resources, we propose to shorten the performance period to coincide with the coupon period by resettling the swap contract at interest payment dates and marking the swap rate to market. The intra-coupon period performance risk can be eliminated through a performance bond. Since this marking-to-market procedure can easily be added to the conventional swap contract, it could allow indebted developing countries access to a deep and flexible market for turning floating into fixed payments over the medium term.

The main drawback of this method is the cash flow requirements inherent in the procedure.[38] However, the internal rate of return on net fixed-rate payments remains equal to the initial swap rate. Furthermore, while the periodic resettlement tends to raise and lower the fixed-rate payments in some periods, it does so in the opposite direction of the movement in rates. For instance, an increase in the long rate would result in payments being made by the floating-rate payor to the country, while a decrease in the long rate would result in payments from the country to the floating-rate payor.

A second drawback is the administrative cost of marking swap contracts to markets. Estimates suggest, however, that such costs would be unlikely to add more than 1 basis point to market swap rates on notional principals in excess of $100 million. It is also possible that if the marking-to-market of interest rate swaps is accepted by the market, the resulting elimination of credit risk and a standardization of contract could lead to an exchange traded contract much like the future contract.

The introduction of a marked-to-market swap contract would allow indebted developing countries to extend the length of the coupon period of their existing external obligation into the medium term at a modest spread above the U.S. Treasury yield curve.[39]

---

[38] Such cash flows are less than would be the case under comparable interest rate hedge constructed with futures contracts.
[39] See footnote 25.

APPENDIX I

Conversions of Yields-to-Maturity to Zero-Coupon-Rates

This appendix shows how the yield-to-maturity of an annual-coupon-paying bond can be converted to corresponding zero-coupon-yields. The correspondence of a yield-to-maturity and zero-coupon yield is based on the equivalence of the two methods of determining the market price of a T-period coupon-paying bond:

$$P_T = \sum_{t=1}^{T} \frac{c_T F}{(1 + r_T)^t} + \frac{F}{(1 + r_T)^t}, \tag{5}$$

$$P = \sum_{t=1}^{T} \frac{c_T F}{(1 + \rho_t)^t} + \frac{F}{(1 + \rho_T)^T}. \tag{6}$$

P_T = price of a T period bond;

F = face value;

c_T = coupon rate on T-price bond;

r_T = yield-to-maturity on T period bond; and

ρ_t = zero coupon rate for discounting payments received in period t.

Let the bond be issued at par, then

$$P_T = F \text{ and } r_T = c_T. \tag{7}$$

After substituting (7) into (6), we get

$$1 = \sum_{t=1}^{T} \frac{r}{(1 + \rho_t)} + \frac{1}{(1 + \rho_T)^T}. \tag{8}$$

Equation (8) can be solved iteratively for ρ_T by letting T go from 1 to the desired maturity. For example, $T = 1$ implies that $\rho_1 = r_1$, that is, in the one-period case the yield-to-maturity is equal to the zero-coupon discount rate. With $t = 2$ and $\rho_1 = r_1$, we have from equation (8)

$$1 = \frac{c_2}{1 + c_1} + \frac{1 + c_2}{(1 + \rho_2)^2}, \tag{9}$$

which can be solved for ρ_2 as a function of c_1 and c_2. This process continues until the desired maturity T, at which point the procedure has computed ρ_1, ρ_2, and ρ_T as the zero-coupon rates.

APPENDIX II

Glossary

Counterparty: The other party to a contract. For exchange-traded futures and options contracts, the counterparty is usually the exchange itself (an exception is LIFFE, where the broker plays this role). For OTC instruments, the counterparty is generally a financial intermediary, such as a major money-center bank, an investment or merchant bank, or a securities company.

Counterparty Risk: The risk that the other party to a contract will not fulfill the terms of the contract. This risk is avoided through the clearinghouse system for exchange-traded instruments; however, it is a relevant source of risk for OTC instruments, such as forward agreements, interest-rate caps, floors and collars, and interest rate or currency swaps.

Credit Risk: Risk associated with the possibility that the other party to a financial contract will be unwilling or unable to fulfill the terms of the contract. Credit risk is distinguished from the risks associated with changes in prices, interest rates, or exchange rates (see also *Counterparty Risk*).

Currency Swap: A transaction in which two counterparties exchange specific amounts of two different currencies at the outset and repay over time according to a predetermined schedule that reflects interest payments and possibly amortization of principal. The payment flows in currency swaps (in which payments are based on fixed interest rates in each currency) are generally like those associated with a combination of spot and forward currency transactions.

Delivery: There are three types of delivery on futures contracts: "current"— delivery during the present month; "nearby"—delivery during the nearest active month; "distant"—delivery in a month further off.

Delivery Date: Date on which the commodity must be delivered to fulfill the terms of the contract.

Delivery Price: Price fixed by clearinghouse at which futures deliveries are invoiced. Also price at which a commodities futures contract is settled when deliveries are made.

Forward Contract: A cash market transaction in which two parties agree to the purchase and sale of a commodity at some future time under such conditions as the two agree. In contrast to a *futures contract,* the terms of a forward contract are not standardized; a forward contract is not transferable and usually can be cancelled only with the consent of the other party, which often must be obtained for consideration and other penalties. Also forward contracts are not traded on organized exchanges.

Forward Rate Agreement (FRA): An agreement between two parties wishing to protect themselves against a future movement in interest rates or exchange rates. In an interest-rate FRA, the two parties agree on an interest rate for a specified period from a specified future settlement date based on an agreed principal amount. No commitment is made by either party to lend or borrow the principal amount; their right (obligation) is only to receive (pay) the difference between the agreed and actual interest rates at settlement. Similar agreements can be made with respect to an exchange rate.

Futures Contract: An exchange-traded contract generally calling for delivery of a specified amount of a particular grade of commodity or financial instrument at a fixed date in the future. Contracts are highly standardized and traders need only agree on the price and number of contacts traded. Traders' positions are maintained at the exchange's clearinghouse, which becomes a counterparty to each trade once the trade has been cleared at the end of each day's trading session. Members holding positions at the clearinghouse must post margin, which is marked-to-market daily. Most trades are unwound before delivery. The interposition of the clearinghouse facilitates the unwinding since a trader need not find his original counterparty, but may arrange an offsetting position with any trader on the exchange (see *Margin*).

Interest Rate Cap: An option-like feature for which the buyer pays a fee or premium to obtain protection against a rise in a particular interest rate above a certain level. For example, an interest rate cap may cover a specified principal amount of a loan over a designated time period, such as a calendar quarter. If the covered interest rate rises above the rate ceiling, the seller of the rate cap pays the purchaser an amount of money equal to the average rate differential times the principal amount times one-quarter.

Interest Rate Swap: A transaction in which two counterparties exchange interest payment streams of differing character based on an underlying notional principal amount. The three main types are coupon swaps (fixed rate to floating rate in the same currency), basis swaps (one floating rate index to another floating rate index in the same currency), and cross-currency interest rate swaps (fixed rate in one currency to floating rate in another).

Long Position: (1) In the futures market, the position of a trader on the buying side of an open futures contract; (2) in the options market, the position of a trader who has purchased an option regardless of whether it is a put or a call. A participant with a long call-option position can profit from a rise in the price of the underlying instrument while a trader with a long put option can profit from a fall in the price of the underlying instrument.

Maintenance Margin: The minimum amount which must remain in the margin account after any market losses are deducted from the initial margin. Once the account declines to the maintenance level, the broker will issue a *margin call,* a request that the client restore the account to its original level. Should the client refuse or default, the position may be closed out by the broker.

Margin: An amount of money deposited by both buyers and sellers for futures contracts to ensure performance of the terms of the contract, that is, the *delivery* or taking of delivery of the commodity or the cancellation of the position by a subsequent offsetting trade at such price as can be attained. Margin in futures markets is not a payment of equity or down payment on the commodity itself but rather is in the nature of a performance bond or security deposit (see *Initial Margin and Maintenance Margin*).

Margin Call: A commodity broker's request to a client for additional funds to secure the original deposits. Margin that must be posted in response to a margin call is known as *Variation Margin*.

Notional Principal: A hypothetical amount on which swap payments are based. The notional principal in an interest rate swap is never paid or received.

Open Interest: The total number of futures contracts of a given commodity which have not yet been *offset* by opposite futures transactions nor fulfilled by *delivery* of the commodity; the total number of open transactions. Each open transaction has a buyer and a seller, but for calculation of open interest, only one side of the contract is counted.

Option: The contractual right, but not the obligation, to buy or sell a specified amount of a given financial instrument at a fixed price before or at a designated future date. A *call option* confers on the holder the right to buy the financial instrument. A *put option* involves the right to sell the financial instrument.

OTC Market (Over-The-Counter Market): Trading in financial instruments transacted off organized exchanges. Generally the parties must negotiate all details of the transactions, or agree to certain simplifying market conventions. In most cases, OTC market transactions are negotiated over the telephone. OTC trading includes transactions among market-makers and between market-makers and their customers. Firms mutually determine their trading partners on a bilateral basis.

Position: A market commitment. For example, one who has bought futures contracts is said to have a *long* position, and conversely, a seller of futures contracts is said to have a *short* position.

Settlement Price: The price of the financial instrument underlying the option contract at the time the contract is exercised. Where necessary, option contracts specify objective standards for determining the settlement price.

Short Position: (1) In the futures market, the position of a trader on the selling side of an open futures contract; and (2) in the options market, the position of a trader who has sold or written an option regardless of whether it is a put or a call. The writer's maximum potential profit is the premium received.

Stack Hedge: A futures hedging strategy that involves taking a large position in an existing contract, and subsequently rolling over part of this position into a later contract month, possibly repeating this procedure several times. This strategy may be used to hedge risks associated with a series of payments or receipts, particularly where these are to occur at dates for which futures contracts are nonexistent or illiquid (see also *Strip, Liquidity*).

Strip: (1) A futures position established by taking the same (long or short) position in a futures contract for a series of delivery dates. This strategy may be used to hedge risk associated with a series of payments or receipts; (2) An options straddle position consisting of the purchase of more puts than calls although all have the same exercise date and exercise price. While the trader expects an increase in price volatility, there is also the expectation that the price of the underlying instrument is more likely to fall than to rise.

Underlying Instrument: The designated financial instruments which must be delivered in completion of an option contract or a futures contract. For example, the underlying instrument may be fixed-income securities, foreign exchange, equities, or futures contracts (in the case of futures option).

Volatility: The price "variability" of the instrument underlying an option contract, and defined as the standard deviation in the logarithm of the price of the underlying instrument expressed at an annual rate. Expected volatility is a variable used in pricing options (see *Standard Deviation*).

References

Bank for International Settlements, *Recent Innovations in International Banking* (Basel: BIS, 1986).

Brignoli, Richard, and Lester Seigel, "The Role of Noise in LDC Growth," unpublished paper presented at Roundtable Conference on Trends in International Capital Markets: Implications for Developing Countries (Oxford, February 1988).

International Monetary Fund, "Managing Financial Risks in Indebted Developing Countries" (forthcoming).

Kopprasch, R., and others, *The Interest Rate Swap Market: Yield Mathematics Terminology and Conventions* (New York: Salomon Brothers, 1988).

Miller, M., "Financial Innovation: The Last Twenty Years and the Next," *Journal of Financial and Quantitative Analysis* (Seattle, Washington), Vol. 21, No. 4 (December 1986).

Stiglitz, Joseph E., and Andrew Weiss, "Credit Rationing in Markets with Imperfect Information," *American Economic Review*, Vol. 71 (June 1981).

Watson, Maxwell, and others, *International Capital Markets*, World Economic and Financial Surveys (Washington: International Monetary Fund, 1988).

Comparing Menu Items:
Methodological Considerations and
Policy Issues

MICHAEL P. DOOLEY AND STEVEN A. SYMANSKY*

It is argued that interest payments and debt buy-backs can be viewed as alternative forms of debt reduction. It follows that the division of available resources between debt reduction and interest payments can be interpreted as a renegotiation of the original contracts. Once the terms of this renegotiation are fully incorporated into market prices, a simple procedure for valuing new money and other menu items is presented. A simulation model illustrates the results of buy-backs under alternative assumptions about expectations of creditors.

A SIGNIFICANT DEVELOPMENT in the implementation of the debt strategy has been the growing emphasis on "broadening the menu" of financing instruments. When employed in conjunction with firm pursuit of growth-oriented adjustment policies, a broader array of financial instruments can be seen as easing the problem of channeling needed finance to heavily indebted countries. The approach of broadening the menu seeks to elicit additional financial flows by appealing to the varying portfolio preferences of creditors and potential creditors. Portfolio preferences can vary for a number of reasons: differing assessments of the economic prospects of debtor countries, different degrees of risk aversion among creditors, different regulatory and tax environments, different perceived comparative advantage and long-term strategies among creditor institutions, and different initial balance sheet structures.

More recently, the recognition has grown that techniques to reduce debt—provided they are market based and voluntary—can help indebted countries return to eventual creditworthiness. Two recent

* Mr. Dooley, Chief of the External Adjustment Division in the Research Department of the IMF, is a graduate of Duquesne University, the University of Delaware, and the Pennsylvania State University.
  Mr. Symansky, a Senior Economist in the Research Department of the IMF, is a graduate of the University of Wisconsin and formerly served with the World Bank and the Board of Governors of the Federal Reserve.

schemes have been the Bolivian debt buy-back and the Mexican debt exchange. In the Bolivian case, additional financing from official sources was used to buy back commercial debt, while in Mexico, an unexpected accumulation of reserves provided collateral for the Mexican authorities to exchange on favorable terms new debt for existing claims. These operations have sparked interest in market-based debt reduction techniques, but they have not as yet led to major additional initiatives.

This paper attempts to deal with methodological issues associated with debt reduction. These issues are particularly significant in cases in which countries need new money to meet a prospective financing gap and in which all parties recognize that future debt service will be so onerous that efforts to reduce debt would be desirable in order to restore a country's external creditworthiness. In such cases, simply adding to existing debt to cover a financing gap compounds the longer-term problems of indebtedness. Nevertheless, countries with a financing gap do not, by definition, have resources readily available to devote to some of the more obvious techniques of debt reduction (e.g., debt buy-backs).

The plan of the rest of the paper is as follows. Section I deals with how debt reduction techniques can be compared with new money. Section II analyzes a stylized financing package containing new money and debt reduction techniques. It focuses therefore on equivalency among financing options from the point of view of creditors once the resources to be used for debt reduction are identified and proposes a simple methodology for evaluating such options.

I. New Money Versus Debt Reduction

In this section, new money and debt relief techniques are evaluated from the points of view of debtors and creditors. It is assumed that the typical debtor faces a "financing gap" in that resources available for debt-service payments are expected to fall short of interest and amortization payments due during a given time period. Thus, a financing package is needed to allow the debtor to satisfy its contractual obligations.

Consider, for example, the case of a debtor who has $10 in interest payments due, but has only $5 in cash flow to finance the payments. (For simplicity, amortization payments are ignored.) Assume further that initial stock of debt is $100 (face value) and that the discount on the debt is 50 percent. With debt reduction techniques included in the menu, the debtor might reason as follows: if interest and amortization payments are limited to, say, $3, then $2 will be available for a debt buy-back. Given the discount at which the debt is being traded, $4 of outstanding debt can be extinguished. Of course, if only $3 is allocated to interest and amortization, a further $7 of new money will have to be borrowed to meet contractual payments. The stock of debt at the end of the period will be $103: the initial $100, *plus* the $7 in new money, *less* the $4 of debt extinguished through a buy-back.

The creditor may have less incentive to agree to the buy-back, essentially because funds used to finance a buy-back would otherwise have been available to meet contractual interest payments. The creditor might prefer to receive the full $5 available in the form of interest payments. He could then lend $5 in the form of new money and complete the period with a claim of $105.

An alternative way of viewing the comparison is to regard both buy-backs *and* contractual payments as debt reduction techniques. In the above example, if the debtor had no resources available for debt service, indebtedness would grow from $100 to $110. The $5 that is available can be applied either to interest and amortization payments or to buy-backs. The difference is that interest and amortization payments follow contractual terms and therefore retire less debt than buy-backs or asset exchanges that follow market prices. For this reason, an offer of a buy-back in a menu may be viewed as a renegotiation of the terms at which debt will be serviced.

It follows that credit items and debt reduction items cannot be made "equivalent," but instead should be viewed as striking a new balance between the interests of debtors and creditors. It might be better to interpret a financing package that includes buy-backs as follows: debtors and creditors, recognizing their common interest in restoring a "sustainable" debt-servicing position, reach agreement on a flow of interest and amortization payments that can be considered appropriate to the circumstances faced by the debtor. Beyond this stream of payments, the debtor (perhaps with contributions from other interested parties) undertakes to make "extra" resources available, provided these "extra" resources reduce debt.

As shown in the technical appendix, the growth of debt relative to debt-service capacity, and thus the market price of debt, can be quite sensitive to this negotiated division of payments by the debtor country between interest payments and buy-backs.

At one extreme, if a debtor devotes all its resources to contractual debt payments, but still has a large financing gap, then new borrowing can cause debt to grow more rapidly than debt-servicing capacity. On the other hand, if a country allocates a relatively small amount to debt service, then the current value of the future stream of debt-service payments will be correspondingly reduced. While it would become easier in these circumstances to buy back the depreciated debt instruments, such a development might be seen as being inconsistent with the cooperative approach.

In the simple examples developed above only one kind of debt is issued by the debtor government. As a practical matter, debtor governments issue a variety of debt instruments in international and domestic markets, and it is important to distinguish between net and gross debt reduction. As is developed in greater detail in the next section, menu items that reduce the gross value of external syndicated debt may do so at the cost of obliging the debtor to increase the value of other internal and external liabilities. A full evaluation of "debt reduction" made possible by a financing plan requires the identification of funds available to finance the debt reduction that are *not* obtained by issuing alternative types of debt.

The successful incorporation of debt reduction techniques in Bolivia, Mexico, and Chile indicates that debtors and creditors have found debt reduction techniques useful. The experience of these cases, however, plus other countries' efforts to incorporate explicit debt buy-back arrangements indicate that it is not easy to obtain creditor agreement, particularly when new money is also required from the creditors. In general, the attractiveness to creditors of debt reduction techniques can be enhanced in the context of a negotiated financing package. In such a package, debtors can provide assurances that improved economic performance will enhance the value of remaining debt. Commitment to a sound economic program, particularly if supported by the Fund and the World Bank, could provide strong incentives for debt reduction techniques. In addition, official creditors can also make clear their own commitment to the debtor's adjustment effort. This might include both financial resources and regulatory initiatives designed to enhance the attractiveness of menu items to private creditors

II. Comparisons of Financing Options

The conclusion from the foregoing is that the negotiated blend of new money and debt reduction techniques will require a negotiated and cooperative agreement among interested parties. In this section, a framework is developed that allows for comparisons among financing options. This framework, it should be emphasized, is illustrative only and does not go into practical detail. In particular, no attempt is made to take into account the wide variety of regulatory and tax structures imposed on banks in different countries or the different attitudes of individual banks toward their long-run involvement with debtor countries. As an example, banks with a relatively small exposure in a given country might find an exit bond more desirable than would be suggested by the calculations presented below since it would reduce the administrative costs of being involved in future financing packages. Such banks would presumably pay a premium for an exit instrument. Moreover, an instrument that allowed creditors greater flexibility in accounting for losses, or greater discretion in establishing reserves against possible losses, might be more valuable to some creditors than the basic "new money" instrument. In this respect, the "terms factor" relevant to a menu item might be enhanced by regulatory authorities in creditor countries. Finally, as with any financial instrument, the tax treatment of earnings and capital gains or losses essentially determines how various potential holders evaluate the contractual terms of alternative menu items. As in any regulatory environment, the tax treatment of a menu item can be seen as an opportunity for creditor governments to enhance the value of menu items.

Characteristics of Menu Items

To keep the exercise simple, it is assumed that investors consider only the expected market value of various options. In practice, menu items with uncertain yields would be less valuable, and this could be considered an additional factor in more realistic exercises. It will be useful to identify at the outset three characteristics of a menu item.

Contractual Terms

Menu items can incorporate many contractual terms. As in conventional credit markets, a variety of debt and equity contracts will appeal to different creditors. Assume that the basic "new money" option is a security with contractual terms identical to existing debt. Consider now a similar credit that carries a contractual interest formula equal to one half that on the basic "new money" instrument. If a prime borrower issues such an instrument, we would predict that the additional discount at which it traded would precisely reflect the fact that the stream of interest receipts was half as valuable. The discount would be greater for a relatively long-lived instrument than for a shorter-dated instrument (since in the former case the share of interest payments relative to amortization payments in the present discounted value of the instrument is greater).

Country Risk

Another important attribute of a menu item is the extent to which interest and principal payments are subject to the risk of default. It is useful to decompose the yield into a part that carries "pure" debtor country risk, defined as having risk equivalent to that associated with existing syndicated credits, and a part that is "risk-free," or is expected to be fully serviced. Since the basic new money instrument is defined as being identical to existing syndicated credits, it carries the same country risk.

A menu item can be differentiated from new money in terms of country risk through subordination, guarantees, or collateral. If investors believe that an exit bond will be serviced in circumstances in which new money instruments will not be serviced, the exit bond will carry less country risk. Subordination of this sort can be associated with any menu item, including debt-equity conversions, and domestic currency bonds. The difficulty in evaluating country risk is its dependence on investors' perceptions that the subordination is credible.

Guarantees by a third party, or collateral held outside the control of the debtor, also reduce the country risk associated with a menu item.

Exchange Ratio

The final important characteristic of a menu item is the exchange ratio offered between the menu item and existing credits. These exchange ratios are sometimes difficult to identify but are implicit in any menu offering. In every case, the menu instrument is offered to discharge a given interest obligation, or what is the same thing, to retire an existing credit. The basic new money instrument is offered at par to discharge an obligation that has accrued or will accrue. On the other hand, if the debtor offers $1 face value of an exit bond to retire $2 of interest due or in exchange for $2 of existing debt, this can be considered an exchange ratio of 0.5.

Illustrative Comparison of Menu Items

Classifying menu items in terms of the three characteristics identified above introduces a flexible way of evaluating financing options. Table 1 presents an illustrative comparison of typical menu items that might be relevant for a typical creditor. For purposes of illustration, it is assumed that the country's existing debt consists of syndicated credits with a contractual yield of 8 percent and that these credits sell at a 50 percent discount in the secondary market.[1] It is further assumed that the "new money" option involves the creditor accepting a new syndicated credit identical to existing credits. This is convenient because it means that if we compare a menu item to the "new money" option, the same comparison will generally apply to an exchange of existing debt for that menu item.

New Money Security

A typical new money option pays a market-related interest rate. For simplicity, it is assumed that the yield is fixed at 8 percent on both existing debt and new money securities.[2] Thus, the new money security carries the same contractual yield as existing debt and its contractual-terms factor is defined as 1.0. Since payment of interest and principal is fully the obligation of the debtor country and because new money is indistinguishable from existing debt, the country-risk factor is equal to the full 50 percent market discount on existing debt, giving a country-risk factor of 0.5. Finally, since the face value of new money security is usually offered to settle an equivalent interest payment, the exchange ratio is 1 : 1 implying an exchange ratio factor of 1.0. In this case, the product of the three factors is 0.5 so that the standard new money instrument is worth 50 percent of a cash interest payment to the creditor.

Exit Bonds

Exit bonds typically carry a lower contractual interest rate, and in this example 4 percent is assumed. If any debtor issues a long-term security with an interest yield half that of similar obligation, the market price of the low interest rate security will be about one half that of the high rate instrument.[3] Thus, the contractual factor is 0.5. The country-risk factor

---

[1] In reality the typical syndicated credit is a floating rate security that carries a spread over LIBOR of ½ to 2½ percent and has a maturity of about seven years. In actual financing packages, these additional details would be important, but the analytical framework is easier to work with if we assume that the benchmark security is a fixed interest perpetual obligation of the debtor country government.

[2] A more realistic example would consider a floating-rate syndicated credit with a fixed spread over LIBOR. While this complicates the arithmetic, it does not alter the results in any important way.

[3] This is strictly true only for consols, but it is approximately true for long maturity securities.

is more difficult to determine. Three cases are examined. In Case 1, it is assumed that exit bonds are believed by investors to carry exactly the same default risk as existing debt. Thus, the country-risk factor for Exit Bond 1 is 0.5. In Case 2, it is assumed that investors expect exit bonds to be repaid with certainty; thus, the country-risk factor is 1.0. A third case is one in which one half of the payments on the exit bond are guaranteed by a collateral, the remaining risk being pure country risk. In this case, the country-risk factor is 0.75. In every case, the exit bond is exchanged for an equivalent face value of existing debt so the exchange factor is 1.0.

Exit Bond 1 carries a combined factor of 0.25 and from the creditor's standpoint is clearly inferior to "new money" since it is simply a low interest variant of the new money security. Exit Bond 2, with a combined factor of 0.5, is equivalent to a new money security or existing debt because the assumed reduction in country risk offsets the low interest rate. Exit Bond 3 is also inferior to new money securities but less so because of the collateral.

Debt Equity Swaps

Although an equity security does not have a contractual rate of return, there will be an expected rate of return, adjusted for project risk. While there may be projects with relatively high risk-adjusted rates of return, it is assumed for simplicity that the expected rate is again 8 percent in terms of U.S. dollars. For Debt Equity Swap 1, it is also assumed that 100 percent of the payments to creditors are subject to country risk. Finally, it is assumed that the debtor government exchanges an equity with a market value of $1 for an equivalent interest payment. Under these conditions, the combined factor is 0.5, and this swap offer is therefore identical to the new money security.

It is possible, however, as in Debt Equity Swap 2, that investors believe that dividend payments on equity are not subject to country risk or that at some point in the near future the equity can be sold for cash without penalty. This implies a country-risk exposure of zero and a combined factor of 1.0—clearly superior to the new money security as far as the creditor is concerned. Debt-Equity Swap 3 reflects the fact that potential investors would be willing to swap $2 in existing debt for $1 in equity if the debtor authorized the conversion rights. In this case, the lower country risk is offset by an exchange factor, so that the cash value is equivalent to the new money security.

Domestic Currency Bonds

The contractual yield on domestic currency bonds must be translated into a dollar equivalent taking into account expected movements in the local currency's exchange value. Again, we assume that the expected value is 8 percent so that the contractual-terms factor is 1.0. Domestic currency obligations of private sector debtors may carry a lower country risk. In particular, if the creditor can induce the private debtor to prepay its obligation, it might be possible to convert the domestic currency into dollars at a parallel market exchange rate. In this example it is assumed that the domestic currency obligation is prepared or sold at par for domestic currency. Thus, the country-risk factor is 1.0, although a 50 percent discount in the parallel exchange market reduces the exchange ratio to 0.5. It follows that the cash equivalent is the same as the new money security.[4]

Cash Buy-Back

A cash buy-back at market prices provides the creditor with the ability to purchase a safe financial asset. As with any cash transaction, the creditor can invest in an instrument with a market-related yield so that the contractual factor is 1.0. Moreover, since the asset carries no country risk, the country-risk factor is 1.0. Finally, the exchange ratio in the case of the cash buy-back is $1:2$ since the debtor is buying its own debt at a 50 percent discount. Thus, the buy-back option priced at the market discount is equivalent to the new money security.

Overview

With this overall framework, there is no difficulty, in principle, in evaluating even very complicated menu options. With more carefully specified and more realistic menu items, the calculation will not produce round numbers—but the methodology will carry through. Still, the problems in making such equivalency calculations should not be underestimated.

Perhaps the most difficult problem is determining a country-risk factor for individual items. Suppose it is true that small issues of exit bonds will be serviced before other debt. Implicit seniority of one type of asset

---

[4] It should be recalled, however, that the buy-back might influence the market discount assumed to hold in this analysis.

means, for a given total availability of resources, a reduced flow of resources to service other assets. This suggests that the discount on other debt will tend to increase and the equivalencies in the table will change. Moreover, since country risk has a large element of subjective judgment, it will be hard to estimate, ex ante, the risk factor attaching to individual assets. This risk factor will be reflected, ex post, in the differential discounts at which different assets trade.

Another difficulty in such exercises is that one cannot determine, by examining a financing package, the overall amount of debt reduction made possible. As discussed in Section I above, the *net* debt reduction depends on the initial blend of new money and debt reduction techniques in the financing package. Any external debt reduction over and above this amount that the debtor is obliged by a financing package to undertake would require offsetting increases in domestic government debt. This could, in turn, alter exchange rates and other factors assumed constant in the analysis. More generally, an important extension of the analysis would involve evaluating each menu item in terms of costs and benefits to the debtor.

III. Conclusions

There is now considerable support for exploring how debt reduction techniques can be included, on an agreed basis, in financing packages. There is also a measure of agreement that debt buy-backs and debt-equity exchanges are promising avenues for reducing external debt. The analysis developed above suggests that a blend of debt reduction techniques and new money can be in the medium-term interests of debtors and creditors. Moreover, once the resources available to support debt reduction are identified, evaluation of alternative menu items is a relatively straightforward exercise.

APPENDIX

This appendix offers some highly simplified examples of the possible effects of buy-backs financed by a portion of a country's resources. Different time profiles for the stock and price of debt are derived that depend on the timing and rules imposed on the buy-back. No attempt is made here to provide realistic scenarios for any country or group of countries.

In every case the debtor country is assumed to devote a fixed share of export earnings to some blend of debt service and repurchases of debt. In the first set of simulations it is assumed that the debtor spreads his buy-backs over time and is not obliged to purchase debt at a price above what would have prevailed in the absence of future buy-backs. This assumption leads to a fall in the initial price of debt as the share of funds used for buy-backs increases. It follows that the stock of debt retired is substantial, and in one case sufficient debt is retired so that the price rises to par after a number of years.

The second set of simulations assumes that the debtor is obligated to utilize the funds that they have set aside for buy-backs. As compared with the first set of simulations, initial prices are higher because creditors fully incorporate future buy-backs into the market value of debt. The initial decline in the stock of debt is nevertheless substantial and, as in the first set of simulations, there are no feedbacks in the model between an improving situation and export performance. If such a feature was added to the model, the benefits of a buy-back would be larger and would occur more rapidly. These scenarios can be expressed more carefully as follows:

1. A debtor country begins with a debt of $1 billion.
2. The debt carries a 10 percent interest rate and infinite maturity.
3. Exports of goods and services are assumed to be $10 billion.
4. The country is expected to utilize 10 percent of exports for interest payments or debt buy-backs. The share of payments for interest, α, and buy-backs $(1 - \alpha)$ is a matter for negotiation. This rule is implemented for 20 years; thereafter α is set to 1. This share is established by negotiating new money equal to $.10 \, D_t - \alpha X_t/10$.
5. The country's debt is the ratio of the present value of payments divided by the contractual value of outstanding debt that remains following that time period's buy-back.
6. In the first set of simulations, it is assumed that future buy-backs are at the discretion of the debtor. In the second set of simulations, the buy-backs are included in the present value calculation. The initial price of debt is set by market participants with full knowledge about the size of the future buy-backs.

These assumptions suggest the following simple models:

$$IP_t = \alpha X_t/10, \tag{1}$$

$$BB_t = (1 - \alpha)X_t/10, \tag{2}$$

$$D_t = 1.10 \, D_{t-1} - IP_t - BB/P_t, \tag{3}$$

$$P_t = PVP_t/D_t. \tag{4}$$

Where IP_t = interest payment

             X_t = exports

             BB = cash used for buy-back

             D_t = debt

             P_t = market price of debt

            PVP = present value of future payments including buy-backs (if known discounted at 10 percent).

The first simulation, Case 1, sets $\alpha = 1$ so that all payments take the form of interest payments. In this case, debt grows more rapidly than the present value of expected payments, so the price of debt falls from $0.38 initially to $0.20 after 10 years and $0.09 after 20 years. (Given these assumptions, the price of debt will approach zero in the long run.)

Case 1: *100 Percent Interest Payment*

Year	Price	Debt	Present value	Buy-Back
1	0.38	1,060.00	399.99	0
2	0.36	1,126.00	399.99	0
3	0.33	1,198.60	399.99	0
4	0.31	1,278.46	399.99	0
5	0.29	1,366.31	399.99	0
10	0.20	1,956.24	399.99	0
15	0.14	2,906.35	399.99	0
20	0.09	4,436.49	399.99	0
25	0.06	6,900.80	399.99	0
30	0.04	10,869.59	399.99	0

Case 2 shows the same country, but now it uses 25 percent of its total payments for buy-backs and 75 percent for interest payments for the first 20 years. Notice that the initial price of the debt, $0.31, is lower than in Case 1 and that the price again declines over time, but less rapidly.

In Case 3, for the first 20 years, half of all payments are interest and half are buy-backs. Again, the initial price of debt is even lower at $0.24, but in this case, sufficient debt is retired so in the short run, the present value of interest payments grows more rapidly than debt, so that the price of debt actually increases to $0.32 after 20 years but again approaches zero in the long run.

Finally, in Case 4, 75 percent of available funds are used for buy-backs and only 25 percent for interest payments. In this case the initial price is quite low, about $0.16, but the buy-back rapidly retires debt so that after 20 years contractual interest payments on remaining debt would be less than 10 percent of exports, the market price of debt would be $1.00, and the debt overhang would be eliminated.

The second set of cases reflects the assumption that the future buy-backs are fully anticipated. In this case the initial price of debt is relatively unchanged since

Case 2: *75 Percent Interest Payment—25 Percent Buy-Back*

Year	Price	Debt	Present value	Buy-Back
1	0.31	1,027.37	314.85	10
2	0.30	1,066.40	316.34	10
3	0.29	1,108.18	317.97	10
4	0.28	1,152.95	319.77	10
5	0.27	1,200.92	321.75	10
10	0.22	1,498.59	335.04	10
15	0.19	1,926.31	356.44	10
20	0.15	2,616.90	390.90	10
25	0.10	3,879.85	399.99	0
30	0.07	6,004.32	399.99	0

Case 3: *50 Percent Interest Payment—50 Percent Buy-Back*

Year	Price	Debt	Present value	Buy-Back
1	0.24	975.11	229.73	20
2	0.24	969.31	232.70	20
3	0.24	964.49	235.97	20
4	0.25	960.74	239.57	20
5	0.25	958.12	243.53	20
10	0.28	965.59	270.09	20
15	0.31	1,018.81	312.88	20
20	0.32	1,199.89	381.81	20
25	0.25	1,621.33	399.99	0
30	0.17	2,366.96	399.99	0

Case 4: *25 Percent Interest Payment—75 Percent Buy-Back*

Year	Price	Debt	Present value	Buy-Back
1	0.16	877.86	144.59	30
2	0.19	795.53	149.05	30
3	0.21	724.00	153.96	30
4	0.24	661.81	159.35	30
5	0.27	607.70	165.29	30
10	0.48	425.80	205.15	30
15	0.80	337.35	269.33	30
20	1.00	321.14	321.13	30
25	1.00	310.25	310.24	0
30	1.00	310.25	310.24	0

Case 5: *75 Percent Interest Payment—25 Percent Buy-Back*
Future Buy-Backs Known

Year	Price	Debt	Present value	Buy-Back
1	0.39	1,034.05	398.50	10
2	0.37	1,080.34	398.35	10
3	0.35	1,129.99	398.19	10
4	0.34	1,183.26	398.01	10
5	0.32	1,240.41	397.81	10
10	0.25	1,594.79	396.48	10
15	0.19	2,097.59	394.34	10
20	0.14	2,809.67	390.90	10
25	0.09	4,295.44	399.99	0
30	0.06	6,673.63	399.99	0

Case 6: *50 Percent Interest Payment—50 Percent Buy-Back*
Future Buy-Backs Known

Year	Price	Debt	Present value	Buy-Back
1	0.39	1,009.16	397.01	20
2	0.38	1,037.76	396.72	20
3	0.37	1,067.67	396.39	20
4	0.36	1,098.94	396.03	20
5	0.35	1,131.62	395.64	20
10	0.30	1,318.42	392.98	20
15	0.25	1,549.79	388.70	20
20	0.21	1,833.27	381.81	20
25	0.15	2,737.57	399.99	0
30	0.10	4,164.68	399.99	0

Case 7: *25 Percent Interest Payment—75 Percent Buy-Back*
Future Buy-Backs Known

Year	Price	Debt	Present value	Buy-Back
1	0.40	985.27	395.53	30
2	0.40	998.01	395.08	30
3	0.39	1,010.95	394.59	30
4	0.38	1,024.08	394.05	30
5	0.38	1,037.39	393.46	30
10	0.35	1,106.21	389.47	30
15	0.33	1,176.89	383.05	30
20	0.30	1,244.72	372.72	30
25	0.22	1,804.35	399.99	0
30	0.15	2,661.72	399.99	0

the present value includes future buy-backs.[5] As can be seen in Case 5, however, the buy-back does succeed in limiting the growth of future debt so that prices fall less rapidly as compared with the baseline scenario.

The larger buy-backs in Cases 6 and 7 tell a similar story. The larger the buy-back, the more slowly prices decline. Notice that the price does not go to par in Case 7 even though the size of the buy-backs were identical to Case 4. Since future buy-backs are assumed known, the debtor country purchases debt at higher prices than the case where the future buy-backs were not reflected in the price.

---

[5] The small rise in the price in the first period is due to the timing of buy-backs and interest payments in the simulation model. Buy-backs are assumed to take place at the beginning of the year, and interest payments are made at the end of the year.

FURTHER READING

Admati, Anat R., and Motty Perry, "Strategic Delay in Bargaining," *Review of Economic Studies* (Edinburgh), Vol. 54 (July 1987), pp. 345–64.

Aizenman, Joshua, "Country Risk, Incomplete Information and Taxes on International Borrowing" (unpublished; Chicago: University of Chicago, 1986).

——, "Country Risk and Contingencies," NBER Working Paper 2236 (Cambridge, Massachusetts: National Bureau of Economic Research, May 1987).

Alexander, Lewis S., "Economic Issues for Debtor Countries Raised by Debt-for-Equity Swaps," (unpublished; Washington: Board of Governors of the Federal Reserve System, September 1987).

——, "Debt-for-Equity Swaps: A Formal Analysis," (unpublished; Washington: Board of Governors of the Federal Reserve System, September 1987).

Borensztein, Eduardo, and A. Rex Ghosh, "Foreign Borrowing and Export Promotion Policies" (unpublished; Washington: International Monetary Fund, 1988).

Bulow, Jeremy, and Kenneth Rogoff, "A Constant Recontracting Model of Sovereign Debt," *Journal of Political Economy* (Chicago), Vol. 97 (February 1989), forthcoming.

Claudon, Michael P., ed., *World Debt Crisis: International Lending on Trial* (Cambridge: Ballinger, 1986).

Cline, William R., *International Debt: Systemic Risk and Policy Response* (Washington: Institute for International Economics, 1984).

——, *International Debt and the Stability of the World Economy* (Washington: Institute for International Economics, 1983).

——, *Mobilizing Bank Lending to Debtor Countries,* Policy Analyses in International Economics, No. 18 (Washington: Institute for International Economics, June 1987).

Cohen, Daniel, and Jeffrey Sachs, "Growth and External Debt under Risk of Debt Repudiation," NBER Working Paper 1703, (Cambridge, Massachusetts: National Bureau of Economic Research, September 1985).

Debs, Richard A., and David L. Roberts, and Eli M. Remolona, *Finance for Developing Countries* (New York: Group of Thirty, 1987).

Dooley, Michael P., "Country-Specific Risk Premiums, Capital Flight and Net Investment Income Payments in Selected Developing Countries" (unpublished; Washington: International Monetary Fund, 1986).

Dornbusch, Rudiger, "External Debt, Budget Deficits, and Disequilibrium Exchange Rates," NBER Working Paper 1336 (Cambridge, Massachusetts: National Bureau of Economic Research, 1984).

——, "Our LDC Debts," in *The United States in the World Economy,* ed. by Martin Feldstein (Chicago: The University of Chicago Press, 1988).

——, "Policy and Performance Links between LDC Debtors and Industrial Nations," *Brookings Papers on Economic Activity: 2* (1985), The Brookings Institute (Washington), pp. 303–68.

————, "The World Debt Problem: Anatomy and Solutions" (unpublished; Cambridge, Massachusetts, 1987).

Eaton, Jonathan, and Mark Gersovitz, "Debt with Potential Repudiation: Theoretical and empirical Analysis," *Review of Economic Studies* (Edinburgh), Vol. 48 (April 1981), pp. 289–309.

————, and Joseph E. Stiglitz, "The Pure Theory of Country Risk," *European Economic Review* (Amsterdam), Vol. 30 (June 1986), pp. 481–513.

Edwards, Sebastian, "Country Risk, Foreign Borrowing and the Social Discount Rate in an Open Developing Country," NBER Working Paper 1961 (Cambridge, Massachusetts: National Bureau of Economic Research, June 1985).

Eichengreen, Barry, and Richard Portes, "Debt and Default in the 1930s: Causes and Consequences," *European Eonomic Review* (Amsterdam), Vol. 30 (June 1986), pp. 599–640.

Enders, Thomas O., and Richard P. Mattione, *Latin America: The Crisis of Debt and Growth* (Washington: The Brookings Institution, 1984).

Feldstein, Martin, "Latin America's Debt; Muddling Through Can be Just Fine," *The Economist* (London), June 27, 1987, pp. 21–25.

————, and others, "Restoring Growth in the Debt-Laden Third World: A Task Force Report to the Trilateral Commission," Triangle Papers, Report 33, (New York: Trilateral Commission, April 1987).

Fisher, Stanley, "Resolving the International Debt Crisis," NBER Working Paper 2373 (Cambridge, Massachusetts: National Bureau of Economic Research, September 1987).

Folkerts-Landau, David, "The Changing Role of International Bank Lending In Development Finance," *Staff Papers*, International Monetary Fund (Washington), Vol. 22 (June 1985), pp. 317–63.

Froot, Kenneth A., David Scharfstein, and Jeremy Stein, "LDC Debt: Forgiveness, Indexation, and Investment Incentives," NBER Working Paper 2541 (Cambridge, Massachusetts: National Bureau of Economic Research, March 1988).

Gale, Douglas, and Martin Hellwig, "Incentive-Compatible Debt Contracts: The One-Period Problem," *Review of Economic Studies* (Edinburgh) Vol. 52 (October 1985), pp. 647–63.

Harberger, Arnold C., "On Country Risk and the Social Cost of Foreign Borrowing by Developing Countries," (unpublished; 1976).

Harris, Milton, and Artur Raviv, "Optimal Incentive Contracts with Imperfect Information," *Journal of Economic Theory* (New York), Vol. 20 (April 1979), pp. 231–59.

Hellwig, Martin, "A Model of Borrowing and Lending with Bankruptcy," *Econometrica* (Evanston, Illinois), Vol. 45 (November 1977), pp. 1879–1906.

Helpman, Elhanan, "The Simple Analysis of Debt-Equity Swaps and Debt Forgiveness," IMF Working Paper WP/88/30 (unpublished; Washington: International Monetary Fund, 1988).

————, and Paul Krugman, *Market Structure and Foreign Trade* (Cambridge, Massachusetts: MIT Press, 1985).

Holmstrom, Benst, "Moral Hazard and Observability," *Bell Journal of Economics* (New York), Vol. 10 (April 1979), pp. 74–91.

Kaletsky, Anatole, *The Costs of Default* (New York: Priority Press, 1985).

Kharas, Homi J., "Constrained Optimal Foreign Borrowing by Less Developed Countries," Domestic Finance Study No. 75 (Washington: World Bank, 1981).

Kletzer, Kenneth M., "Asymmetries of Information and LDC Borrowing with Sovereign Risk," *Economic Journal* (London), Vol. 94 (June 1984), pp. 287–307.

Krugman, Paul R., "Prospects for International Debt Return," in *International Monetary and Financial Issues for the Developing Countries,* UNCTAD/ST/MFD/4 (New York: United Nations, United Nations Conference on Trade and Development, 1987).

————, "Financing vs. Forgiving a Debt Overhang," *Journal of Development Economics* (Amsterdam), forthcoming.

————, "International Debt Strategies in an Uncertain World," in *International Debt and the Developing Countries,* ed. by Gordon W. Smith and John T. Cuddington (Washington: World Bank, 1985), pp. 79–100.

Lancaster, Carol, and John Williamson, eds., *African Debt and Financing,* Special Report No. 5 (Washington: Institute for International Economics, 1986).

Lessard, Donald R., and John Williamson, *Financial Intermediation Beyond the Debt Crisis,* Policy Analysis in International Economics, No. 12 (Washington: Institute for International Economics, September 1985).

Lindert, Peter H., "Relending to Sovereign Debtors," Research Program in Applied Macroeconomics and Macroeconomic Policy Working Paper Series (Davis, California: University of California-Davis, 1986).

————, and Peter J. Morton, "How Sovereign Debt has Worked," Institute of Government Affairs Working Paper Series No. 45 (Davis, California: University of California-Davis, 1987).

Makin, John H., *The Global Debt Crisis: America's Growing Involvement* (New York: Basic Books, 1984).

Marquez, Jaime, and Caryl McNeilly, "Income and Price Elasticities for Exports of Developing Countries," *Review of Economics and Statistics* (Cambridge, Massachusetts), forthcoming.

Morrison, Thomas, and Michael Wattleworth, "The 1984–86 Commodity Recession: An Analysis of the Underlying Causes," IMF Working Paper WP/87/71 (unpublished; Washington: International Monetary Fund, 1987).

Rogerson, William P., "Repeated Moral Hazard," *Econometrica* (Evanston, Illinois), Vol. 53 (January 1985), pp. 69–76.

Rubinstein, Ariel, "Perfect Equilibrium in a Bargaining Model," *Econometrica* (Evanston, Illinois), Vol. 50 (January 1982), pp. 97–109.

Sachs, Jeffrey D., *Theoretical Issues in International Borrowing,* Princeton Studies in International Finance, No. 54 (Princeton, New Jersey: Princeton University, July 1984).

———, "Conditionality, Debt Relief, and the Developing Country Debt Crisis," NBER Working Paper 2644 (Cambridge, Massachusetts: National Bureau of Economic Research, July 1988).

———, "Managing the LDC Debt Crisis," *Brookings Papers on Economic Activity: 2* (1986), The Brookings Institution (Washington), pp. 397–431.

———, ed., "Developing Country Debt," NBER Conference Report (Cambridge, Massachusetts: National Bureau of Economic Research, 1987).

Sappington, David, "Limited Liability Contracts Between Principal and Agent," *Journal of Economic Theory* (New York), Vol. 29 (February 1983), pp. 1–21.

Smith, Gordon W., and John T. Cuddington, eds., *International Debt and the Developing Countries* (Washington: World Bank, 1985).

Sobel, Joel, and Ichiro Takahashi, "A Multi-Stage Model of Bargaining," *Review of Economic Studies* (Edinburgh), Vol. 50 (July 1983), pp. 411–26.

Spear, Stephen E., and Sanjay Srivastava, "On Repeated Moral Hazard with Discounting," *Review of Economic Studies* (Edinburgh), Vol. 54 (October 1987), pp. 599–627.

Watson, Maxwell, and others, *International Capital Markets: Developments and Prospects,* World Economic and Financial Surveys (Washington: International Monetary Fund, January 1988).

Williamson, John, *Voluntary Approaches to Debt Relief,* Policy Analyses in International Economics (Washington: Institute for International Economics, forthcoming 1988).

Worrall, T., "Debt with Potential Repudiation: Short-Run and Long-Run Contracts," University of Reading Discussion Papers in Economics, Series A, No. 186 (Reading: University of Reading, 1987).